Hawker Typhoon, Tempest and Sea Fury

HAWKER TYPHOON, TEMPEST AND SEA FURY

KEV DARLING

The Crowood Press

First published in 2003 by
The Crowood Press Ltd
Ramsbury, Marlborough
Wiltshire SN8 2HR

www.crowood.com

British Library Cataloguing-in-Publication Data
A catalogue record for this book is available from the British Library.

ISBN 1 86126 620 0

Acknowledgements

A work of this nature could not be completed without the help of a great many people, for
both photographs and information. As regards photos, Peter Russell Smith yet again let me
rampage through his collection for hidden gems, while Nick Challenor also provided many.
Museum curators were very generous: thus thanks are due to Christine Gregory and her staff
at the Royal Air Force Museum, and to Jerry Shore and his team at the Fleet Air Arm
Museum at Yeovilton. From other parts of the globe Thomas Genth in Germany delivered a
set of rare photographs covering the Sea Fury with the DLB, while from America Nick
Veronico came up with illustrations of the Reno racers. Others who contributed to this work
include Michael Baldock, W. A. 'Bill' Harrison, David Howley, Dennis R. Jenkins, Peter R.
Arnold, whom I managed to wrench away from his precious Spitfires, and finally Damien
Burke.

Information on all three types of aircraft would have been very hard to come by without
assistance from numerous organizations and individuals. Organizations that assisted, either
directly or indirectly, included the associations of Nos 3, 197, 486 (NZ) and 609 Squadrons.
As ever, the RAF Museum at Hendon and the FAA Museum at Yeovilton proved stalwart
allies, as did the Air Historical Branch and the Public Records Office. People who came
forward with much needed information and encouragement included Allan Smith, who came
all the way from New Zealand to fight and fly in Typhoons before returning home; he then
took the time to relate his experiences and share his photographs with me – many thanks,
Allan. I am also particularly grateful to Dave Gilmour, Alan Hall, Les Bywaters, Gorden
Sumner and Ray Sturtivant. Other snippets came from people too numerous to mention,
and to those I say here a big 'Thank You!'.

Kev Darling
Wales 2003

Designed and typeset by Focus Publishing, 11a St Botolph's Road, Sevenoaks,
Kent TN13 3AJ

Printed and bound in Great Britain by Bookcraft, Midsomer Norton

Contents

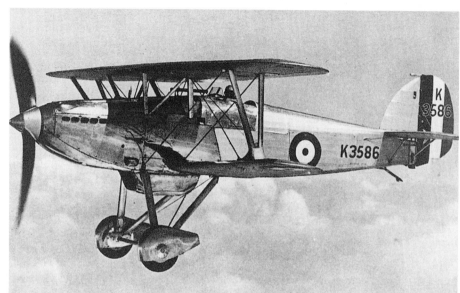

Above Hawker's would build a fighter equivalent of their biplane bombers, this being the Fury series of fighters. Here No. 25 Squadron scrambles, as part of an air defence exercise. Big Bird Aviation Collection

Left The Hawker Fury II, K3586, was constructed to Specification F14/32 and could lay claim to being one of the fastest biplanes in military service. After initial flight trials, the aircraft was used as a Merlin test bed; the engine was then installed in the forthcoming Hurricane fighter. Big Bird Aviation Collection

Below The Hawker Demon was also used extensively by the Royal Air Force light bomber squadrons. Although the biplane bombers were speedy, their days were numbered due to the advent of the monoplane fighters. Big Bird Aviation Collection

CHAPTER ONE

Hawker Engineering: Early History and Evolution

From the era of the biplane to that of the jet aircraft, the name Hawker has been synonymous with the Royal Air Force and the air wing of the Royal Navy, the Fleet Air Arm. There is even a connection, via Sopwith Aircraft, to the events that unfolded between 1914 and 1918, before a degree of sanity returned on 11 November 1918.

The formation of Hawker Aircraft in 1920 would come as a shock to many in the world of business as Great Britain struggled to restart its economy after World War I. Allied to this, the government appeared to have no coherent policies regarding aviation of any kind, and military aviation as applied to the newly emergent RAF in particular. Into this area of uncertainty stepped H. G. Hawker Engineering Ltd on 15 November, complete with a capitalization of £20,000 in £1 shares. The persona behind this almost bald statement were F. I. Bennett, H. G. Hawker, T. O. M. Sopwith, F. Sigrist and V. W. Eyre, all of whom had connections with either engineering or aviation, or both.

Although H. G. Hawker Engineering had ostensibly been formed to manufacture motorcycles originally designed and patented by F. I. Bennett, there were inklings towards the manufacture of aircraft. However, this was against a background of rapid contraction of the Royal Air Force, where operational units were disbanding on an almost daily basis until the air defence of Great Britain rested on a single squadron of Sopwith Snipe fighters. With a depleted complement of front-line aircraft, the few remaining manufacturers were reduced to modifying machines from the vast surplus left over from the war for further service.

One of the companies struggling to survive was Sopwith's, which in order to exist had turned to the manufacture of motorcycles and car bodies; Tom Sopwith had nevertheless continued to advocate the development of civil aviation, to which end the company had placed various products on this emerging market. All would have been well had the Treasury not decided to invoke the Excess War Profits Duty act, which resulted in a large claim against Sopwith's. Add to the equation an increase in trading losses, and it was inevitable that a receiver would be required to preserve the interests of the company's creditors. Careful economies by the company allowed for all debts to be cleared satisfactorily, thus allowing Tom Sopwith to take part in the formation of Hawker's. As part of the deal, Hawker's took over a substantial part of the Kingston premises and Canbury Park offices, the latter remaining in use until 1959.

Although the purported role of the company was that of supporting the motor trade, Hawker's quickly entered the aviation business when it secured contracts for the refurbishment of war-surplus Sopwith Snipes and various de Havilland aircraft.

Hawker Engineering suffered its greatest loss on 12 July 1921 when Harry Hawker died at the controls of a Nieuport Goshawk that he was testing from

---

Thomas Octave Murdoch Sopwith

Seen as one of the denizens of British aviation history Thomas Octave Murdoch Sopwith was born in London on 18 January 1888. Thomas Sopwith's interest in aviation began in 1906 when, aged 18, he was hooked by the bug while racing cars at Brooklands, soon to become famous as one of the earliest aerodromes. His first aircraft would be a 40 hp Howard Wright monoplane with which he would attempt to obtain his pilots certificate. This flight on 22 October 1910 would end in a crash however this minor set back would be overcome by the purchase of another aircraft, a biplane of unknown origin. During November Thomas Sopwith would gain his pilots certificate, No.31, and would carry his first legal passenger that same day. Four days later he would establish a British duration record of 108 miles in 3 hours 12 minutes. Further aviation success would come quickly as on 18 December 1910, he won the Baron de Forrest prize of 4,000 Lire for the longest flight from England to the Continent, flying from Eastchurch to Tirlemont, Belgium, in three hours, a distance of 161 miles.

A trip to the United States of America during 1911 would see him winning numerous flying competitions across that vast country. Upon returning to Britain Thomas Sopwith would found the Sopwith Aviation Co. Ltd in 1913 as well as a Flying Training School. Also in 1913 Thomas Sopwith would win the first British Aerial Derby. His company's innovative designs caught the eye of the War Office who would place an order for twelve aircraft. Within twelve months a Sopwith aircraft would win the Schneider Trophy in Monte Carlo.

The outbreak of the war in Europe in 1914 would see massive contracts placed with Sopwith's at Kingston on Thames for a variety of aircraft designs. These included such famous names as the Pup, Triplane, Camel, Snipe, Dolphin, and Salamander which were delivered in vast numbers. By the end of the four year conflict Sopwith Aircraft had delivered approximately 18,000 machines to the Royal Flying Corps and the embryonic Royal Air Force. However the requirements of the postwar RAF would result in the cutting of outstanding contracts to the bone which in turn led to serious financial difficulties for Sopwith Aircraft. Eventually the company was wound up being replaced by H G Hawker Engineering Ltd.

As a founder member of this organisation Thomas Sopwith would become a full director during 1920. This would be followed by the Chairmanship of the Society of British Aircraft (later Aerospace) Constructors during 1925 to 1927. As Hawkers expanded into Hawker Siddeley it was felt that the enlarged group would require a well respected figure as its Chairman, a role that Thomas Sopwith would fill admirably from 1936. Further honours would be bestowed for services to aviation by the award of a Knighthood during 1953. During 1979 Thomas Sopwith was inducted into the International Aerospace Hall of Fame at San Diego. Always a respected figure within British Aviation Sir Thomas Octave Murdoch Sopwith would pass away at his home at Kings Sombourne on 27 January 1989.

Harold George Hawker

Although he would never live long enough to see the success of the company that would bear his name Harold George Hawker would have been proud of the achievements wrought in his name. Born on 22 January 1889 in Moorabbin, Victoria, Australia he would undertake a basic education before beginning work as a trainee mechanic at the Melbourne branch of Hall & Warden bicycle depot during 1901. He would stay in Melbourne for the next three years before moving onto the Tarrant Motor and Engineering Company where he would qualify as a motor mechanic. His sojourn would last from 1905 to 1907 when Harry Hawker would leave Tarrants to set up his own workshop at Caramut in Western Australia. This period in Hawkers life would last for four years although it was not all work as he found time to join the St Kilda Brass Band during 1908.

A need for travel and adventure would bring Harry Hawker to Britain during 1911 where, for the next twelve months, he would undertake work for the Crommer Car Company as well as Mercedes and the Austro-Daimler Company. It was during this period that Harry Hawker developed a passion for aviation which would lead him to the Sopwith Aircraft Company during 1912 where he was involved with the Sopwith-Wright biplane. Impressing Thomas Sopwith with his skills and strong desire to fly Harry Hawker would soon become the Chief Test Pilot for the company as well as the chief designer. This would be followed in 1913 by his winning a £1,000 prize for the first flight of 1,000 miles on an outward course. During the period Hawker would also find time to design the Sopwith Tabloid which would be shipped to Australia during 1914 for the purpose of displaying aircraft as a practical means of transport and communication. During these display flights many Australian notables were given their first taste of the potential of aviation.

After the war in Europe ended in 1918 Harry Hawker was one of those few who graced numerous newspapers in the immediate drab postwar years. During 1919 he would enter a number of speedboat and motor racing events and would win £5,000 from the *Daily Mail* for the first pilot to fly over 1,000 miles of water without touching down. His would be the second plane to attempt the non-stop crossing of the Atlantic Ocean and the first to fly from west to east in the great race. Piloted by Harry Hawker and Kenneth Grieve flying the aptly named Sopwith Atlantic, this was a land-based biplane of some 350 horsepower. Part of this aircraft could form a boat that could be detached in case they ran into trouble over the ocean. They would depart from a field in Mount Pearl on 18 May 1919 jettisoning the undercarriage to reduce weight and drag. The wheels were later recovered by local fishermen and are in the Newfoundland Museum in St. John's.

Several hours into the flight, problems occurred with the wireless being followed by overheating problems with the engine which forced them to ditch in the Atlantic some 14.5 hours into the flight. They abandoned their plane and were rescued by the Danish ship SS *Mary*. Since the Danish ship carried no wireless, their safe rescue could not be reported and no wreckage was found. Word was received in Britain on 25 May with the aviators landing on British soil a few days later courtesy of the Royal Navy.

As the aircraft company of his old boss Thomas Sopwith was encountering financial difficulties Harry Hawker formed the H G Hawker Engineering Company in 1920. Although there were tough times ahead as Hawker struggled to find work for his workforce and to help Thomas Sopwith out of his difficulties he did find time to be the first person to drive a car above 100mph. His untimely death on 12 July 1921 at Hendon was a result of excessive 'g' forces being applied to a spinal tumour which would cause him to lose control of his aircraft and crash. Although not celebrated widely in Britain for his outstanding contribution to the British aviation heritage Harry Hawker is remembered more fondly by the citizens of the City of Moorabbin where his exploits are commemorated by a memorial at the local airport.

Hendon, prior to taking part in an Aerial Derby scheduled for some ten days later. Subsequent investigations revealed that Harry Hawker had been suffering from a tubercular disease of the spine, which had haemorrhaged under a high 'g'-loaded turn; so the pilot was already dead before the aircraft hit the ground.

The loss of Harry Hawker did not damage the prospects of the company, which had reached firmer financial ground having managed to capture enough aircraft refurbishment contracts to continue in business. The management team in 1922 consisted of Fred Sigrist, Tom Sopwith, V. W. Eyre, F. I. Bennett and Capt L. F. Peaty, with the appointed chief designer being Capt B. Thomson.

Thomson and his growing team of draughtsmen were somewhat underemployed, as the few Air Ministry specification sheets being offered to manufacturers were at best vague in outline, and would result in a plethora of prototypes totally unsuitable for aerial warfare. Also shackling the Royal Air Force were the entrenched attitudes brought over from the army and Sir Hugh Trenchard, whose ongoing effort to safeguard the RAF as a bomber force put fighters of any sort well down the list of priorities.

The first practical design from Hawker's was the Woodcock, which in essence was no more than a rework of the Sopwith Snipe. When Thomson decided to leave Hawker's he was replaced by W. G. Carter, once the chief draughtsman at Sopwith. Carter's first task was to redesign the Woodcock from the ground up. This was successfully accomplished over the following six weeks, when drawings for a single-bay biplane powered by a Bristol Jupiter engine were produced. Once prototype flying at Martlesham Heath had ended, Hawker's was rewarded with a small contract for ten aircraft, designated the Woodcock II.

Sydney Camm Joins the Team

Although Carter had successfully revamped the Woodcock for production, he would be joined in 1923 by a brilliant young designer named Sydney Camm. Destined to guide Hawker's for many years, Sydney Camm's first contribution to the company was the Cygnet light aircraft. Following on from that came a range of military aircraft, including the Danecock, the Horsley, the Hedgehog, Heron and Hornbill.

The first project in which Sydney Camm was involved as lead designer was that of the Danecock, a re-engined version of the Woodcock destined for the Royal Danish Air Force. This machine differed from the RAF original in that it was powered by an Armstrong Siddeley Jaguar engine. Only three machines were constructed by Hawker's; the remainder were built under license in Denmark at the Royal Danish Naval Dockyard.

Sydney Camm would have influence over another Hawker design, the Horsley. This was intended as a joint venture aircraft for both the RAF and the Fleet Air Arm, whose equipment was controlled by the Air Ministry. The premise behind the Horsley was that of a medium bomber for the RAF and a torpedo bomber for the FAA. The initial design of wooden construction was found to be too bulky for carrier operation, and too heavy to carry enough fuel for the air force. The answer put forward by Sydney Camm was to utilize a metal framework for the fuselage structure that allowed the overall size of the airframe to be reduced whilst still allowing sufficient fuel to be carried. The result of this rework saw Hawker's awarded a contract in 1926 to supply aircraft to the Royal Air Force, delivered during 1927, and the Fleet Air Arm, delivered throughout 1928.

Camm would also put forward the idea of manufacturing metal framework structures that would be bolted together instead of being welded. Not only was this perceived as an advantage in construction, it also meant that the RAF, short of experienced metal workers, could maintain aircraft built in this manner. Developed throughout 1925 by Camm and Sigrist, this method would be employed on all Hawker aircraft up to 1943, and would lead to the famous Sigrist quote 'Find me a chippy with a spanner and we'll mend the aeroplane'.

The framework developed consisted of steel or duralumin tubes swaged to a rectangular section at the end. Joints were formed by riveting a steel plate to the tube ends, to which another similar assembly could be bolted. In this manner a fuselage frame could be constructed whose tension and bracing were courtesy of cross-bracing wires tensioned by turnbarrels for any required adjustments. Two of the most famous exponents of the metal framework approach were the Hart and the Fury. The former was designed and built as a day bomber, whilst the latter was an interceptor fighter. Both would be seen in public for the first time at Olympia in July 1929.

The design of both these significant aircraft had begun in 1925, both incorporating metal framework for the fuselage assembly. Other innovations included a development of the Falcon inline engine designated the F.XI, which would eventually evolve into the Rolls-Royce Merlin powerplant. Supplying the engine was a pump-operated fuel system instead of the original gravity feed so popular in earlier machines. Improvements were also made to the undercarriage, which employed Vickers oleo-pneumatic shock absorbers strengthened by a cross-bracing strut.

The Success of the Hawker Hart

Deliveries of the Hawker Hart began in 1930, to 33 Sqn at Eastchurch. The advance in performance of the Hawker product meant that the top speed of the bomber outstripped the in-service fighters by 30mph (50km/h). So successful was the Hart that every day bomber squadron in the UK was equipped with it, plus many of those overseas. The last in-service Harts left the front-line squadrons in 1939, although a career as trainers soon

Above **The Audax was the epitome of style and aviation grace, as this view exemplifies. Under the skin, this two-seat light bomber was built around the unique braced tubular framework developed under the guidance of Sydney Camm.** Big Bird Aviation Collection

---

Sir Sydney Camm

Sydney Camm was born in Windsor in 1893, and his aviation career spanned the earliest days of flight. While at the beginning it was characterized by 'stick and string' biplanes, in the year of his death Mach 2 fighters were the norm, and similar capabilities were under development for the civil market in the shape of the Anglo French Concorde.

His first venture into the world of aviation design began in 1912, when he and a group of fellow enthusiasts from the Windsor Model Aeroplane Club designed and built a man-carrying glider, although no record exists of its success or otherwise. After this initial project, Sydney Camm joined Martinsydes, where he would gain valuable experience in the essentials of factory production techniques. From here he was promoted to the design department, where he would stay until moving to another early aircraft manufacturer, Handasyde Aircraft, in 1921. During 1922, Sydney Camm and a colleague, Fred Raynham, would refurbish a Martinsyde F.3, with which they would gain a creditable second place in the very first King's Cup Air Race. To complement his powered flight success, Sydney Camm would also design and largely build a glider that would also prove successful in the International Gliding Meeting at Itford Hill.

Having proved his talent, it should come as no surprise that Sydney Camm was lured to the design department of H. G. Hawker Engineering Co. Ltd during 1921. Within two years Camm would find himself involved in the development of the Hawker Cygnet, and in 1924 the full responsibility for its continued progress was placed in his hands. During 1925 Sydney Camm would replace E. R. Carter as the chief designer at Hawker's, his first full project in charge being the Danecock, the re-engining of the Woodcock for export to Denmark.

Under Camm's leadership the company would develop such famous biplanes as the Hart, Nimrod, Demon, Audax, Hind and Fury, before the monoplane Hurricane appeared on the drawing board. Having launched the Hurricane successfully into RAF service, where it would become the unsung hero of the Battle of Britain, the Camm design team would turn its attention to creating another dynamic fighter. Via the Tornado development programme the Typhoon would emerge, with Camm pushing on his team mercilessly. Although a perfectionist and no sufferer of fools, Sydney Camm worked the same long hours as his team, and was more than willing to listen to ideas from team members. Even though seen by some as a difficult person to work both for, and with, everyone involved with him realized his brilliance as a designer and engineer.

When the Typhoon entered service with the Royal Air Force, its early teething problems were understandably a cause of concern for Camm. Hours were spent in trying to find solutions to the Napier Sabre engine failures, while the detachment of the rear fuselage for no apparent reason also gave serious cause for concern. Eventually the former would be brought under control by better metal treatments, while the tendency for the tail units to come adrift was addressed by the addition of strengthening plates to the rear fuselage tail unit joint and careful rerigging of the elevator controls, although there were still some instances of this occurring. Following on from the Typhoon would come the Tempest and the Sea Fury for the Royal Navy.

During 1935 Sydney Camm became a director of Hawker's, and would follow this up postwar in 1949 by being awarded a British gold medal for aeronautics. During the period 1951 to 1953, Sydney Camm was appointed chairman of the technical board of the SBAC, this being followed in 1953 by a well deserved knighthood for services to aviation. In the following two years Sir Sydney Camm would be appointed as the president of the Royal Aeronautical Society, while in 1959 he would be appointed as chief engineer for the Hawker Aircraft Group. Sir Sydney Camm CBE FRAES would never have the chance to take up any form of retirement, as he would die 'in harness' on 12 March 1966. Possibly the best description of Sydney Camm's work is attributed to the man himself: 'If it looks right – it *is* right!'.

followed. After the Hart came a fighter development that would be named the Demon: this was fractionally slower than the bomber due to the increased weight of the installed Kestrel engine. A further development saw the introduction of the Audax for use in the bomber role. This, too, caused embarrassment to the fighter force, as its deployment to the day bomber squadrons brought about another increase in speed.

In parallel with Hawker's developments for the Royal Air Force, the company was also providing aircraft to the Royal Navy: ships for the RN were under the control of the Admiralty, whilst aircraft procurement was the responsibility of the Air Ministry in a misguided attempt at standardization. The first fruits of their labours appeared in 1932 when the Osprey was chosen to equip the fighter squadrons aboard the fleet carriers HMS *Furious*, *Glorious* and *Courageous*. Changes to the original Hart specification included folding wings, for which purpose each mainplane structure was strengthened, whilst the undercarriage was reinforced to cope with the shock of landings aboard ship. Further trials also introduced floats for operations from non-carrier class warships. The Osprey would leave FAA service at the outbreak of hostilities in September 1939.

The two final Hart variants to enter RAF service were the Hind and the Hector. The former was a refined version of the Hart, which entered service in 1935 and numbered some 527 production aircraft. The Hector was designed for use in the army co-operation role, where it would supplant the earlier Audax; it remained in service until 1940, when it was superseded by the Westland Lysander. Overall the Hawker Hart and its various offspring provided work for the whole of the company as well as shoring up the fortunes of others, which would allow them to continue in business and play their significant parts in the events of 1939 to 1945.

The Fury

Although Hawker's was a modest organization when production of the Hart began, Sydney Camm had always believed that fighter development was the catalyst for aeronautical developments. Pursuing this goal began in 1927 when Camm and his team began to study two specifications,

N.21/26 and F.20/27. Both designs seemed unrelated, as the naval 'N' requirement called for a radial-engined aircraft, whilst the 'F' specification required an aircraft with an inline engine. Development of two prototypes, known as the Hoopoe and the F.20/27 interceptor, would lead on to the appearance of the most significant single-seat fighter able to satisfy both naval and air force requirements.

Powered by a Rolls-Royce F.XIS, the Hornet biplane – later renamed to the more familiar Fury – was able to achieve a top speed of 200mph (320km/h) fully fuelled and armed. Not only did the power of the engine contribute to this excellent top speed, but careful aerodynamic refinements also played their part. The Fury underwent comprehensive testing at the A&AEE, although entry into service would be delayed as the pressure upon Rolls-Royce to produce enough engines, especially the Kestrel IIS, meant that the Fury would not join the RAF until 1931.

Once the Fury had become established with the Royal Air Force during 1932 it became the élite fighter force within the service. Such was its impressive performance that overseas sales were soon forthcoming. However, many of these machines were powered by radial engines: thus the Norwegian aircraft had the Armstrong Siddeley Panther engine, the Persian machines a Pratt and Whitney Hornet, whilst a further batch for the same country featured the Bristol Mercury, the most successful of all the conversions.

The Hurricane Makes its Debut

Following on from the first variant came the Fury II, which had the Kestrel VI engine installed, and which entered RAF service in 1936 when five fighter squadrons were equipped. Their tenure in service would be short, however, as another Hawker product, the Hurricane, was in the process of making its service debut. Regarded as a development of the Fury, the Nimrod for the Royal Navy was in fact developed in parallel with its land-based counterpart. Changes included an upper wing that was slightly lowered in height, a requirement necessary to clear the limited roof heights available aboard these early-build carriers, plus a strengthened airframe to accommodate the forces generated not only by landing aboard a carrier, but those of being pulled up short by the arrestor hook mounting points. Deliveries began in 1932, and equipped units aboard the main fleet carriers HMS *Courageous* and *Glorious*. Following on came the improved Nimrod II, which featured slightly swept-back wings; it entered service in 1934 and would equip three squadrons. Although one of the fastest naval fighters in service, it was slightly slower than its land equivalent due to the weight of the installed naval equipment.

The aircraft that would follow on from the two seminal Hawker biplanes would feature heavily in the Battle of Britain,

Below When Hawker's created the monoplane Hurricane it inherited the tubular structure of the earlier biplanes and their ventral radiator. Big Bird Aviation Collection

Right **The final version of the Hurricane was dedicated to the ground-attack role, for which purpose the machine guns were replaced with cannon, whilst extra firepower could be supplied by the Vickers guns under the wings.** Big Bird Aviation Collection

and yet in many ways it was a continuation of all the ideas developed during the biplane period.

The aircraft was, of course, the Hawker Hurricane, created in response to the specification issued in 1930, F.7/30. This had called for a high performance fighter armed with four machine guns instead of the normal two; it was also required to have a top speed of at least 250mph (400km/h). The response from Hawker's would be a monoplane fighter whose starting point would be the Fury biplane. The first evolution featured a low cantilevered wing with tapered leading and trailing edges which ended in rounded tips. The powerplant was the steam-cooled Rolls-Royce Goshawk, which would eventually be dropped from the development programme as totally unreliable. The undercarriage was of the fixed spatted type, whilst the cockpit was covered by a sliding hood. The rear fuselage and tail feathers remained virtually unchanged from the Fury. The proposed armament consisted of four machine guns, two in the wing roots and two in the fuselage. The construction of the said fuselage was of the standard Hawker framework with fabric covering to the rear, whilst the forward fuselage was metal clad.

Although the design would progress no further, the appearance of the PV.12 liquid-cooled engine from Rolls-Royce allowed Camm to redesign his interceptor monoplane to take the new powerplant. During 1934 the Experimental Drawing Office began to rework the design, and this would result in the creation of a $\frac{1}{10}$th scale model that would undergo tests in the National Physical Laboratory wind tunnel. As the testing proved successful, the Air Ministry drew up draft

Specification F.5/34 to cover further development. By August the submitted design was accepted by the Air Ministry: therefore Specification F.36/34 was issued to cover the construction of one high speed monoplane.

One bone of contention between Camm and the Ministry was the aircraft's armament, which the designer wanted to increase whilst using Colt machine guns instead of any of the normal British favourites. Another area that Camm was pushing was the ability of the new fighter to mount a compact block of weapons in the relatively deep wing, which would fire from outside the propellor arc. Given this capability, the proposed eight gun installation was adopted instead of the original earlier proposal.

Construction of the prototype had advanced enough in September 1935 for the newly named Rolls-Royce Merlin to be installed in the airframe, the whole being rolled out to public view on 23 October; the first flight was undertaken on 6 November. The resultant aircraft, later named Hurricane, continued with the tubular steel framework pioneered by the earlier biplanes, although in this case the forward covering to the fuselage was metal-sheathed, while that from the cockpit aft was fabric-covered. This method of construction meant that the Hurricane was far easier to repair, a boon to the fighter squadrons engaged in the Battle of Britain. The wing was also of similar construction, being twin-sparred with interspar girders for strength and shaping purposes. As with the rear fuselage, the wings were fabric-covered, as were the components attached to the rear fuselage.

The armament in these early aircraft was established as eight .303 Browning

machine guns, although this would later change to four Hispano cannon, an alteration much appreciated by those units employed in the ground-attack role. One other major innovation that appeared on the Hurricane was that of the retractable undercarriage, the mountings for which were set quite a distance outboard. Such a wide track ensured great stability under most conditions.

While the Hurricane was slower than its contemporary the Supermarine Spitfire, the stability of the aircraft on the ground was put to good use by No. 46 Sqn aboard the carrier HMS *Glorious* during the campaign to defend Norway in May 1940. Both take-offs and landings were undertaken by the fighters with very little difficulty. The first version of the Sea Hurricane was deployed aboard the catapult-armed merchantmen, but this was an altogether hazardous duty for the pilots, as it was a one shot flight for the aircraft, whilst the pilot had to take to his parachute and pray for rescue. As this was wasteful in both machines as well as the occasional pilot, an alternative was required. The advent of the converted merchantman aircraft carrier for escort duties would provide the answer, allowing the Hurricanes deployed by the now independent Fleet Air Arm to take off, attack any intruder, and 'and back on their bobbing and bucking postage stamp upon the ocean. In this role the wide track of the undercarriage was a definite bonus, a fact that would not be lost on Hawker's when the time came to develop the Sea Fury. Other innovations developed for the Sea Hurricane that would be taken into the Sea Fury in one form or another were the launch spools and arrestor hook.

CHAPTER TWO

A Powerplant for the Tornado

Most aircraft constructors preferred to rely upon dedicated manufacturers to provide powerplants for their latest designs, apart from the occasional one-off by such companies as de Havilland or Bristol. And even this area had its acknowledged favourites. Rolls-Royce became one of the best known engine builders, although Armstrong Siddeley and Napier also figured in the plans of many airframe designers, including Hawker's.

Napier Engines

Napier engines had begun to move into the aero engine business during 1917, after years as a manufacturer of civil and military vehicles. This first effort was named the Napier Lion and was initially rated at 450hp, although through further development this was soon increased to 1,400hp. Its arrival was too late for the events of 1914–18, however it would provide a staple for the Royal Air Force and the growing civil airline market. One of the best known airframes that the Lion was bolted onto was the Fairey IIIF series of aircraft, as well as the early entries for the

Schneider Trophy races. The Lion powered the Supermarine S.4 and S.5 racers, plus the entries from Glosters, the IV and VI. One of the Lion engines' biggest successes came in 1927 when the Napier-engined S.5s of the RAF High Speed Flight were the only entries to complete the course.

Continued development by Napier resulted in the appearance of the 395hp Rapier engine, the first successful twin crankshaft, multi-cylinder aero engine. Due to its layout, this series of engines and their subsequent developments became known as the 'H'-type powerplant. The first application of the Rapier was in the Fairey Seafox fleet spotter aircraft. Although Napier's seemed to have the edge in the development of liquid-cooled engines, the upstart newcomer Rolls-Royce was well on the way to delivering the Merlin engine to power the Spitfire and the Hurricane for RAF use, the design having progressed from the earlier Kestrel V via the PV.12.

The chief designer at Napier's, Frank Halford, had realized that the Rapier was capable of further enlargement: thus the 1,000hp Dagger was born. Larger, but simi-

lar to the Rapier, the Dagger was used to power the Hawker Hector and the Handley Page Hereford, although it was not an out-and-out success. However, the team at Napier had realized that the 'H'-type engine layout was capable of further development. This new design first appeared on the drawing boards in 1935, and was seen as a 2,000hp sleeve-valve powerplant. The engine that finally appeared in 1938 was a twenty-four-cylinder, twin crankshaft, liquid-cooled, sleeve valve powerplant, with a two-speed supercharger. The cylinder blocks were located on either side of the vertically split crankcase in four banks of six in an 'H' formation. The twin crankshafts rotated in the same direction, being positioned one above the other, with the two pistons on each crankshaft operating in horizontally opposed cylinders.

The pistons were connected by conventional plain and fork connecting rods, and each piston had three rings, one a gas ring, the next a gas/scraper ring, and the third a wedge-shaped scraper at the inner end. Four separate induction manifolds, each incorporating a pair of coolant runs to provide cooling flow, were bolted to each bank of cylinders. Exhaust was through ejector-type exhausts that were fitted into a recessed face on the outer side of each cylinder block. The valve sleeves were manufactured from chrome molybdenum and were nitrided, a form of metal hardening, and lapped for hardness before assembly. Driving the cranks were bronze worm wheels, flange-bolted into position, these being driven in turn by a worm shaft. This assembly was manufactured in two parts, these being joined by an external sleeve. The twin torsion shafts ran inside a hollow-sleeve drive shaft that transmitted the power from the reduction gearing to the supercharger. Located to the rear of the supercharger was a hydraulic clutch that translated the input into the impeller, using either of the two set speeds.

Engine-system lubrication oil was delivered at a pressure between 60–90psi, by a

Below The Fairey IIIF series II was powered by the Napier Lion engine; it was one of the company's earliest steps into the aero engine business. Big Bird Aviation Collection

single stage pump housed in the sump. The primary system operated at maximum system pressure while the low-pressure system, controlled by two pressure-reducing valves, lubricated other components around the engine. Those items not covered by direct lubrication were lubricated by both the splash- and mist-dispersion methods. Oil returning to the bottom of the engine was collected by two scavenge pumps, one located at the front of the engine to return oil to the main sump, while the remainder was collected and returned to the sump by the main scavenge pump. The other primary system bolted onto the engine was the pressurized, liquid cooling system that enabled high temperatures to be combated at all altitudes and speeds. The auxiliary components for the engine were located at the top and bottom of the crankcase: the upper unit contained the drive shafts for the magnetos, the distributors, and the ignition servo control unit; and located under the bottom component housing were the drive shafts and gear trains for the oil, fuel and coolant pumps.

The way that the various systems were mechanically interconnected by linkages meant that control of the engine was possible by the use of a single lever; although the down side to such a system was a tendency for the powerplant to be cantankerous under certain conditions, especially when components had become worn. The reasoning behind such interconnections was to relieve some of the pilot's workload, although provision was made for disconnection should the pilot so desire. The starting of the engine was by courtesy of the Coffman cartridge system, consisting of a starter unit, cartridge breech, safety relief valve and connecting pipework. The starter unit consisted of a large-diameter piston fitted into a cylinder that had a combustion chamber at its head. When the cartridge was ignited, the gases generated were directed into the cylinder. The resultant forces were then converted into a rotary motion, courtesy of a screw drive. This in turn generated enough torque force to provide a high turning rate strong enough to turn over the largest engines, although the available power was available for only a short period of time. On average, the Coffman starter unit was capable of generating 25hp at its peak of 0.75sec.

As starting an engine using this system could be tricky, the cartridge breach

Above **The Schneider Trophy saw Supermarine building three S.5 aircraft, N219 to N221, powered by the Napier Lion engine to Specification 6/26. The success of this attempt further cemented Napier's reputation as an engine manufacturer.** Big Bird Aviation Collection

contained five cartridges in five separate barrels, each of which, upon selection, would rotate to the firing position and seal against the face of the outlet tube. Once in position the cartridge could be fired from the cockpit using a selector switch. To prevent a misfire should foreign matter become lodged in the breech, an automatic safety cut-out was installed, that stopped the operation of the firing pin. As the gases generated by an ignited cartridge could reach up to twenty tons' pressure on the piston, it was important that safety mechanisms were built into the unit. The first was a differential safety valve fitted between the breech and starter, which would release the cordite gases should the pressure rise too high, whilst the final release was a bursting disc that would rupture should all else fail.

This, then, was the first of a new type of engine from Napier that rejoiced in the name of the Sabre I.

The Rolls-Royce Vulture

While Napier were working towards a high performance engine, Rolls-Royce were also engaged in creating a similar powerplant. Named the Vulture, it was in fact two Kestrel engines driving along a common driveshaft, the whole being arranged in an 'X' formation and having twenty-four cylinders in total. The engine was constructed using two aluminium alloy crankcases complete with integral

heads with steel cylinder liners. Each cylinder was fitted with two exhaust valves operated by an overhead camshaft. Operational development and subsequent testing began in 1937, with flight-testing being undertaken in the Hawker Henley prototype.

An Improved Fighter

During 1937 the Air Ministry began to cast about for a fighter that would improve on the performance and armament of both the Hurricane and the Spitfire. The specification called for an aircraft capable of reaching 400mph (640km/h) whilst toting an armament of twelve .303 Browning machine guns; the machine was also required to be a stable gun platform. When Hawker Aircraft began developing an aircraft to Specification F.18/37 it was drafted as a single seat interceptor, designed to be powered by either the Napier Sabre or the Rolls-Royce Vulture. To cater for both engines, Hawker's were contracted to build four prototypes, those for the Sabre being known as the 'N-type' whilst those for the Vulture became the 'R-type'; eventually the former became the Typhoon, while the latter became known as the Tornado. The proposals were presented to the Ministry in January 1937, being accepted on 22 April 1938. As Hawker's were at maximum capacity building Hurricanes for the Royal Air Force, the Air Ministry requested that

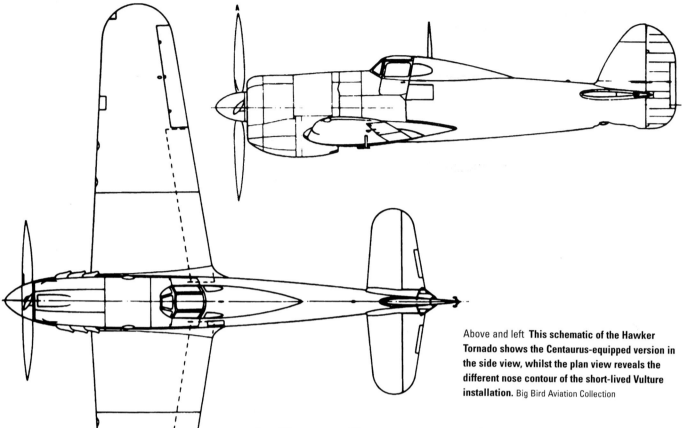

Above and left **This schematic of the Hawker Tornado shows the Centaurus-equipped version in the side view, whilst the plan view reveals the different nose contour of the short-lived Vulture installation.** Big Bird Aviation Collection

another group company, 'A. V. Roe', would build the production Tornado, although design management would rest with the main company.

The Tornado Prototype

Confirmation orders for the four aircraft were issued by the Air Ministry on 30 August 1938; they were issued as separate contracts for development, with that for Vulture-powered aircraft being given preference, as Napier's were encountering some problems with the Sabre. Construction of the first prototype began in March 1938 at the Carbury Park Road

premises, Kingston-on-Thames; its powerplant was the twelfth production Vulture engine, which arrived for installation in December 1938. Complete with its engine, the first hand-built Tornado prototype, P5219, was rolled out at Kingston in December 1938. From Kingston the aircraft was sent by road to Langley on 31 July 1939 for final assembly and testing. Upon arrival the airframe was assembled and tested at the new experimental flight department. Taxi trials of the Tornado began on 1 October on the Langley grass airfield; these were confined to short runs to test the braking and to record the engine temperatures. Satisfied that the brakes and engine appeared to be behaving normally, a series of high-speed runs was carried out on 3 October.

Its maiden flight was undertaken by company test pilot P. G. Lucas on 6 October 1939, and was described as uneventful. To get the Tornado airborne required some imaginative effort by Phillip Lucas, who drew his inspiration from the pilots of the Schneider Trophy seaplanes. As the Tornado suffered from a lack of directional stability and excessive engine torque during the take-off run, Phillip Lucas would carry out engine and magneto checks at full power at an angle

to the runway. Once completed, he would maintain full power and begin his take-off at an arc. By the time the Tornado was pointing into the wind, the aircraft was close to reaching take-off speed. Even when first airborne, the fighter still needed to achieve 150mph (240km/h) for the rudder to become fully effective. Of course, such a technique was fine for test pilots such as Lucas and those flying the Vulture-Henley; however, it would never be an option for service pilots, especially when airfields with concrete runways were built.

The engineers from Rolls-Royce were obviously concerned about the behaviour of the Vulture engine, as thermocouples had been installed on six of the engine cylinders, these being distributed between all four banks of cylinders. Their purpose was to monitor the whole of the engine's temperature range throughout the flight, and they rose quite quickly to the permitted maximum temperature before dropping back slightly. This would be maintained until landing, when the temperature rose again. On subsequent flights P. G. Lucas managed to push the Tornado up to a maximum speed of 370mph (595km/h) at 15,000ft (4,500m), although after this effort the engine began to run roughly. Inspection on the ground revealed that there were metal particle traces in the oil filter; analysis suggested that these were coming from the bearing races.

Ground running was another area entirely, as any power running was limited to a maximum of five minutes, otherwise the whole aircraft would be enveloped in clouds of oily smoke. Investigations by both Hawker's and Rolls-Royce engineers revealed that improvements in engineering tolerances between the pistons and their rings needed tightening up. Oil consumption was also causing concern, because it wasn't just being consumed by the leaky rings: the overall consumption rate meant that 50 per cent was used after no more than thirty minutes running. Nevertheless, on the strength of the first flight and subsequent flights, an Instruction to Proceed was issued, which contracted Hawker's to manufacture 500 Tornados, 250 Typhoons and another 250 machines whose powerplant would be selected later.

Details of the Tornado Prototype

As the Vulture was destined to power both the Tornado and the Manchester bomber, later to be revamped as the more famous Lancaster, Hawker's were concerned enough to convert the Henley prototype, K5115, to act as an engine test bed. As this engine required extensive cooling, the Hawker engineers fitted a generous radiator under the fuselage, while a further intake was mounted above the cowling.

The airframe followed Hawker's previous practices, using a metal-braced structure of tubular construction for the fuselage, although the original fabric covering was replaced by aluminium sheet flush-riveted to the framework. The numerous access panels let into the fuselage were of close tolerance, to reduce airflow turbulence. The cockpit canopy sections were backed by a distinctive fairing that would terminate in tail surfaces similar in outline to the earlier Hurricane. The powerplant in this prototype was the Rolls-Royce Vulture II, rated at 1,760hp, which in turn enabled the Tornado to achieve a maximum speed of 423mph (680km/h) at an altitude of 23,000ft (7,000m).

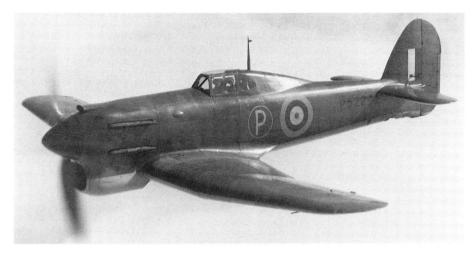

Above **One of the most fervent pilot complaints concerning the Tornado and the early Typhoons was the original canopy, which featured heavy framing and a solid metal rear fairing: both conspired to restrict vision.** Big Bird Aviation Collection

The wings were built as separate assemblies, and were attached to the fuselage by four bolts, two for each wing spar. Each wing section was cranked, the inner section with an anhedral set at 1 degree, whilst the outer sections featured a dihedral of $5\frac{1}{2}$ degrees. Incorporated into the inner sections were the undercarriage bays, which held the strongly built undercarriage legs. Fuel was carried in self-sealing tanks in the leading edge of this section, whilst situated in the outer panels were the armament bays, and the landing lights in the leading edge. Of the flight controls, only the rudder was fabric-covered, the fabric tightened with cellulose dope, whilst the remainder, including the split flaps, was metal-

covered. When attaching the wings to the Tornado, they had to be mounted some 3in (8cm) lower, as the Vulture could not be accommodated over the main spar as the Sabre could.

Test-Flying the Tornado Prototype

Given the shortage of room at Hawker's production facility, the majority of Tornados were built at the premises of A. V. Roe at Manchester, after the initial batch had been constructed at Hawker's Langley factory. During initial test-flying the prototype had its radiator bath posi-

Below **In this view of the Tornado, the windows at the rear of the main canopy are clearly visible, as is the landing light and its cover let into the leading edge of the port wing.** Big Bird Aviation Collection

tioned under the fuselage centre section in a manner similar to the Hurricane; however, the onset of compressibility at high speeds was found to cause adverse airflow conditions around the fairing, which in turn increased the engine's operating temperature. Also there was a sharp increase in drag, accompanied by a violent shuddering and vibration at speeds approaching 400mph (640kph) IAS.

Confirming this phenomenon was a sequence of photographs that revealed the wool tufting applied around the airframe being drawn forwards by the turbulence. To sort out this problem the radiator assembly was moved to a position under the engine. In its new configuration, P5219 undertook its maiden flight on 6 December 1939, thereby establishing the now familiar, under-the-nose radiator

position. This modification, plus the associated strip-down and rebuild, was completed in a week.

The test-flying revealed that although the cooling around the oil cooler had improved, the down side was that the longitudinal stability had deteriorated. To see by how much, wind-tunnel tests using a scale model were carried out, and these revealed severe airflow instabilities just aft of the radiator exit vent; these were further exacerbated by turbulence in the vicinity of the uncovered area of the mainwheels when they were retracted. In flight this was made apparent by a low-frequency rumble that seemed to reach back as far as the rudder. In an effort to reduce these airflow disturbances, small sprung doors were mounted on the main gear doors, closing upon retraction. Although at slow speeds this modification improved the handling of the Tornado, they would misbehave as speeds increased. Eventually these doors would be removed, as they had been on the Henley, Hurricane and Typhoon prototypes, as mud and other debris kept getting wedged in the sprung section, thus causing the door to remain in the airflow. Eventually 'D' doors would be mounted on the inner edges of each bay, hard by the aircraft's centreline.

Having spent January 1940 testing undercarriage improvements, in the following month P5219 was engaged in general handling trials, which would be followed throughout March by Lucas

Above **P5224 was the second Tornado prototype built to Specification F18/37. As airflow problems had been encountered with the ventral radiator installation, it was moved to the more familiar chin-mounted position.** Big Bird Aviation Collection

Below **This side-on view of Hawker Tornado P5224 reveals the supplementary cooling intake mounted above the nose cowling panels, and the double row of engine exhausts applicable to the Vulture engine installation.** Big Bird Aviation Collection

pushing the Tornado to the edge of the flight envelope; this included its maximum performance at 20,500ft (7,000m) in fully supercharged mode. Although the aircraft reached a top speed of 384mph (620km/h), the control instability was even more marked; however, an extension of the under-engine radiator fairing by 3in (7.5cm) smoothed out many of the airflow instabilities. By 9 May, P5219 was the only F.18/37 prototype available for flight trials, as the prototype Typhoon had suffered near catastrophic structural failure that day. With the Typhoon undergoing rebuild, it was the task of the Tornado to flight-test a rudder of increased area: this first flew on 16 May, and was an immediate success as stability was improved. On 12 June a further series of test flights was undertaken to assess the behaviour of the recently added tailwheel doors, both modifications being adjudged successful.

Having pushed the Tornado flight envelope as far as possible, it was time to see if the Vulture engine could be pushed further. To that end P5219 was despatched to Rolls-Royce Hucknall, where engine No. 12 would undergo a series of progressive modifications centred around the oil cooling system, and flight trials to see if the Vulture would perform better. After Rolls-Royce had completed their modifications, the Tornado was returned to Langley in mid-July, complete with a Rotol propeller of 13ft 2.5in (4m 3cm) in diameter, which seemed to improve the engine output absorption. On 27 July, Tornado P5219 made its first flight at its intended all-up weight of 10,225lb (4,638kg): this consisted of the basic aircraft, to which had been added a full fuel load, twelve Browning machine guns, and ballast to represent ammunition. In this condition the aircraft returned a top speed of 396.5mph (638km/h) at 20,800ft (6,340m), while the climb-to-height measured to 20,000ft (6,000m) took just over six minutes – which was considered outstanding for a fighter of this power and weight. However, this period of glory was short-lived as the Vulture would suffer a catastrophic failure on 31 July when at least two connecting rods fractured. In the subsequent crash landing the airframe would also be damaged, although it was quickly repaired.

The second prototype, P5224, made its maiden flight on 5 December 1940 and was also powered by a Vulture II; this

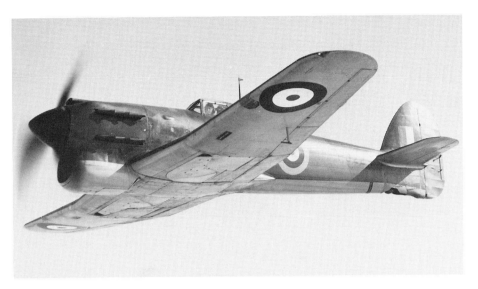

Above **This view of P5224 emphasizes how much of the technology behind the Hurricane was adopted for the Tornado and Typhoon prototypes. This included the concept of the thick wing to house the armament, and a similar wing planform.** Big Bird Aviation Collection

Above **Photographed in October 1941, this official portrait of the Tornado P5224 prototype reveals the cranked wing and the definitive undercarriage door arrangement adopted for both the Typhoon and the Tempest.** C. P. Russell Smith Collection

Specification – Tornado	
Type:	Experimental single-seat fighter
Powerplant:	P5219, 1,760hp Vulture II; R7936 1,980hp Vulture V; HG641 2,210hp Centaurus CE 4S
Weights:	Empty 8,377lb (3,800kg); loaded 10,668lb (4,840kg)
Dimensions::	Span 41ft 11in (12.78m); length 32ft 10in (10m); height 14ft 8in (4.47m); wing area 283sq ft (26.29sq m)
Performance:	Max. speed 398mph (640km/h) with Vulture V, 402mph (647km/h) with Centaurus; rate of climb 7.2min to 20,000ft (6,000m) with Vulture; 8.4min to 20,000ft with Centaurus; range not specified; service ceiling 34,900ft (10,640m)
Armament/fuel tanks:	none

Above **This three-quarter rear view of the Centaurus-powered Tornado reveals that this installation was not as neat as that applied to the Tempest and Sea Fury.** Big Bird Aviation Collection

machine had a Rotol constant speed propellor, which increased the all-up weight to 9,600lb (4,355kg). Other changes from the first prototype included new canopy windows and an altered rudder. In contrast to the first Tornado, this machine had provision for four Hispano cannon instead of the earlier aircraft's twelve machine guns. To simulate an aircraft with a full weapons' load, a full fuel load plus ballast was carried, which pushed the total operating weight up to 10,580lb (4,800kg). In March 1941 the original Vulture II engines in both prototypes were replaced by the intended production engine, the Vulture V, rated at 1,980hp. Testing was undertaken at A&AEE at the end of 1941, and it was established that this version of the Tornado could easily achieve 398mph (640km/h) at an altitude of 23,300ft (7,100m). In contrast to the Typhoon, the Tornado had better longitudinal stability, a slower stalling speed and slightly better vision over the nose.

The Tornado is Aborted

Although the Vultures in the Tornados were behaving reasonably well, those in the Vulture-Henley as well as those installed in the Avro-Manchester bombers were suffering serious problems, although it had successfully passed its type test in 1939. These centred around fractures of the connecting rod bolts, which resulted in failure and in some cases fire; also the cooling system was found to be inefficient, whilst failures of the oil lubrication system contributed to the big-end failures, thus

adding to the fire hazard. As pressure was mounting on Rolls-Royce to increase production of the Merlin engine, it was decided to cease development of the Vulture, and it was abandoned. As an alternative to the Vulture it was proposed to install the Wright Duplex Cyclone Type C engine, or the Fairey Monarch in the Tornado. Design work for this change began in January 1941 at Kingston, and would continue until July when the Ministry of Aircraft Production ordered that all such development work would cease.

Not all traces of the Tornado programme would disappear, however, as Avro had already started production, completing its first machine, R7936, at Woodford, which would undertake its maiden flight on 29 August 1941. A further four were already on the jigs close to completion, whilst a further set of detail parts for 100 more were in stock at the Yeadon factory. Unlike its predecessor, it was built with the chin radiator from the outset. Once Avros had completed test-flying of this machine, it was flown to Langley. Its stay with Hawker's was short, as two days later it was on its way to Rotol Propellors Ltd at Staverton, Glos. From Staverton, R7936 was passed on to de Havilland Propellors Ltd at Hatfield; at both locations its role had been that of development test-flying of various types of propellor. During an eighteen-month period this machine was the recipient of a variety of six-bladed contra-rotating propellors from both manufacturers. Both Tornados, R7936 and R7938, continued in use with RAE during 1943, before being withdrawn in 1944 for disposal.

When it became obvious that the Tornado programme was going to be aborted, Sydney Camm had suggested that at least one Tornado should be used in the development work of the new Bristol Centaurus eighteen-cylinder engine then under development at Filton. As other work was taking precedence, it was not until April 1940 that further steps were taken to progress this idea, when an additional prototype was ordered. In the event, however, only a new centre section was constructed, as the remaining major components were drawn from stock at Langley. Serialled HG641, this new machine, complete with a Centaurus CE.45 engine rated at 2,210hp, was rolled out for its maiden flight by P. G. Lucas on 23 October 1941. Unfortunately initial test flights revealed serious problems, with the engines cooling as the exhaust collector ring was carried forward of the powerplant, this culminating in a single exhaust which vented under the port wing. To counter this, the exhaust pipes were split in two and vented under the aircraft's centre section, while the cowlings themselves were modified to accept the changes. Another modification applied to the cowling was the oil cooler intake, which was extended to the cowling lower edge to improve the cooling airflow.

The Rotol propeller assembly fitted to HG641 featured a large spinner that covered the complete hub. After the modifications had been applied to HG641, its performance and behaviour improved markedly, so much so that a small contract for a further six was placed in early 1942. The revamped engine installation allowed the Centaurus Tornado to resume flying again in November 1942. During these flights a maximum speed of 412mph (663km/h) was achieved, at an altitude of 18,000ft (5,500m).

Although these test flights were successful, no more would be built: the six Centaurus-powered Tornados would be cancelled because the test-flying of a Centaurus in the Typhoon II was proving it to be a far more capable aircraft. The sole Centaurus Tornado continued in use as a test bed until August 1944, when it was scrapped.

Hawker's new fighter might have been cancelled, but its contribution to the subsequent Typhoon, Tempest and Sea Fury development programmes cannot be underestimated.

CHAPTER THREE

The Typhoon in Development

At the same time as Hawker's were busy developing the Tornado, they were also proceeding apace with the alternative version, then known as the Type 'N', but soon to be renamed the Typhoon; this was also being hand built by the experimental staff at Canbury Park Road, Kingston. The contract – 815124/38, for the two Typhoon prototypes to works order No. 5232 – was issued to Hawker's on 3 March 1938. The resultant prototype, P5212, powered by a Sabre engine rated at 2,200hp, made its maiden flight with P. G. Lucas at the controls on 24 February 1940.

To get the aircraft to this stage the Hawker design team, led by Camm, had had to exercise extreme ingenuity to shoehorn the Sabre into the airframe. Complicating the installation was the need to move the engine backwards some 7in (18cm) to maintain the centre of gravity. To accommodate this change the engine bearer structures, secondary structural components, connections and all the various fairing panels underwent complete redesign. Although this sounded complicated, it did in fact make installing the Napier Sabre a far easier task, as it allowed the deletion of various structural components that had been required for the Rolls-Royce Vulture. Overall these changes would result in an aircraft some 120lb (55kg) lighter and a few inches shorter. The down side was that mounting the engine virtually onto the main spar accentuated the effects of undampened engine vibration, and led to secondary harmonics transmitting along the inboard wing structure and rear spar to the centre and rear fuselage.

Test-Flying the Typhoon

First taxi trials were made on 23 February 1940, as well as a short airborne hop that would confirm that the prototype Typhoon, in common with the prototype Tornado, was short on longitudinal stability. In fact Philip Lucas would later report

that even at 70mph (112km/h) on the ground, the rudder was so ineffective that the Typhoon would continue to turn to port even with the rudder fully deflected in the opposite direction. In fact Lucas made strong representations to Napier's about the vibration and noise generated by the Sabre, although they continued to deny his allegations. Eventually the complaints were written into a formal report that not only mentioned these two major faults, but would also highlight the fact that as the upper ranges of rpm were reached, the vibration became so bad as to make the cockpit instruments unreadable, this being accompanied by a persistent, severe, low frequency buzz throughout the cockpit. In an attempt to reduce these effects the instrument panel mountings were tightened, rubber bungee grommets were installed on the pilot's seat, while the wheel-mounting spigots were shortened slightly. Changes were recommended for the exhaust system, as it was admitted that they were inadequate for the Typhoon, and also for the engine and its oil system. It was suspected that under proper flight conditions, the engine temperatures might rise dangerously high.

This machine led a fairly adventurous life, as it would lose part of its undernose fairing during the second flight on 1 March. The cause was never completely discovered, but the panel fasteners were changed as a precaution. During the remainder of the month the Typhoon was flown a further eight times, and Lucas was able to report that the modifications had reduced the various faults, though to a barely acceptable level. During these flights Lucas pushed P5212 to a maximum speed of 376mph (605km/h) at 20,400ft (6,220m). At the end of this sequence the engine was throwing oil, indicating that the header tank pressure-relief valve was blowing off; also fuel consumption was far higher than predicted, especially at constant engine outputs.

P5212 was then fitted with Sabre 1 No. 95005, and test-flying was resumed. By 4 April a new fuel pump, complete with lowered gearing and simplified piping, was test-flown, and found to give better performance in the subsequent test flight. This engine was then removed for its twenty-five-hour strip examination, and replaced with another whose mountings had been changed from the original solid type to a

Above **This side-on view of Typhoon 1A, R7579, reveals that this first batch was fairly basic in comparison to the versions that followed. Changes included installation of cannon armament, strengthening of the rear fuselage, modification of the elevator control balance, and more significantly, the fitment of a clear vision canopy.** Big Bird Aviation Collection

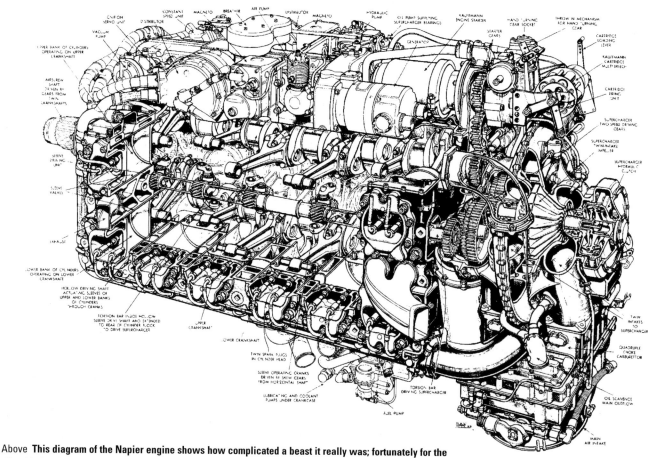

Above This diagram of the Napier engine shows how complicated a beast it really was; fortunately for the pilot, his involvement required no more than the operation of a few levers. Courtesy Rolls-Royce

dampened version mounted on shock-absorbing rubber pads. Coupled to this fitment was the installation of a Vibrograph on the behest of the RAE.

Flying with the new engine resumed on 7 May, and Lucas reported that engine and airframe vibration seemed to have been reduced. But just two days later, on 9 May, whilst flying P5212 for Vibrograph tests, the aircraft suffered partial structural failure of the rear fuselage at a speed of 270mph (434km/h) at an altitude of 10,500ft (3,100m). Unaware of the damage caused, the pilot, P. G. Lucas, turned the prototype towards Langley where he made an excellent landing, keeping the undercarriage and flaps retracted until the last moment, even though the controls felt loose and sloppy with a distinct tendency to drift to port. Investigation revealed that two of the primary structural members aft of the cockpit had failed, which in turn had placed great strain upon the monocoque rear fuselage, which had begun to come apart. For his efforts in returning the prototype

Typhoon safely to *terra firma*, Lucas was awarded the George Medal. Strangely enough it was deduced that the primary cause of the failure was the engine vibrations, which had literally shaken the structure apart.

The aircraft was safely recovered, and rebuilt with redesigned engine mountings; it went on to test numerous Sabre engines, including the Mk II S.322 during May 1942. But on 7 July, P5212 again suffered an engine failure, obliging the pilot to make a hasty landing at Langley. Yet again the aircraft was repaired, and whilst in the process of this, the opportunity was taken to fit an enlarged tailplane to see if it would improve stability and handling. In contrast to the second prototype, this machine had mountings incorporated for twelve Browning machine guns. The initial test flights were seen as promising, so Lord Beaverbrook, the Minister of Aircraft Production, made arrangements for Napiers to have enlarged premises so that production of the Sabre could begin

en masse. However, there would be no avalanche of engines, as the requisite airframes did not exist, there being only the two prototypes.

The second prototype, P5216, made its first flight on 3 May 1941; it was also piloted by P. G. Lucas, and featured extended wingtips. The engine fitted for this flight was development Sabre No. 95018, but a few months later it would be replaced by a production version Sabre II, No. S.322, while armament in the form of four 20mm Hispano cannon was fitted on 27 April 1941. By this time the Typhoon had followed the soon-to-be-cancelled Tornado on to the list of aircraft to be manufactured for war service; the selected manufacturer was the Gloster Aircraft Company Ltd, based at Hucclecote in Gloucester.

While production lines were being established for both the engine and airframe, the prototype Typhoon was running into trouble, the main cause centring around the Sabre engine; this was proving temperamental, especially at altitudes above 20,000ft

(6,000m). However, the airframe was also behaving less well than expected, as manoeuvrability, and especially the roll rate, was sloppy. During 1941 attempts were made to improve the behaviour of the airframe, these being centred around both extending and clipping the wingtips. Both proved to be viable prospects, but neither would be adopted, because the resultant loss in performance was not acceptable. Further attempts to improve the behaviour of the airframe included a six cannon installation that was abandoned at the mock-up stage, and an exhaust-driven supercharger that was also trialled, but in the event was abandoned.

When the second prototype Typhoon, P5216, made its first flight in May 1941, it was fitted with one of the recommended armament installations, in this case four 20mm Hispano long-barrel cannon, two per wing. Each weapon was belt-fed, and each had 140 rounds. Changes from the first aircraft included the deletion of the small windows in the canopy fairing, as these were found to be of little use. The fairings for the undercarriage were also modified. The original set-up had hinged fairings attached to the main doors, but these had a tendency to become damaged by the build-up of mud and grass when operating from unprepared airfields; a 'D' door was therefore installed at the fuselage wing root joint.

The First Production Aircraft

Even though the Typhoon prototypes were experiencing performance and behaviour troubles, enough progress was being made with the various modifications to allow

Above **This underside view of a Typhoon IA reveals the crank built into the wing, plus the layout of flaps, and also the construction of the radiator under the nose, and the location of the flap that could be opened to improve the airflow on take-off and landing.** C. P. Russell Smith Collection

production by Gloster Aircraft to proceed. The first production aircraft, R7576, made its first flight on 27 May 1941, just over three weeks after the second prototype had flown. This machine was very similar to P5216, except that it featured machine-gun armament instead of the preferred cannon, as the cannon-feed mechanisms manufactured by Chatellerault were in seriously short supply due to service requirements elsewhere. After manufacturers' flight trials, the first production aircraft would be operated mainly by the Royal Aircraft Establishment, although some time was spent with No. 56 Sqn for

front-line evaluation. To differentiate between the machine-gun version and the cannon-armed machines they were designated the Mark 1A and Mark 1B respectively. As Browning machine guns were easier to obtain, much of the early production was delivered as the Mark 1A variant. When the cannon and its feed mechanisms became more plentiful, the Mark 1B replaced the earlier version on the production line. Altogether 110 Typhoon IAs were manufactured, although some would later be reworked to Mark 1B standard.

It was during this early period in the

Right **Typhoon IB, R7700, was employed by the A&AEE for use in carbon monoxide leaks trials, radio and IFF tests, engine cooling, fuel consumption, plus climb and speed trials. This portrait reveals that this aircraft has had the first tail unit strengthening modification carried out. This was a one-piece steel band that was later replaced by fishplates. As this was a Typhoon IB, the aircraft sports four cannon, and the first attempt to improve the pilot's vision.** Big Bird Aviation Collection

Typhoon's development that the Luftwaffe began to deploy a fighter that was far more potent than the Messerschmitt Bf 109. This was the Focke-Wulf Fw 190, which was faster and more manoeuvrable than the current RAF front-line fighter, the Supermarine Spitfire V. To find a counter to this new threat, the fifth and sixth airframes were despatched to the Air Fighting Development Unit at Duxford, where they were flown in competition against a Spitfire V. They had to use these two brand-new machines because all the others were heavily involved in trials work at the manufacturers, the A&AEE and RAE. In the comparative flights between the Spitfire and Typhoon, the latter outperformed the former by some 40mph (65km/h), especially at altitudes of 14,000ft (4,200m) or below. In common with other agencies, the AFDU found the Typhoon to be less manoeuvrable than the Spitfire, although its high speed would be noted as useful in low level combat.

Even though the AFDU report had been encouraging in places, overall the Royal Air Force had not yet envisaged a role for such a heavyweight fighter – which was unfortunate, as the production rate at Hucclecote was increasing. While complete aircraft were stacking up awaiting usage, the design teams at Hawker's and Napier's, as well as at Gloster's, were also in the throes of trying to improve the reliability of the engine and airframe. The first defect to be looked at was a problem with carbon monoxide fumes leaking back into the cockpit through the front bulkhead. Careful investigation and sealing of the bulkhead helped reduce the fault, and pilots were instructed to wear oxygen masks wherever possible.

Serious Problems with Structural Failure

The next fault to appear was far more serious and took some time to rectify satisfactorily. On 29 July 1942 a pilot undergoing conversion training with No. 257 Sqn was killed when the complete tail unit of his Typhoon, R8633, detached whilst the plane was making a turn during a shallow dive; the machine plunged away out of control, coming to earth just south-west of High Ercall. Within two weeks a further tragic loss occurred when a Hawker test pilot, Ken Seth-Smith, was killed

when his Typhoon IB, R7692, also suffered a catastrophic failure of the tail unit; the wreckage landed near Staines. At the time the aircraft was being put through a series of spinning trials. A third loss occurred in the following week when an aircraft flying in a No. 56 Sqn formation disintegrated in mid-air, killing the pilot.

The reaction to this failure was to ground the Typhoons immediately until a fix could be applied. Investigations revealed that under certain flight loadings excessive pressures were being applied to the transport assembly joint, the interface between the rear fuselage and the tail unit. Whilst waiting for a fully developed modification, a temporary repair was applied, in which a steel butt strap was wrapped around the whole joint. This, however, was heavy, cumbersome, and also caused some trim problems, so another repair was developed that was lighter but just as strong. Known as Mod 286, this consisted of twenty high-tensile steel plates that were riveted to the airframe at equidistant points around the transport joint. The civilian working parties from the manufacturers were mainly assisted in this task by No. 13 Maintenance Unit at Henlow; they undertook the programme on at least 300 airframes from December 1942 until March 1943. On the production line the modification was introduced as standard from the 820th aircraft onwards.

Although the stress analysts at Hawker's and their counterparts at the RAE were fairly sure that the tail-shedding problem had been resolved, further investigations were made. Close examination of the recoverable wreckage seemed to indicate that the transport joint might not have been the cause of the failures. To test out this theory, Typhoons fitted with stress and strain gauges underwent a series of airborne tests; these mainly consisted of diving up to maximum speed, close to 500mph (800km/h), then executing a violent manoeuvre as if to escape enemy AAA fire. Given the speed of these dives and the gyrations undertaken afterwards, it is immediately obvious that these pilots were putting their lives on the line for what became a set of inconclusive results.

Attention then turned to the operational squadrons, especially Nos 181 and 182 Squadrons who were using their Typhoons in the dive-bombing role; close inspection of these machines revealed a

slight buckling of the rear fuselage in the area of the transport joint. However, ground trials of these machines soon established that the structures were more than capable of accepting the loads imposed. Another area of the airframe placed under closer examination was the elevator mass balance, carried centrally in the fuselage. It was discovered that under great stress the mounting bracket could fail, thus rendering the elevators uncontrollable due to induced flutter.

While these investigations were proceeding, further Typhoons were being lost due to structural failure: by May 1943 the total had risen to thirteen, with only one pilot surviving, a Pilot Officer Kilpatrick of No. 192 Sqn, who somehow managed to fight his way clear of his tumbling fighter to parachute to safety. What confused the issue even more was that some of these machines had undergone the structural modification process. At this point the investigators changed their approach, preferring to look at other causes. Amongst the main areas to come under scrutiny were the elevator and rudder. The former was definitely seen as a prime candidate, as this was the particular surface that had been used just before the transport joint failed, and the balance mounting bracket had failed. Flutter or harmonic vibrations were now suspected of being the primary cause of the crashes, therefore the focus moved to the mass balance weights attached to the elevators.

After numerous flight trials with weights of different mass and size, a modification programme was undertaken to fit all new and surviving machines with the new items. On the whole it seemed to be a success, although the occasional single aircraft, possibly more, arriving back at base would report elevator control problems having exceeded 500mph (800km/h) in a dive. When inspected, the lightening holes that the elevator rods passed through in the fuselage were found to be distorted, and in some cases cracked due to the deflection loads placed upon the control rods when pulling out of a dive.

Evidently this situation could not be allowed to continue because of possible problems with pilot morale, so the decision was taken to fit production Typhoons with the Tempest tailplane of increased span, which, it was confidently predicted, would eliminate the tail-end failure

Above **This three-quarter forward view of a Typhoon IB shows the striping under the wings that was applied to stop various Allied forces trying to shoot the type down. This aircraft also sports a white nose, although this modification was quickly removed as it compromised the effectiveness of the camouflage.**
Big Bird Aviation Collection

completely. This modification came on stream at the beginning of 1944, and was followed by another later that year, which changed the elevator mass balance shape again. Overall the accident rate for the Typhoon was reduced considerably, although there were a final three crashes in 1945: as far as these were concerned, reports seemed to indicate that one or both main undercarriage units were becoming unlocked in flight and dropping into the airflow, and the ensuing turbulence was suspected of placing unacceptable loads upon the airframe, which would then break up. However, no further action would be taken to solve the Typhoon's departing rear end since it was leaving RAF service in 1945 as more and more Tempests became available.

The Sabre Gives Cause for Concern

Whilst the rear end of the airframe was causing considerable trouble, things were not going so well under the engine cowlings, either. The Sabre engine, although powerful, was giving everyone concerned with the Typhoon development programme serious cause for concern. Not only was it temperamental, but Napier's were unable to manufacture enough to keep up with airframe production, so

Gloster's were faced with the situation of either having engineless aircraft cluttering up Hucclecote, or removing them to maintenance units where they could be stored while awaiting powerplants. The latter was the preferred option, although it did mean a perpetual cycle of engine changes, where the delivered aircraft would land at the MU and have its engine removed, this then being returned for use in the next airframe. The engine shortage also caused problems with the completion of the test-flight schedule, and any rectification required at turnarounds tended to be rather quick.

In front-line service, too, the behaviour of the Sabre was proving rather worrying. The cause was centred around the sleeve valves, which were seizing after a few hours of flying time. To counter this, a rigorous series of inspections was put in place, though this meant pulling the engine from the airframe every twenty-five hours, which reduced the available operating fleet. The situation improved in May 1943 when the inspection schedule was increased to the thirty-hour flying mark; however, this was only achieved by careful husbandry, which included keeping the engine warm by the use of external hot air blowers.

Obviously such a situation could not be allowed to continue, and Napier's therefore began a programme of research to resolve this problem. Consultation with

Bristol Engines of Filton helped provide the answer, as this company had extensive experience in the production of sleeve-valve engines. The solution was to select the right material for the task, and apply such treatments as nitriding and lapping the valves before assembly. Once the full permutation of metal alloys had been explored and the right one selected, Napier's then embarked on a massive modification programme to install the new valves. This in turn temporarily reduced the availability of Typhoons, so the fighter squadrons had their flying hours cut to 300 per month, whilst those undertaking the more strenuous art of dive bombing were restricted to 200 hours per month. But the restrictions were worth it in the long run, as Sabre reliability improved far beyond the original availability figure – although, in common with other piston engines, it could still be a temperamental beast.

In an effort to improve the performance of the Sabre engine and the Typhoon in general, in 1943 Napier's fitted Tornado R8694 with version IV of the Sabre engine. The major change from the earlier version was the installation of an annular radiator instead of the characteristic chin type. Test-flying by Napier's produced a reported top speed of 452mph (727km/h); however, because the Tempest programme was well on in its development, the Typhoon with its modified engine was no more than an interesting sideline.

Shortcomings in the Airframe

While the manufacturers and the various test organizations were struggling to rectify the more obvious defects that had beset the Typhoon, the operational units were also voicing their complaints – the main one being the terrible all-round pilot's vision. The first step in resolving this fault involved replacing the solid metal rear cockpit fairing that featured on the early-build machines with a single-piece perspex canopy. Having dealt with one area specifically to improve the pilot's vision, Hawker's then turned their attention to improving the remainder of the canopy, whose heavy framing also restricted the outlook. Initially the plan was to develop a lightweight windscreen assembly with a smaller frame, which would be allied to a revamped main canopy. Although the new windscreen assembly would eventually be introduced, the remainder was superseded by a one-piece blown canopy designed to slide to the rear; this would replace the car door and multi-part original. Initial flight trials were undertaken using airframe R8809; test-flying began in January 1943.

From the outset the new canopy was praised by all involved with the trials, which had included pilots seconded to the manufacturers, the RAE and the AFDU. Further trials began at Northolt in February using service pilots who would also heap praise upon the redesigned canopy. The modified machine was greeted with delight by all who flew it; however, it actually took until November 1943 for it to come on line.

One further attempt to extend the pilot's vision was to fit a rear-view mirror under a small perspex blister on top of the canopy. However, in service this was found to be less than useless because of vibration, and failures to the canopy finally led to it being abandoned. In parallel to the new canopy being introduced on the production line, a programme was put in motion to modify as many of the older machines as possible. However, this did not start until September 1943, which meant that on D-Day some aircraft were still flying on operations with the original heavy-framed 'coffin hood' canopy assembly.

Pilots were also responsible for the next modification, which involved replacing the original rigid seat with a sprung assembly. This was needed in order to counter the excessive high frequency vibration experienced at certain engine settings. When the four-bladed propellor modification was introduced in 1944 it was hoped that this would completely eliminate the vibration; however, the handling was found to be unacceptable. The cure for this would be the installation of the Tempest tailplane, with its increased span.

The modified aircraft began to enter squadron service from February 1944. Except for a slight tendency for the tail unit still to come adrift, this final version of the modified Typhoon was a vast improvement on the original. Other modifications were applied as the war progressed: these included cannon barrel fairings, the fitment of exhaust stub fairings, and the replacement of the aerial mast by a whip aerial. Only one was subsequently removed, and that was the exhaust stub fairings, which were found to be less than beneficial in use.

Above Standing on pierced steel planking, this Typhoon IB epitomizes the pinnacle of the type's development: thus it sports the extended span Tempest tailplane, a four-bladed propeller to better absorb the Sabre engine's prodigious output, a full-blown canopy plus a full spread of rockets mounted on rails under the wings. Of note is the incomplete D-Day striping under the wings. Real Wings Collection

Alternative Roles for the Typhoon

Although the Typhoon was intended as a fighter or fighter bomber, there were attempts to fit it for other roles, such as night fighting. In June 1942 Typhoon R7651 was withdrawn from No. 266 Sqn and delivered to the Fighter Interception Unit at Ford for trials in the night-fighting role. In contrast to the Spitfires and Hurricanes that had already been tried, the Typhoon was found to be easy to fly at night, especially on instruments. However, to fit it for the night-fighter role proper, a series of modifications was suggested. These included a sliding clear canopy for improved all-round vision, improved and redesigned cockpit lighting, and improved braking. Further trials involving Typhoon R7630 were begun in August 1942 at the FIU, in conjunction with a Turbinlite twin-engined Boston. This particular type of aircraft was fitted with AI radar aerials and a powerful searchlight in the nose; when in range of its target as detected by the radar array, the accompanying fighter would theoretically shoot it down. But the trials involving the Typhoon were a mismatch, as the cruising speed of the Boston was only just above the Typhoon's stalling speed, which made it extremely difficult to maintain any form of formation. Even so, the high speed of

the fighter meant that it could hit a detected target hard and fast.

In order to remove the disparity, plans were put in hand to create a proper night-fighting Typhoon. The trials aircraft was R7881, converted by Hawker's as the prototype Typhoon NF.1B. To create this version the port wing main fuel tank was removed to allow for the installation of the AI Mark VI transmitter and receiver boxes, whilst the radar aerials themselves were mounted on the leading edges of both wings. Although at first sight the deletion of a primary fuel tank could be seen as retrograde, there was in fact compensation in the form of a pair of under-wing fuel tanks, each of which could contain 45gal (205ltr) of fuel. After company flight trials, the Typhoon was passed on to the RAE at Farnborough in April 1943 for assessment of the aircraft, and of the radar's performance.

As these trials were successful, another series of night-fighter trials was carried out over London by pilots of the FIU. These would prove uneventful, with no 'trade' being available, although the trials were deemed a success. The report after the trials was very positive, praising as it did the aircraft's speed, which allowed for quick interceptions to be made. Coupled to this was the efficacy of the AI system, whose range was effective between 500 and 9,000ft (150 and 2,750m); and the aircraft's manouvrability that allowed good tracking of a target during the interception phase. Oddly enough, although R7881 had proved the concept of the Typhoon night fighter, this one machine would remain a 'one-off', being stripped of its radar equipment and then passed to No. 3 Tactical Exercise Unit at Honiley in July 1944. Why the Typhoon was chosen for this task is a mystery, since the night-fighter versions of the Mosquito and the Beaufighter were much better suited to the role, and as they carried two crew, were more than up to the task.

The Typhoon as Ground-Attacking Fighter Bomber

The role that would come to epitomize the Typhoon's role in RAF service was that of ground attack as a fighter bomber. Although it was originally conceived as a pure interceptor fighter, its performance at altitudes above 14,000ft (4,270m) was not very good, which meant that its future was at lower levels. The original concept of the fighter bomber had been proven by the

Hawker Hurricane, once its days as a front-line fighter had ended.

To see if the Typhoon was a suitable aircraft, R7646 was passed to the A&AEE in August 1942 for trials. For this purpose it was fitted with a faired bomb rack under each wing, each rated to carry one 500lb (225kg) general-purpose bomb. The flight trials revealed that in straight and level flight there appeared to be little alteration to the aircraft's handling and performance; however, when entering a dive, airframe buffeting ensued at an indicated air speed of 350mph (560km/h), which in turn would place a maximum limiting speed of 400mph (640km/h) on the Typhoon in operational use. When flown within these limits the Typhoon experienced no noticeable change in trim once the bombs had been released. As well as carrying out trials using 250 and 500lb (110 and 225kg) general-purpose bombs, R7646 was also employed in gun-heating tests, and the testing of a signal discharger.

Further trials were undertaken in October using the same machine; by this time the aircraft had been modified with extended ejector slots under the wings to

assist in the clearance of spent cannon cartridges away from the bombs and mounting racks. One of the first trials undertaken using R7646 was the measurement of the Typhoon's maximum speed in level flight fully loaded. This showed that a clean Typhoon travelling at an altitude of 8,000ft (2,500m) was capable of a True Air Speed of 372mph (599km/h), but whilst loaded the True Air Speed dropped to 336mph (540km/h).

Judged as successful, the fighter-bomber version of the Typhoon was passed for production. Hawker's would begin fitting bomb-carrying equipment to production airframes in mid-October 1942, although production would be split between both fighter and fighter-bomber versions until the middle of 1943, when the fighter-bomber version would become standard. Trials with 500lb general-purpose bombs were successful, although a modified anti-shimmy tailwheel and tyre were required, to stop the tail wagging with the heavier load. After service trials in March 1943, the latest modifications were embodied on the production airframes from the 1,001st aircraft onwards, whilst as many as possible of the original machines already in service were brought up to the same standard. First service deliveries were made to No. 181 Squadron.

Extending the Typhoon's capabilities to carry a heavier load was the next step. During April 1943, the production Typhoon DN340, fitted with a four-blade propeller, was passed to the A&AEE for trials with 1,000lb (450kg) general-purpose bombs. With a full load of fuel and bombs, the Typhoon weighed in at 13,250lb (6,010kg) AUW. In contrast to the service norm of taking off from grass or PSP planked runways, the trials aircraft used the concrete runways at RAE Thruxton, to eliminate the tendency of a loaded Typhoon to nose-down before rotation. During these trials, take-offs were executed with the flaps set at 15 degrees down. Behaviour was similar to a lightly loaded aircraft without any external weapons, although it required a slightly longer run. In the air, the aircraft with its increased bomb load behaved much as had the Typhoon with 500lb bombs, although the top speed reached by DN340 was held at 390mph (630km/h) IAS.

The trial reports cleared the new combination for service usage, although doubts were raised about the performance of the

Below **This close-up view of the aerial installation fitted to R7881 also shows the cylindrical 45gal (200ltr) external fuel tanks that were permanently carried, as one of the wing tanks had been removed to accommodate the radar transmitter and receiver equipment.** Real Wings Collection

four-bladed propeller with the shorter span tailplane, and some problems were experienced with the bomb-release mechanisms. Putting right these problems meant that the service entry of the Typhoon in its modified form was delayed until April 1944, when No. 143 Wing received the first machines. The ability to use both types of bomb gave the mission planners greater flexibility for each target. The performance and stability of the Typhoon was further improved when the increased span tailplane of the Tempest was fitted, which allowed the top speed in dives to be increased. Trials were carried out during June 1944, and would clear the Typhoon for a top dive speed of 450mph (725km/h) maximum. Only one other type of bomb would be cleared for use by the Typhoon before it was retired from RAF use, this being a 520lb (235kg) anti-personel bomb, consisting of twenty-six 20lb (9kg) segments.

The Typhoon and the Unguided Rocket

Having proved itself as a fighter bomber, it is hardly surprising that Hawker's and the Air Staff would cast about in an effort to extend the Typhoon's capabilities even further, and a weapon that was subsequently adopted as standard was the unguided rocket. The first operational use of such a weapon had been undertaken in 1942, when they were deployed under the lower wings of the Fairey Swordfish. During 1943 the unguided rocket was also applied successfully to another Hawker product, the Hurricane. Even as the Hurricane was using the rocket offensively, in June 1943 Hawker's fitted Typhoon EK497 with a set of Mark 1 rocket rails, capable of toting eight 3in (8cm) RPs. After its period as a trials machine, EK497 would be returned to active service; however, while on active service with No. 183 Sqn, it was lost on 1 January 1945 when a USAAF North American P-51 Mustang shot it down by mistake while the British fighter was in circuit waiting to land at Y.29 near Asche.

Trial firings under the aegis of the A&AEE and the AFDU were adjudged so successful that an immediate modification programme was instituted to convert as many aircraft as soon as possible. Running parallel to the aircraft programme was one

to train pilots in the use of the new weapon. This entailed learning to use the gunsight in a new manner in order to place the rockets on target. Such were the resources put into this programme that the first unit to equip, No. 181 Squadron, received its first machines in October 1943. By the time D-Day missions began on 6 June 1944, the 2nd Tactical Air Force was able to deploy eleven squadrons flying rocket-equipped Typhoons that worked in concert with seven Typhoon fighter-bomber units.

Having cleared the rocket installation for use, attention now turned to the rocket rails themselves. The original Mark 1 units were made from steel, which made them very unwieldy as they weighed over 400lb (180kg). Such heavyweight items had a detrimental effect upon both the ground-crew and the performance of the Typhoon, so they were quickly redesigned. The resultant Mark III rail assemblies were made from aluminium and weighed in at 240lb (110kg); they were first test-flown during mid-1944, and entered operational service with the squadrons of the 2nd TAF in December. Another benefit of the change to aluminium in the rails' construction was a welcome increase of 15mph (24km/h) in top speed.

The introduction of the lighter rail assemblies was not the end of development in rocket technology. In an effort to increase the firepower available to the Typhoon, trials were undertaken with the rockets double-banked vertically. In this form they were linked together using a Duplex No. 2 connector, and were launched together when the sequence was initiated. To give greater flexibility the Duplex No. 3 connector was developed, which allowed rockets to be fired either singly or in salvoes. The first test flights of the Duplex rocket-equipped Typhoon were undertaken in August 1944, when MN861 was transferred to A&AEE at Boscombe Down for evaluation.

The post trials report stated that the handling characteristics were satisfactory, and that the new rail assemblies were more that capable of withstanding dives of 450mph (725km/h) IAS. Take-off performance from grass runways was also deemed satisfactory, although it was slightly longer than before. Further evaluations were then undertaken by the AFDU at Wittering using Typhoon EK290, although their report differed from that prepared by the A&AEE in that the take-off and landing

runs were longer, the climb-to-height speed was sluggish, and the top speed had been reduced to 310mph (500km/h). After both reports had been weighed up, the 2nd TAF erred on the side of caution and decided not to proceed with their use on operations generally, although some partial installations were deployed against specific targets.

Trials with Napalm

Having cleared fairly conventional weapons for use by the Typhoon, the AFDU became involved in trials involving napalm during late 1944. First test drops were made over the Holbeach ranges, and were followed by attacks against dummy trenches and pillbox fortifications at Collyweston. Mustangs as well as Typhoons were involved in these trials, both using modified versions of their own specific fuel drop tanks. Compared with the sophisticated weapons deployed in Vietnam later on, the bombs tested in 1944 were quite crude in comparison, consisting of napalm gel in the tanks ignited by white phosphorus grenades.

The initial tests were completed in January 1945, and overall were seen as disappointing due to the small quantity of napalm gel in the fuel tanks. To increase their effectiveness, new containers containing 1,000lb (450kg) of gel were constructed. But service trials against live targets were less than satisfactory, as on the first run the tanks failed to ignite. The second run was more successful, however, and the target was completely destroyed. A third attack was made on 12 April 1945: this involved eight Typhoons against a target near Arnhem and was even more effective, especially as it was followed up by a bomb strike. The use of napalm by the Royal Air Force was not extensive, however, and would come to an end in early 1946.

Carrying fuel for napalm bombs was not the primary role of the tanks under the wings of the Typhoon. Hawker's heavyweight began trials with underwing tanks, each containing 45gal (205ltr), that had originally been developed for the earlier Hurricane. Typhoon R8762 was used for each test flight in December 1942. Without external tanks the nominal range for the Typhoon was some 600 nautical miles, depending on external weapons, engine throttle settings and altitude.

Above **This head-on view of a Typhoon FR.1B reveals the modifications carried out to create this version: only the outer cannons still remain, the inner one on the port side having been removed to allow for the carriage of reconnaissance cameras, whilst the starboard one has been replaced by a forward-facing camera gun.** Big Bird Aviation Collection

When the external tanks were installed, the Typhoon's range was extended by 50 per cent, the trials using R8762 showing that 1,090 nautical miles were possible at an altitude of 5,000ft (1,500m), although to achieve this the tanks had to be dropped once empty.

After completion of the conventional fuel tank trials, R8762 was then flown with a single drop tank and a single 500lb bomb. Once these were completed, further trials were carried out using a single 500lb bomb. All these trials centred upon the behaviour of the rudder with these various loads, the ensuing deflection requirements later being passed on to the front-line pilots. Once production plumbing had been designed, installation was started on new build aircraft, whilst those already in service were modified as soon as the opportunity arose. The increase in range then allowed the Typhoon to roam over France, Holland and Germany attacking designated or random targets at will.

The Typhoon as Fighter Reconnaissance

Whilst steps were being taken to extend the combat capabilities of the Typhoon, its possible use in the fighter reconnaissance role was also being investigated. The primary aircraft assigned to this mission was the North American Mustang I powered by the Allison engine: the latter had been found wanting in combat at altitude, but had proved supreme in the reconnaissance role. Following the Mustang I into RAF service came the Mustang III, powered by a Packard-built Merlin engine. This latter machine was withdrawn from the fighter reconnaissance role due to a more pressing requirement for long-range escort fighters. This left the earlier Mark 1 to shoulder the burden – although stocks of these machines were running low, and no replacements were forthcoming.

The Air Ministry therefore cast about for a suitable replacement to supplement the surviving Mustangs. The first aircraft to feature a reconnaissance fit was JR207, which underwent trials with No. 400 Squadron during January 1944. Post-trial reports were obviously successful, as production orders were placed for 200 conversion kits to create the Typhoon FR1.B. The camera installation consisted of one 14in (35cm) and two 5in (13cm) focal length cameras installed in the port wing inner cannon bay. The first conversion was MN315, which became the production prototype in February 1944. The majority of the aircraft were drawn from those engineless aircraft that were still held in various maintenance units around the country. Although the Typhoon FR.1B entered service with the 2nd TAF, this organization decided that their greater priority was for ground-attack machines: therefore suitably modified versions of the Spitfire Mark IX and the Griffon-powered Mark XIV were deployed instead. Even so, some Typhoon FR.1Bs were deployed on operations from July 1944, when No. 268 Squadron received a handful of aircraft.

In service the 'Tac R' Typhoons were found to be less than suitable for the role compared with the Mustang I: comparisons between the two were invariably made, and the former was found wanting. The Typhoon might have been a good ground-attack platform at a reasonable altitude, but at low level and at high speed it was unstable and not as manoeuvrable as the American product. Coupled to this was the vibration experienced at low level, not only in flight, but when the cannon were fired. This resulted in blurred and indistinct photographs, also the yaw caused by the cannon firing muddied the images. No. 268 Squadron continued to use their Typhoon FR.1Bs until November 1944, when they were replaced by the Mustang II. Only a handful of Typhoon FR.1Bs would remain in service for use in the post strike role, for which they were modified by the replacement of the original camera installation by a single F.24 long-lensed camera coupled to the gunsight. In contrast to the straight reconnaissance Typhoon, this version was successful and produced excellent combat photographs.

27

Other Underwing Loads

As well as the more conventional weapons deployed with the Typhoon there were trials involving other underwing loads. In early 1944, Typhoon JR307 was fitted with M.10 smoke tanks for trials at A&AEE Boscombe Down. As these were successful in laying down an effective smoke screen, it was postulated that a force of Typhoons would be ideal for laying a dense smoke screen to hide the movements of the invasion fleet on D-Day. However, JR307 was not so lucky as it broke up recovering from a high speed dive on 26 March 1944, the wreckage landing near Crichel Down, Dorset. In the event a force of Douglas Boston bombers was deployed, as the fighters were required for a far more aggressive role.

Less violent but deemed just as necessary were the missions involving the dropping of canisters filled with propaganda leaflets that urged the German forces to surrender, these beginning in August 1944. Eight months later Typhoons would be engaged in sorties that were in direct support of SAS troops operating behind enemy lines. Travelling hard and fast, the Typhoons were very successful in their mission. Another mission deemed absolutely necessary was that of transporting beer in barrels mounted onto the wing bomb pylons, a duty shared with some Spitfires. The contents were reported as somewhat metallic in taste, but welcome nevertheless. Other weapons trialled on the Typhoon by the A&AEE included smoke bombs, Mk.VIII mines and practise bombs, the latter being adopted for use by the Typhoon training units , four being carried under each wing.

Much of the history of the Typhoon revolved around refining the aircraft, its systems and its weaponry; however, on at least one occasion the type was used by the scientists based at the Telecommunications Research Establishment at Malvern for use in the 'Abdullah' trials. This strangely named project was engaged in the development of a radar homing device that was required to locate German 'Wurzburg' radar transmitters. Trials undertaken during April 1944 were carried out using a suitably modified Typhoon against a captured 'Wurzburg' radar by pilots of the FIU. The trials proved that the Abdullah detector was capable of detecting a transmitter from 50 miles (80km) away, providing that the approach was over the sea. Only a handful of Typhoons were converted for this task, and these were used to attack German coastal radars prior to the invasion of Europe. To operate these machines No. 1320 Flight was formed, using pilots drawn from the Fighter Interception Unit.

Only one other version of the Typhoon was mooted, this being the Sea Typhoon, which could be seen as a precursor of things to come. Put forward by the Admiralty as Specification N.11/40, the Hawker P.1009 Sea Typhoon would be powered by a Napier Sabre II rated at 2,140hp. Folding wings and arrestor hook were fitted as standard, although the original early hard canopy was still retained. Armament was set at four Hispano cannon as per the Typhoon IB, although there were drastic changes wrought to the wings, where the flaps had to be redesigned into six separate sections, and the undercarriage was moved further outboard, each leg being of a longer stroke than that of its ground-based counterpart, and capable of absorbing the impact of a carrier landing. All this movement of major components meant that the wing fuel tanks had to be relocated into the deepened wing roots. All of this design work was in vain however as the Admiralty decided to stay with the Sea Hurricane.

Addressing the Shortcomings

Although the Typhoon eventually made its mark as a ground-attack aircraft, there were some serious shortcomings that needed addressing. The problem with the manoeuvrability and the drag coefficient generated by the thick wing section was one that Sydney Camm and his team were already investigating. The resultant redesign of the wing had a semi-elliptical planform and was far thinner in section. After presenting this new development to the Ministry of Aircraft Production in mid-1941, Hawkers was rewarded with a Letter of Intent for development specification F.10/41, which was placed in November 1941.

Designated the Typhoon II, this machine was seen purely as a development of the earlier Mark 1, although the projected powerplant was to be a developed Napier engine, the Sabre IV. In common with other Sabre versions, this uprated powerplant would also run into problems when testing began in early 1942. To alleviate the potential shortage of engines for the new airframe, other powerplants were investigated. One of the first was the Rolls-Royce Griffon II, which was a Griffon 61 with a two-stage supercharger. Also considered was the Bristol Centaurus radial engine, which in the event would become the chosen alternative. As the redesigned aircraft progressed, it was felt that it would benefit from a rename to differentiate it from its predecessor. The chosen name was Tempest – of which more anon.

Left The final expression of the Typhoon was this hybrid assemblage of parts better known as HM595, which later became better known as the Tempest prototype. C. P. Russell Smith Collection

CHAPTER FOUR

The Typhoon Uncovered

When it was initially rolled out, at first glance the Typhoon presented a smooth aerodynamic shape to the waiting world. However, under the skin it exhibited many of the techniques developed during the age of the biplanes of the interwar years, techniques that were carried on through the Hurricane. In order to understand this unique fighter bomber fully, it will be discussed section by section.

The Typhoon Fuselage

The fuselage was basically constructed in three sections. First was the forward unit, starting at the engine bulkhead and ending to the rear of the pilot's seat at the armoured bulkhead; it was based around a tubular framework. This consisted of a rectangular structure, that in turn comprised steel tubes assembled together with flat plate fittings and machined stampings that were covered by alloy skin panels mounted on curved frames.

The aft section to the rear of the pilot's cockpit was a monocoque stressed structure, consisting of straight longitudinal stringers riveted to shaped frames, all being covered by an alloy skin flush-riveted to reduce drag. This section terminated in a transport joint, to which was riveted a quite muscular butt strap on which the tail section was mounted. This was the last section of the Typhoon's fuselage, and incorporated the fin within its make-up. The fin itself had horizontal ribs above the upper surface of the fuselage, which were riveted to a vertical fin post. The whole was covered by an alloy skin, with the leading edge being protected by shaped and formed panels. Fitted on the fire-proof engine bulkhead were the mountings for the engine and the connections for the fuel and electrical systems, plus the linkages for engine management. Bolted on to the lower portion of this bulkhead were the tubular frames that supported much of the engine's weight.

Underneath these beams were the mountings for the radiator assembly, as

fitted to the production Sabre engines. Covering the engine and its ancillaries was a series of specially shaped panels and fairings, the latter being removable for access to the engine itself. The chin radiator was also covered by a specially manufactured and shaped fairing, which featured a retractable flap to the rear. Given the stresses and strains surrounding the engine area, it is hardly surprising that many of these panels and fairings were subject to cracking; therefore many hours would be spent in repair and maintenance.

Wing Assemblies

As the Typhoon was a low-wing cantilever monoplane, the corresponding attachment points were set low on the fuselage. Each was manufactured as an individual item, and featured primary and secondary main spars that tapered from the root to the tip. At the outer end of the wing were the mounting points for the removable rounded wing-tips, whilst at the inner end were the fuselage/wing mounting points. These were attached to the fuselage by close tolerance bolts that fitted through steel bushes that were designed to absorb many of the stresses and strains generated by combat flying. To ensure that the bolts stayed in place, they terminated in castellated nuts fixed with a split pin.

Along the leading edge of the wings were specially shaped ribs that were riveted to the front face of the forward main spar. Between each of the spars were six heavy-duty main ribs interspersed with lighter ribs that shaped the wing and provided further mounting points for the alloy skin. The inner sections of the spars were extruded during manufacture and were 'N'-shaped in section. Outboard of these inner sections the spars were on an extruded 'T'-section with a single web plate riveted to the lower face. As the gun bay by its very requirement was a relatively large open space, a single 'D'-section member took the torsional loads and

Below **This cutaway model of a Typhoon was prepared by Hawker's to show the internal construction of the aircraft and equipment fitted. It was last reported at the Science Museum.** Real Wings Collection

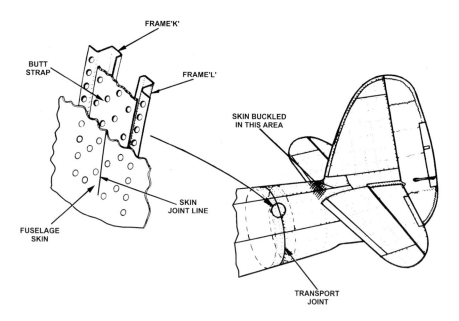

Above **In the early Typhoon years a pilot's greatest fear was the tendency for the rear fuselage to fail, thus casting the rudder and elevators adrift. In most cases the results were fatal, although at least one pilot managed to survive this catastrophe. The modifications carried out to fix the problem included strengthening of the interface between the centre and rear fuselage assemblies, and a complete reworking of the elevator balance system to reduce control surface flutter.** Big Bird Aviation Collection

provided structural strength. Close by, the wing root forward of the spar was the space for the wing fuel tank, which terminated at the rib; this in turn provided the outer edge for the main undercarriage bay.

The outboard sections of the wings were of normal stressed skin construction, with reinforcing stringers for strength and to maintain the wing's shape. The leading edges of the wings were clad in specially shaped alloy skins that featured cutouts for the landing light glazing, and removable panels at the front of the gun bays. The type of armament installed in the gun bays would depend on whether the panel required two clearance ports, or six. On early production Typhoons there was also a cutout panel on the outer section that allowed access to the camera gun. Mountings were provided on the wing's trailing edge for the Frise-type ailerons and the split flaps.

The Tail Unit

The Typhoon tailplane was of the cantilever type with two spars, one mainly for structural strength, the other to mount the elevators on. To give strength and shape to the tailplanes a series of ribs was placed between the spars, while specially shaped ribs were riveted to the forward face of the front spar. Overall the tailplane was clad with alloy skinning, with access panels for the flight controls and associated trim tabs. The leading edge was manufactured from specially shaped panels that were riveted to the ribs. Mounting was courtesy of close-tolerance bolts in a similar manner to the mainplanes.

Flying Controls

The ailerons, elevators and split-type flaps were of all-metal construction, whilst the rudder consisted of a metal framework covered in fabric stretched tightly over the surface by the action of a cellulose linen dope. Each of the primary surfaces was constructed in a similar manner: a spar to which were attached rounded ribs to the fore, while aft of the spar the ribs were more tapered. To reduce weight, each of the ribs was pierced by lightening holes, a technique practised throughout the entire airframe wherever possible. Let into each flight-control surface was a trim tab. On the ailerons and elevators one tab was a ground-only adjustable balance tab, whilst the other, a trim tab, could be adjusted by the pilot. That on the rudder was adjustable by the pilot for balance and

trimming.

Operation of the flight controls was by cable: those to the elevators and rudder led up to bellcranks that led in turn to torque tubes that moved both the rudder and elevators, the latter being coupled together and held in place by locked nuts and bolts. Protecting the cables were guides that prevented any form of excess movement, and protected the airframe structure from rubbing. Operation of the rudder was achieved by the use of rudder pedals, whilst the elevators were controlled by fore and aft movements of the control column. The ailerons were also cable-operated, running from the cockpit to the flight surface itself. The cables terminated in change-of-direction pulleys, from which further cables were attached to the control surface itself. The pilot-adjustable trim tabs were also cable-operated, and were attached to trim-wheels in the cockpit and to mechanical rotary jacks close by the relevant control surface. The trim-tab rotary jacks were connected to the port elevator and the starboard aileron respectively. Also part of the flight-control system was the elevator balance weight housed in the rear fuselage, and that for the rudder affixed to the forward face.

The range of movement for each of the flying control surfaces is as follows: ailerons deflected up 18 degrees, and down 18.5 degrees about the datum, whilst the elevators deflected 24 degrees up and 24.5 degrees downwards. Rudder deflection was 27 degrees each way. The flaps when set at fully down reached 80 degrees.

The final flight-control surfaces were the hydraulically driven flaps. These were operated by a lever located on the left-hand sloping panel, being moved to the rear to deploy the flaps. The flaps could be set in any position when the lever was reset to the 'valve shut' position, all being displayed on an indicator fitted into the instrument panel. In the event of an engine-pump failure the pilot was recommended to pump them down using the hand pump.

The Undercarriage

Both main and tail undercarriage units were retractable, all being housed in specially shaped bays under the wings and tail unit. Those under the wings retracted inwards and were enclosed by fairings; the

Above **With its engine panels removed, this Typhoon IB exemplifies the final state of the type, featuring the extended span tailplane, the four-bladed propeller and the one-piece blown canopy.** David Howley Collection

Right **Typhoon IB EK183 was serving as 'US-A' of No. 56 Sqn when this portrait was taken. It was later operated by No. 609 Sqn, before being retired on 16 July 1945 as 5323M.** Big Bird Aviation Collection

main fairings were attached to each leg, whilst the inboard doors retracted slightly later in the sequence, courtesy of a hydraulic jack. Originally there was no inboard door on the prototype, the wheel being covered by spring-loaded fairings mounted at the base of each door. However, rough field trials found that mud collected around the doors and caused them to jam, so they were quickly removed and the undercarriage bays redesigned. The tailwheel leg retracted forwards. Production aircraft were not fitted with fairing doors, although the prototype was fitted with them. The main legs were carried on reinforced mountings, the forward of which was attached to the rear face of the front spar. The tail leg was mounted on specially reinforced attachments, all three units incorporating bearings to reduce wear.

Each main undercarriage leg was manufactured by Vickers; they were of the oleo-pneumatic shock-absorber type, and were fitted with Dunlop wheels and tyres coupled to pneumatic brakes. The tail-wheel unit was manufactured by Dunlop-Ecta, and incorporated a wheel and pneumatic tyre manufactured by the same company.

Operation of the undercarriage was by a selector lever located on the left-hand side of the pilot's panel. This lever operated in the natural sense: thus 'up' required it to be pushed up and forwards. To raise the undercarriage, the knob mounted on the

lever had to be rotated clockwise to release the lock. Further insurance against an inadvertent 'up' selection required that a safety catch be moved to the 'free' position; this automatically returned to the 'lock' position when the lever was moved to the 'down' position.

In the event that the undercarriage would not lock down, the first choice of action was to switch to the secondary set of indicator lights. Should these still not show red for an unlocked undercarriage, the pilot was blithely instructed to use the hand pump or emergency release pedals. Operation of the former required that the undercarriage be left selected in the 'down' position while the pilot pumped until he felt resistance. At this point, in theory, the lights should be green and the gear down and locked. The unlock pedals were required if the undercarriage lights failed to illuminate after twelve strokes of the hand pump. To be effective the pilot was advised to fly straight and level without pulling any 'g' forces, although he was allowed to push either pedal separately or together as needed. The range of movement needed to operate this release mechanism was some 3–4in (7–10cm). In theory this should release the undercarriage 'up' lock mechanism. To assist the undercarriage in locking down, the pilot was advised to skid the aircraft from side to side, the forces generated being estimated as enough to lock the legs down and produce the required green lights.

Undercarriage indications were both electrical and mechanical. The electrical visual indicator was mounted on the main instrument panel, and comprised three green lights for both the main and tail undercarriages, plus two extra for the main legs only. To further confirm to the pilot that each undercarriage leg was down and locked, there was a mechanical indicator button that protruded through the upper wing skin when the corresponding main leg was down. To stop our intrepid aviator from making a mistake with the undercarriage selection, there was a warning horn located behind the headrest, where its impact would be strongest. There was also a red indicator light, and both would be activated should the throttle be set to less than one third power with the undercarriage in the unlocked position. To ensure that the system was not malfunctioning, a test button was incorporated, mounted on the main pilot's panel.

If at any time the pilot needed to undertake a forced landing, the glide path needed to be extended, and this could be achieved by pulling the propeller speed-control lever fully aft. With the flaps and undercarriage in the 'up' position, the glide path was very flat, at about 150mph (240km/h) IAS. To make the pilot's life even more interesting, it was recommended that should a tyre burst on take-off, no attempt at landing should be made with the undercarriage lowered. Instead the pilot was instructed to make a belly landing, as less damage would result to both aviator and aircraft.

Primary Systems

The primary services aboard the Typhoon centred about the hydraulic, pneumatic and electrical systems. The hydraulic system was powered by an engine-driven pump that was capable of maintaining a system pressure of 1,800psi. This system drove the undercarriage legs and the inner doors, plus the wing flaps and radiator shutter.

Pneumatics also played an important part in providing services aboard the Typhoon. As with the hydraulics, the pump was engine-driven, and maintained a working pressure of 450psi. Systems that utilized this service included the main wheel-braking and gun-firing mechanisms. Indications for the pilot came via a triple-pressure indicating gauge mounted in the cockpit instrument panel. Operation of the wheel brakes was by a lever mounted onto the control column spade grip, with differential braking being achieved by a relay valve connected to the rudder bar. A catch to hold the brake lever in the parked position was located near the brake lever pivot. Indication of the systems pressure, and that for each brake, was provided by a triple pressure gauge in the cockpit.

The on-board electrical system was based around a 24-volt, engine-mounted generator that charged two accumulators that operated the complete electrical system. Control was via a main on–off switch complete with voltmeter mounted on the right-hand side of the cockpit. On later-build aircraft a 'power failure' light came on when the generator was not charging the accumulators.

The fuel system consisted of four self-sealing tanks in each mainplane, with the fuel being delivered to the carburettor by an engine-driven pump. To supplement the main fuel system, provision was made for two auxiliary jettisonable tanks, one under each wing. This modification was only available on the Mark 1B, the earlier machine gun-equipped Mark 1A not having such provisions. Transference of fuel from these tanks was achieved by the use of air pressure from the engine-driven pump. The total fuel load without drop tanks was 154gal (700ltr), whilst with drop tanks fitted the total increased to 244gal (1,109ltr). The fuel was carried in two main wing tanks capable of holding 40gal (180ltr) each, while the two nose tanks contained 37gal (168ltr). The auxiliary tanks were rated to carry 45gal (205ltr) each.

In common with other fighters of the period, the fuel aboard the Typhoon was susceptible to boiling off in warm weather at high altitudes. To counter this possibility – which could result in the engine cutting out – the tanks could be pressur-

Below **This view of the Typhoon cockpit shows the main flying panel, situated above the control-column spade grip; directly above is the gunsight and protective padding.** Damien Burke

ized, although this was only effective above 20,000ft (6,000m). When this system was operated, it impaired the effectiveness of the self-sealing of the fuel tanks; therefore its use was recommended only when the fuel pressure had fallen below 1.5psi, when the warning light illuminated, or when the auxiliary fuel tanks were emptied.

Controlling the fuel system was a single three-position switch that could select either the nose tanks or the main tanks for fuel feed, but not at the same time. Control of the auxiliary tanks was via another three-way cock that catered for three positions: 'port', 'starboard' or 'off'. Close by this cock was the tank jettison lever, although it could not be operated until the system was set to 'off'. When the lever was operated, the air supply was automatically cut off.

The Cockpit

The cockpit is located in the forward section of the fuselage, and contained between the fireproof bulkhead and the rear armoured bulkhead. As such there was no floor to the cockpit, there being a pair of footplates that led from under the pilot's seat to the rudder pedals. The pilot's seat was adjustable in the up and down directions, and was sprung to reduce the vibrations generated by the Sabre engine. Facing the pilot was a primary panel containing the major instruments:

the airspeed indicator, the artificial horizon, rate-of-climb indicator, direction in-dicator, and the turn-and-bank indicator. On each side of the primary panel were the secondary panels: the starboard one held the engine instruments, whilst the port contained the instrumentation for the brakes and radio, amongst other systems.

Located on the left-hand side of the cockpit was a semi-angled panel that housed the engine controls, above which were the canopy winding handle and the weapons selector for the Mark 1B. On the right-hand side in a similar position were the fuel system control cocks, the cylinder priming pump, and the Very pistol and its cartridges. Down and to the right of the pilot were located the switches for the Typhoon's electrical systems and the radio control box.

Protecting the cockpit was the canopy. On earlier machines, access was gained via a car-type door located on the starboard side of the fuselage. However, the very first production Typhoons had an even more complicated assembly consisting of two car doors, one per side, both with windable windows, and all being topped off by a hinged top panel. The rear canopy fairing on the first-build Typhoons was an alloy structure, although this was soon changed to perspex, being known as the 'Stage B' modification. However, the heavy framing was frequently complained about by pilots, therefore a single-piece blown perspex canopy that slid back for access was

provided which improved all-round visibility dramatically. The canopy was opened by a handle located on the port cockpit wall. To open the hood a knob was pulled out and the handle rotated anti-clockwise. The hood could be locked into any intermediate position by releasing the knob.

To escape from a doomed Typhoon could be quite a difficult exercise, especially in the early aircraft fitted with car doors. In an emergency the door would need to be jettisoned, therefore levers were provided on the front and rear door posts, which needed to be pulled down and inwards simultaneously to release the door. To gain greater purchase for release it was recommended that a crossed arm position be adopted, as failure to release the door would stop the roof panel from automatically detaching. To escape from a later-build aircraft with a sliding canopy, a single lever needed to be pulled: this was located at the bottom of the instrument panel close to the blind flying panel.

In the event of needing to ditch whilst flying over the sea, the canopy or door needed to be jettisoned; however, it was recommended that baling out was a far better option. If hitting the sea was inevitable, it was suggested that the pilot should pull the aircraft nose upwards. While the aircraft was climbing, the Sutton harness and the helmet plus the R/T plug had to be disconnected. Once this was achieved, it was recommended that a final bailout attempt be made. If this

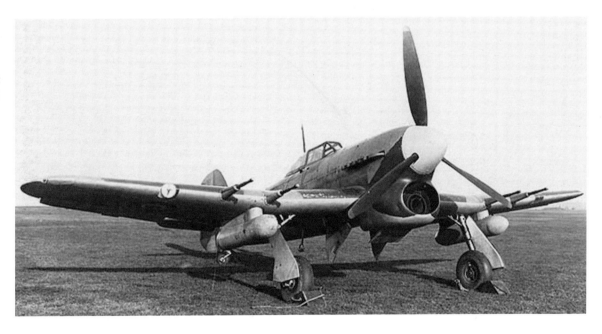

Right **This forward view of Typhoon IB reveals it to be a second-stage conversion machine. It already sports the first attempt at improving the pilot's vision, as well as a pair of underwing 45gal (205ltr) fuel tanks.**
Real Wings Collection

Above **An excellent shot of Typhoon IB JR128 'HF-L' when it was serving with No. 183 Sqn. On 18 August 1944 the aircraft was shot down by flak near Livarot. The pilot, Flying Officer W. Grey, was taken as a prisoner of war.** Big Bird Aviation Collection

Powerplant

Powering the Typhoon was the 24-cylinder Napier Sabre IIA/B, rated at 2,200hp, an H-type liquid-cooled sleeve valve engine that was mounted onto the front spar and was supported by a braced cantilevered tubular structure that was also bolted to the front spar. To provide a housing for the radiator and the oil cooler there was a low velocity duct assembly mounted below the engine. The powerplant drives a de Havilland three-or four-bladed Hydromatic propellor depending on modification state. Lubrication oil for the engine was housed in a tank located aft of the fireproof bulkhead that contained 16gal (72ltr) of oil and a 1gal (4.5ltr) airspace. Indication for the pilot was courtesy of gauges in the cockpit, whilst the cooler formed an integral part of the radiator matrix.

The coolant system was thermostatically controlled, with the radiator being kept in bypass mode until the coolant had reached its nominal operating temperature. Controlling the airflow around the chin-mounted radiator was a lever in the cockpit that used a narrow bore hydraulic jack to move the radiator flap. When 'down' was selected the shutter opened, whilst 'up' moved it in the opposite direction. Should the hydraulic system fail for any reason, the flap could be operated by use of the hand pump in the cockpit.

Although the Sabre engine was theoretically capable of being operated by the use of one lever, the cockpit was fully equipped with a selection of levers and controls that allowed the pilot a fair amount of flexibility. Principal amongst these were the throttle and mixture controls. During operation the throttle was moved forwards to the climb and take-off positions, the latter being gated against inadvertent selection. Incorporated into this was a friction adjuster that also managed the propeller control. On the Mark 1B aircraft a bomb-release button was incorporated into the top of the lever. Located close by the throttle lever was a mixture lever that was moved forwards to operate. The first selectable location was for a weak mixture that automatically became rich when the throttle lever was between the closed and 14-degree position. Between this point and fully open, the pilot was able to set the mixture control as he saw fit to match the circumstances. On earlier aircraft the mixture lever moved to the rich position

was still not possible due to circumstances such as engine failure, the flaps should be lowered to the halfway point, and the crash landing made with the tail held as far down as possible.

Armament

The Typhoon's fixed armament consisted of twelve Browning 0.303in machine guns as installed in the Mark 1A, six per wing. The guns in each bay were set out in an arc, both banks being located outside the propeller's diameter. In a similar manner the Mark 1B had its cannon mounted in the same gun-bay location, two per side, the magazines being located outboard. To remove the empty cartridge cases after firing, each cannon was fitted with a clearance chute; this was designed to clear any external mounted underwing armament. Access to both sets of armament was through a large removable panel in the upper wing surface. Control of the wing guns was via a push button on the control column spade grip; the guns themselves operated pneumatically.

Also installed in the Typhoon was a camera gun; this was originally located in the port outer wing, but was moved into the radiator fairing because pilots complained that it was not capable of recording results accurately from that location. It was operated by the same push button as for the wing guns. When

the button was depressed, a succession of exposures was made until the button was released. To help the pilot gauge the contents of the camera gun magazine there was a footage indicator and an aperture control switch in the cockpit close by the camera selector controls. There was also a button on the spade grip that would operate the camera gun independently, should the pilot have so wished.

External weaponry was only carried by the Typhoon IB, most of it on a single pylon under each wing. This aerodynamic fairing was plumbed for a manual release mechanism, fuel and pneumatics. The stores that could be carried included a 45gal (205ltr) fuel tank, a 1,000lb (450kg) bomb, a 500lb (225kg) bomb, a 250lb (110kg) bomb, plus a practice bomb rack capable of carrying small smoke and flash bombs. The bombs were released mechanically while the fuel tanks required the fuel and air connectors. In place of the wing racks, four rockets rails could be installed under each wing, these capable of carrying either 25lb (11kg), 60lb (27kg) or armour-piercing rockets. Originally these were mounted singly, although later developments allowed for carriage in pairs. Release of the bombs for the Typhoon IB was controlled by two selector switches, one for each side, plus two nose and tail fusing switches. The bomb-release push button was incorporated in the top of the throttle lever.

Right **Typhoon IB DN406 was serving with No. 609 Sqn as PR-F in May 1943. Its career was short from this point, as it was transferred to No. 56 Sqn and was struck off charge soon after, on 31 August 1943.** Big Bird Aviation Collection

Right **The Napier Sabre engine in all its glory, complete with engine bearer frame; prominent are the plug leads to both banks of cylinders.** Real Wings Collection

Below **This close-up view of a Typhoon reveals much detail, even though the engine is running. The pilot is climbing into the cockpit after one of the groundcrew had got the cantankerous Sabre running. Prominent in this photograph is the oil cooler in undernose air intake.** David Howley Collection

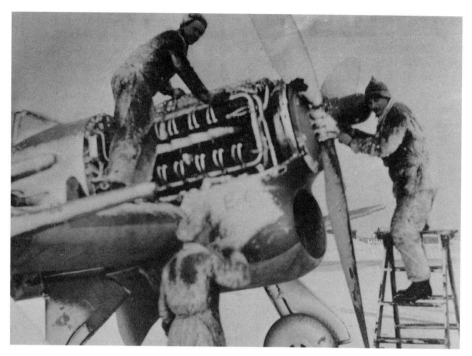

Above **No matter what the weather, the servicing went on, as this scene of engine fitters in the snow shows: even they have been coated by the blizzard.** David Howley Collection

when the throttle was moved beyond the climb position.

The pilot also had a lever to control the propeller settings. The speed control lever in the engine control box varied the governed speed from 3,700 down to 2,000rpm. And just to confuse matters, some lever slots on early aircraft were marked with the legend 'Positive Coarse Pitch', although there was in fact no such setting available on the propeller.

To give the Sabre engine an extra boost, a supercharger was installed. The lever in the engine control box was moved downwards to select the 'full' (S ratio) supercharging, and upward for 'moderate' (M ratio) supercharging. To assist the pilot in engine starting, there was a starting and slow-running cutout control, located on the left-hand sloping panel. This had three positions: 'start', 'normal' and 'cutout'. When 'start' was selected, a stop was introduced into the throttle quadrant to give the throttle setting for starting, although there was a safety catch that had to be de-selected so that 'start' could be used.

Also part of the engine start sequence was the priming of the cylinders and carburettor. Two pumps were provided for this task, the inner of which primed the cylinders, whilst the outer did the same for the carburettor. To operate the pumps they needed to be released by first unscrewing and then screwing back down again after usage. Engine starting was controlled by the ignition switches located on the left-hand side of the instrument panel. These were prevented from moving by a sliding bar that was integrated with the undercarriage indicator, which in turn was required to be in the 'on' position.

Close by the engine ignition switches were those that controlled the cartridge starter. There were two switches, one of which controlled the cartridge starter itself, while the other operated the booster coil. To be effective, both switches needed to be depressed at the same time otherwise the engine would not start, being inclined to misfire if incorrectly operated. As production of the Typhoon continued, the switches were moved across to the right-hand side of the instrument panel. To move the cartridge selector there was a reloading control that was also located on the right-hand-side sloping panel, and was used to rotate the cartridges into the starter breech. There was one other switch in the cockpit that frequently confused pilots, this being an oil dilution switch located on the right-hand console. However, it wasn't until late in the production run that this system was installed.

Flight Controls

The primary flight controls were operated by a spade-grip pattern control column attached by cables to the ailerons and elevators, whilst the rudder was operated by two position rudder pedals that could be adjusted for reach using a foot-operated wheel on the rudder bar. Incorporated into the control column spade grip were the gun-and cannon-firing buttons, depending on the model of aircraft.

As unrestrained flight controls can cause damage to an airframe in high winds, the Typhoon came complete with its own surface-control locking kit that was housed in a bag on the left-hand side of the cockpit. This kit consisted of a hinged clamp and four cables. The clamp was used on the control column, its locating lugs coming into contact with the aileron fork end locking nuts of the tie rods. Two of the cables were clipped from the hinged clamp to the rudder pedals, whilst the other cables were clipped onto the clamp, then to the seat, which had to be raised to the third notch from the top via the adjuster lever. Cable-tensioning was achieved by extending the rudder pedals and raising the seat.

Flying the Typhoon

Preliminary Inspections

The Typhoon was like any other piston-powered aircraft in that it could be a handful if not handled correctly. Except for emergency scrambles when it was necessary to get airborne as quickly as possible, pilots followed a set sequence of actions before taking to the skies. As always, each pre-flight began with a walk-round, when the pilot inspected the entire aircraft for defects such as loose or missing panels, cracks and dents, and anything else that might be a potential problem. Close attention was paid to the undercarriage, and in particular the tyres for wear, cuts and embedded debris. One final check before boarding was to ensure that the elevators, ailerons and rudder moved in a full and free manner.

Once satisfied with the serviceability of the aircraft, its fuel and weapons load, and happy with the paperwork, the pilot would sign off the F.700 form accepting the Typhoon. Entrance to the cockpit was achieved via the starboard wing root trailing edge. To assist air-and groundcrew to reach the wing safely, a retractable stirrup-type footstep extended below the fuselage wing joint. Once settled into the cockpit, strapped in and connected to the mic-tel lead, the first task was to check the position of the undercarriage lever: this had to be in the 'down' position, with the locking catch in the 'lock' position. Once he was satisfied that the mechanicals were correctly set, the pilot would then turn on the undercarriage indicator to ensure that the green lights illuminated. Next was to make sure that the cabin roof panel was locked properly on both sides, also that the cockpit doors were locked, and that the footstep was in the retracted position.

At this point the pilot would establish whether his aircraft was pre-, or post-modification 293. If the former, the pilot was required to fit his oxygen mask and begin breathing the gas straightaway at a setting of 15,000ft (4,500m). This was because there was a very real risk of carbon monoxide poisoning in aircraft that had not been modified, and which therefore did not have the better sealed engine mounting bulkhead.

The final check before engine start was to adjust the rudder pedals to a comfortable setting that would allow for full deflection of the surface to counteract the propeller torque generated on a full power take-off.

Once satisfied with the condition of the aircraft, the pilot would signal the groundcrew to point the Typhoon into the wind. Should the engine run be required for engineering purposes, the tail had to be tied down with restraints. In any event, other aircraft and personnel should be well clear of the machine waiting to start.

Starting Up

To start the engine, the following sequence had to be followed. First, the ignition switches needed to be in the 'off' position, as did the fuel cocks for the main tanks, and the pressurization and underwing drop tanks. If the Typhoon was of a late enough build or modification, the mixture control had to be set to 'rich', whilst the propeller speed control needed to be fully forward. Also requiring a pre-start check was the supercharger control, which had to be set at 'moderate', whilst the radiator shutter had to be in the 'down' position. One other point the pilot needed to note was the requirement for the fuel system to be set to nose tanks should the main fuel system be less than half full.

The engine wasn't always easy to start in cold weather ñ indeed the Sabre was renowned for being exceptionally cranky if not nurtured in adverse conditions. During the early days of the Typhoon's service any aircraft required for flight the

next day was either lagged to keep the cold at bay, or kept warm by a hot air blower. As the engine became more reliable, the only instruction given to the pilot was to shut the radiator flap to prevent the radiator coolant freezing.

Before starting the engine the pilot had to ensure that there was no live cartridge in the breech; only then would he signal for the propeller to be turned over by the groundcrew. The starting lever would be moved to 'start', and the throttle advanced to the stop; then the carburettor could be primed until the fuel pressure reached a minimum of 1.5psi, after which the pump would be screwed down. The next step was to load the cartridge starter, then switch on the ignition. Once all this was done, the cylinders needed to be carefully primed with the priming pump. If the aircraft had been standing for less than half an hour, only one pumpful would be needed, otherwise two were required at any point under the hour.

Once priming was completed, the booster coil and starter buttons needed to be pushed simultaneously and held in while further priming of the cylinders was carried out using the other hand. Once the engine was running steadily the priming could stop, the buttons be released, and the start lever set to normal. Given the Sabre engine's propensity to misbehave, a follow-on start did not require any further priming, otherwise the possibility of fire was increased – although vigorous priming was recommended once the engine had caught.

Below **Up on jacks, panels are off, flaps are down, and the Typhoon IB MN716 'F3-A' – named 'Diane' of No. 438 'Wildcat' Sqn, RCAF – undergoes much-needed maintenance.** David Howley Collection

With all this fuel priming it was not surprising that the greatest fear of any pilot was fire. If the Typhoon engine did start to burn, the groundcrew would warn the pilot, who had to turn the ignition switches to 'off'; he would then place his hands outside the cockpit to show that the engine was safe, after which the fire extinguishant was released down the radiator intake. Assuming that the fire was only excess fuel burning off, and that it was successfully extinguished, the pilot was advised to run the engine in the 800–1,000rpm range until the oil pressure had dropped below 100psi. Once this point was reached the throttle could be further advanced to 2,000rpm, which had to be maintained until the oil temperature had dropped to 40/C. Once satisfied that the engine was behaving correctly, whatever the circumstances surrounding the start, the pilot was recommended to test all the engine controls and systems with the proviso that full power was only applied for the briefest of times.

Once cleared to depart, the pilot would taxi out of the dispersal with the warning not to use the brakes too much as they could easily overheat and become inefficient, this being exacerbated should they be new.

Preparing for Take-Off

Having negotiated the perimeter track, the pilot then had to prepare the Typhoon for take-off. The mnemonic for the sequence of actions required in this procedure was TMPFF: trim tabs, elevator to neutral and rudder fully offset to port, the mixture control to rich, the propeller control to fully forward, fuel-pressurizing cock to off and the drop tanks to off, flaps to 10 to 15 degrees down for normal airfields, and to 30 degrees for shorter runways. The final two checks were to ensure that the supercharger was set to moderated, and the radiator shutter in the 'down' position.

Even this phase of the departure had certain exigencies: +4psi boost for take-off, and the tail had to be held down for as long as possible, thus allowing the aircraft to fly itself off the ground. Further instructions were issued to cover the take-off performance, with the flaps at the 30 degree position. At this setting, however, the Typhoon had a strong tendency to swing to starboard, and to counteract this departure the throttle needed to be advanced progressively, which allowed the rudder to maintain control effectiveness up to take-off. Once airborne, the flaps needed to be raised between 200 and 300ft (60 and 90m); a steep climb was not to be undertaken until a speed of 150mph (240km/h) was reached. The recommended speed for maximum rate of climb was 185mph (300km/h) IAS up to 16,000ft (4,800m).

The Typhoon in Flight

In flight the Typhoon's behaviour was very stable directionally and laterally, although there was a slight tendency for it to be unstable longitudinally; this improved, however, as its speed increased. The ailerons remained light and responsive throughout the speed range up to the maximum, although they were known to be sluggish at very low speeds and when carrying bombs. Elevator control was considered rather light for an aircraft of the Typhoon's type, and pilots were warned not to operate them too harshly – although that advice was not always heeded if there was an Fw 190 in pursuit. In a loop the Typhoon had a tendency to tighten up as the loop progressed, which could induce a black-out. In that situation the pilot, having recovered, was advised to move the control column forward to stabilize the aircraft.

Trim changes whilst flying the Typhoon were fairly minor in nature, thus lowering the flaps produced no change; on the other hand, when the undercarriage was lowered and the radiator shutter retracted, the aircraft had a tendency to pitch nose down. Other factors that could affect the trim of the Typhoon included variations in airspeed and throttle settings; thus the rudder trim tab would be used to avoid the possibility of sideslip. However, pilots were warned that the trim tab had to be used carefully, as it was very sensitive. To reinforce this fact, over-use of the tab could induce changes in fore and aft trim of the aircraft – thus left yaw produced a tendency for the nose to drop, and right yaw had the opposite effect.

The pilot was also warned that the radiator shutter should be in the 'up' position except for taxiing, take-off, climbing, and flying with flaps down, and that careful attention needed to be given to the engine's oil temperature. Finally he was advised to use the main fuel tanks first, to maintain a stable centre of gravity.

Flying at varying speeds also produced a whole raft of regulations, the most important of which concerned variations in altimeter readings at high speed. Low speeds in the region of 155mph (250km/h) IAS, with the flaps set at between 30 and 40 degrees, required the radiator flap to be open, and the propeller control adjusted to produce a speed in the region of 3,100rpm. When flying in formation, however, the propeller speed control needed to be maintained at above 2,600rpm.

Left Captured running up to full power is Typhoon IB MN264 of No. 222 Sqn, on the ground at Eindhoven. Prominent under the wings are a full set of rocket projectiles. Peter R. Arnold Collection

Problems: Stalling and Spinning

Having got his Typhoon into the air, our intrepid aviator had other things to contend with, one of which was stalling, when either wing would drop sharply with flaps up or down. With bombs loaded and everything up, the limit was between 90 to 100mph (145 to 160kmph), whilst in landing condition this dropped to 70 to 75mph (113 to 120kmph). When flying at normal weights without external stores, these figures dropped by 10mph (16kmph) across the board; a further drop of 10mph occurred when the Typhoon was flying virtually unladen.

In common with many combat aircraft of the period, the Typhoon could be induced to spin; however, this was not overly recommended, and was completely forbidden while carrying bombs or external fuel tanks. In the allowed condition the spin had to be undertaken between 15,000 and 20,000ft (4,500 and 6,000m), with recovery action to be initiated within one rotation. Other factors also governed the behaviour of the Typhoon in the spin: one of these was applying full rudder in the opposite direction, whilst the control column was pushed forward slowly until the spin stopped. To assist in counteracting a spin to the left, the engine could be used, although in practice it was not necessary.

The Typhoon was known to have a tendency to enter a flat spin at altitudes above 25,000ft (7,500m). To counter this, the pilot needed to apply full opposite rudder, and the control column had to be rocked fore and aft ñ although it was commonly recognized that this was difficult, as movement was restricted in this kind of spin. In theory these movements should force the nose down, by which time some 8,000 to 10,000ft (2,500 to 3,000m) of altitude would have been lost. In all cases, the dive after the spin had to be maintained until a speed of 200mph (320kmph) IAS had been reached, otherwise the Typhoon might stall again.

Controlling a Dive

During combat missions the Typhoon was frequently placed into a dive to attack selected targets, and even this manoeuvre required certain actions by the pilot, the most important being to ensure that the radiator shutter was closed in the 'up' position. Trying to do this when the dive was

already begun would result in a violent nose-down pitch. In contrast, during a normal dive, speed increased and the Typhoon became tail heavy – although not to the extent that re-trimming would be required, especially as the elevator tabs were very sensitive. Trimming of the rudder would be necessary as the speed increased, however, as the aircraft had a tendency to yaw to port.

Aerobatics

Throughout the conversion phase the trainee Typhoon pilot would be encouraged to practise aerobatics, training that would serve him well in combat. During these manoeuvres, large amounts of height could be lost or gained, although the Typhoon was easy to handle. Loops had to start with full engine power and a minimum speed of 350mph (560kmph), and the controls operated gently otherwise a high-speed stall might ensue. If the aircraft was to be rolled, the forward speed needed to be at least 250mph (400kmph), and the roll needed to be 'barrelled' enough to keep the engine running and to maintain oil pressure. Further loops and rolls were authorized, although a speed of 400mph (640kmph) needed to be maintained to keep up forward momentum. Aerobatics were officially banned when the aircraft carried external loads, although dodging flak and fighters might induce the pilot to forget these instructions. Finally, a short, bald statement at the end of the pilot's instructions stated categorically that 'Flick manoeuvres are not permitted'.

Preparing to Land

Having survived his flight, our pilot then had to complete certain checks before he

was allowed to land. First, he had to check the state of the fuel tanks: if the mains were less than half full, the nose tanks had to be selected in order to maintain the aircraft's trim. Once the aircraft's speed had reduced to 160mph (260kmph), the undercarriage was selected 'down' and checked for three greens, the mixture control was moved to rich, the propeller control was pushed fully forward, and the supercharger to moderate. Finally the flaps had to be placed in the fully 'down' position, whilst the radiator shutter also needed to be 'down'. The pilot by this time in his training regime was aware that the aircraft would yaw as the undercarriage moved to the 'down' position, although stability returned when the gear was down and locked. The flaps also had quite an effect upon the behaviour of the Typhoon, as their size when presented fully down to the airflow would increase the rate of descent dramatically.

Once the aircraft had touched down, the pilot was expected to bring it to a standstill before proceeding to dispersal. During this short break the flaps would be raised.

Shutting Down

Once in the correct parking space, the engine would be shut down. To do this successfully the throttle needed to be retarded to the slowest speed possible before being blipped up to 1,000rpm, then the starting lever moved back to cut off. Once the engine had shut down the ignition switches could be switched to 'off', as could the fuel cocks.

Although the foregoing might make the Typhoon seem a bit of a beast, it was in fact seen as a steady and reliable ground-attack aircraft by the pilots that flew it.

Specification – Typhoon	
Type:	Single-seat fighter/fighter-bomber
Powerplant:	2,100hp Sabre I, 2,180hp Sabre IIA, 2,200hp Sabre IIB, 2,260hp Sabre IIC
Weights:	Empty 8,840lb (4,000kg); loaded 13,250lb (6,000kg)
Dimensions:	Span 41ft 7in (12.67m); length Typhoon IA 31ft 10in (9.7m), Typhoon IB 31ft 11½in (9.74m); height 15ft 4in (4.67m); wing area 279sq ft (25.92sq m)
Performance:	Max. speed with Sabre IIB 412mph (663km/h); rate of climb 5min 50sec to 19,000ft (5,800m); range 510 miles (820km) with 2 × 500lb bombs, 980 miles (1,580km) with 2 × 45gal (200ltr) drop tanks; service ceiling 35,200ft (10,730m)
Armament (fixed):	Typhoon IA 12 × Browning 0.303in machine guns with 500 rounds each, Typhoon IB 4 × Hispano 20mm cannon
Armament (disposable)/ fuel tanks:	Typhoon IA none, Typhoon IB 8 × rocket projectiles or 2 × 1,000lb bombs or 2 × 45gal (200ltr) drop tanks

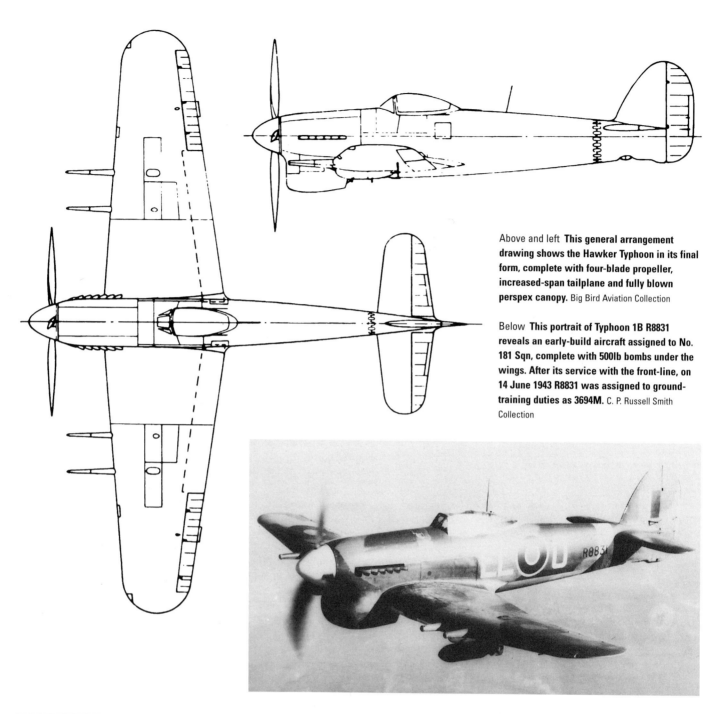

Above and left **This general arrangement drawing shows the Hawker Typhoon in its final form, complete with four-blade propeller, increased-span tailplane and fully blown perspex canopy.** Big Bird Aviation Collection

Below **This portrait of Typhoon 1B R8831 reveals an early-build aircraft assigned to No. 181 Sqn, complete with 500lb bombs under the wings. After its service with the front-line, on 14 June 1943 R8831 was assigned to ground-training duties as 3694M.** C. P. Russell Smith Collection

Left **This rear quarter view depicts R8224, a Typhoon 1B. This was one of the few aircraft actually built by Hawker's, and was paid for by public subscription. It would carry the name 'Land Girl' on the port cockpit door, whilst the starboard door had the name plus badge applied. When this portrait was taken the aircraft was on the strength of No. 56 Sqn; it moved on to No. 609 Sqn. It would be withdrawn on 13 September 1943 after being overstressed during aerobatics.** RAF Museum Collection

CHAPTER FIVE

The Typhoon at War

Being the first unit to receive a new type of aircraft is an unnerving experience, especially for the pilots, and it is quite a steep learning curve for the groundcrew, too. No. 56 Sqn, commanded by Sqn Ldr Peter Prosser Hanks, at Duxford, received its first Typhoon IAs on 11 September 1941, with the others arriving throughout that month; the last one flew in at the beginning of October, to make sixteen on strength. The squadron was converting from another Hawker product, the Hurricane.

Initial Problems and their Outcome

The squadron was soon placed on alert by Fighter Command for Operations *Circus* and *Ramrod* cross-Channel raids, but in fact this never happened because the Typhoon was exhibiting some distressing faults, especially the Sabre engine, and the airframe was also manifesting serious shortcomings. Napier's finest powerplant, as yet untried and untested in combat, had begun to exhibit a distressing habit of failing in the most embarrassing manner. The groundcrew did their best to alleviate this

problem by wrapping it up in blankets and rugs, and using hot air blowers to keep the engine warm and the oil moving freely, but it was discovered that the problems centred around the lubrication system, and putting it right would involve serious investigation. Further, the squadron's pilots complained about poor visibility, engine-starting difficulties, and draughts in the cockpit.

When No. 56 Sqn finally began to undertake combat missions with its Typhoons, another problem appeared. This centred around the drag coefficient of the thick-sectioned wing, which was tending to seriously compromise the aircraft's performance at altitude. The ability to perform at altitude was vital in the air war being waged above Europe, and the failure of the Typhoon in this respect meant that it needed to be found another role. Furthermore, its manoeuvrability by comparison with the Spitfire and the Hurricane, and hence the fighters of the Luftwaffe, was also causing concern – although to its credit the aircraft was a very stable gun platform.

These early Typhoons were built with heavily framed cockpit canopies and, in the earliest instances, a rear fairing of metal construction. This arrangement

allowed the pilot reasonable vision to the front, although to the rear, any manner of view was completely obscured. Given these obvious shortcomings, it is surprising that the Typhoon actually progressed any further in Royal Air Force service; however, the type had a few saving graces, these being a heavy armament in the cannon version, outstanding acceleration in the dive, good stability as a gun platform, and an outstanding turn of speed at low level.

Training for the pilots of No. 56 Sqn continued unabated until 1 November 1941, when one of their aircraft crashed with fatal consequences: this was R7592, piloted by Pilot Officer J. F. Deck. Investigations revealed that the Typhoon cockpit was very vulnerable to carbon monoxide fumes, which in this case had completely overwhelmed the occupant. In an attempt to rectify this problem the port access door was permanently sealed, the exhaust stubs were extended, and the engine bulkhead sealing was improved. These modifications did alleviate this defect to a certain degree, although all pilots were urged to wear oxygen masks from take-off to landing. Curing the carbon monoxide leaks meant that the squadron's aircraft were grounded for a

Right **Typhoon 1B R8852 'US-Y' of No. 56 Sqn was an indirect victim of structural failure when it was hit by pieces of the disintegrating DN265 which was flying in the same formation. The pilot of R8852 was fortunate enough to bale out of his damaged aircraft; that of DN265 was less fortunate.** RAF Museum Collection

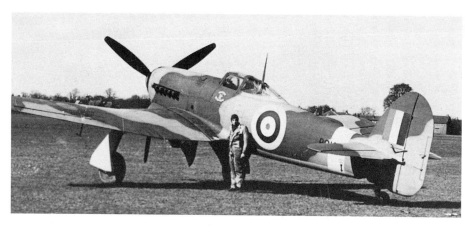

Above **Paid for by subscription by the good citizens of the Borough of Sutton and Cheam, this Typhoon IB R8199 was part of the batch built by Hawker's. R8199 was on the strength of No. 56 Sqn as 'US-E'; it was shot down by Spitfires on 1 June 1942 near Dover, and the pilot killed.** Big Bird Aviation Collection

Below **Seen from above, this Typhoon IB of No. 56 Sqn sports identification stripes over the wings in an attempt to dissuade anti-aircraft gunners and Allied fighter aircraft from shooting it down.** Big Bird Aviation Collection

month; however, flying resumed from Duxford in December. At the beginning of 1942 a second unit at Duxford was re-equipped with the Typhoon, this being No. 266 (Rhodesia) Squadron, which had previously flown Spitfires.

One benefit of No. 56 Squadron's experience was soon evident on the production line where, from the 163rd aircraft onwards, the rear cockpit fairing was modified, the original metal assembly being replaced by a clear perspex one, whilst the armour plate behind the seat was cut and reshaped to allow for better vision all round. As the newly modified machines became available, the originals were withdrawn for modification; by the middle of April 1942, No. 56 Sqn had eighteen on strength. One further modification also came on line at this time, namely the Hispano cannon-equipped Mark 1B version of the Typhoon, which would quickly replace the earlier machine gun-fitted Mark 1A machines.

Into Combat

On 10 April 1942 the final unit that was required to form the Duxford triumvirate began to exchange its Spitfires for the Typhoon IA. This was No. 609 (West Riding) Sqn, previously based at Digby in Lincolnshire. The following month the Wing began combat operations when a No. 266 Sqn machine was launched to intercept an incoming target – which turned out to be a Spitfire. These sorties and their attendant training missions were not without incident, however, as 56 Sqn found when two of their Typhoons were shot down by Spitfires, both chasing a group of incoming intruders. On the training front, all three units were losing aircraft, some to engine problems and others to airframe faults; the final number was eight all told in these early days.

Although the first Typhoon Wing was experiencing problems, the conversion process would continue in July 1942. The first to convert was No. 1 Sqn, based at Acklington, and it was quickly followed by No. 257 at High Ercall, and No. 486 (New Zealand) Sqn based at Wittering; all of these relinquished Hurricanes for the new type, and became operational in September. Their intended original role was that of night fighting, in concert with Turbinlite Bostons; however, the Typhoon was too fast for the converted day bomber, and the experiment was soon abandoned.

Combat success eventually came to the Typhoon, on 9 August 1942, when a pair of patrolling aircraft from No. 266 Sqn managed to intercept and shoot down a Ju 88 over the North Sea. Further sorties involving the available Typhoons took place over wartime Europe, culminating in their participation in Operation *Jubilee*, the landings at Dieppe that began on 19 August 1942. Authorization for such missions was required from No. 12 Group HQ, and because the authorities didn't want any of the new aircraft to fall into enemy hands intact, pilots of stricken machines were requested to abandon them at height, and over the sea if possible.

Operation *Jubilee*

This was to be Fighter Command's biggest-ever air-defence operation of World War II, and it involved the whole of the Duxford Wing. The first sortie departed at 11.00hr, local time, and it required the Typhoons to act as a feinting probe towards the enemy forces grouped around Ostend. Although there were no Luftwaffe takers, the entire wing continued its patrol before returning to West Malling for refuelling.

After a re-brief and a quick lunch, the Wing's Typhoons were in the air again, at 14.00hr local time. Their designated operating altitudes ranged between 15,000 and 17,000ft (4,500 and 5,000m), and the three squadrons patrolled from Le Touquet to Le Treport with little enemy trade – although they did try a high speed, low level run over Dieppe in an effort to open the Typhoons' combat account over Europe. In the resultant mêlée, Flt Lt Dawson of No. 266 Sqn claimed one confirmed, whilst another probable was claimed by Plt Off Munro from the same squadron. Other aircraft from the Duxford wing would claim bits of various Fw 190s, although there were no more confirmed.

On their way home the Typhoons ran into the perennial problem of being misidentified for the very aircraft they had been hunting, the Fw 190; this time it was Flt Lt Dawson who took the brunt of this mistaken attack.

A third and final mission was flown by the Wing that day, although this was uneventful as the cloud cover had spread across the entire area. One of the pilots of

No. 609 Sqn involved with these sorties was a certain Flt Lt R. P. Beamont; after the war he would make history as a test pilot with Hawker's and its successors.

A General Move-Around

Although Typhoon operations to date had engendered some success, it was obvious that greater results could be achieved. To this end a report was commissioned from the Typhoon squadron commanders, in which they were asked to describe both the good and bad points of the type, and how they thought it should be deployed. The crux of the plan was a suggestion that the Typhoon squadrons should be re-deployed to Coltishall, Tangmere and Exeter, with dispersed sections at advanced landing grounds. Fighter Command seemed happy with this idea and sanctioned a general move-around; this began on 18 September 1942 with the

disbandment of the Duxford Wing. No. 609 Sqn moved to Biggin Hill, No. 486 Sqn took up residence at North Weald, No. 266 Sqn dispersed to Warmwell, No. 257 Sqn moved west to Exeter, whilst No. 56 Sqn was based at Matlask in Norfolk.

With the established Typhoons safely ensconced at their new bases, it was the turn of Nos 181 and 182 Squadrons to trade in their original Spitfires and Whirlwinds for Typhoons. No. 181 Sqn, commanded by Sqn Ldr Dennis Cowley-Milling, began re-equipping at Duxford on 7 September, whilst No. 182 Sqn did the same at Martlesham Heath on 12 September. Both units were intended to act in the fighter-bomber rôle, although the aircraft they received to begin with were a motley collection that had seen better days. But this was only a temporary arrangement, as Hawkers were hurriedly manufacturing bomb racks for the new aircraft that both units were scheduled to receive.

Above **Surrounded by the debris of maintenance is Typhoon IB JP380, seen on the ground at New Romney whilst in service with No. 182 Sqn. After combat use the Typhoon saw service with No. 56 OTU, before being struck off charge in 1946.** C. P. Russell Smith Collection

Further Problems

Other concerns were also starting to occupy those at Fighter Command and Hawker's. The first was the tendency for home-defence fighter units to shoot at the Typhoon, due to its resemblance to the Fw 190. In an attempt to identify Hawker's product, Fighter Command stipulated that a yellow band should be painted around the wings, although this was soon changed to a sky band around the rear fuselage, and yellow leading edges to the mainplanes, the wraparound bands being dispensed with.

The other problem that appeared at this time was far more serious in nature: it concerned the distressing tendency for the rear fuselage to fail. Initially the squadrons did not know why some of their pilots were failing to return from their assigned missions. This changed, however, when at least one formation, flying straight and level, saw one of its number suffer a catastrophic failure of the rear fuselage. Once this weakness in the structure became common knowledge, the morale of the pilots plummeted quickly in response. Initially a steel band was used as a temporary fix, until a more permanent solution was instigated, the definitive, morale-boosting fix known as Mod 286, featuring fishplates riveted around the joint. Although this modification in fact had only a limited effect on the rate of struc-

tural failures, it did seem to reassure the pilots.

While the Typhoon was still suffering from engine problems and structural failures – though was still out looking for defensive fighters and anti-aircraft gunners to shoot down – production rates were increasing enough to replace losses and allow new units to form. Thus during November and December of 1942, a further five squadrons came on stream: No. 183 Sqn at Church Fenton on 1 November; No. 195 Sqn at Hutton Cranswick on 27 November; No. 197 Sqn at Drem on 28 November; No. 198 Sqn at Digby on 8 December; No. 193 Sqn at Harrowbeer on 18 December; and No. 245 Sqn at Charmy Down on the penultimate day of the month.

A Change in Rôle: Night Flying

The Typhoon squadrons were beginning to have an effect upon the Luftwaffe's low-level raiders. In those last two months of 1942, a Ju 88 and numerous Fw 190s were to fall to the cannons of the Typhoon. A further change to the type's role was put forward by Sqn Ldr Roland Beamont, who suggested to Fighter Command that possibly the Typhoon might return to its night-fighter rôle. Having carried out

similar missions with some success while flying Hurricanes, he postulated that the Typhoon could cause havoc amongst enemy forces during night attacks. Beamont himself would fly the first mission, codenamed *Rhubarb*, on 17 November 1942, when he and his small force attacked a train near Abbeville. The success of this mission was enough to convince Command that further pilots should be trained in night flying and attacks. Thus No. 609 Sqn concentrated upon the night-time Operations *Rhubarb*, while No. 56 Sqn would do the same during daylight hours.

The latter's first sortie involved strafing Messerschmitt Bf 109s on the ground near Vlissingen: the result of this was that not only were enemy aircraft destroyed, but more importantly, confusion was caused amongst the ranks of the German forces as they realized that they were now vulnerable to attack at any hour of the day.

While the Typhoon units were making their presence felt across Europe, they were also coping rather well with the continued flood of Luftwaffe attackers. During December, pilots from both Nos 486 and 609 Sqns successfully brought down at least four Messerschmitt single-seaters, a pair of Dornier Do 217 twin-engined bombers, and four Fw 190s – although at least one Typhoon was lost in these combats.

Typhoon Strength in 1943

At the beginning of 1943 the future of the Typhoon was in doubt, as continued losses due to structural failure and engine shutdowns were still giving rise for concern; therefore a meeting was held at Fighter Command HQ at Bentley Priory to discuss the type's future. Many at the meeting were for removing the Typhoon from the inventory straightaway; however, other arguments were put forward concerning success already achieved, and this led to a stay of execution so the aircraft could be further evaluated. Recommendations were made concerning improving the Typhoon for the ground-attack mission: these included structural strengthening so that a greater weapons load could be carried, and the provision of a better canopy for all-round pilot vision.

Typhoon strength at the beginning of 1943 stood at fourteen squadrons, either operational or about to achieve opera-

Above **The code 'PR' indicates that this Typhoon IB, R7752, is on the strength of No. 609 'West Riding' Sqn. The nominated pilot for the aircraft was Sqn Ldr R. P. Beamont, and it would remain in use until struck off charge on 25 August 1943.**
RAF Museum Collection

Right **Typhoon IB JR504 and its pilot await clearance to start. The codes worn indicate ownership by No. 197 Sqn, who would pass it on to No. 137 Sqn, where it became 'SF-E'. The aircraft's fate was to be shot down by flak on Boxing Day 1944 near Schlieden.** C. P. Russell Smith Collection

tional capability, divided into four combat groups. The first of these was No. 10 Group, whose area of responsibility covered the south-west of Britain. This group consisted of four flying units: No. 257 Sqn based at Exeter, No. 266 Sqn at Warmwell, No. 245 Sqn at Charmy Down, and No. 193 Sqn at Harrowbeer. At the opposite swing of the compass was No. 11 Group, whose defensive responsibility covered the south-east of the UK; it consisted of just two operational units: No. 609 Sqn at Manston, and No. 486 Sqn at Tangmere. The Midlands were the responsibility of No. 12 Group, consisting of six squadrons (although three of these were on 'rest and recuperation'): No. 56 Sqn was based at Matlask, No. 181 Sqn at Snailwell, No. 182 Sqn. over at Sawbridgeworth, and No. 183 Sqn at Church Fenton. The final two units in the group were No. 195 Sqn at Hutton Cranswick, and No. 198 Sqn at Digby in Lincolnshire. The final group was No. 13 Group, whose responsibilities included the north of Britain; it had two units: No. 1 Sqn at Acklington, and No. 197 Sqn on rest and recuperation at Drem.

The year 1943 would prove to be significant for both air forces involved with the European conflict. For the Luftwaffe this meant a re-jigging of the units engaged in the hit-and-run strikes across south and east Britain. The two original specialist Jagdgeschwarden, Nos JG 2 and JG 26, had their primary role changed to that of air defence, whilst the raiders, equipped with the bomb-carrying Fw 190A-4/U8, were transferred to Gruppen I and II of Schnellkampfgeschwader 10, whose primary airbase was located at Amiens.

The Typhoon in Air Defence Patrols

Across the Channel, reorganization was also the order of the day for Britain's air defence forces. Although both the chain home low-level radars, as well as their counterparts in the Royal Navy surface watch patrols, were picking up incoming raiders, the lack of an IFF system meant that each target had to be investigated. To help counter this waste of man-hours and materials, Operation *Totter* was conceived. This required the assistance of the Observer Corps and the coastguard, who added the Mark 1 to the defence chain. The premise was that when an intruder was spotted, a large pyrotechnic rocket, known as an 'Eyeball Snowflake', would be launched, to indicate the position of the

Above **'ZX-N' was a Typhoon IB belonging to No. 247 Sqn when this photograph was taken. The pilot had obviously not read the pilot's notes, as the undercarriage has been retracted very quickly after take-off.** David Howley Collection

Left **Seen after their interception of a pair of Messerschmitt Bf 109s over the Channel are Frank Murphy on the left, and Allan Smith to the right, pictured at Tangmere. Both ended the war as Squadron Leaders.** Allan Smith

Below **Although the camera has stopped the propeller's rotation in this photograph, this Typhoon IB, RB389 'I8-P' of No. 440 Sqn RCAF, prepares to depart on another mission. As this is a precision strike mission, the aircraft is armed with a pair of tail-fused 1,000lb bombs.** David Howley Collection

confirmed intruder. Archaic as this may sound to modern conceptions, this system actually worked quite well, and enabled the patrolling fighters to intercept intruders who might have evaded the defence net completely.

The primary aircraft assigned to these standing air patrols was the Typhoon, the duty being known as 'anti-*Rhubarb*', the reference being to their own hit-and-run raids. This mission only took effect during daylight hours, and required pairs of aircraft to patrol off the coast on a regular basis. The Typhoon's beats typically consisted of Ramsgate to Dungeness, Dungeness to Beachy Head, Beachy Head to Shoreham, Shoreham to Selsey Bill, and Selsey Point to St Catherine's Point. Other patrols covered the coastline sectors that reached to Start Point in Devon. Although seemingly a quiet existence, these patrols were not without peril, as the altitude most were flown at was between 10 to 200ft (3 to 60m) above sea level. This kind of flying required a high level of concentration, but it was necessary because the Luftwaffe raiders came in at these heights; but after 75min of it, pilots were glad to return to base.

More Problems with the Sabre Engine

As well as the ever-present dangers of either flying into the sea, or into the guns of an Fw 190, there was also the apprehension that was felt concerning the Sabre engine's lack of reliability: if it failed at that altitude, it meant certain death. In order to assuage pilots' fears and improve reliability, a regime was instituted that required each engine to be pulled after twenty-five hours of running time for a complete strip-down and overhaul. Obviously this placed a great strain on the ground engineering team, although the complement of engineers on each unit was increased to match the workload. Also increased was the number of Typhoons per squadron, so that typically, each boasted an extra 50 percent above establishment.

In an effort to improve availability, servicing procedures for the Sabre engine were modified slightly, which allowed running hours to increase to thirty – although this would soon be compromised when Napier's began the Sabre engine modification programme. This would

result in a sharp reduction in available flying hours per squadron, each of which was limited to no more than 300 hours per month in total. Fortunately the Germans were not fully aware of the parlous state of Britain's air defences during the opening months of 1943, otherwise Jabo activity would most certainly have been higher. Nevertheless, even with the restrictions on flying hours in force, and the massive amounts of maintenance being carried out on each Sabre, losses due to engine failure continued to mount: fifty aircraft crashed during these early months of the year, whilst others were damaged during heavy landings and were removed from the active inventory for repairs.

Typhoon Successes

Some compensation for these losses in aircraft and pilots were the successes scored by the Typhoons of Nos 10 and 11 Groups: thirty-two Fw 190s, eight Messerschmitt Bf 109s, plus a single Junkers Ju 88. Other combat claims included probables against four Fw 190s, one Bf 109 and a single Dornier Do 217. Damages included a further eleven Fw 190s and a Do 217. The high scorer in this table was No. 609 Sqn, whose tally included nineteen Fw 190s and three Bf 109s; whilst at the other end of the scale,

the New Zealanders of No. 486 Sqn brought down three each of Messerschmitts and Focke-Wulfs, plus a single Ju 88 as their confirmed kill tally.

One of the most successful interceptions of 1943 was made on 29 April, by the then Fg Off Allan Smith (a major contributor to this book). Based at Tangmere with No. 486 Sqn, Allan Smith and his wingman Flt Sgt Frank Murphy were scrambled on the orders of 'Blackgang', a chain home radar station located at Blackgang Chine on the Isle of Wight. As was the norm for these flights, the intercepting pair flew low across the water whilst awaiting orders from the plotters assigned to 'Blackgang'. The orders soon came, as 'bandits' were plotted coming from the south; a navigation 'vector' was therefore issued, that put the pair between the 'bandits' and their route home to the French coast. Two further 'vectors' came from 'Blackgang' that would put the Typhoons behind the 'bandits'.

Once in position the controllers issued the code 'Buster': this was to go for full throttle and the final run-in to the intercept. As the fighters began their run-in towards the incoming 'bandits', Allan Smith radioed the 'tallyho' signal to the Blackgang controllers, meaning that the enemy aircraft were sighted and being intercepted. As the two Typhoons closed in, the 'bandits', by now identified as

---

Squadron Leader Allan Smith DFC*

Born in Auckland, New Zealand on January 12th 1921 he would grow up during the depression years and when his secondary education finished started work with the NZ subsidiary of the American Meat Packer; Wilson & Co attending classes at Auckland University at night where he graduated as a Bachelor of Commerce in 1940.

He joined the RNZAF in March 1941 doing his elementary training in New Zealand, his Wings training in Canada where he came top of his course and his OTU training in England. In March 1942 he was posted as a foundation member of No.486 (NZ) Squadron and stayed with this Squadron until his tour of operations was completed late January 1944. During this period the Tangmere Typhoon Wing was led in turn by Des Scott and Denys Gillam. Smith was a Flight Commander on No.486 Squadron and on 29 April 1943 was credited with one Me 109 destroyed over the English Channel. In the latter months of 1943 the Wing were converted to Typhoon bombers and made a number of dive bombing attacks on the V-1 sites in Northern France.

On a rest period Smith was posted as a Test Pilot to Gloster Aircraft Co and during this period married Irene Duddleston who had been a WAAF transport driver attached to 486 Squadron. From July 1944 to December 1944 he was the Commanding Officer of No.197 Typhoon Squadron flying from the Normandy Beachhead, Lille and Antwerp as close support ground attack for the Canadian Army. He led the No.5 Squadron attack which destroyed the German 15th Army Headquarters at Dordrecht in Holland on October 24th 1944 killing 2 Generals 70 Officers and 200 other ranks.

Smith flew over 400 missions and was finally shot down by flak on December 31st 1944 during a low level bombing attack on a bridge in Holland. He crash landed successfully and was taken POW. Squadron Leader Smith was Mentioned in Despatches in 1944, awarded the Distinguished Flying Cross in 1944 and in 1945 a Bar to the DFC.

Back in New Zealand after the war Smith resumed his position with the Wilson Company and in 1955 was made General Manager for New Zealand operations and retained that position in the highly successful Company until he retired in 1987.

Messerschmitt Bf 109s, began to take evasive action, which included a turn towards the French coast. In Allan's words, 'We tucked in behind them, which made it difficult for them to cover each other's tails as they were flying too close together.'

At a height of approximately 10ft (3m) above the sea, and racing onwards with the Sabres bellowing under full throttle, Allan Smith directed his wingman to take the trailing Bf 109, while he dealt with the lead aircraft. However, his wingman, Frank Murphy, was having serious problems with the reflector gunsight, and was reduced to tracking the cannon shell strikes on the water's surface to bring his guns to bear on the fleeing German fighter. Rudimentary though this method was, it had some success, as shell strikes were seen on the wings and fuselage. Damaged, the Bf 109 pulled away to port – and into the gunsight of Allan Smith, who promptly opened fire. Obviously these short bursts were enough to disable the Messerschmitt completely, as it crashed soon afterwards. Returning to the leader, Allan found himself dead astern of the remaining German fighter. From such an advantageous position he promptly opened fire, the shell strikes peppering the wings and fuselage, with panels being literally blown clear.

As the damaged fighter began to lose airspeed, Allan Smith manoeuvred his Typhoon alongside the stricken German: 'It was my first face-to-face meeting with a German, and I will remember that face till the day I die.' He remembers thinking at the time, that had he been in a similar position he would have tried to ram his enemy; however, the Bf 109 pilot appeared to be unable to do so, therefore the Typhoons pulled clear and tracked the German fighter until it crashed into the sea; after which they returned home to Tangmere.

Further Engagements

Combat patrols by the Typhoon units continued, with No. 257 Sqn, operating out of Warmwell, picking up the patrol duties in the Portland to Isle of Wight sector. It was during the anti-*Rhubarb* period of the Typhoon's history that it was realized that it was up to 100mph (160km/h) faster at lower altitudes than its Luftwaffe opposition. This advantage

came to the fore when an unannounced attack was made on Torquay by a twenty-strong force of 'Jabos'. A five-section scramble was made from Warmwell to intercept the departing fighter bombers. The Typhoons gave chase at low level across the channel. As their top speed was approaching 350mph (560km/h) they began to overhaul the fleeing Fw 190s, whose top speed was limited to a maximum of 320mph (510km/h). In the engagement that followed at least one enemy fighter was brought down, whilst others were claimed as damaged.

In a further engagement on 1 June 1943, at least five Focke-Wulf Fw 190s were shot down by pilots of No. 609 Sqn. This was to be the high point of the German hit-and-run raids upon Britain, as the main units involved were then posted to Sicily to reinforce Luftflotte 2, leaving only thirty fighters in France to continue the raids upon Britain. This reduction in the number of attackers, plus the improvements made to radar detection and reporting procedures, meant that airborne standing patrols could also be reduced, to a pair of Typhoons waiting in readiness at the end of various advanced landing grounds, the pilots sitting in the cockpit. Joining the original Typhoon squadrons were No. 197 Sqn based at Drem, which re-equipped with the Hawker fighter during November 1942, and No. 198 Sqn, formed at Digby on 7 December 1942; later it was moved to Manston to join No. 609 Sqn. No. 193 Sqn became operational at Harrowbeer, relinquishing its Hurricane night fighters during January 1943 before moving to Gravesend.

The final squadron to join Fighter Command during this period was No. 174 Sqn, which changed over to the Typhoon in April 1943. The final defensive combat undertaken by the Typhoon squadrons took place on 21 October 1943, when a pair of aircraft from No. 1 Sqn shot down a single Fw 190 off Beachy Head. From this moment on, the Typhoon squadrons would switch to the attack role, taking the war to the enemy in preparation for the invasion of Europe.

Combat in Europe

The initial attacks upon targets of opportunity in Europe were undertaken as *Rhubarbs*. Their impact had more of a propaganda value than tactical, as losses

due to flak were higher than those due to engine or structural failure. The number of raids at the end of 1942 and the beginning of 1943 was also affected by the winter weather, which was quite severe. However, from April and as spring advanced, *Rhubarb* missions increased. The RAF also created a whole raft of code-names to cover a number of missions that varied in target type and the number of aircraft deployed.

The first of these offensive sorties was called *Circus*: it involved a handful of bombers that were essentially being used as bait, accompanied by a significant force of fighters, the purpose of the operation being to draw into combat as many enemy fighters as possible, and destroy them. The ground-attack version of this was called *Ramrod*, and placed the emphasis on the bomber force destroying a ground target. For targets at sea the codename was *Roadstead*; it essentially featured a low-level attack on shipping and coastal defences.

The next two operations were pure fighter sweeps, these being *Ranger*, a freelance fighter sweep with no specific target, while *Rodeo* was similar, but featured a defined target or goal. The final fighter operation was flown purely at night and was the dark hours' version of a *Rhubarb*, being designated *Intruder*. If these types of operation were not enough, the Typhoon squadrons were also allocated to shipping reconnaissance missions sometimes called *Lagoons*, and to protecting convoys, plus air-sea rescue duties.

At the heart of the attacks on Europe were two Typhoon squadrons, Nos 181 and 182 Sqns; these had finally received their new Typhoons complete with Hawker's hastily manufactured underwing bomb racks. Early in 1943 they were joined by three other units whose Typhoons were configured for the fighter-bomber role. No. 183 Sqn would form at Church Fenton on 1 November 1942, commencing operations from Colerne in April. No. 3 Sqn, based at Hunsdon, was flying Hurricanes until February 1943, when it re-equipped with Typhoons, beginning operations in May. The final fighter-bomber unit to trade in its Hurricanes was No. 175 Sqn, who received their Typhoons at Colerne in April 1943.

When combat sorties began, the Typhoons – or Bombaphoons – were armed with general purpose 250lb bombs,

Right Typhoon IB EK183 was serving as 'US-A' of No. 56 Sqn when this portrait was taken. It was later operated by No. 609 Sqn, before being retired on 16 July 1945 as 5323M.
Big Bird Aviation Collection

though these were soon replaced by 500lb bombs. Strikes carried out by these squadrons were normally escorted by other Typhoons from the pure fighter squadrons. Nevertheless, once they had disposed of their underwing loads, the fighter bombers were more than capable of fighter-like performance, as the drag coefficient of the bomb racks had a minimal effect upon performance. Early targets attacked by the fighter bombers included airfields in France; initially those in the area of Poix and Abbeville were favourites, although attacks against shipping anywhere off the European coast were soon added to the inventory, as the Typhoon with or without bombs was a hard-hitting adversary.

However, not everything went the way of the Typhoon, as they began to fall victim to their greatest enemy at low level, German flak, which was especially lethal up to 6,000ft (2,000m). Not only were the German guns frequently radar guided, but the defences were built up in belt formation: at lower levels small calibre weapons were used, whilst at greater heights the 88mm general purpose gun was deployed. Typhoon pilots were advised to fly as low and as fast as possible to bypass the flak – although this advice came to naught should the aircraft take a hit in a vital area. In such circumstances the chances of a successful abandonment were virtually nil.

These operations against Europe were mainly the province of the southern-based units such as No. 3 Sqn, and Allan Smith's No. 486 Sqn. Shipping attacks would become the province of the two Norfolk-based units, Nos 56 and 195 Sqns, whose remit was the whole of the North Sea. As before, missions were flown at low level to confuse any enemy radar with ground clutter returns; however, this did have its down side in that occasionally aircraft came back with bent propeller tips. The formation normally adopted was either a loose line-abreast pair, or a group of four, which allowed all in the formation to keep a good lookout for enemy fighters. When an attack was initiated, the idea was that all aircraft would attack in a short space of time to divide the ship's defences, hopefully completing the sinking of the vessel after one concerted pass; all the Typhoons would then describe violent rudder-driven manoeuvres to get clear.

A New Format

With the Typhoon squadrons at last coming into their own after a shaky start, there would be a reappraisal of their operations and how they were conducted. Originally squadrons were liable to be moved from station to station as requirements altered; however, in the early days of July 1943, a completely new concept

came into being: that of combat wings whose complement of squadrons remained virtually unchanged. The original idea had been formed around an 'airfield', in whose structure were included both the flying and support units, all capable of packing up and moving as a body to where their services were required next. This concept of self-containment was very appealing, especially as planning for the invasion of Europe was already under way, and the mobile, self-contained airfield/wing was seen as a kingpin in any such undertaking. The constituent wings/airfields were No. 121, based at Lydd and which comprised Nos 174, 175 and 245 Sqns; while Nos 181, 182 and 247 Sqns would form the basis of No. 124, based at New Romney. The respective wing leaders were Wg Cdrs Crowley-Milling and Ingle.

In this new format the wings operated as either individual or combined formations for *Ramrod* operations, which would result in some losses to enemy fighters. On 13 August No. 266 Sqn lost their CO, Sqn Ldr MacIntyre, as well as two other pilots. Four days later another *Ramrod*, run by No. 182 Sqn, lost 50 percent of its despatched strength: only three of its fighters returned, after being bounced by German fighters.

Although the Luftwaffe was a constant danger, the losses to flak would total some thirty-three aircraft; these were lost during the period 1 June to 30 September 1943, from a total of sixty-six machines. On each occasion probably no more than one or two machines went down – although Allan Smith's No. 486 Sqn was very unlucky to lose three aircraft on 16 September on a *Roadstead* to Le Havre – but it was a form of attrition that was a constant drain on resources.

Attack on the *Munsterland*

As if attacking well defended ground targets, and being the butt of the attentions of Focke-Wulf and Messerschmitt fighters was not enough, the Typhoon wings were also sent to attack shipping that was just as well defended. Possibly the hardest target detailed to the wings was the transport *Munsterland* that had been spotted docked at Cherbourg. This was one target that no squadron wanted to attack because it was so heavily defended; however, the authorities decided that the

prize was worth the effort. Thus No. 263 Sqn, flying the Westland Whirlwind, and the Typhoons of No. 183 Sqn flying from Warmwell, were ordered to attack the ship. The first attack was begun early on the morning of the 24 October. The incoming wall of flak did not deter the squadrons, and a couple of hits were scored, although two Whirlwinds and a Typhoon were lost.

The Unguided Rocket

On 25 October the Typhoon added another weapon to its armoury: the unguided rocket. It was deployed by No. 181 Sqn under the wings of six aircraft against the power station at Caen, in an operation that involved all the squadrons allocated to the two combat wings. The plan was that No. 174 Sqn would dive-bomb the marshalling yards at Caen, escorted by No. 245 Sqn, whilst Nos 175 and 182 Sqns made dummy runs over

Caen in an effort to draw the enemy's flak and fighters. No. 181 Sqn was charged with actually hitting the power station, and would be escorted by No. 247 Sqn, whose task was to draw the flak from the attackers. But as so often happens with even the best laid plans, it went adrift, and No. 181 Sqn found itself exposed and would lose three aircraft, one of the pilots being killed.

Fighter Command was quite rightly becoming concerned about the losses of highly trained pilots involved in these *Rhubarb* operations, so the decision was taken to restrict these flights to special missions only, against high value targets.

Having cleared both rockets and bombs for use with the Typhoon, the 45gal (200ltr) long-range tanks were introduced, and these would result in changes to the way the aircraft was deployed. Using these tanks, the Typhoon's range was extended from 610 to 980 miles (980 to 1,575km), although their introduction was not without incident. This was because the layout of the fuel system meant that in theory the drop tanks would be emptied first, before switching to the main tanks; however, a fault in the design of the fuel-switching cock sometimes meant that the non-return part of the valve did in fact allow fuel to seep back from the full wing tanks into the empty drop tanks. If this was allowed to continue, or if the pilot failed to notice this return transfer, the result was frequently engine stoppage due to fuel starvation. At medium to high altitudes the pilot had the

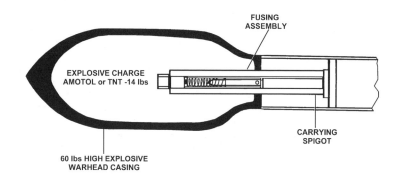

Above The 60lb (27kg) warhead was possibly the most effective type fitted to the unguided rocket, and became a very effective Jack-of-all-trades weapon. Big Bird Aviation Collection

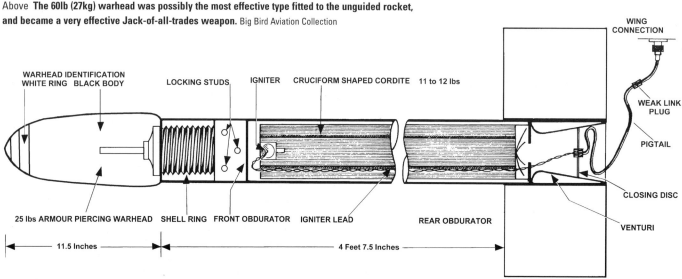

Above This diagram shows the complete unguided rocket, its components and the method of connecting the weapon electrically to an aircraft. Big Bird Aviation Collection

The Underwing Rocket Projectile

The use of underwing rockets by the Royal Air Force had first been investigated by the Projectile Development Establishment at Fort Halstead, Kent prior to its move to Aberporth in Wales during 1940 where they would join up with the Rocket Research Establishment. Together these two departments would create the first examples of the unguided rocket. Once successful trials had been completed the first production examples were rushed out to the Middle East for use by the Hurricane squadrons whose primary task was to support the units of Montgomery's Eighth Army.

Originally the ground units had been equipped with anti tank guns – these plus the tanks own guns – were found to be ineffective against the their opposite numbers of the German Afrika Corps. Mounted on the original Mk.1 underwing rails these early unguided rockets were found to have an effect upon the older Panzer Mk.IV tanks, however they had little or no effect upon the seven inch armour applied to the newly arrived Tiger tanks. These results were greeted with mixed concerns at the Air Ministry who were initially pleased with the early results however the lack of success against the heavier Tiger were very disappointing, especially as the Ministry had hoped that this weapon would be the fix-all for the tank problem. The result was that the newly established production facilities were asked to halt production of rocket motors and warheads until ordnance experts could find a way of improving the performance of the warhead.

It was about this time that the Royal Navy reported that the version developed for their use was proving ineffective as the 60lb high explosive warhead as fitted was only capable of causing superficial damage above the waterline. This was disappointing as the warhead was designed to penetrate the hull of a ship and explode. In some government circles the failure of these weapons was greeted with some glee – senior officials were said to doubt the wisdom of spending money and research time on these 'new fangled weapons'. However it would not be the research experts who would guide the answer – but a howitzer battery in the Western Desert who had found that their thin walled shells had blown the tracks and turrets of a handful of Tiger tanks by the application of brute explosive force. This warhead was in complete contrast to the original armour piercing rocket which had a hardened steel and tungsten nose cap that was intended to penetrate the tanks hull and ricochet around the inside.

The scientists then took another tack and attached a modified howitzer shell that could be driven by the three inch rocket motor. To test that the new rocket would work some prototype 60lb HE warhead fitted rockets were despatched to the trials department of the Rocket Research Establishment at Aberporth for firing trials. Not only were these successful it was also shown that these new rockets could be carried and fired by the existing aircraft mounting rails. Even as examples were being sent to the Hurricane squadrons in the Middle East for immediate use test specimens were on their way to Boscombe Down to see if they worked properly! Fortunately for all concerned there were no trajectory problems after launching and the new rockets could knock out Tiger tanks. The only problem reported by the pilots was one of

accurate sighting as the heavier 60lb warhead had a tendency to drop further upon release thus tests at Boscombe Down showed that the lighter 25lb round dropped some forty feet over a distance of 323 yards while the heavier weapon descended ninety feet over the same distance.

To counteract this problem squadron armourers rigged up a make shift sight that was graduated for various ranges which, although not perfect, was adequate for the purpose until a production version was developed. The success of the 60lb rocket meant that it quickly established itself as the primary weapon for ground attack use which meant that most of the heavy calibre underwing guns were retired except for the Vickers Type 'S' of 40mm calibre which was retained for use in the Middle East. When the Allied Army hit the beaches of Normandy in June 1944 the Typhoon and Tempest rocket equipped squadrons of the 2nd TAF were to the fore scoring some noticeable successes such as against the German armoured units at Mortain.

While the rockets were undergoing development so were the rails that they were carried on. Originally the Mk.1 rails were three steel tubes linked with cross bracing mounted on a heavy steel shielding plate under the wing. The rockets themselves were hung from two hook assemblies fitted into the rails. Mounted from the rail to the rocket motor was an electrical connection which was placed to the front of the cordite charge, firing was carried out by using a panel in the cockpit upon which was mounted a master switch, a pairs or salvo switch and a firing button. The original electrical circuit needed to be modified as loading accidents saw premature ignitions on the ground. Correction of this fault meant that a multiple socket was fitted under the wing which needed a shorting plug inserting by an armourer just prior to take off.

With the minor faults concerning the rocket and its rails being dealt with, it was time to concentrate upon creating a weapons aiming sight that could deal with both the launching of rockets and the aiming of wing armament. After much deliberation and experimentation the Mk.II reflector sight was fitted with an adjustable reflector screen. Adjustment was via a knurled knob at the front of the sight base which allowed the pilot to depress the sight line downwards by up to five degrees for rocket firing.

Developing the rocket further led to the double mounting of 60lb rockets using a Duplex mount. Initially there were problems with this double launch system as the lower rocket exhibited a tendency to cartwheel into the ground. Modifying the Duplex launcher to allow single rocket launches meant that the problem was reduced to acceptable limits. With these double rocket assemblies fitted the Typhoon could fly at speeds up to 450mph IAS as long as no violent manoeuvres were attempted. The original Mk.1 rocket rail assemblies were the next items to be looked at and these were quickly modified to Mk.II standard by the removal of the heavy steel mounting plate which improved aircraft performance and handling. Following on from this came the Mk.III which are better known as the Zero length launchers and would serve the forces well until the mid 1950s.

---

time to rectify the situation; at low level, however, the outcome was normally disaster. Those aircraft already in service had the fuel tank modification added retrospectively, while from the middle of 1943 Hawker's were building new aircraft with these fitments embodied as standard.

A New Role for the Typhoon Squadrons

With all machines being brought up to nearly the same standard, it was now time for the Typhoon squadrons to begin training for a new role. The first signs that the Typhoon's role was changing came when Exercise *Spartan* was mounted. Designed to prepare all the designated forces for combat in France, this exercise involved four of the six units, these being Nos 181, 182, 183 and 247 Sqns. In order to reinforce the results of this exercise, all six squadrons would become truly mobile: thus living under canvas became the norm, as did packing up and moving to a new location at short notice. All these preparations would eventually result in Fighter Command announcing the creation of the Second Tactical Air Force, whose role would be to provide support for

the ground forces as they moved across Europe.

The date of the 2nd TAF's creation is given as 13 November 1943, when Fighter Command revealed it as a component of the Allied Expeditionary Air Force. The Typhoon units allocated to the AEAF/2nd TAF comprised the six squadrons of Nos 121 and 124 Airfield/Wings based at Westhampnett and Merston respectively, whilst the remaining twelve squadrons were allocated to the remainder of Fighter Command, by now renamed the Air Defence of Great Britain. The first commander of 2nd TAF was Air Vice Marshall Arthur Coningham; his deputy

Above and left **The Typhoons of No. 438 Sqn RCAF, part of No. 143 Wing, continued their combat operations even though their airfield was heavily flooded in early 1945. In these views, R6207 'F3-T' is photographed during its departure. Of note is the pilot paddling across in a survival dinghy to reach his machine.** Both David Howley Collection

commanders were AVM Harry Broadhurst, in command of No. 83 Group, formed to support the British Second Army; and AVM Brown, whose command was No. 84 Group, formed to support the Canadian First Army. This brought the total of operational groups up to three, the other organization in the 2nd TAF being No. 2 Group. The two Typhoon wings would be allocated to No. 83 Group for the duration of the European campaign, although control would remain vested in 11 Group until the invasion began.

For the Typhoon squadrons, life would continue as before, with strikes being carried out against ground targets in France and the low countries. As always,

losses were accumulating as accurate German flak took its toll – although in return they managed to bring down a Ju 88 and four Fw 190s. During the period covering the end of 1943 and the beginning of 1944, Hawker's began to deliver Typhoons capable of firing rockets, whilst in-service machines underwent conversion – as did the pilots, who had to learn to use their gunsights for aiming, while attempting to calculate offsets to improve accuracy.

Improvements in the reliability of the Napier Sabre also led to an increase in Typhoon production, which meant that most squadrons began to receive new machines, whilst the older aircraft were transferred to Operational Conversion

Units for further service. Those that had been in long-term storage were also dragged out for upgrading at Gloster's, who re-manufactured each and every one to the latest standard, including the sliding blown canopy. All designated squadrons would be fully equipped with the right version of aircraft by April 1944.

The increased availability of Typhoons allowed for an increase in the number of operational units: hence Nos 137, 164, 184 and 263 Squadrons reformed with the Hawker product in January 1944, January 1944, March 1944 and December 1943 respectively. In addition, three RCAF units also gained Typhoons, these being Nos 438, 439 and 440 Sqns, who equipped in January, February and March 1944; these became No. 143 Airfield/Wing. After a period of working up to operational standard, they transferred to Hurn to begin combat missions.

The tenor of the Typhoon's sorties also changed, as photo reconnaissance flights over the Pas de Calais had revealed a series of concrete structures that were eventually identified as the launching pads for the Fiesler Fi-103 flying bomb, better known later as the V1. Intelligence gathering soon revealed that these structures (known as 'Noballs') were vulnerable to direct hits by bombs of 500lb or higher, so various heavy bombers and Typhoon fighter bombers were sent on missions to destroy them. During December 1943 and July 1944, all the identified sites were attacked relentlessly, with some aircraft being lost to the intensive flak surrounding some locations. Given that the invasion was scheduled to take place in 1944, the participation of the Typhoon squadrons in these attacks began to diminish in the first quarter of 1944; however, some sorties were still flown when required, although the original sites were soon abandoned for others that were smaller and better camouflaged.

In early 1944, all rocket-equipped Typhoon squadrons began to attend Armament Practice Camps to hone their accuracy with the rockets. The first would be No. 174 Sqn, whose pilots went to Eastchurch aerodrome for further training. Other APC units, at Llanbedr and Hutton Cranswick, dealt with the training of other squadrons in rotation: Nos 175, 181, 182, 184, 245 and 247 Squadrons of 83 Group, and Nos 164, 183, 198 and 609 Sqns and No.137 Squadrons of 11 Group. Those squadrons not required for rocket projectile training would remain in the fighter-bomber role.

Changes in the formation of the Typhoon wings began in March 1944, when Nos 198 and 609 Sqns were transferred from 84 Group directly into the control of the 2nd TAF. These two units would form the nucleus of No. 123 Airfield/Wing at Tangmere; their replacements were Nos 197 and 183 Sqns. The former squadron later returned to Tangmere, where it would be joined by Nos 257 and 266 Sqns, all three moving to a location near Beaulieu, where No. 193 Sqn would join up with them to form No. 146 Airfield/Wing. In the meantime No. 183 Sqn would join up with No. 164 Sqn

to form No. 36 Airfield. All these revamped formations were under the control of No. 20 Wing. Changes in the way the groundcrews were organized also came into effect at this time, when they were renamed as servicing echelons. The theory was that each echelon would follow behind the invasion forces and establish forward landing grounds for aircraft that required servicing. Initially this separation led to a deterioration in morale, although in reality each echelon stayed in close contact with their original aircrew and aircraft.

As invasion day drew closer, more and more units went through APC, until by April all had undergone rocket training. It was during this month that the Canadian No. 143 Airfield/Wing became operational under the command of Wg Cdr Davidson. The rearrangement of squadrons and aircraft continued as units traded in their Typhoons for the new Tempest: thus No. 3 Squadron flew its last Typhoon sortie on 24 March 1944, whilst No. 486 Sqn did the same on 14 April; and No. 1 Sqn changed over at the beginning of April, while No. 56 Sqn changed over in May 1944.

These various swaps and changes would be the last before the invasion of Europe, hence eighteen Typhoon-equipped units were allocated to Nos 83 and 84 Groups within the 2nd TAF. The other two Typhoon units, Nos 137 and 263 Sqns,

remained on the strength of the ADGB based at Manston and Harrowbeer respectively, the former being rocket-equipped while the latter retained the bomber role. Both these squadrons mainly concentrated on anti-shipping sorties along the length and breadth of the Channel.

Offensive against Enemy Radar Installations

The role of the units allocated to the embryonic 2nd TAF was to attack various ground installations in an effort to soften up the German defences. Not only were 'Noball' missions continued against the V1 sites, but a new type of target presented itself for attention by the rocket-equipped Typhoons: the radar installations that stretched from the Pas de Calais to Brittany, and these were given some serious attention. Many were taken out of commission during the first attack that was driven through heavy defences; however, some of these sites needed a second visit, and this allowed the German defences to be better prepared, and as a result the number of casualties increased. Fortunately the 60lb (27kg) rockets were successful in their application, and the great majority of these radar sites were heavily damaged. At the beginning of June, all the Typhoon squadrons flew

Below **Typhoon IB EK427 spent some time with the A&AEE undergoing FR.1B trials; it then served successively with Nos 268 and 4 Sqns, before being struck off charge in February 1946 during the great Typhoon cull.** C. P. Russell Smith Collection

intensive sorties against the remaining radar sites; some 694 missions were flown.

In between these sorties, during the final three days before the invasion, orders were received from Command to apply, as neatly as possible, the well known black and white Invasion stripes under the wings and rear fuselage of each aircraft destined to take part in Invasion operations.

Invasion Day

On 6 June 1944 at 07.25hr, one day later than originally planned, the Allied forces began their assault on the Normandy beaches: 'H' hour had arrived. Operating in support of the troops hitting the beaches in their landing craft were nine of the eighteen Typhoon squadrons assigned to 2nd TAF. Designated for 'Air Alert' duties, the squadrons were assigned to support the British and Canadian forces, although they were briefed to contact the HQ ships upon arrival in case the primary targets had changed. As new orders were not forthcoming, the Typhoon squadrons divebombed their allotted targets near Le Hamel/La Rivière, better known as Gold Beach, Courseulles designated as Juno Beach, and Hermaville known as Sword Beach.

The nine remaining Typhoon squadrons were also allotted German targets, namely four gun sites plus two Army HQs, at Château-le-Parc and Château-le-Meauffe. Once the squadrons had destroyed their targets, calls were put out for attacks on a radar station near Le Havre; this station was directing coastal guns against the Invasion force, as well as other sticking points, and this was slowing down the Allied advance. As the expected 'trade' had failed to materialize, the Typhoons were despatched on armed reconnaissance to the south of Bayeux, their purpose being to disrupt any attempt by the Germans to reinforce the Normandy area, and to suppress any intervention by the Luftwaffe.

The Battle for France

The next day saw the Typhoon squadrons airborne again, although the cloud base was down to 1,500ft (450m), and stretched upwards the same distance. By this time the beach-heads were well established, so the construction units moved on to the Normandy fields to carve out advanced landing grounds, which were then surfaced with PSP matting to provide a runway and hard standings. This allowed the squadrons and their mobile servicing echelons to begin combat operations close to the front line. One of the biggest sorties flown that day was against the HQ of Panzer Gruppe West based at Château-le-Caine. In this aerial assault, over seventy Mitchell bombers and forty Typhoons hit the orchards surrounding the château, destroying the HQ's vehicles and killing the chief of staff General von Dawans. A further assault of a similar nature would take place on 27 June, when a mixed force of Mitchells and Typhoons struck the HQ of Lieutenant General Dohlman, commander of an infantry division. The ensuing strike killed the general and his entourage, thus reducing the effectiveness of the troops.

Full-scale operations from the advanced landing grounds (ALGs) known as B.2, B.3 and B.6 began during the second week of June, with Nos 181, 174 and 247 Sqns taking up residence at their new bases, in that order. Their tenure would be short, as the German forces had managed to come in range with their artillery and began shelling the ALGs. As there was no protection for the aircraft or personnel, it was decided to withdraw the advanced forces back to Britain.

Upon arrival, the Napier Sabre engines of the survivors were subjected to a major overhaul, as there had been a spate of serious failures. Investigation revealed that fine dust had been entering the engines and causing wear to the moving parts. This had been caused by the dust created when the airfields in Normandy had been built, as the stable topsoil had been removed. The answer was to fit a hastily contrived, mushroom-shaped dust deflector, which diverted the heavier particles clear of the carburettor. The down side to this modification was that the Sabre would occasionally backfire, and in doing so would launch the deflector across the airfield. Eventually a purpose-designed, tropical-type filter was developed for use in Normandy.

The Typhoon squadrons would return to Normandy by the end of June; thus No. 121 Wing was based at B.5, No. 124 Wing at B.6, and No. 143 Wing at airfield B.9. Joining these units would be No. 123 Wing, which arrived at B.10. All the operating squadrons were desperately short of aircraft and pilots, as more than seventy Typhoons had been lost in action. However, this reduction in strength did not deter the Typhoons from carrying out their allotted task, that of hitting road and rail targets, and thus appreciably delaying much needed German reinforcements.

Below Reconnaissance photographs were vital to the work done by the Typhoon squadrons. This view is of a French château in use by the Wehrmacht as a command headquarters just prior to attack by the 2nd TAF. Allan Smith

Above **Complete with a full array of underwing identification striping, this early-build Typhoon awaits its bomb load before departing on another mission over Europe.** Real Wings Collection

Above **The other favoured underwing load carried by the Typhoon was the unguided rocket; here, D-Day striped examples are loaded with the ubiquitous 60lb (27kg) warhead variant.** Real Wings Collection

Right **Seen through the gun camera of another Typhoon, an aircraft pulls up after releasing a salvo of rockets against a railway.** Big Bird Aviation Collection

Above **Once operational in Normandy, the role of Typhoons altered slightly to encompass attacks against softer targets. As if to emphasize this, two armourers add the nose and tail to a segmented anti-personnel bomb, for use against such targets as trucks.** Big Bird Aviation Collection

Above **For use against harder targets such as bunkers and pillboxes, high explosive bombs were preferred. Here, two armourers finish loading a 500lb bomb.** Real Wings Collection

their participation was in the form of attacks against the launch sites themselves.

Continued Assaults

During July and August the Typhoon squadrons continued their assaults upon designated targets, and also those of a more opportune nature. The rocket-equipped aircraft were very effective against soft-skinned transport, whilst the bomb-carrying aircraft were used against harder targets. To increase their effectiveness, the 'Bombphoons' began toting 1,000lb general-purpose munitions, as their close proximity to the battlefield allowed for their carriage. This capability, plus that of the rocket Typhoons, was severely put to the test on 7 August, when the German forces began a full-scale breakout in the area of Mortain. But as the German Panzer divisions and their supporting infantry pushed forward, they were moving into a carefully prepared trap. No. 197 Sqn would be one of the lead Typhoon bomber squadrons throughout this period, an activity that they would develop into a speciality.

To make their attacks more effective, they were flown at low level, with the bomb fuses set to 11sec. Where possible, stereoscopic pictures of a static target were obtained, and an approach path determined that would place the heavy fighter at an altitude below the height of the building. Using this approach, and releasing the bombs at the last possible moment, the certainty of a hit was assured.

The air component of the defensive counter attack consisted of Republic P-47 Thunderbolts and Lockheed P-38 Lightnings operating in the bomber role, whilst the 2nd TAF supplied rocket-equipped Typhoons, whose task was to destroy the German armour. Indeed, they had plenty of targets to choose from – in fact there were so many tanks and trucks that an attack shuttle service evolved to cater for the constant stream of aircraft landing at the ALGs for rearming and refuelling. The concentrated firepower of both the USAAF and the 2nd TAF soon reduced the German forces to a smoking ruin. To achieve this, however, over 300 sorties were flown, the Typhoon/rocket combination being seen as a particularly lethal combination.

Whilst the other squadrons plied their normal trade, No. 137 Sqn was given another task: to intercept V1 flying bombs that were being launched from the Pas de Calais towards London; these were known as *Diver* patrols. Their participation was on an 'as and when' basis, much of these intercepts being carried out by Mustangs, Spitfires and Mosquitos. Many of the other Typhoon squadrons were also involved with destroying the V1 menace, although

The defeat of the German forces at Mortain was the final fling for the Allied forces, as their destruction meant that a breakout was now possible. As the Germans retreated, the various Army Corps pushed forwards after them; and the 7th German Army suffered serious casualties as it travelled through the narrow Normandy lanes. In response, the Typhoon squadrons were committed to providing air attack in order to slow down their escape, and it was during this period of intense operations that the squadrons would suffer their highest losses: more than ninety were lost in August alone, mainly due to flak and persistent small-arms fire. 18 August would see the highest peak, when seventeen were shot down.

The German anti-aircraft set-up was one of the more efficient parts of their air defence organization, as many pilots would find out. From zero to 6,000ft (0 to 2,000m) the Germans used both 20mm and 40mm cannons, while above that altitude they favoured the deadly 88mm gun. Once the Typhoon wings were established in Europe, they found themselves under intensive fire at all times, in some cases from take-off to landing. What exacerbated the situation was the introduction of proximity fuses, which made the practice of flying straight and level distinctly inadvisable.

Attack on a Railway-Mounted Gun

On 18 August, No. 197 Sqn was tasked to take part in an attack on a railway-mounted gun being used by the Germans to shell the *Mulberry Harbour*, moored off the invasion beaches. This monster gun only emerged at night, and was hidden during the day in a railway tunnel near Pont L'Évèque. Careful study of the target zone revealed that the preferred method of divebombing to collapse the tunnel roof would probably be ineffective, therefore the attack needed to be carried out at low level. Each aircraft would be armed with 1,000lb bombs with the fuses set at 11sec, and four Typhoons were assigned to strike at each end of the tunnel. The direction of the attack was straight down the railway line, with the intention of bringing down one end of the tunnel, when the next four aircraft would attack the other end. The flight leaders for this attack would be Allan Smith and the Wing Leader Johnny Baldwin, the former having to attack the more heavily defended end.

The first four Typhoons succeeded in their attack without loss, and the tunnel end duly collapsed. At the other end of the tunnel the flight led by Johnny Baldwin was not so lucky, as every flak gun opened up on the four Typhoons. However, their perseverance paid off, as the last group of bombs successfully brought down the other end of the tunnel roof. To assist the attacking fighters the first flight attacked the anti-aircraft guns, which distracted them enough to let the second flight fly clear. Even so, the Typhoon piloted by Johnny Baldwin was hit by flak, but did manage to land back at B.3.

Into Europe

With much of the battle for France over, the Typhoon wings turned their attentions to the German forces occupying the rest of Europe. By this time the two Typhoon squadrons assigned to ADGB had been released to the 2nd TAF, while some of the bomber Typhoon squadrons underwent APCs for conversion to rocket attacks.

While the German forces were in constant retreat towards their own borders it was a fairly orderly affair, so on 17 September, Operation *Market Garden* was put into action. With the intention of cutting off some of the retreating enemy and inducing the rest to rout, the plan was to drop US paratroops at Grave and Nijmegen, and the British 1st Airborne Division at Arnhem. To pave the way for this assault, over 100 Typhoon sorties were flown to neutralize the German defences. After the airborne forces had successfully landed, the Typhoon squadrons set up a 'cab rank' system of attacks. Upon arrival, any available targets would be attacked, after which the Typhoons would orbit for a short period while waiting for designated or opportune targets to appear. This continued throughout 17 September, but inclement weather the next day reduced Typhoon sorties to a minimum. Although for the time being Arnhem would be retained by the Germans, the attack had opened up the route to Holland via Grave and Nijmegen; Arnham would be claimed at a later date.

With the Netherlands now open to Allied forces, ALGs were quickly established; one of the first was B.78 at Eindhoven, which became the home for No. 124 Wing and No. 143 Wing; No. 121 Wing would take residence at Volkel. 83 and 84 Groups now parted company, the former continuing in support of the advancing forces, while the latter turned their attention to those pockets of resistance that had been bypassed by the Allied units.

The Typhoons meanwhile were putting their anti-shipping skills to good use, attacking the enemy garrisons that prevented the Allies using the Port of Antwerp, and their attentions were quite quickly rewarded by German surrender.

Below **In lighter moments, happy snaps were taken as mementos of the experience in Europe. This group are from No. 197 Sqn.** Allan Smith

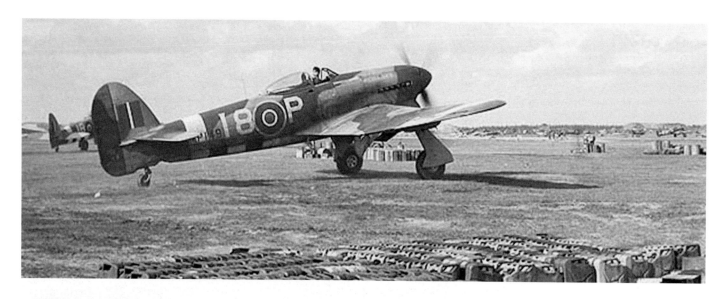

Above **Typhoon IB MP149 '18-P' was on the strength of No. 440 'City of Ottawa' Sqn of the Royal Canadian Air Force when this portrait was taken. Nicknamed 'Pulverizer IV', the fighter bomber was being prepared for its next flight at B.100 Goch in April 1945. Of note are the neat rows of jerry cans to the front.** Public Archives of Canada

Left **The groundcrew are just finishing connecting the underwing fuel tanks, before electrically connecting the rockets on this Typhoon IB, the cables of which are seen dangling below the wing.** Big Bird Aviation Collection

Below **Although its serial has been censored, this Typhoon is in fact RB402 '5V-P' of No. 439 Sqn, landing at B.100 Goch during April 1945. This aircraft would remain with the Canadians until it was withdrawn on 15 November 1945.** Public Archives of Canada

On 29 September they were in action again, though this time their role was purely of intimidation. Canadian forces had negotiated a truce with the garrison holding Boulogne, to allow the civilian population to escape. A short time before the truce ended, the Typhoons formed a circling 'cab rank' above the town, which was enough to force a surrender – although the flak gunners could not resist loosing off a few shots.

Once Antwerp had fallen into Allied hands, the Typhoons moved in to occupy airfield B.70 at Deurne. However, this was on the flight path of the V1s being launched towards the Allied forces occupying the city and docks of Antwerp – in fact, it was not unusual to see three or four at a time overflying the airfield during the day, while a far greater number were launched at night. Although most of these weapons were aimed past the airfield, a few, whether by accident or design, would cut their motors in the vicinity of B.70 and plunged to earth. These hits were close by, which tended to shake the occupied buildings, but fortunately missed the aircraft. At one stage the intensity of the bombardment was such that the pilots of No. 486 Sqn considered it was safer to be airborne than on the ground. The 'V2' was also posing a serious threat during this period, and at least one landed

Above **Mass briefings at Antwerp were frequently held out in the open, and involved a gathering of pilots around the briefing officer and his board of maps and reconnaissance photographs.** Allan Smith

Below **Wearing the personal code of the No. 143 Wing leader, Wg Cdr F. G. Grant taxies out in RB205 for another mission at B.78 Eindhoven in December 1944. To assist the pilot in avoiding obstacles on these forward bases, it was normal practice for groundcrew to ride on the wing-tips. This aircraft was destroyed on 1 January 1945 in an air raid at Eindhoven, together with another seventeen aircraft.** RAF Museum Collection

in the B.70 maintenance area, wounding some personnel and badly damaging aircraft already under repair.

As the winter of 1944 set in, the Typhoon squadrons were involved in consolidation sorties, winkling out the few pockets of Axis resistance that remained behind the Allied lines. On the first day of 1945 the Luftwaffe would have one last fling, a significant force of fighter bombers striking at the Allied airfields in the area of the Ardennes. Codenamed Operation *Bodenplatte*, this would be a costly attack for the Germans, as their losses of aircraft and pilots would far exceed the aircraft they destroyed. One of their most successful forays was against Eindhoven, where Nos 124 and 143 Wings and their eight squadrons were stationed. As the fighters of Jagdgeschwader 3 struck, there was a mission on the runway preparing to take off, and of the four aircraft to get airborne, only one would survive. At the end of the attack the Typhoon squadrons had lost nineteen aircraft destroyed, and a further dozen damaged. The reduction in strength for the Typhoon squadrons was short-lived, however, as within days the pilots had been flown by transport to No. 83 GSU to collect replacement machines.

Into Germany

Better weather arrived as the year progressed, and so the Typhoon squadrons continued to provide support as the Allied armies continued their advance, with all manner of targets being attacked. By this time the 'cab rank' operation was an established method of providing close air support to the ground forces, and it would be an essential component in the final mass crossing of the Rhine.

On 24 March 1945 the anticipated crossing of the Rhine began, the final hurdle into Germany. As before, the Typhoons operated in the 'cab rank' role, although some were allocated a far more hazardous task, that of flak suppression. This was a dangerous task, but thankfully only a handful of Typhoons were lost, and fortunately most of the pilots were able to bale out over Allied-held territory.

With the Rhine safely crossed, the British and Canadian forces continued their thrust after the retreating German army. As well as providing support for the advancing armies, the Typhoons were also sent to attack the remaining Luftwaffe airfields, although these were heavily defended by automatic flak installations. However, these attacks proved fruitful in depleting the strength of the Luftwaffe, therefore they would continue, as would attacks on any road vehicles and trains found to be moving in German-held territory. Ships, too, of all description were seen as legitimate targets, and were attacked without respite. These sorties in the last few weeks of the war saw an increase in the number of casualties amongst the Typhoon squadrons, as the German defenders threw all they had against the fighters in an attempt to stop the inexorable advance of the Allies. During the month of April and the first week of May 1945, forty-five Typhoons would be shot down by flak.

Left **Briefing facilities in the field were by necessity rough and ready. The central figure in this picture taken at Antwerp is Flt Lt 'Tommy the Spy' Thomas, the intelligence officer for No. 146 Wing. The other two are both pilots, the one on the right being an Australian, 'Cobber' James, who frequently flew as No. 2 to Allan Smith, and would tell his wife that the pilot was fine after his aircraft was shot down.** Allan Smith

Above **During Operation *Bodenplatte* this Typhoon IB 'XM-K' of No. 182 Sqn was attacked as the pilot tried to take off. Struck by cannon fire, the pilot subsequently crashlanded the Typhoon and vacated the cockpit in a great hurry. To the rear, a pair of No. 440 Sqn machines were also damaged in the attack.** David Howley Collection

Below **Roaring down the runway at B.91 Kluis at full power, this Typhoon IB of No. 183 Sqn is on the point of rotation. The underwing fuel tanks and the lack of external weaponry indicate that this aircraft was on a routine air patrol.** RAF Museum Collection

Above **On the left, Sqn Ldr Arthur (Spike) Umbers, DFC & Bar, was a Flight Commander on 486 Sqn, then went on rest as a test pilot at Hawker's. Returning to 486 Sqn, he was made CO in December 1944. He was shot down by flak and killed in February 1945. On the right is Sqn Ldr Harvey Sweetman DFC: he started flying Spitfires with 485 Sqn, and was then posted as a foundation Flight Commander on 486 Sqn. When his time on tours expired, he went as a test pilot at Hawker's. He returned to 486 Sqn until he was posted as CO of 3 Squadron; he stayed with them until the end of the war.** Allan Smith

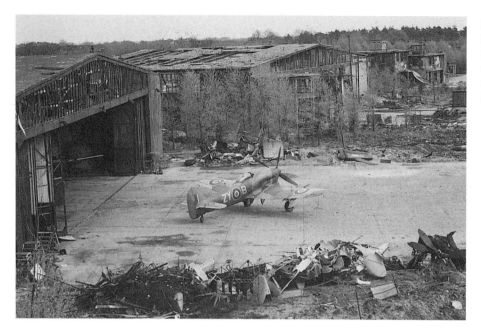

Left **Ah, luxury! This Typhoon IB, RB458 'ZY-B' of No. 247 Sqn, sits amongst the cleared wreckage of Lubeck airfield during the closing days of the war. Although not the most salubrious of scenes, the location is a change from the muddy fields of Normandy.** RAF Museum Collection

A Misplaced Attack

Having been part of a victorious hard-fought campaign across Europe, it is a great shame that the Typhoon would end its part in the war in the execution of a distressing and misplaced attack – although the blame would appear to lie at the door of British Intelligence, who either ignored the information they were given, or were unaware of their mistake until the events here related took place.

On 3 May 1945 Typhoons belonging to No. 83 Group, 2nd Tactical Air Force,

were briefed to carry out missions over northern Germany, to destroy any form of transport attempting to leave the country. In the northern port of Lubeck the camouflaged ocean liner *Cap Arcona*, once the queen of the southern seas, plus the freighters *Athens* and *Thielbeck*, had embarked aboard the survivors of a death march from the SS concentration camps at Auschwitz and Majdanek. Over 10,000 died on this forced march; 8,000 survived to be forced aboard the three ships by the SS guards. Then on the afternoon of 3 May, three Typhoons saw the ships

anchored in the harbour. Diving into the attack, all three aircraft fired their rockets and cannon, striking the ships repeatedly. The *Athens* sank quickly, and the *Cap Arcona* rolled over, blazing furiously. The *Thielbeck* took 45 minutes to go down, and it is reported that the few survivors from the attack came from this vessel. Even so, their chances of escape were remote, as the SS guards machine-gunned those struggling ashore, whilst the coldness of the water claimed many others. Once the British government realized that the ships were in fact carrying concentration camp

Typhoon Combat Victories

As the Typhoon and its pilots concentrated mainly upon ground attack it is hardly surprising that their record of air combat victories is low. However there were eight pilots that managed a reasonable total each out of a total of 250 confirmed, possibles and probables. The first victory was placed on 9 August 1942 and was a Junkers Ju 88 claimed by Pilot Officer N J Lucas of No.266 Sqdn flying Typhoon R7696 'ZH-C'. The

final Typhoon claim was placed on 3 May 1945 and was shared by twelve pilots from No.193 Sqdn, the victim being a Bv 138.

Flying Officer C F J Detal was killed on active service while Sqdn Ldr R Van Lierde would also claim at least forty 'V1' flying bombs while flying Tempests with No.3 Sqdn.

Pilot	Nationality	Unit(s)	Victories	Shared	On Ground	Probables
Grp Capt J R Baldwin DSO DFC*	British	Nos.609, 198 Sqdns No.146 Wing	15	1(0.5)	0	0
F/O C F J Detal	Belgian	No.609 Sqdn	6	1(0.5)	1	0
Sqdn/Ldr R Van Lierde DFC *	Belgian	Nos 609, 164 Sqdns	6	0	1	0
Sqdn/Ldr W F Stark DFC*	British	Nos.609, 263, 164 Sqdns	5	1(0.50	1	0
Sqdn/Ldr R A Llalemant DFC	Belgian	Nos. 609, 198 Sqdn	4	1(0.5)	1	
Sqdn/Ldr J Niblet DFC*	British	No.198 Sqdn	4	1(0.5)	1	0
Pilot Officer F Murphy DFC	New Zealand	No.468 Sqdn	4	1	0	0
Flt/Lt J Davies DFC	British	No.609 Sqdn	4	0	0	0

Right **Not all maintenance was carried out in the open: some units were fortunate enough to have mobile servicing hangers in which to attend their Hawker-built charges.** RAF Museum Collection

victims, and not fleeing German military personnel, the whole incident was placed under a 'D' notice and was struck from the record.

Epilogue

On 4 May 1945 the German armies in Holland, Denmark and northern Germany surrendered, whilst the remainder of their armies would complete the surrender process some three days later. During the Typhoon's part in the invasion of Europe, over 200,000 rocket projectiles had been fired, and an immense tonnage of bombs had been dropped. The claims made against this massive expenditure of weaponry included one hundred German aircraft destroyed, plus uncountable numbers of trucks, tanks and trains. In return the Typhoon units had lost over 500 aircraft, with as many more damaged. The remaining Typhoons would leave RAF service very promptly, as they were quickly replaced by Spitfires and Tempests. Placed in storage, the more serviceable Typhoons, some 674 in number, would eventually be scrapped during 1946 and 1947. Those considered too war weary for any form of further usage were virtually scrapped where they stood.

Below **Its fighting days over, this Typhoon IB lingers at Locking as a training aid. EK326/5446M had once been on the inventory of Nos 609 and 56 Sqns before joining No. 55 OTU, whose coding it wears.** C. P. Russell Smith Collection

CHAPTER SIX

The Development of the Tempest

While the Typhoon was adequate for the task presented to it, Hawker's were more than aware that the design had reached the end of the road. The fuselage still bore traces of its biplane ancestry, whilst the wing section was very deep in section to NACA 22, which meant that it generated a high level of drag. Technically at 30 per cent chord, the thickness/chord ratio at the root was 19.5 per cent, which petered out to the tip at 12 per cent. Such a design guaranteed great structural strength and plenty of room for any internal armament and fuel; however, the maximum speed was 400mph (645km/h). In a dive, however, the story was different, as the maximum speed that could be achieved without buffeting and trim changes was 500mph (800km/h).

Hawker's had already noted the performance available to the Spitfire with its thinner section wing, and had begun to investigate the design of a new wing in March 1940. The Battle of Britain interfered with the development of the new wing, as Hurricane production was of the highest priority, therefore it was not until September of the following year that design work began. The new design featured the maximum depth set further back, at 37.5 per cent chord, while the thickness/chord ratio was set at 14.5 per cent at the root, tapering out to 10 per cent at the tip. The physical sign of these numbers was that the new wing was some 5in (13cm) thinner at the root compared to that of the Typhoon. During the redesign the planform was changed to a semi-elliptical shape, radically different to the mild taper built into that of its predecessor.

These changes also meant that space was not available in the wing structure for the same amount of fuel, therefore an extra fuel tank would be needed in the fuselage of the new fighter. This was based on the earlier Typhoon, although the addition of an extra fuel tank required that any proposed engine installation had to be moved forwards by 21in (53cm), which allowed for a quantity of 76gal (345ltr) to be carried in a tank located between the firewall and the oil tank. The new wing also allowed for a new undercarriage, as wide-tracked as that of the Typhoon. The proposed powerplant was the Napier Sabre Mark IV.

A Design for the New Fighter

The design of the thin wing Typhoon described above was known as the EC.107C, and once it had been presented to the Air Ministry, a specification, F.10/41, was issued in August 1941. It covered the construction of two prototypes designated the Typhoon II; the prototype production contract would follow in November. As the design of the new fighter entered the definition stage, Sidney Camm approached the Ministry of Aircraft Production with a modified proposal for the cooling of the engine. His idea was to place radiators in the wing leading edges, in a similar manner to that employed by the de Havilland Mosquito. The removal of the bulged radiator under

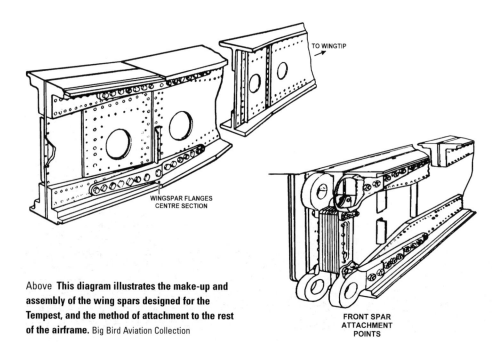

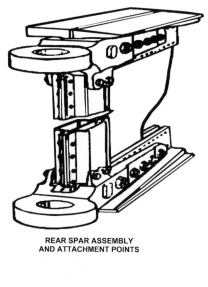

TO WINGTIP

WINGSPAR FLANGES
CENTRE SECTION

FRONT SPAR
ATTACHMENT
POINTS

REAR SPAR ASSEMBLY
AND ATTACHMENT POINTS

Above **This diagram illustrates the make-up and assembly of the wing spars designed for the Tempest, and the method of attachment to the rest of the airframe.** Big Bird Aviation Collection

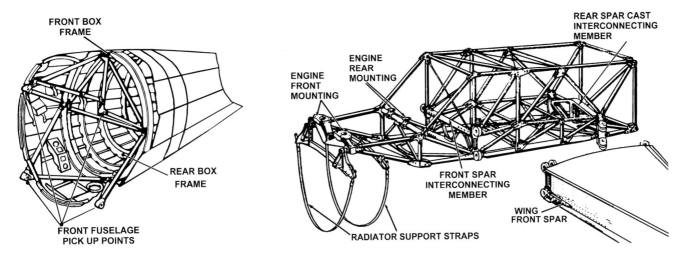

Above As the cockpit area of the Tempest was tubular in construction, the attachment of the rear monocoque fuselage required a tubular attachment framework for connection. Big Bird Aviation Collection

Above This diagram shows the arrangement of the Tempest forward tubular fuselage framework as applicable to the Mark V, and the layout of the fuselage to wing spar attachments. Big Bird Aviation Collection

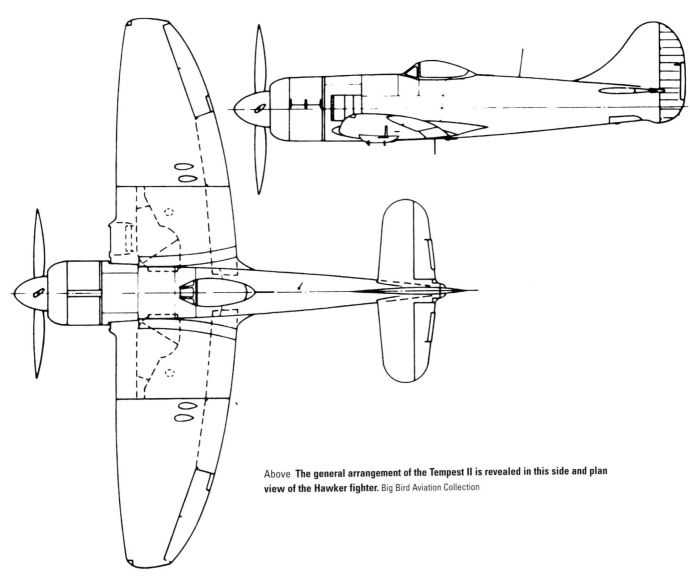

Above The general arrangement of the Tempest II is revealed in this side and plan view of the Hawker fighter. Big Bird Aviation Collection

the nose allowed for an engine installation that was tightly cowled, and hence neater and more streamlined. Wind-tunnel tests by Hawker's seemed to show little difference in the drag coefficients between both types of cooling installation; however, the RAE at Farnborough begged to differ, as their calculations showed that the drag would be reduced by two-thirds. Development of the wing radiator layout would therefore continue.

An Engine for the Typhoon II

During this period, problems had begun to arise with the in-service Napier Sabres, and this cast doubt upon the use of this engine in Hawker's new fighter. As added security, the company began to look at the Rolls-Royce Griffon as an alternative. To prove the new installation, a Typhoon I airframe was modified to accept the Rolls-Royce engine, and taken by road to Derby for a trial fit. Whilst this machine was being prepared for trials, one of the proposed Typhoon II airframes had the design of its firewall changed to accommodate the Griffon. Also looked at was the

Bristol Centaurus, although this would not be adopted at this stage in the proceedings, as the engine was in the earliest stage of development.

With two engines proposed for the Typhoon II, it was decided to double the number of prototype aircraft ordered, as a form of insurance. The breakdown of this revised order was that two machines would be powered by Rolls-Royce Griffon engines, two would feature the Napier Sabre, whilst a further two would be ordered two months later to act as test beds for the Bristol Centaurus. The Napier engines selected for the Typhoon II were the Mark V and the Mark VI, although the latter was seriously delayed, so a standard Typhoon engine, the Mark II, was used instead.

A New Name for the New Fighter

A further change was to the aircraft's name, which became 'Tempest' as the Typhoon was going through its bad technical patch when engines were failing and rear fuselages were coming adrift under mysterious circumstances. It was also thought necessary as the revamped aircraft was different enough to justify a name change. A series of mark numbers was also issued to cover the different versions: the Mark 1 with the Sabre IV, the Mark II with the Centaurus IV, the Mark III with the

Griffon IIB, the Mark IV with the Griffon 61, and the Mark V fitted with the Sabre II engine.

The last designated airframe would be the first to fly, as development troubles and delays were plaguing both the Sabre IV and Centaurus engines, whilst the redesign of the airframe to accept either version of the Rolls-Royce Griffon was even further behind schedule. It was also felt that the Tempest V would be the easiest to develop, as the proposed Sabre engine would fit into the new airframe without too much difficulty, allowing that confirmation of the wind tunnel data concerning the new wing was correct. Even as the prototype contract was being placed, Hawker's were being warned to tool up for the production of 400 Tempests, beginning in July 1942.

Test-Flying the Tempest V Prototype

On 1 September 1942 the prototype HM595 was rolled out at Langley for taxi trials; on 2 September it made its first flight, piloted by Philip Lucas. Changes from its predecessor included a four-blade de Havilland Hydromatic propeller, previously test-flown on Typhoon R9198, and the substitution of the earlier direct-acting oleo undercarriage units by levered suspension units. In its first incarnation, this aircraft was fitted with a Typhoon tail

Below **HM595 was constructed as the Tempest V prototype, although in reality it owed more to the earlier Typhoon, only the wings exhibiting any real changes. After numerous trials it would be retired for instructional purposes as 5940M.** C. P. Russell Smith Collection

unit and the early style of heavily framed cockpit canopy, although a bubble-hood sliding canopy was under construction, and a new tail unit was also in the design stage.

Having completed its first flight without incident, on the second day of flying Philip Lucas took the aircraft up to an altitude of 10,000ft (3,000m) and to a speed of 300mph (480km/h), during which limited manoeuvres were carried out. Stalling was checked at 5,000ft (1,500m): with the Tempest weighing in at 10,550lb (4,785kg), this gave a measured stalling speed of 90mph (145km/h) with undercarriage and flaps deployed. In this guise the elongated nose presented its own set of problems, inducing longitudinal instability and a neutral performance throughout the full range of movement and speed. As a temporary measure to counteract this, a metal plate was riveted to the trailing edge of the rudder; however, a more positive solution was required, and to this end a quite ugly fin fillet of 2.7sq ft (0.25sq m) was fitted, as was a tailplane of increased span. Production aircraft would also receive a fin fillet of the same area, although it was a far more refined design, while the rudder was also increased in area. With these modifications incorporated, the Tempest was far more stable while airborne, although Philip Lucas did mention in one post-flight report that the elevator response had become heavier, and that the aircraft had a tendency to stay airborne even with full opposite elevator applied.

Having shown that, by increasing the areas of both the fin and rudder, the Tempest prototype was more stable, HM595 underwent further modifications during September. This involved increasing the size of the fin by some 1.44sq ft (0.13sq m), to give a total of 15.54sq ft (1.4sq m), reducing the rudder range of movement by 10 per cent and modifying the trim tab. The first flight in this new guise was on 2 October, during which Lucas would push the Tempest up to 430mph (690km/h) TAS at 20,300ft (6,200m). Further minor adjustments were made to the trimming throughout November until the balance was right. Unfortunately the original method of trimming was a small sheet of alloy that was susceptible to accidental adjustment by the groundcrew. These tribulations notwithstanding, the pilots assigned to fly the Tempest praised it for its improved

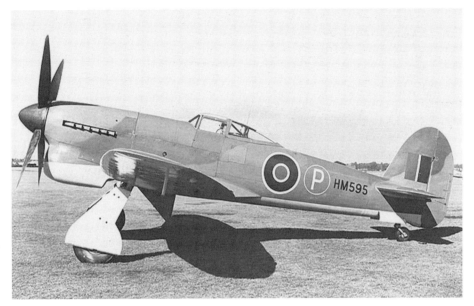

Above **On rollout, the prototype Tempest V sported a set of Typhoon tail feathers, which gave it a similar appearance; however, HM595 was fitted with Tempest wings and had fully retractable doors to cover the tailwheel when it was up and locked.** Big Bird Aviation Collection

handling. To counter these inadvertent trim-tab alterations, a system of pilot-controllable tabs was installed, although these were no more than a stopgap before the definitive spring-balance tabs were developed for the production versions.

On 12 December Philip Lucas departed Langley to test the aircraft in a controlled dive from 27,000ft (8,200m). By the time the 19,000 to 20,000ft (5,700 to 6,000m) band had been reached, HM595 was travelling a true airspeed of 575mph (925km/h), equivalent to Mach 0.76. The pilot reported that there was an increase in nose heaviness, and that the airframe vibrated as this speed was reached. Unfortunately this was the maximum it did reach on this occasion, as the engine failed and the starboard undercarriage unlocked, forcing Lucas to make a careful emergency landing at Langley. HM595 was fitted with a new Sabre, while the original was removed for investigation – although no real cause for its failure could be found. After ground functionals and inspections, the Tempest was cleared for further flying, and test flights resumed on 23 December.

Yet again the aircraft was put through a series of test dives, and achieved the same speed at the same height; this time the engine behaved itself. One slight niggle arose, concerning the canopy: HM595 was fitted with the early type of Typhoon

canopy, and an unseen defect resulted in the starboard window being sucked out of its mounting. This was not considered a serious problem, however, as production aircraft would be fitted with a sliding canopy, which had already passed its flight test successfully.

Armament for the New Fighter

Even though the airframe was slightly unstable, the new wing was behaving exactly as predicted, giving an increased top speed coupled with crisper and smoother handling; furthermore, the vibration that had beset the Typhoon had completely disappeared. As HM595 was seen as no more than a development prototype, no armament was carried; however, various specifications had been suggested for installation in the production versions. These had included three Hispano 20mm cannon per wing, or what became known as the 'Universal Wing': this could tote either a pair of cannon per wing, or one cannon plus a single .50in calibre machine gun, or a pair of machine guns per wing. After much discussion, the final choice was the pair of cannon per wing: not only did the effects of the weaponry play a part in this decision, but the logistics of organizing the stores for two types of ammunition also played a part.

Left **The second prototype Tempest constructed was HM599; it was intended to trial the Napier Sabre IV engine, although this version used leading-edge radiators in the wings for heat dispersion and conversion. After service trials the prototype Mark 1 was retired as 6442M.** Big Bird Aviation Collection

Test-Flying the Mark I

February 1943 proved to be an interesting month for the new Tempest, as the Mark I version made its flying debut on 24 February, having successfully accomplished the obligatory taxi trials to test the brakes, engine and other systems. As before, the test pilot Philip Lucas put the new prototype through its paces. His initial report stated that the Mark I had improved stability, although elevator control decreased in effectiveness as the speed dropped off, becoming non-existent below 110mph (177km/h).

During March 1943, Napiers finally issued clearance for the Sabre IV to run at 4,000rpm with +9 lb boost, although the engines with Hawker's were not capable of such a performance. HM599 was grounded

during May whilst waiting for a new engine, so the opportunity was taken to overhaul the airframe and install a bubble-hood canopy. Once these modifications had been completed and a new engine installed, HM599 was cleared for flying. The pilot this time was Bill Humble from the flight-test department; he would undertake these duties while Philip Lucas was in the Middle East carrying out tropical trials on the Typhoon.

The new Tempest was an immediate success with the pilots; the subsequent post-flight reports on the whole praised the type's handling, although there was a comment with reference to elevator control response at low speed, and the time taken by the engine to respond to throttle inputs. The wing-mounted radiators, which had proved troublesome to

manufacture, plus the tightly cowled nose, gave the Tempest I a top speed of 466mph (750km/h) at 24,500ft (7,500m). Further tweaking of the airframe's finish, plus the fitment of a tailplane with a thickness/chord ratio of 11.5 per cent, allowed the Tempest 1 to be pushed to 472mph (759km/h) during September 1943. However, the Air Ministry still had serious doubts about the Sabre IV engine's reliability, therefore this avenue of development would stop in December as funding was discontinued.

On the face of it, the Sabre IV seemed to be the engine that Napier's had been looking for; however, the standards being achieved by the manufacturers were not good enough. One of the most obvious signs of this problem was the tendency for the engine to throw large amounts of oil at

Left **Tempest 1 HM599 was built as the test bed for the Rolls-Royce Griffon engine. It made its first flight in this guise on 24 February 1943, and remained in use until withdrawn from service in 1946.** Big Bird Aviation Collection

any speed above 3,750rpm. It also failed to reach the much desired target of fifty running hours between inspections, even though as a pre-series powerplant it was virtually hand built. That being said, Bill Humble would heap praise upon the Tempest I, especially in the region above 20,000ft (6,000m), where it outshone any other fighter in the Allied inventory.

The other event that shaped the early days of the Tempest was the test-flying undertaken by pilots from the A&AEE, who were compiling a report for the Air Ministry using Tempest V prototype HM595. Overall the report was as favourable as that for the Tempest I, although a slight heaviness in elevator behaviour was noted. Once the Tempest I programme had been cancelled, the jigs already manufactured were reworked for the forthcoming Mark V contracts.

Further Trials for the Mark V Prototype

Running in parallel to the Mark I programme, Tempest V prototype HM595 was undergoing further trial flights during February 1943 – only by this time the airframe had been cleaned up, and so the aircraft was capable of achieving 438mph (705km/h) IAS at 22,000ft (6,600m). Fitment of an inertia damper operated by a lever on the control column meant that the Tempest could be prevented from tightening in turns up to a loading of 5g. In this condition the Tempest was passed to Boscombe Down for evaluation and

appraisal, complete with Sabre IV No. S76. During this period, HM595 was flown at 459mph (738km/h) IAS at 24,900ft (7,200m) by Bill Humble on 17 June. Although there was ballasting installed to represent the guns and ammunition, the blisters that would cover the cannon breeches were not fitted, thus the indicated speed was between 7–10mph (11–16km/h) faster – therefore higher than that postulated for the production machines. Yet again during these flights the cockpit windows were sucked out of the early-type canopy.

In the event the Air Ministry decided to push on with the Tempest V, as the chin-cooled radiator and engine were already in service with the Typhoon, and were reasonably well understood. Of the remaining prototypes, the Centaurus-powered Tempest II was retained because engine development was progressing well, and preliminary results looked promising; however, both the Tempest III and IV would be axed, as the Rolls-Royce Griffon powerplant had been earmarked for the second tranche of Spitfires and thus was not available to Hawker's. To speed up the development of the Centaurus, one of the Tornado prototypes was being utilized as a flying test bed prior to it being installed in the Tempest II prototype. The priority therefore would be to get the Tempest V refined enough to enter production, with the Centaurus-powered version being seen as its replacement in the longer term. Although the Griffon-powered programme had been cancelled, at least one prototype, Tempest III LA610, was fitted with a Griffon 85 engine, to become the

Hawker Fury prototype. It would later have a Napier Sabre VIII powerplant fitted, and distinguish itself as Hawker's fastest piston-engined fighter, achieving a maximum speed of 483mph (777km/h).

The Tempest V Series I into Production

While decisions were being made concerning the prototypes of the various engines, production contracts had been placed with Hawker's, authorizing them to start construction of the Tempest V. The first machine appeared on 21 June 1943: JN729, which made its maiden flight piloted by W. 'Bill' Humble. The contract was for 100 machines, and these aircraft were designated Tempest V Series 1: they differed from later production aircraft in having long-barrelled versions of the Hispano II cannon, which extended beyond the wing leading-edge skin by nearly 9in (23cm).

It took until October for a specimen of the Tempest V to reach A&AEE at Boscombe Down for trials flying. The aircraft nominated for this task was JN731, and it was put through all its paces, including general handling and performance. The reports were very favourable, although it was mentioned that at speeds above 500mph (800km/h) the ailerons became heavy due to aerodynamic forces, though some movement was still possible. The biggest criticism was the poor rate of roll, although this would be quickly resolved by the installation of spring tabs

Right **The Hawker Tempest V JN757, a Series 1 production aircraft, as evidenced by the cannon barrels protruding from the wing leading edge. After service with No. 3 Sqn, the Tempest was passed on to the AFDU, with whom it stayed until struck off charge on 6 October 1947.** C. P. Russell Smith Collection

to the ailerons. One of the positive comments concerned the canopy, which was of the new, single piece, bubble sliding type already earmarked for the Typhoon: as in the case of its predecessor, it elicited praise from all for its excellent all-round visibility. Performance figures quoted for JN731 included maximum speeds of 376mph (605km/h) at sea level, increasing to 432mph (695km/h) at 18,400ft (5,570m) with an intermediate speed of 411mph (661km/h) being recorded at 6,000ft (1,800m). Service ceiling was set at 34,800ft (10,460m).

Having impressed the test pilots at Boscombe Down, the aircraft now had to do the same with those assigned to the Air Fighting Development Unit at Wittering, where another production Tempest V, JN737, arrived on 8 January 1944. This aircraft differed from its sibling in that it had the spring-tabbed ailerons and new-type canopy already fitted. A series of tests would be conducted against current RAF fighters and captured examples of the enemy's machines, the first against the Typhoon.

The Typhoon used by the AFDU featured the earlier type, heavy frame canopy, and this, coupled to the earlier machine's various vices, meant that the new Tempest easily out-performed its Hawker sibling. Most impressive was the rate of roll, which had improved dramatically above 250mph IAS. In comparison to the Typhoon, the flight controls were better balanced, the test reports commenting on the positive, crisp behaviour about all three axis.

Also improved was the maximum top speed of the Tempest, which was found to be some 15 to 20mph (25 to 30km/h) faster at all altitudes than the Typhoon – although in fairness to the latter it did have the capacity for more fuel, carrying some 154gal (700ltr) as opposed to the Tempest's 132gal (600ltr). The refined wing, however, paid off in this respect, as the given range for each type was roughly the same, though the Tempest had a better rate of climb – some 300ft (90m)/min faster that the thicker-winged Typhoon. Other benefits noted during this preliminary evaluation included excellent diving characteristics, steadiness as a gun platform, and the ability to take great advantage of a zoom climb after a dive.

With comparison tests against the Typhoon completed, it was time to try out the new fighter against other machines on the inventory of the AFDU. The chosen guinea pigs were a Packard Merlin-powered Mustang III, a Griffon-powered Spitfire XIV, plus a Messerschmitt Bf 109G, and a Focke-Wulf Fw 190A. In combat flights against both Allied and German types, the Tempest outperformed them all up to an altitude of 20,000ft (6,000m). Against the British and American fighters its speed was faster by some 15 to 20mph (25 to 30km/h), while the German aircraft were outclassed by some 40 to 50mph (65 to 80km/h). Above 20,000ft (6,000m) the Allied fighters began to outstrip the Tempest, whilst of the German aircraft, the Messerschmitt was close in performance, although the Fw 190 was slower.

In combat manoeuvring the Tempest was out-turned by both the Mustang and the Spitfire, while against the Fw 190 it was on a par. The Bf 109 was completely outclassed, as its leading-edge slats had a tendency to open as the turn tightened and stalling speed approached, thus causing the pilot of the German fighter to break away or lose control. On the other hand, in the performance of roll rate the Tempest was slightly laggardly, falling behind both Allied fighters and the Fw 190 at low speeds, although above 350mph the Tempest would again come into its own, with only the Bf 109 coming close – though even this could be countered by a quick change of banking angle and direction. The conclusion drawn from these evaluations was that the Tempest was far superior to the Typhoon, and completely outperformed all other fighters up to medium altitudes.

The AFDU also recommended that units already equipped with the Typhoon would gain the most from the Tempest. However, this was not to be, as only three squadrons that had previously flown the Typhoon would re-equip, as pilots could not be spared by 2nd TAF to undertake conversion training. The first unit to try out the new Hawker fighter was No. 486 (RNZAF) Sqn, which received a handful at Tangmere in January 1944 – although their tenure was short, as No. 3 Sqn would take them on and become the first squadron to officially operate the Tempest.

Left **This slightly nose up Tempest V JN802 is a Series 2 aircraft, evidenced by the lack of protruding cannon barrels. Although the aircraft's outline reveals its ancestry, the Tempest was a far more refined machine than the Typhoon.** Big Bird Aviation Collection

The Tempest V Series 2

During 1944, the short-barrel version of the Hispano 20mm cannon, the Mark V became available in sufficient numbers to be fitted to aircraft on the Tempest production line. The resultant aircraft was then designated the Tempest V Series 2. As before, each cannon was a self-contained unit complete with ammunition tank, feed, and link disposal chute. Also incorporated into the Tempest from this point was the plumbing required to mount external 45gal (205ltr) fuel tanks. These were different from those fitted to the Typhoon and the earlier Hurricane in that they were streamlined in shape, not cylindrical, which was the type preferred by the Ministry of Aircraft Production. The argument put forward by Sidney Camm was that the new tanks generated less drag. Once cleared for production, initial flight trials revealed that the tanks would need internal damper walls installed to stop fuel surging in the tank during manoeuvres, and thereby unbalancing the aircraft.

The Centaurus-Powered Tempest II

While the Tempest V was the chosen production version for use by the Royal Air Force during the remainder of the war, it was the Centaurus-powered Tempest II that was recognized as the definitive version. In fact it nearly failed to evolve at all, as Sydney Camm was not too keen on a radial-engined version of the Tempest. However, the arrival of Oberleutnant Faber and his Fw 190A at Pembrey, in mistake for his home base in France, revealed that putting a radial engine on the front of a high performance, well designed airframe was entirely feasible. Thus the first prototype, LA602, made its maiden flight on 28 June 1943, and in common with the Tempest I and V prototypes, emerged with a set of Typhoon tail feathers. The installed engine was the Bristol Centaurus IV, an air-cooled, radial powerplant rated at 2,520hp; it was mounted to the bulkhead using rigid mounts, and drove a four-bladed propeller.

The engine installation had thrown up some weight and balance problems, therefore the engine itself was mounted a whole 1ft (0.3m) further forward; the exhaust

Above **At least one early Series 1 Tempest V was employed in the trials concerning the Hawker-designed 45gal fuel tanks. This unidentified example, possibly JN730, was photographed while on charge with the A&AEE.** Peter R. Arnold Collection

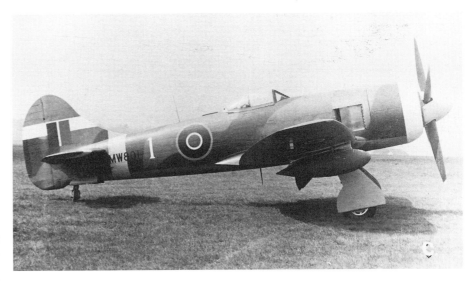

Above **Hawker Tempest II MW801 would never see service with the RAF, being employed by the A&AEE at Boscombe Down for armament trials. It is depicted here sporting a pair of Hawker-designed 45gal (205ltr) tanks that were intended to replace the earlier cylindrical types.** Peter R. Arnold Collection

collector ring was moved as far back as possible, while the oil coolers were installed in the wing roots. This set-up was soon found to suffer from excess vibration, therefore the second Tempest II prototype, LA607, was assigned to the engine development programme. Its primary purpose was to find out why the powerplant was generating so much vibration, and more importantly, how to rectify it. The cure owed much to the rubber-dampened undercarriage units as developed by de Havilland: thus the original eight-point

rigid mountings were replaced by six dampened rubber bush assemblies.

The change in the number of mounting points meant that the Centaurus XII originally planned for the production version of the Tempest was replaced by the Centaurus V, which had a similar power output to the Mark IV. The problem with the Mark XII was not as serious as it first appeared, as the engine itself was suffering from development delays. Also trialled on the development aircraft was a five-bladed propeller, seen as another potential vibra-

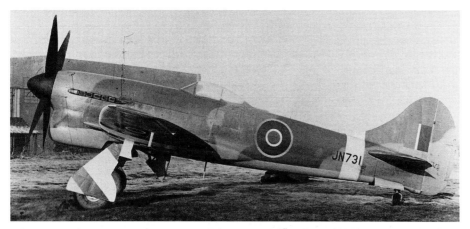

Above **Complete with prototype marks is the Tempest II prototype LA602, modified to the latest standard which includes a single-piece blown canopy, and a full Tempest fin and fillet, although it still retains the Series 1 cannon installation.** Peter R. Arnold Collection

Left **Tempest V JN731 would spend much of its life with Hawker's as a trials machine. During this period it would be used for general handling, plus development flying of modified ailerons and control surface spring tabs.** Peter R. Arnold Collection

tion cure; in the event, however, the production machines would be equipped with a balanced, four-blade unit.

Other Problems

Having sorted out the vibration problems, attention was now turned to dealing with other faults that were occurring regularly; these included engine overheating, crankshaft lubrication, and reduction gear seizure, all of which conspired to delay the production version from entering service. Even though there were concerns about the excessive vibration, which required the installation of the Vibrograph, the handling reports indicated that the aircraft and engine behaved as well as expected – although the problem concerning fumes in the cockpit had arisen again. The cure for this was to rework the two lower exhaust pipes and fit them with

extensions. On 1 July 1943 Philip Lucas was airborne again, undertaking the third test flight. Having achieved an altitude of 10,000ft (3,000m), the engine speed was set at 2,400rpm and a test run began. But within a minute there was a loud knock, after which the Centaurus began to vibrate violently. Suspecting drastic engine failure, the pilot throttled back and made an immediate emergency landing. Investigation of the powerplant on the ground revealed that the sleeve valve drive to one of the cylinders had failed. After replacement, LA602 resumed flying in December, with no reports of the engine misbehaving.

Although the Mark II was suffering from production delays, it was felt that LA602 was close enough to the production version to be despatched to A&AEE at Boscombe Down for initial type evaluation. Differences from the projected

production aircraft included the early type engine mountings, inherent exhaust system difficulties, and the armament, which was still the earlier long-barrelled Mark II Hispano cannon. In spite of these differences, the aircraft was still put through a thorough workout, which revealed a few niggling faults. The first of these was the vibration level, which was quite excessive below 2,000rpm and above 2,400rpm, although the noise level was lower in comparison to the Typhoon, thus making the Tempest less tiring to fly.

The general handling was found to be satisfactory, although as this was before the introduction of the spring balance tabs, the aileron and roll control were rather heavy. Rudder movements were light for small movements, whilst the loading increased as the deflection increased. In contrast, the elevators appeared to behave themselves throughout their full range of movement;

thus only slight changes were required to the longitudinal trim of the aircraft, and only at higher speeds.

When an approach and landing were attempted, both were found to be relatively easy, although with the engine throttled fully back, elevator control was reduced to marginal and therefore insufficient control was available to force the tail down for a three-point landing.

The Tempest II and V Compared

Dimensionally the Tempest II was similar to the Mark V in that it shared the same wingspan, although the Centaurus engine meant that the former aircraft was slightly longer, at 34ft 5in (10.5m), whilst its height datum was slightly lower at 15ft 10in (4.8m), although this was dependent on loading. Strangely the overall fully loaded weight had only increased by 20lb (9kg) to 14,500lb (6,580kg). The greatest gain came in performance, the Mark II achieving a top speed of 442mph (711km/h) at 15,200ft (4,630m), whilst the climb time to this height took no more than 4½min, which put the Mark V's time of 5min to shame. Service ceiling was also increased to 37,500ft (11430m).

To clear the Tempest II for service, the reports recommended that the aileron loads be reduced: this was achieved by implementing the spring balance tab modification, while the engine vibration problem was solved by incorporating rubber damper bush mountings.

Tempest II into Action

Even though Hawker was the design authority, its workload was such with the Tempest V that production contracts for the Tempest II would be subcontracted to the Gloster Aircraft Company at Hucclecote, part of the Hawker Group of companies. However, this organization was also experiencing problems, as its own workload was increasing as the invasion of Europe continued, and the requirement for further Typhoons to replace the losses experienced by 2nd TAF was putting available resources under pressure; moreover, Gloster's were also in the process of designing the Meteor jet fighter. The construction contract for 300 aircraft was

therefore further subcontracted to Bristol Aircraft at Filton; in this way the production of both the airframe and engine would be under the control of one company.

However, delays would also be the lot of the Bristol Aircraft Company, as a whole new manufacturing facility was being built at Banwell to build the new fighter, the original facility being fully occupied in constructing the Bristol range of twin-engined aircraft. These delays meant that the first Bristol-produced aircraft would not roll off the Banwell production line until February 1945.

By contrast, the Hawker production line at Langley had begun to build Tempest IIs in parallel with the Tempest V, and their first Centaurus-powered machine would roll out during October 1944 (although this was much later than planned). Given the performance benefits of the Centaurus-powered Tempest, it is hardly surprising that all concerned with the aircraft wanted to hurry it into RAF squadron service as rapidly as possible. To this end the two prototypes, JN750, a Mark V converted Mark II standard, plus the first six production aircraft were allocated for trials and evaluation work.

With the Typhoon and Tempest V operating successfully over Europe, thought was given as to how best to employ the Tempest II. The most obvious area would be the Far East, where there was a need to replace the elderly Hurricane and Lend Lease Republic P-47 Thunderbolts already in use. Originally hot and high trials were planned to take place in this theatre, possibly in India, but these plans were abandoned in

favour of the far more stable Middle East as the preferred location to try out the new type. Hence six machines, MW801 to MW806, were despatched to Khartoum in April 1945 to undertake intensive flight trials. These were not without incident: one aircraft, MW806, was damaged beyond repair during a landing accident when it swung into soft ground and overturned; while another, MW801, failed to return home because the engine caught fire during the ferry flight back to Britain on 5 August, resulting in the aircraft being abandoned near Marble Arch, Libya. Eventually some 740 flying hours were managed using the test group Tempests.

Overall the reports rated the Tempest as more than satisfactory, especially in the low-level ground-attack role; however, a series of minor modifications – twenty-nine in number – were recommended to make the Tempest a more efficient aircraft.

The recommendations from the test group pilots were applied where possible to the first production Tempest IIs being held in storage at various maintenance units around the country, prior to these being released to operational squadrons. The first to become operational was No. 13 Operational Training Unit based at Harwell; it received its first examples in June 1945, and deliveries to fighter-bomber units began not long afterwards. However, the original re-equipment plan was hastily revised after the surrender of Japan, and many new Tempest IIs would find themselves placed in long-term storage awaiting a decision as to their fate.

Below Complete with identity bands is the first production Tempest II, MW735, which was loaned to the Bristol Engine Company after flight trials by Hawker's for use in the Centaurus development programme.
Big Bird Aviation Collection

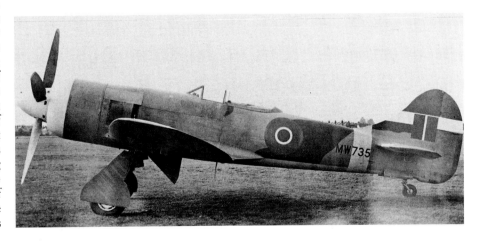

The knock-on effect of the cessation of hostilities was that production orders were also reduced; therefore Bristol Aircraft's production would amount to only fifty machines, of which the final twenty would be assembled by Hawker's using Bristol-manufactured assemblies. Hawker's, too, would feel the effects of this peace, as the final production run for the Tempest II would only achieve 452 aircraft, of the thousands ordered and planned.

The Tempest VI

Running in parallel to the Centaurus-powered Tempest II was the production of an upgraded Tempest V, designated the Mark VI. The need for this version had arisen due to the foreseen shortage of Centaurus engines, and with this in mind, Napier's were encouraged to push the Sabre design a little further to increase its power. The resultant engine, the Sabre V, was able to deliver an extra 10 per cent more output than the previous Sabre II. To trial the new powerplant, the original Sabre II Tempest prototype, HM595, was fitted with a Sabre V and a proper single-piece sliding canopy; it made its maiden flight on 9 May 1944. As this engine delivered 2,340 horsepower, its cooling needs were naturally greater; therefore the oil cooler and carburettor air intakes were relocated from the underslung nose intake, the resulting enlarged area being occupied by a radiator of increased dimensions. The new location for the carburettor air intakes was in the leading edge of the wing close by the root, while the oil cooler was repositioned behind the radiator.

Trials in the Middle East

Thought was also given to the employment of the new fighter, and as the Middle East had no new aircraft planned for introduction in the immediate future, it was on this area, and its attendant problems, that Hawker's and Napier's were asked to concentrate. To hurry the process along, a single Tempest V, EJ841, was converted to Mark VI standard and despatched to Khartoum, in company with a Tempest V, EJ759, for comparison purposes. Operating throughout the normal temperature range experienced every day in the region, the aircraft's cooling system was found to struggle in the greatest heat, so an extra oil cooler was installed in the leading edge of the starboard wing, as in the Tempest II.

The air cleaner/filter assembly was a very clever design, and was based on that fitted to the Typhoons for use in the dusty Normandy airfields. It was located beneath the fuselage between the wings, and would be in use during ground running and taxiing. In this manner, air was drawn into the carburettor via the filter system, although this would cease to operate when the undercarriage began its retraction cycle. As the gear moved into the closed position, the air intake filter system would transfer its task via a series of linkages to the intakes located in the wing leading edges. As the undercarriage was lowered, a reversal of the foregoing process occurred, although the changeover to the wing leading-edge intake could be overridden by a switch in the cockpit should the pilot consider this necessary.

To reinforce the projected desert-flying role of the aircraft, the trials machines were equipped with desert survival equipment in the form of two crash-proof water containers located behind the pilot's seat head armour.

Production of the Tempest VI was initially set at 250 aircraft, although as the war in Europe and the Far East had ended, so had the need for this quantity of aircraft; the order was therefore reduced to just 142 machines. Under normal considerations this particular version of the Tempest would have been cancelled, as there was no real requirement for it, since the Royal Air Force had more than enough Tempest IIs and Vs. However, Napier's would have been in serious financial trouble if the Sabre programme had ended so suddenly, as other projects under development by the company were not ready for production. Production of the Tempest VI began in the early months of 1945, with the first seven service-ready machines – NV997 to NV999, plus NX113 to NX116 – appearing during July and August of the same year.

Further Desert Trials

With production versions of the Tempest VI proceeding steadily, it was time to put another machine through desert hot and high trials. To this end, aircraft NX119 was despatched to Khartoum, where it would arrive in December 1945. The trials would last until February 1946, and included a full evaluation of the whole airframe and its systems. During this period the Tempest VI, complete with its Sabre V engine, achieved a top speed of 438mph (705km/h) at an altitude of 17,800ft (5,425m), whilst its service ceiling was set at 38,000ft (11,600m). The final report stated that the aircraft performed more than satisfactorily, so it was cleared for service usage. Deliveries of production aircraft to RAF squadrons took place during 1946, with five units in the Middle East receiving the Tempest VI.

Below Seen from a three-quarters front angle is this Tempest VI. The differences between this and the Mark V included the auxiliary cooling intake located in the port wing leading edge. C. P. Russell Smith Collection

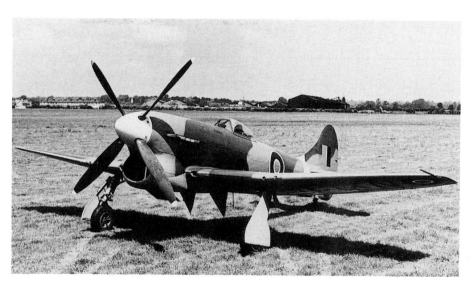

Right **Although it bears no serial, this aircraft is in fact HM595 that has been converted to be the Mark VI prototype. It made its first flight in this guise on 9 May 1944, after which it was despatched to Boscombe Down for evaluation trials.** Big Bird Aviation Collection

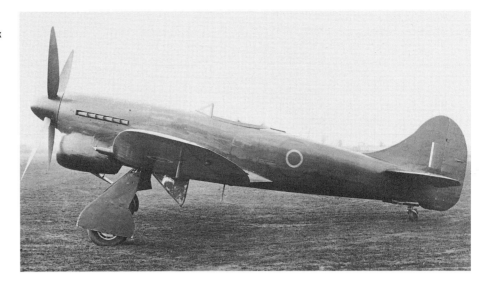

Right **For the whole of its useful life Tempest VI NX116 was employed by Napier's on Sabre engine development trials, a role it maintained until it was dispensed with in March 1959.** Big Bird Aviation Collection

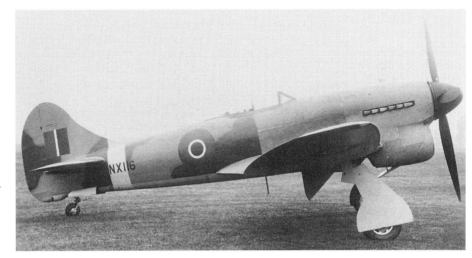

Below **Seen from a slightly rear angle is this Tempest VI NX135 photographed at the makers prior to delivery to the Royal Air Force. In service it would be flown by Nos 6 and 249 Sqns in the Middle East; it was withdrawn in May 1951.** Big Bird Aviation Collection

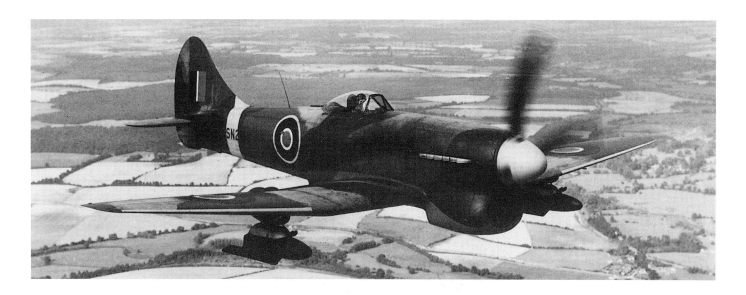

Fitting Tempest Armament

Although the wing fitted to the Tempest was different to that on the Typhoon, it was thought that it could be cleared to carry the same range of stores without too much trouble. During mid-1944 Hawker's, in conjunction with the A&AEE, used some of the aircraft retained for trials purposes to test the full range of bombs, rockets and other stores originally cleared for the Typhoon. As expected, the fitment of bomb racks under the wings reduced the top speed of the Tempest by no more than 10mph (16km/h), although adding a pair of 500lb (225kg) GP bombs would bring this down by up to 30mph (50km/h), depending upon altitude. When lightweight Mark III rocket rails were fitted,

Below **Tempest V EJ891 was by the A&AEE for various weapons delivery trials. Here it is seen sporting a pair of mines under the wings.** Peter R. Arnold Collection

the top speed fell by up to 16mph (25km/h); and when 60lb (27kg) rockets were added, a further drop of 21mph (34km/h) was experienced.

The drop in top speed was the only effect that external stores had upon any version of the Tempest, handling appearing to be unaffected. A further store added to the inventory after the war was the 1,000lb GP bomb. Further experimentation with unguided rockets and their carrier rails resulted in the Zero length rail, which quickly replaced the Mark III type in early 1946.

Other weaponry trialled on the Tempest included the Vickers 'P' gun, a development of the earlier Vickers 'S' gun, which had been used with some success by Hawker Hurricanes in the Western Desert in the ground-attack, anti-tank role during 1943. Although the trials were successful, the Royal Air Force would persevere with its use of unguided rockets in the ground-attack role, in preference to underwing gun pods.

Above **Complete with a light bomb carrier under the wings, Tempest V SN219 is here under test with the A&AEE at Boscombe Down. It would later be converted to target-towing 5 standard, and serve with the APC at Acklington and No. 233 OCU, before being sold to the MoS in November 1955.** RAF Museum Collection

Engine Experimentation

As there was a surplus of Tempests available after the war, it was not surprising that some were diverted to various manufacturers for related trials. One of the recipients would be Napier's, who received two Tempest V's, EJ518 and NV768, for engine experimentation. The latter aircraft was already fitted with a Sabre V engine; this was taken out and the machine soon fitted with a huge ducted spinner with an air intake forward of the propeller blades. As with many experiments, the resulting flight trials were successful, although no further develop-

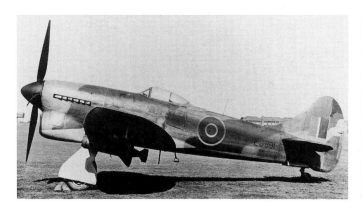

ment would occur as the idea was considered to be too radical for general service usage.

Even less likely to enter service was the proposed Hawker P.1027, which never even left the drawing board. This version of the Tempest would have been powered by the Rolls-Royce 46 Eagle powerplant, rated at 2,690hp, and attached to a six-bladed contra-rotating propeller assembly; the radiator was moved to a ventral position under the fuselage, as in the North American P-51 Mustang.

Designs for the Hawker Sea Fury

Only one other version of the Tempest would take to the skies, this being the Tempest lightweight fighter, developed to specification F.2/43. This version of the Hawker fighter featured a reduced wingspan achieved by removing the full-width centre section, and replacing it with one of reduced span, to which the wing outer panels were then bolted. Allied to the new wing was an all-new fuselage of monocoque construction. The engines proposed for the new fighter were the Napier Sabre, the Rolls-Royce Griffon,

Above Once NV768 had been successfully flight-trialled with the annular radiator, Napier's then fitted it with a ducted spinner to improve engine cooling. Big Bird Aviation Collection

Below Photographed in formation are two versions of the Tempest. The furthest machine is a Mark VI, NX121, that was permanently bailed to the engine manufacturers Napier's. The aircraft in the foreground had started life as a standard Mark V that had seen service with No. 274 Sqn before being bailed to Napier's for trials. In this view, NV768 sports an annular radiator instead of the normal underslung housing. Big Bird Aviation Collection

and the Bristol Centaurus. Eventually, after many trials and tribulations, the design would enter production as the Hawker Sea Fury and Fury, the latter intended for export purposes. The Royal Air Force, however, declined to accept the lightweight Fury, as it had more than enough Tempests available to satisfy its current and future requirements.

Tempests Surplus to Requirement

This surplus of Hawker Tempests resulted in stocks building up at No. 5 Maintenance Unit at Kemble, and No. 20 MU at Aston Down. Both held stocks of the Tempest V, which had been retired from front-line service in favour of the Centaurus-powered Tempest II. During 1947 the Royal Air Force began to cast around for a new target tug to replace the original incumbent in the job, the Miles Martinet. Although this machine had proved adequate for the task during the war years, after the war its lack of top speed was seen as a hindrance, when aircraft speeds were increasing due to the new jet fighters entering service, and anti-aircraft guns having better radar guidance.

The Tempest V was seen as the ideal solution to the requirement, so a single example, SN329, was refurbished by Hawker's. Complete with newly installed target tow equipment, the re-designated Tempest TT.5 underwent a full evaluation at the Airborne Forces Experimental Establishment at Beaulieu, an organiza-tion charged with the testing of all types of towing trials, including those for gliders. These trials were undertaken during 1948, and continued until 1949 when the Tempest was transferred to A&AEE at Boscombe Down for evaluation and service pre-release trials. A few minor modifications were required to the target tow equipment, and SN329 was cleared for service in 1950.

To cover the target tow requirement for the RAF, a total of eighty airframes was withdrawn from the maintenance units for conversion by Hawker's at Langley to TT.5 standard; this whole process took until May 1952 to complete. This particular version of the Tempest was the last to remain in service with the RAF, the final example not retiring from No. 233 OCU at Pembrey until July 1955.

The Tempest TT.5

Serial numbers of the Tempest TT.5's included:

EJ580, EJ585, EJ598, EJ631, EJ643, EJ660, EJ663, EJ667, EJ669, EJ740, EJ744, EJ753, EJ758, EJ786, EJ801, EJ805, EJ807, EJ839, EJ846, EJ862, EJ875, EJ879, EJ880, JN807, JN871

NV645, NV661, NV664, NV665, NV669, NV671, NV699, NV704, NV711, NV723, NV725, NV762, NV778, NV780, NV781, NV793, NV917, NV922, NV923, NV928, NV937, NV940, NV960, NV962, NV965, NV974, NV975, NV978, NV992, NV994, NV996,

SN127, SN146, SN209, SN215, SN219, SN227, SN232, SN259, SN260, SN261, SN271, SN274, SN289, SN290, SN321, SN326, SN329, SN331, SN332, SN333, SN340, SN342, SN346, SN354

Acklington APC 'WH'	Sylt APC		226 OCU 'XL'	229 OCU 'RS'	233 OCU	CGS 'FJU'
EJ580	EJ585	NV780	EJ669	EJ660	EJ580(2)	EG667
EJ598	EJ667(2)	NV793(2)	EJ862	EJ663	EJ598(2)	EJ740
EJ744	EJ740	NV922		EJ669(2)	EJ631	EJ879
EJ805	EJ753	NV928	NV671	EJ744(2)	EJ669(3)	
EJ839	EJ758	NV937	NV699		EJ805(2)	NV664
	EJ786	NV940	NV711	NV645(2)		NV793
JN807	EJ801	NV960	NV923	NV669	NV711(3)	
JN871	EJ807	NV962	NV992	NV671	NV778	SN215
	EJ839(2)	NV974		NV699(2)	NV917(3)	SN261
NV645	EJ846	NV975	SN326	NV762	NV965	SN321
NV711(2)	EJ875	NV994		NV917(2)	NV996	
NV781	EJ879			NV923(3)		
NV917	EJ880	SN289		NV978	SN127	
NV923(2)		SN290		NV992	SN219(2)	
NV965	JN871(2)	SN321(2)			SN259	
		SN327		SN146(2)	SN274	
SN146	NV661	SN329		SN260(2)	SN331(2)	
SN209	NV664(2)	SN333		SN271(2)	SN332(2)	
SN215	NV665	SN342		SN326(2)		
SN219	NV704	SN346		SN340(2)		
SN227	NV723			SN354		
SN232	NV725					
SN260						
SN271						
SN274						
SN331						
SN332						
SN340						

(2) Second user unit. (3) Third user unit.

Tempest Under the Skin

Even though structurally the Tempest in all its versions bore a striking resemblance to the earlier Typhoon, in comparison to the earlier fighter it featured numerous improvements. The fuselage was of all-metal construction and consisted of four major assemblies. The forward section contained the cockpit, all encased in a box-like tubular structure, clothed by light alloy fixed and detachable panels. To the fore of this assembly was the armoured firewall, in front of a bay containing the main fuselage fuel tank, its filler cap at the top for easy access. Also located in this bay was the oil-petrol engine priming tank, located on the starboard side, whilst to port was the de-icing tank.

Between the fuselage fuel tank and the windscreen mounting frame was the engine oil tank, below which was mounted the hydraulic system reservoir and the brake accumulators. The Vokes tropical air filter was mounted in the fuselage underbelly of the Tempest V and VI, whilst in the Tempest II, with its Centaurus engine, it was located in the upper fuselage centre section. Fronting the cockpit was a three-part bullet-proof windscreen backed by a single-piece, blown, fully transparent perspex canopy that would slide aft. The canopy was mounted onto rails fixed into the cockpit walls, there being a third guiding rail mounted on top of the fuselage just aft of the cockpit.

The centre windscreen section consisted of two layers, the outer one 1.5in (3.7cm) thick, while the inner pane was thinner at 0.25in (6mm) in thickness. In the event of an emergency, the movable canopy could be jettisoned, as could a panel on the starboard upper side of the cockpit.

Located to the rear of the pilot's seat was a two-piece set of armoured plates, 0.75in (19mm) in thickness. Aft of the cockpit was the radio and navigation equipment bay, which had an access panel for maintenance purposes located on the port side of the fuselage. Mounted in the same bay

was the cylinder for the Tempest's pneumatic air system. For those aircraft destined for use in the desert, mounting locations were supplied for water bottles as part of the survival kit.

The rear fuselage assembly was of monocoque construction, consisting of eleven alloy frames to which were riveted support stringers and longitudinal stringers for strength. The skin covering was light alloy, each panel being lap-jointed, with the higher located plating pieces overlapping those lower down.

Connecting the forward and aft fuselage sections together were four equally spaced mounting bolts, each being of an interference fit. Located within the lower rear section of this structure was the tail-wheel bay, above which were the mountings for the vertical fin. On the Tempest V Series 1, the dorsal fin was a permanent fixture, whilst those of the Mark V Series 2, Mark VI and the Mark II were detachable. On the earlier aircraft the fuselage joint was strengthened by the use of fishplates

riveted to the structure, while on the later machines the structural strength was embodied by increasing the thickness of the cladding material. During the design stage of the Tempest, great attempts were made to eliminate the problem of carbon monoxide leaking into the cockpit, but although extra sealing was applied around the control access points in the bulkhead, there was still a small problem with carbon monoxide ingestion, which meant that pilots were advised to wear oxygen masks.

The Cockpit Assembly

Inside the cockpit the pilot was faced by a myriad of dials, knobs and switches, all of which either supplied information concerning the behaviour of the aircraft, or allowed the occupant to communicate, navigate or dispense items of weaponry. As always, the centre block of instruments were those needed for basic flying and included the airspeed indicator, artificial

Below This diagram reveals the layout of the underlying structure as applied to all three main versions of the Tempest. Big Bird Aviation Collection

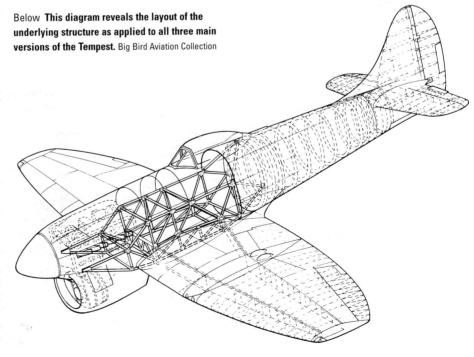

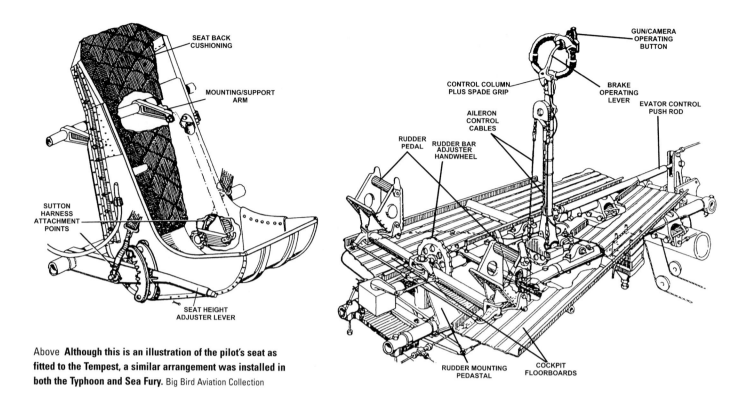

Above **Although this is an illustration of the pilot's seat as fitted to the Tempest, a similar arrangement was installed in both the Typhoon and Sea Fury.** Big Bird Aviation Collection

Above **Neither the Typhoon Tempest nor the Sea Fury had a proper built-in floor, but instead relied on floorboards leading from the seat to the rudder pedals. Although this gave better access to items below floor level, it did leave parts of the flight-control system open to foreign object damage.** Big Bird Aviation Collection

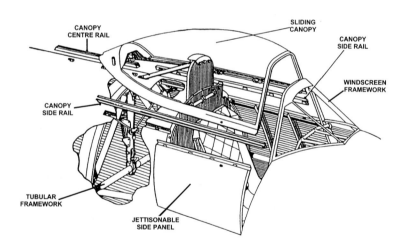

Left **The canopy fitted to the production Tempests was similar to that already installed in the earlier Typhoon, thus both used similar mechanisms for operating and emergency purposes.** Big Bird Aviation Collection

horizon, altimeter, direction indicator plus the turn and bank indicator. In the panel to the left were mainly the engine start switches and controls associated with the propeller, while in that to the right were indicators for the various fluids that allowed the Tempest to operate: thus fuel and oil contents were visible here. The fuel-system gauge was of the direct-reading type: the largest part of the gauge recorded the main fuel tank contents, whilst the other smaller sections recorded the contents of the nose and interspar tanks.

Just below the left-hand panel were the throttle handle, plus friction control; this also contained the propeller speed control lever, the undercarriage lever, supercharger lever, canopy winding lever, radiator shutter control and the gunsight control weapons selector. The throttle lever was gated at the climb position, and had the bomb release switch incorporated in the top of the lever. The propeller speed control was located inboard of the throttle lever, and operated in the natural sense, being pushed forward to the 'Increase Revs' position. The propeller was governed down to 1,600rpm to allow a glide to be stretched out in an emergency after engine failure, although system oil pressure had to be available. In normal operation for ground and flight use, the normal available minimum was 2,000rpm. The supercharger control lever was located behind the engine control box, which was moved downwards for 'S' ratio, and upwards for 'M' ratio.

Located on the left sloping panel was the radiator shutter control, which moved 'Down' to open the shutter, the reverse movement closing the shutter. In the event of a failure of the engine-driven hydraulic pump the shutter could be operated by use of the hand pump. When the time came to start the engine, use was

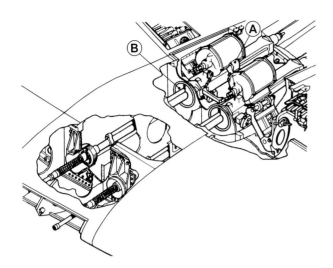

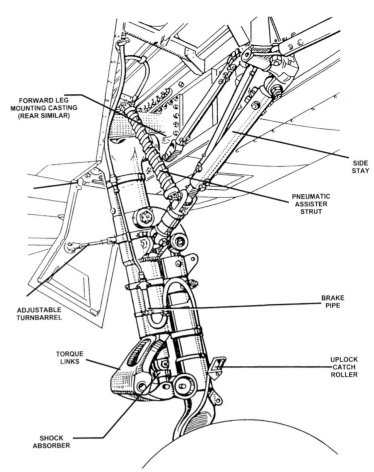

FORWARD LEG
MOUNTING CASTING
(REAR SIMILAR)

SIDE
STAY

PNEUMATIC
ASSISTER
STRUT

ADJUSTABLE
TURNBARREL

BRAKE
PIPE

TORQUE
LINKS

UPLOCK
CATCH
ROLLER

SHOCK
ABSORBER

Above **The layout of the Tempest wing structure meant that the Hispano cannon could be set further back. This in turn meant the cannon breeches and feed mechanisms required bulged covers on the upper surfaces.** Big Bird Aviation Collection

Right **The undercarriage legs fitted to the Tempest were manufactured by Dowty and were of the lever link suspension type; thus the great majority of shock absorbing was taken by the upper section.** Big Bird Aviation Collection

Below **The Tempest series of fighter bombers used a similar layout for lights and aerials, although the variations between each version are clearly illustrated here.** Big Bird Aviation Collection

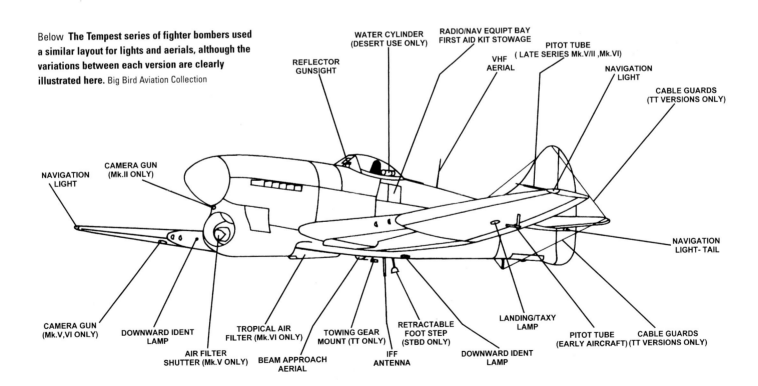

WATER CYLINDER (DESERT USE ONLY) — RADIO/NAV EQUIPT BAY FIRST AID KIT STOWAGE — PITOT TUBE (LATE SERIES Mk.V/II ,Mk.VI) — REFLECTOR GUNSIGHT — VHF AERIAL — NAVIGATION LIGHT — CABLE GUARDS (TT VERSIONS ONLY)

NAVIGATION LIGHT — CAMERA GUN (Mk.II ONLY) — NAVIGATION LIGHT- TAIL

CAMERA GUN (Mk.V,VI ONLY) — DOWNWARD IDENT LAMP — AIR FILTER SHUTTER (Mk.V ONLY) — TROPICAL AIR FILTER (Mk.VI ONLY) — BEAM APPROACH AERIAL — TOWING GEAR MOUNT (TT ONLY) — IFF ANTENNA — RETRACTABLE FOOT STEP (STBD ONLY) — DOWNWARD IDENT LAMP — LANDING/TAXY LAMP — PITOT TUBE (EARLY AIRCRAFT) — CABLE GUARDS (TT VERSIONS ONLY)

made of the starting and slow-running cut-out control lever, which had three designated positions: 'start', 'normal' and 'cut-out'. At the 'start' point there was a stop in place to accurately delineate the proper position; however, the safety catch beside the lever needed to be moved down before the process could begin.

The two 40cc priming pumps were mounted vertically on the right-hand sloping panel. The upper pump handle primed the engine cylinders with fluid drawn from the priming tank, while the lower pump was used to prime the carburettor with fuel drawn from the main supply. To release the pump handles required them to be unscrewed, whilst they needed to be screwed to the shut position after use.

To start the engine there were ignition switches located on the left-hand instrument panel, these being prevented from careless operation by the use of a sliding bar that required the undercarriage indicator switch to be on. To test the system there were four ignition test buttons located on the left-hand side of the cockpit. In the event of an ignition problem causing a drop in rpm, use of these buttons would enable the pilot to reproduce the power loss for repair purposes. When the cartridge starter and booster coil were

required during the start cycle, their push buttons had to be depressed at the same time so that engine start could be achieved. Should there be a failure in the first cartridge start, the starter reload control would allow one of the next five cartridges to be used.

Further equipment located in the cockpit included a modified seat harness on which all four restraining straps could be adjusted. After adjustment the pilot was recommended to locate the junction box just below that of the parachute quick-release box. Until modification 103 was introduced there was no quick harness release available, therefore care was required should they be loosened.

Above the pilot was a single-piece canopy whose winding gear was located on the port side of the cockpit. To open the canopy the spring-loaded knob on the winder crank required pulling inboard and holding against the spring while the crank was turned. Once the knob was released, a pin at the bottom engaged in one of the holes in the locking plate, which locked the canopy into position. When egress of the cockpit was planned, the knob on the handle needed to be pulled out as far as possible and rotated until a projection on the knob engaged with a small recess on the crank lever, thus holding the pin free

of the holes in the locking plate: this permitted the hood to be opened from the outside by hand.

To lock the canopy from the outside, a spring-loaded bolt located on the starboard side needed to be released whilst the canopy was slid to the closed position. Once the canopy was closed the bolt was released and locked into a cut-out in the hood bottom mounting rail.

Forward of the canopy was the windscreen assembly, which on earlier aircraft was of the dry-air sandwich-type. This was connected by rubber tubing to a rubber expansion bag, which was contained in a fibre cylinder located immediately below the windscreen. The pilot was advised that should the screen mist up, the tube needed to be disconnected, and should remain that way until the screen demisted, after which the tube should be reconnected.

To enable the pilot to operate in all conditions, the cockpit was well equipped with lighting. Two lamps were fitted to the top of the instrument panel, these being controlled by two dimmer switches. A third lamp was located above the electrical panel, this being controlled by a dimmer switch. A similarly controlled lamp was located above the trim tab control box. The final cockpit light illuminated the compass, and was also controlled by a dimmer.

Having provided the pilot with many aids, Hawker's also installed cockpit heating, controlled by a lever close to the

Below Tempest V, JN729, was built as a Series 1 machine, hence the protruding cannon barrels. Aerials present on this aircraft include an IFF under the fuselage, and a radio whip aerial aft of the canopy.
Big Bird Aviation Collection

starboard cockpit wall. Only two positions were available, these being 'on' and 'off'. Two ventilators were provided, one each side of the instrument panel.

Just behind these controls, to the side of the pilot, were the hydraulic hand pump and the elevator trim wheel. All trim wheels acted in the natural sense, with the tab position indicators being fitted between them. On the right-hand side of the cockpit, the panel below the fuel/oil contents panel, were the fuel system control cocks, with one lever each for the inter, main and nose fuel tanks, these being closed when the levers were aft. In the small console to the right of the pilot's seat were the switches for the aircraft's electrics: these included the pitot head heater switch, camera master, navigation lights and the TR.1143 radio master switch.

Just forward of this console was the mounting for the cylinder priming pump and the carburettor priming pump handle. The mixture used in the priming system consisted of 70 per cent fuel, with the remainder being 30 per cent oil contained in a tank that had a capacity of 5 pints (3ltr), this being located on the starboard side of the main tank in the fuselage. Above the side console were the mounting clips for the Very pistol cartridges.

In common with the earlier Typhoon, the Tempest did not have a proper floor: the pilot rested his feet on two ribbed plates that led up to the adjustable rudder bar assembly. Between these two floor panels was the control column, topped by a spade grip. In this were the buttons for the gun control and the radio 'press to talk' switch. Located under the ribbed floor panels were the control runs for the ailerons, elevators and rudder, plus various components belonging to the aircraft's electrical and radio systems, all of which were accessible.

Also located in the cockpit was a bag stowed on the left-hand side, containing the flying control locking kit. This consisted of a hinged clamp and four cables, and installation involved the clamp being fitted to the control column with the projecting lugs in contact with the fork end nuts of the aileron tie rods, while two of the cables were hooked onto the rudder pedals. With the seat-adjusting lever locked in the third notch from the top, the rear cables were hooked to each side of the seat and tensioned by adjusting the rudder bar, and then adjusting the seat.

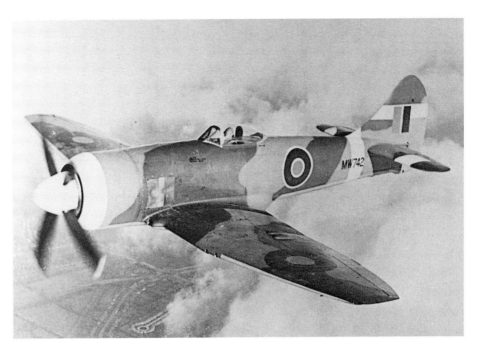

Above **In common with many Tempests built after the war, MW742 would see no service with the Royal Air Force, being sold instead to the RIAF as HA566 during May 1948. Taken prior to that date, this view reveals the camouflage pattern and identification stripes as applied to the Tempest.** Big Bird Aviation Collection

The Wing

The three-section wing was of a semi-elliptical shape in planform, and was of a laminar flow section, the outer panels ending in blunted wing-tips. The centre section had the outer wing panels bolted on at an anhedral angle of 5 degrees and 30 minutes. The thickness chord ratio varied from 14.5 per cent at the root, to 10 per cent at the tip, with a maximum thickness at 37.5 per cent measured from the leading edge, at which point it produces peak suction.

The profiles used to build the wing were H.14/14/37.5 at the root, decreasing to H.14/10/37.5 at the wing-tip joint. The wing centre section was attached to the fuselage at the front and rear spar pick-up points. These were held onto the fuselage by interference-fitted bolts pushed through stress-relieving bushes, these being capped by torque-loaded nuts split-pinned for locking purposes. When the first Tempest V Series 1 aircraft were being constructed, the rear wing to fuselage pick-up points were mounted onto the fuselage tubular assembly; on later build machines this was replaced by a single-piece casting which made mounting of the wing easier.

Each wing consisted of three sections assembled as one unit. The primary structural components were the two main spars, with ribs and alloy skins reinforced by spanwise stringers; further reinforcing was carried out at the wing root to compensate for the impact of personnel getting in and out of the cockpit. On the forward face of the front spar were shaped riblets riveted into position, although these were missing in the area of the wing tanks located in the inner area of the centre section. This omission was catered for by specially formed skins of increased thickness, whereas those further outboard were of a lesser gauge. The front spar ran from each wing-tip mounting rib to the other wing-tip mounting rib, whereas the rear spar was cranked forward within the centre section. This started at the fuselage mounting point, and continued to where the outer panel began, from which point the angle reduced considerably. The spars formed a torsion box and were free from unnecessary cut-outs, which obviated the need for any structure aft of the rear spar in the area of the cannons. This layout allowed for easy access to the cannon for servicing and rearming of the weapons. The panel between the wing spars outboard of the dihedral point helped form the torsion box skin and was of a heavier gauge than that in other areas of the wing.

There were two interspar wing fuel tanks, and a single nose fuel tank in the

Above **This fine portrait of Hawker Tempest II MW742 reveals an outstanding amount of detail, such as the fuselage access step to the cockpit, the covers over the cannon breech housings, plus the oil cooler intake and anti-slip walkway on the starboard wing.** Big Bird Aviation Collection

leading edge of the port wing. The leading edges of the Tempest II and the Mark VI were modified to incorporate the carburettor air intakes in the roots and an additional oil cooler radiator in the starboard wing. The wing trailing edges incorporated hydraulically operated, four-section landing flaps. The Frise-type metal-covered ailerons extended from the sixth outboard rib on the dihedral wing panel to the wing-tip mounting rib. On early-build aircraft the ailerons had ground-adjustable tabs, although these were later replaced by spring-loaded tabs on later build machines. Located underneath the port wing, forward of the aileron leading edge, was the retractable landing/taxi lamp, whilst in a similar location under the starboard wing was the downward identification light.

The Tailplane

The tailplane was constructed as a single assembly, and consisted of two spars interspersed with shaped ribs punctured by lightening holes to reduce weight. Mounted on the forward face of the front spar were shaped ribs which decreased in size towards the tip. On the rear spar were located the mountings for the elevators which were connected together by a torque tube, in the centre of which were the operating bellcranks. The elevators were identical, and were therefore interchangeable, as were the tabs let into the trailing edges. Both the tailplane and flight control surfaces were covered by stressed alloy skins. To fit the tailplane it is slid through a cut-out in the rear empennage, and locked in place by nuts and bolts. Surrounding the tailplane were fairing panels which helped reduce the turbulence in that area. The fin was built integrally with the fuselage, being sheathed with an alloy skin riveted to the front spar rib and the interspar ribs. Those on the forward face of the front fin spar reduced in depth as the tip was reached.

The rudder consisted of a single spar, to which were attached nose ribs and the main ribs which helped form the surface's aerodynamic shaping. In contrast to the other flight control surfaces it was fabric covered, with an adjustable trim tab inset into the trailing edge. This unit was aerodynamically and mass balanced for smooth operation throughout the full range of movement. In common with all the primary flight control surfaces fixed stops were incorporated into the system to ensure that the surfaces were not excessively deflected, which could lead to overstressing of the airframe.

The Undercarriage

The main undercarriage legs were manufactured by Dowty, and used levered suspension units for shock-absorbing purposes. The advantage of such a unit was that it was manufactured in two sections, both being connected by lever links. The upper section acted as the shock absorber, whilst the lower section carried the gear unit and main wheel. The main legs were mounted at a point just inboard of the dihedral junction where the outer wing panel joined the wing centre section. The forward mounting was attached to the rear face of the front spar, whilst the rear mount sat on a false spar, both leg-mounting pins running in large diameter bearings. Each undercarriage leg retracted inwards, activated by a hydraulically driven undercarriage jack which operated against a lever on the leg, and on the 'up' selection broke a mechanical lock that allowed the leg to retract.

Attached to the leg was the main fairing, above which was a movable door attached at the top to the wing by a hinge, and to the leg by adjustable turnbarrels. The wheels were either four- or five-spoked, the former being fitted to the Tempest V Series 1 aircraft only. These were 34in by 11in (86 by 28cm) in size, while those fitted to the later versions were 30in by 9in (76 by 23cm) in size.

The pneumatic brake system was manufactured by Dunlop. Completing the main undercarriage were the 'D'-shaped doors that were hinged at the wing roots, retracting with the aid of linkages. The tailwheel unit consisted of a Dowty oleo pneumatic anti-shimmy strut that retracted forwards into the rear fuselage. The wheel itself was either a Dunlop tyre of plain design or a twin contact Dunlop Marstrand tyre.

Covering the leg were a pair of doors that closed as the leg moved into the bay. The undercarriage lever moved forwards for 'up' selection and travelled aft for a 'down' selection. To enable the lever to move, a safety catch had to be pushed to the 'free' position before an 'up' selection was made, and it returned to the locked position when the lever was moved to the 'down' position. The undercarriage indicators used three green lights to indicate that both main gears and the tail leg were safely down and locked; during undercarriage transitions two reds are displayed for the main legs only. When all the lights were out it indicated that all three undercarriage units were up and locked. Should there be a failure of the primary set of indicator lights, a secondary set could be selected by pulling and turning a knob on the light array. Should the throttle be less than one third open and the wheels not locked down, a red warning light mounted on the instrument panel would come on.

The Tempest Engines

The Sabre Mark V and VI engines fitted to the Tempest were mounted on cantilever tubular steel supports attached to the two upper fuselage longerons and to the front spar pick-up points, while the engine itself was located on the front and rear mounting pads. In contrast, the Sabre Mark II powerplant installation was mounted onto tubular steel struts with six-point rubber-packed mountings. Aircraft fitted with the Sabre Mark II had a bay to the rear of the engine that housed a filtered air intake, the carburettor intake ducts, and the coupled exhausts. In contrast, the Sabre Mark V and VI engines would exhaust through six twin-branched stub manifolds on each side.

Both engine types were surrounded by contoured nose cowlings, into which were inset quick access panels for ease of engine maintenance. Engine starting was by a Coffman Type L.4S multi-breech cartridge starter. The propeller units were either de Havilland or Rotol four-bladed, variable-pitch, constant-speed, left-hand airscrews with a diameter of 14ft (4.3m), the former applicable to the Marks V and VI, whilst the latter, as fitted to the Tempest II, had a diameter of 12ft 9in (3.9m). The Tempest VI had its propeller assembly mounted 2.5in (5.5cm) further forward in contrast to the Tempest V, which required a slightly longer spinner to compensate.

Fuel for the Tempest

The aircraft's fuel was carried in four internal self sealing Linatex or Sorbo tanks, these were located in the main fuselage, two interspar tanks and a nose tank located in the port wing leading edge. Capacities of each tank installed in the Tempest V were 76gal (345ltr) in the fuselage, while the interspar tanks held 28gal (127ltr), with the nose tank holding a further 30gal (136ltr). Similar capacities were available for the Tempest II and VI, which were armourplated for protection, but which reduced the nose tank contents to 28gal (127ltr).

Starting with the Tempest V Series 2, provision was made for the carriage of external streamlined fuel tanks that could hold either 45 or 90gal (205 or 409ltr) respectively. Delivering the fuel to the engine were Pesco pumps that were pressurized at high altitudes. This function was required to stop the engine cutting out in warm weather due to the fuel boiling off. On earlier build aircraft this became operative above 15,000ft (4,500m), although on later machines this dropped to 10,000ft (3,000m). However, there was a downside to this application, in that the self-sealing capability was impaired, therefore the pilot was instructed to turn off the pressurization should a tank be holed.

Fuel grades as specified by the Directorate of Technical Developments were set at 87 octane to Spec DTD 230, and 100 Octane 100/130 grade to DTD 2473, for all versions of the Napier Sabre, while the Bristol Centaurus was confined to using DTD 2473 only. Fuel consumption with the mixture set to rich for the Sabre Mark V at 3,500rpm was 150gal (680ltr) per hour at 5,000ft (1,500m), while the Centaurus operating under similar conditions consumed 210gal (955ltr) per hour.

The lubricating oil tank for the Tempest V had a capacity of 16gal (73ltr) with a 2gal (9ltr) air space, whilst that of the Tempest VI had its capacity increased to 22gal (100ltr) of fluid with a 2.25gal (10ltr) air space. To control the temperature of the oil a thermostatic valve opened an oil outlet when temperatures rose above 50 degrees. There was a separate relief valve that was set at 55psi to blow off pressure; it was located between the scavenge pump and the oil cooler, which prevented damage to the oil cooler when starting the engine in cold weather. The relief valve effectively short-circuited the entire oil system, which discharged the oil into the suction side of the engine-oil delivery pump. The oil tank fitted to the Tempest II was smaller than that required for the Sabre engine, holding only 14gal (64ltr) of oil with an air space of 4gal (18ltr).

The oil cooler for the Tempest V was incorporated in the central core of the Serck compound radiator mounted beneath the engine, while that of the Mark VI was repositioned to the rear of the coolant radiator, which covered the whole

Below **The Napier Sabre in all its glory. This example is mounted on the front of a Tempest V of No. 16 Sqn. The oblong shapes around the perimeter of the removed panel landings are the mountings for the fasteners. Also clearly visible are the pipes for the coolant and lubrication system, plus the extensive cabling for the ignition system.** Michael Baldock

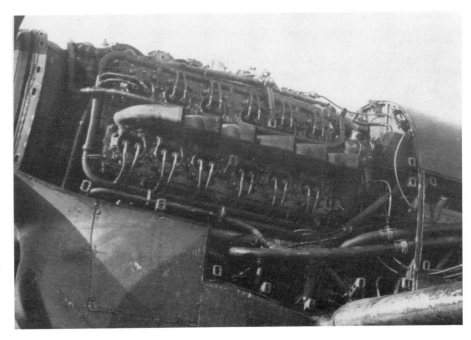

duct cross-section. Assisting the cooler was an auxiliary mounted in the starboard wing leading edge. The cooler arrangement for the Tempest II required only the wing-mounted radiator. The coolant system was thermostatically controlled, the radiator being bypassed until the system coolant temperature reached 85 degrees. The thermostat became fully open at 105 degrees. Control of the radiator shutter was by hydraulic means.

The Hydraulic System

The hydraulic system as fitted to all versions of the Tempest was powered by an engine-driven Dowty 5700RH pump that maintained a system pressure of 1,800psi. This system drove the flaps and the oil cooler shutter, plus the undercarriage and associated doors. The filler for the hydraulic reservoir was located on the port side of the fuselage, just below that of the oil-tank filler point. In the event of a hydraulic system failure there was a hand pump located on the port side of the cockpit. Also mounted on the engine was the Heywood compressor that maintained an

air cylinder charged to an operating pressure of 450psi. This system provided the power for the braking system, the gun-firing mechanism and the undercarriage assister.

The assister was the final option available to the pilot to lower the undercarriage should the engine-driven pump fail and the hand pump prove ineffective. In this event the main legs could be lowered by gravity assistance, once the mechanical uplocks had been released by the operation of two red-painted foot pedals located under each sloping panel. When the wheels travelled past the vertical, a pneumatic assister jack was operated to finally lock the legs down. The tailwheel lowered automatically during this process, and would lock down when the aircraft landed. During this operation the main leg indicator light should come on, although the tailwheel light might be intermittent.

Flap control was by a lever on the left hand sloping panel, the positions being marked on the scale as 'up', 'down' and 'valve shut'. The flaps could be stopped in any position by placing the lever in the 'valve shut' position, this being a necessity when fully lowered. This was required, as in

the down position the blow-off pressure was lower than that required for retracting the undercarriage. As with the undercarriage, the flaps could be lowered by use of the hand pump. The wheel brakes were operated by a cylinder that was maintained by the engine-driven pump. Differential braking was achieved by use of a relay valve connected to the rudder bar, while indications were given on the triple pressure gauge that showed the cylinder contents and the pressure available at each brake.

The Electrical System

The final system installed in the Tempest was the electrical supply system. When the engine was running, power was supplied by a twenty-four-volt engine-driven generator that supplied a pair of twelve-volt accumulators wired in series: these supplied the entire aircraft electrical requirements. To indicate a system failure, there was a power failure warning lamp mounted on the instrument panel, which would light up when the generator was not charging the system. For power supplies on the ground without engine-driven power there was a socket mounted in the starboard side of the fuselage located just below the jettisonable cockpit panel. Power for the aircraft on the ground was supplied by a twenty-four-volt 'trolley acc' accumulator.

Below Tempest II PR533 turns towards the camera on a test flight from Hawker's prior to delivery. Clearly visible beneath the wings are the streamlined bomb carriers. This particular aircraft served with the A&AEE on trials work until passed on to No. 33 Sqn, with whom it stayed until withdrawn in March 1951.
Big Bird Aviation Collection

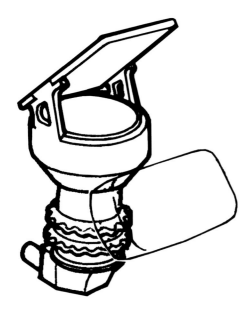

Above **The gunsights fitted to the Tempest included the Mark III, which had an adjustable head that catered for the use of both cannon and rockets. It was most commonly fitted to early build Tempest Vs.** Big Bird Aviation Collection

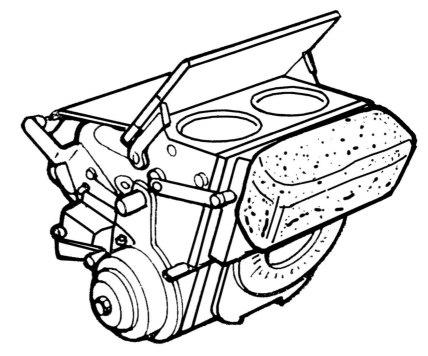

Above **The Mark II gyro-stabilized gunsight was mainly installed on the Tempest IIs and VIs.** Big Bird Aviation Collection

Tempest Armament

The basic armament fitted to the Tempest consisted of four license-built 20mm Hispano cannon, these being housed in pairs in the outer wing panels. The ammunition bays were located behind the rear spar on the inboard and outboard sides of the gun bay, each ammunition feed drum being covered by a distinctive blister fairing. The cannons as fitted to the Tempest V Series 1 and the Mark II prototypes were fitted with the longer-barrelled Mark II cannon, while the later versions – the Mark V Series 2, the production Mark II and the Mark VI – were fitted with the shorter-barrelled Mark V version of the cannon, which meant that none of the barrel extended beyond the wing leading edge.

Ammunition carried by the Tempest V and VI amounted to 200 rounds per gun; the Mark II carried 162 rounds in the inboard drum, while the total was reduced to 156 rounds in the outboard drum. Firing of the cannon was achieved electro-pneumatically, the operation being controlled by a push button on the control-column spade grip. There were two positions, 'safe' and 'fire', and to achieve the latter the button needed to be pushed clockwise. The source for the pneumatic pressure was

the same as that for the brake supply, the available pressure being shown on a gauge located on the instrument panel.

Aiming of the cannon was via a Type Mark II* or a Mark IIL fixed reflector gunsight in the later models of the Tempest, whilst the earlier versions used the Type I Mark I or the Mark III projector gunsight; a modified version of this sight was used on some Series 2 machines, although the reflector screen was normally removed and the graticle was projected directly onto the windscreen. With the introduction of the Tempest VI and II aircraft, the gunsight was changed to the Type Mark IID gyro gunsight. To enable the pilot to use the gunsight under all conditions, a dimmer controlled light labelled 'off', 'night' and 'day' was provided.

Supporting the aircraft's weapons was a Williamson G.42 or G.45 cine combat camera to record each sortie. On the Tempest V and VI the camera was mounted inside the starboard radiator fairing, while in the Mark II it was in the starboard wing outboard of the oil cooler. The camera was operated by use of the gun-firing button, and ran for the entire length of time that the button was depressed. To keep the pilot informed about the state of the camera there was a

footage indicator and an aperture control switch located on the right-hand side of the control panel, with the camera switch itself being located on the electrical panel. Should there be a need to use the camera gun for recording rocket attacks without the cannons being used, there was a separate switch on the spade grip.

To enable the Tempest to carry out its ground-attack duties it was fitted with aerodynamic bomb racks that could carry either a pair of 500lb general purpose, medium capacity or semi armour-piercing bombs, or 1,000 GP or MC bombs. For pilots undertaking weapons training, the Tempest could have a light bomb carrier attached to the rack; this could carry either 28lb smoke and flash, high explosive or general purpose bombs. The first version of the Tempest to be built directly for the fighter-bomber role was the Mark II Series 2, later to be designated the fighter-bomber Mark 2. The earlier versions would be retrospectively modified at the manufacturers, the maintenance units, or where possible the operating units where wiring and structural modifications were applied.

All versions of the Tempest, once modified, were able to carry 200lb smoke floats, 1,000lb Type A mines, 45gal (205ltr) napalm bombs, 1,000lb ANM 59 or ANM

Above **This portrait of Tempest II MW801 clearly shows the location of the pitot head fitted directly to the leading edge of the port wing of both the II and VI. MW801 was one of the six aircraft sent to Khartoum for tropical trials, hence the 45gal (205ltr) tanks under the wings required to give maximum range. Unfortunately the Tempest would be abandoned in Libya after the engine caught fire during the ferry flight.**
C. P. Russell Smith Collection

65 cluster bombs for use as incendiary or oil bombs, or 1,000lb incendiary bombs Mark II. For use in special purposes the Tempest could carry smoke-curtain installation smoke-generating canisters, or M. 10 smoke tanks could be fitted. Further weapons for use in the ground-support role could include the Type R, C or CLE Mark III parachute supply containers that weighed in at 300lb (135kg) each.

During February 1945 the Tempest V was cleared for firing rockets: these included the 3in (7.5cm), 25lb (11kg) and 60lb (27kg) or concrete practice versions of unguided projectiles. Carriage was on Mark III rails of lightweight construction; the original were of the heavyweight Mark I variety. All were eventually replaced by the Mark VIII zero-length launch rail.

During its career the Tempest was cleared to carry two types of 45gal (205ltr) tank: the first was an aerodynamic tank complete with internal dampening walls designed by Hawker's specifically for this aircraft, while the other was more of a generic cylindrical type that could also be used as a napalm bomb if required. For ferry or extended patrol purposes, a pair of 90gal (410ltr) fuel tanks could be installed, although their fitment required a rearrangement of any underwing impedimenta. Their use was mainly confined to the Tempest II and VI.

When the Tempest was selected to undertake target-towing duties, a Malcolm Type G Mark II wind-driven target winch was installed under the port wing of the prototype target-towing Mark V, while an appropriate balancing store such as a fuel tank was located under the starboard wing. In the event, a far simpler installation was actually used, namely a simple drogue attachment that was bolted under the lower fuselage beneath the cockpit. The Swiss-built installation would eventually find further usage with the Hawker Sea Furies operating on behalf of the West German armed forces.

Communication Systems

Communication equipment was located to the rear of the pilot's seat and was accessed through a panel on the port side of the fuselage. The array consisted of a Marconi TR 1143 VHF transceiver, whose whip or blade aerial was located on the fuselage spine behind the canopy. An A.1271 Standard Beam Approach radio navigation unit – either the R.3090, R.3121 or the Type BC-966 A receiver – was installed in a mounting tray under the radio. Externally the only visible sign of its fitment was a small bulged fairing with a small horizontal aerial located under the centre fuselage section. If required, 'Identification Friend or Foe' equipment could be installed, the aerial, either a Type 90 or 93, placed alongside the Standard Beam Approach fairing. When the Tempest target-towing Mark V entered service, one of the modifications carried out was to remove the Standard Beam Approach antenna and replace it with the IFF aerial, as the SBA was not required for the target-towing role. As well as the attack weaponry, the Tempest also carried a variety of survival and rescue equipment which included a Very signal pistol and cartridges, a crowbar, flying control locking kit, and for desert operations, a desert survival kit.

Pilot Training

Once our pilot was familiar with the many components and systems that made up all versions of the Tempest, he would then be schooled in handling the aircraft. First he would have to concentrate on the fuel system, which needed care in its management to maintain the aircraft's centre of gravity. The first fuel management technique taught to the pilot was that of flying the Tempest without external drop tanks. When the fuel tanks were full, the aircraft could be taken off using any combination of fuel tanks, but pilots were recommended to have all tanks selected on. Once airborne, the main fuselage tank had to be switched off and used as a reserve, otherwise, due to it being a gravity-feed tank, it would drain first. To complicate matters further, if any wing tank were less than half full, take-off using all tanks was forbidden, therefore departure had to be made using the main fuselage tank only.

Once airborne, the fuselage tank could be switched off and the wing tanks used instead. During normal flying the interspar and nose tanks could be used as a collective group, and only in the event of a tank being punctured in combat should it be switched off. Once the wing tanks were emptied, it was the turn of the main tank in the fuselage to be used, although the others had to be switched off first. If the main fuselage tank were drained inadver-

tently, it had to be turned off before the wing tanks were selected.

In the event of the engine cutting out due to lack of fuel, the following strategy had to be followed. First the throttle should be closed, the fuel contents should be checked and any empty tank turned off, then a full tank selected. With fuel available, the rpm control lever could be advanced to the maximum position, then the throttle should be opened slowly, then closed, until the engine picked up. During the landing phase the wing tanks must be turned off and the main fuselage tank used. This particular tank differed from the others in that it had a deep sump that could drain completely in yaw and steep approach angles without suffering an air lock. In contrast the wing tanks, being shallow, were susceptible to air locks when close to empty during yaw manoeuvres.

Just to keep our intrepid pilot on his toes, Hawker's and the Air Ministry came up with a completely different set of rules for flying the Tempest with underwing tanks fitted, the first of which stated that maximum diving speed should not exceed 450mph (724km/h) IAS up to an altitude of 15,000ft (4,500km/h). Above this level the dive speed was reduced to 50mph (80km/h) below the permissible speed for a clean aircraft. Jettisoning of the fuel tanks should not be attempted above 400mph (650km/h), and only in straight and level flight; also their release had marginal benefits in increasing range, and

there was always the cost of replacement. A far more cryptic note states that spinning was not permitted, probably due to the unbalanced nature of the airframe in this condition.

Engine starting and departure was very similar to that of flying clean, although the wing tanks had to be in the 'off' position until airborne. As it was recommended that the external tanks be used first, the pilot was instructed to turn on the port-wing tank prior to selecting the mains 'off'. Once the port tank was empty, some swift work with the switches was required to change over to the starboard tank. Once both were drained, the main system could be used as before. In common with the operation of the main fuel system, the drop tanks required pressurization above 10,000ft (3,000m).

Flying the Tempest

With the complexities of ground school and fuel system management safely covered, our intrepid aviator was then presented with the task of actually entering the cockpit and flying the Tempest. Checklists, as always, played a major part in this process, the first two on the list being the most obvious but the easiest to forget: the undercarriage lever had to be checked in the 'down' position, while the locking catch had to be at 'lock'. With the lever and its catch checked and external power available, the three greens of the undercarriage indicator were checked and confirmed. Given that piston-engined aircraft, especially the Sabre powered machines, could give off quite a display of pyrotechnics it is hardly surprising that the next instruction was to ensure that the canopy was in the locked open position, and that the fuselage footstep was in the retracted position, as its continued extension posed a safety threat to ground-crew – trapped fingers and suchlike, and would cause problems with shutting the canopy.

By the time the Tempest became available for operational usage, many of the techniques for engine starting had been improved, although the machine still needed turning into the wind for starting, and lashing down for ground running. Once in position, the ignition switches had to be set to 'off'; all fuel tanks, except externals, had to be in the 'on' position while the flaps were retracted. Once these

Below **With its access panels removed, this Tempest II shows the mounting of the Centaurus engine and the forward oil and coolant tank. The removal of the fuselage side panel reveals the tubular framework underneath an idea inherited from the Hawker biplanes of the 1930s.** Michael Baldock

Above **This head-on view of the Bristol Centaurus 18 reveals this mighty powerplant in all its glory. The protruding shaft facing forward is the splined drive upon which the propeller assembly was mounted.**
Big Bird Aviation Collection

Below **Close observation of this side-on shot of a Centaurus reveals the way that the exhausts are cleverly worked to bring both sets of pipework to a single termination point on each side of the engine.**
Big Bird Aviation Collection

items were confirmed, the propeller speed control was set to fully forward, the supercharger control was up in the 'M' position, while the radiator shutter was open in the 'down' position. To protect the ground-crew, the cartridge starter was confirmed empty: this allowed the propeller to be swung manually to ensure that the engine was free to turn.

With all the conditions required for a safe start satisfied, the pilot would then select a cartridge to be loaded into the starter breech whilst setting the 'cut-out' lever to the start position and pushing the throttle lever forwards up to the first stage stop. With the levers set, the carburettor and cylinder priming pumps were then operated until all lights were out. As soon as the priming was complete and all handles safely stowed and locked down, the booster-coil buttons and start buttons were pushed at the same time. If all went well, the engine would start: however, there was an obvious problem should the exhaust emit white smoke, or if the propeller started to slow down instead of picking up speed. In both cases the recommendation was to shut down, although only in the case of the former was a restart allowed; the latter was more than likely due to a seized valve sleeve, a known problem with the Napier Sabre when cold. In the case of a sticky or seized sleeve valve it was recommended that some gentle easing be tried before a restart was attempted.

If the engine behaved itself and all was well, the cut-out lever was returned to 'normal' while the buttons were released and the priming pump screwed shut. If, however, the engine decided to misbehave by bursting into flames, the application of a fire extinguisher to the air intake was required. Hopefully the fire would be extinguished, and the powerplant run up to 1,000rpm so that the oil pressure could drop below 100psi. Once stabilized, the speed could be increased to 2,000rpm, and all magnetos and systems checked, after which the Tempest was cleared to depart.

Having left the dispersal, the pilot could then taxi his aircraft to the runway threshold where another series of vital checks was needed. These included the trim tabs, the elevator being set at 1.5 divisions nose down, and the rudder being offset fully to port to counteract the engine torque. Next came the propeller, which needed its control setting fully forward, whilst the fuel tank cocks needed to be set correctly for take-off. The flaps had to be in the 'up' position, while the supercharger was set to 'M' and the radiator shutter was selected to the 'down' position for increased cooling. Once the pre-flight checks were complete, a short full-power run at 2,500rpm was required – after which the aviator was encouraged to clean the windscreen of any oil splashes, should it be necessary.

Cleared to take off, the throttle could be pushed to maximum, although little would have been gained if a higher boost, above +4psi, had been used. Flaps could also be used with their setting placed at any point between 20 and 30 degrees, although the Tempest would then exhibit a marked tendency to swing to the right.

Once airborne, the undercarriage had to be selected 'up' as soon as possible, although the aircraft should be kept in the 145 to 150mph (230–240km/h) band to ensure a positive lock-up. If flaps had been used to assist in the take-off, it was known that the undercarriage red lights would be slow to go out, as the hydraulic system struggled to cope with the demands placed upon it; thus the flaps would complete their retraction first before the undercarriage.

Specification – Tempest	
Type:	Single-seat fighter/fighter-bomber
Powerplant:	Mk II, 2,520hp Centaurus V/VI; Mk V, 2,180hp Sabre IIA, 2,200hp Sabre IIB, 2,260hp Sabre IIC
Weights:	Empty Mk II 8,900lb (4,040kg), Mk V 9,000lb (4,080kg), Mk VI 9,150lb (4,150kg); loaded Mk II 13,250lb (6,000kg) with 2 × 90gal (400ltr) drop tanks, Mk V 13,540lb (6,140kg) with 2 × 1,000lb bombs, Mk VI 13,700lb (6,200kg) with 2 × 1,000lb bombs
Dimensions:	Span 41ft (12.5m); length Mk II 34ft 5in (10.5m), Mk V 33ft 8in (10.26m), Mk VI 33ft 10½in (10.33m); height Mk II 15ft 10in (4.83m), Mk V/VI 16ft 1in (4.9m); wing area 302sq ft (28.06sq m)
Performance:	Max. speed Mk II 442mph (710km/h), Mk V 426mph (685km/h), Mk VI 438mph (700km/h); rate of climb Mk II 4.5min to 15,000ft (4,500m), Mk V 5min to 15,000ft, Mk VI 4.6min to 15,000ft; range Mk II 1,640 miles (2,640km), Mk V 1,530 miles (2,460km), Mk VI 750 miles (1,200km); service ceiling Mk II 37,500ft (11,430m), Mk V 36,500ft (11,125m), Mk VI 38,000ft (11,600m)
Armament (fixed):	Mk II, V, VI 4 × 20mm Hispano cannon
Armament (disposable)/ fuel tanks:	2 × 500lb bombs or 2 × 1,000lb bombs or 8 × rocket projectiles, or other cleared stores

The Tempest in Flight

The Tempest in flight was quite a sprightly performer, therefore its limiting speed up to 20,000ft (6,000m) was restricted to 185mph (298km/h) IAS, and was best achieved by selecting the 'S' ratio setting once 10,000ft (3,000m) had been reached. Once straight and level, stability was recorded as good directionally, although there was a slight tendency to misbehave longitudinally. The flight controls themselves were recorded as being excellent, although there were some provisos. The first of these was that the ailerons became sluggish at low speeds, while a similar affliction affected the elevators once the undercarriage and flaps were fully deployed. The rudder remained effective throughout the speed range, although all movements had to be executed firmly.

Aerobatics in the Tempest could be performed without restrictions, except those generated by common sense and height requirements. Stalling, on the other hand, was something that all pilots had to look out for, that of the Tempest giving no obvious clues whilst flying at low speed, except that the left wing would drop suddenly. In contrast, the Hawker fighter could also stall at high speed should excessive 'g' be generated in a turn. This would lead to an aileron snatch, which, if not dealt with correctly, could lead to the aircraft becoming inverted and spinning; however, correct application of the recovery procedure would lead to a safe return to normal flight.

Landing the Tempest

Having survived the vagaries of flight, the pilot then had to prepare to land, which involved more checks. Fortunately these were minimal: the undercarriage had to be selected down and three greens obtained, the propeller control lever placed fully forward, the supercharger put in 'M' ratio, the flaps and the radiator shutter fully down. With all these conditions satisfied, the pilot could then attempt his landing, which took place between 100 and 120mph (160 and 190km/h), depending on flap position.

Emergencies occurred, however, even with the Tempest, and centred mainly around the undercarriage. One of the greatest concerns was that of the gear either not deploying correctly, or not locking down. If there was a red undercarriage light, and the engine pump seemed unable to drive the gear fully down, the pilot had a choice of using the hand pump, or operating the release pedals and pneumatic assister system.

If the pilot needed to abandon the aircraft, the first requirement was to jettison the canopy. This was done by pulling the red handle on the instrument panel, and as the hood departed the aircraft, the starboard side panel went with it. Once the canopy had departed the aircraft, the pilot could be faced with the possibility of ditching, especially if he was flying at low level – although in fact he was exhorted to climb to height and bale out, if at all possible. If that option was not available, the aircraft flaps had to be lowered to half down, and the touchdown made at the lowest speed possible. Just before hitting the water, the drop tanks had to be jettisoned, and then the Tempest placed in a tail-down position just before impact.

Surviving a Crash Landing

Forced landings and their survival were also taught to the budding Tempest pilot. The first given instruction was to try to lengthen the glide by pulling the propeller speed control as far back as possible, although there had to be oil pressure available for this to happen. In extending the length of glide it was also recommended that the undercarriage and flaps be kept retracted, which gave a very flat glide angle with a speed of 170mph (275km/h) IAS. This procedure was mandatory in the event of a mainwheel tyre bursting, as the deflated tyre could make the aircraft uncontrollable on the ground.

Once our trainee pilot had mastered all these techniques and instructions at the operational training unit, he would then be considered competent enough to join a front line squadron.

CHAPTER EIGHT

Tempest in Combat

The Hawker Tempest's combat service during the period April 1944 to May 1945 may have been short, but it was a formidable aircraft, and its addition to the strength of the 2nd TAF was a positive asset. However, its appearance was the result of some strenuous efforts by the Royal Air Force and Hawker's to clear the type for service and produce sufficient aircraft to undertake air superiority missions during the D-Day landings and their aftermath. The proposal, as suggested by the AFDU, was to create at least one wing to operate the new fighter, the chosen route being to re-equip a Typhoon wing, thus reducing the conversion time.

The first unit to receive a handful of these new machines was No. 486 (NZ) Sqn, whose initial examples arrived at Tangmere in January 1944. Their tenure with the New Zealanders was short, as No. 3 Sqn at Manston would end up being the first unit to fully convert after a move to Bradwell Bay on 6 March 1944. Once the initial work-up had been completed, the squadron transferred to the Ayr APC, where it arrived in April to undertake weapons training, returning to Bradwell Bay on 14 April. Having successfully

completed both phases to become operational, the squadron undertook its first combat sortie on 23 April in support of an air-sea rescue sortie. From Bradwell Bay, No. 3 Sqn moved on to Newchurch a fortnight later, before settling at Matlask in September.

Although No. 486 Sqn's initial time with the Tempest had been short, that would quickly change, because when it moved to Castle Camps during March 1944 it finally traded in its Typhoons for the more potent Tempest V. Once again, a trip to the Ayr APC was undertaken after the successful completion of the initial work-up. With both phases complete, the squadron would move to join No. 3 Sqn at Newchurch in Kent on 29 April 1944, where they would form No. 150 Airfield. The third unit destined to join No. 150 Airfield was No. 56 Sqn at Acklington; it had just received a fairly new batch of rocket-firing Typhoons during March, although these were quickly exchanged with No. 137 Sqn, who passed on their older, unmodified aircraft. Eventually No. 56 Sqn would re-equip with Spitfire IXs, and it was still equipped with these when it moved south on 28 April to become

part of No. 150 Wing, as part of No. 85 Group.

The delay in Tempests becoming available for the third squadron had been caused by industrial action at Hawker's Langley factory over pay rates offered to those building the new type. The commander of this slightly mixed bag of aircraft was none other than Wing Commander R. P. Beamont DSO, DFC, who had already spent some time flying the Tempest as a test pilot at Hawker's.

Combat operations by the Tempests of No. 150 Wing initially involved armed anti-shipping reconnaissance, plus some strafing sorties. However, the problems with the Napier Sabre had started to plague the Tempest, with two being forced to make emergency landings after engine failure. As before, strenuous efforts were made by all concerned with maintaining the aircraft to reduce this problem to a minimum. Overall this was a successful strategy, although No. 150 Wing had to wait until the invasion was well under way on 8 June before they could join the action. Ostensibly they had been kept in reserve in the event of the Luftwaffe attempting to intervene in any strength during the initial stages of the invasion. On that date, Wing Cdr Beamont led nine of No. 3 Squadron's aircraft on a sweep over the landing beaches close by Rouen. Here they encountered five Messerschmitt Bf 109s, and shot down two of them, Beamont himself taking one of them.

Whilst most of the pilots had been involved with intercepting the five German fighters, the remainder had been circling clear to provide any required cover – and it would be required, as two other Messerschmitts tried to bounce the formation already in contact. But the Luftwaffe attempt was foiled by Pilot Officer Whitman, who brought down one aircraft and scared the other away. After these initial successes the Luftwaffe stayed away, although the Tempests were fully employed in supporting the Allied ground forces.

Below **The Focke Wulf Fw 190 was one of the main adversaries to face the Tempest in the war over Europe. However, it was consistently outflown by the British fighter, especially below 20,000ft (6,000m).**
Big Bird Aviation Collection

Destroying the German Flying Bombs

As there was sufficient air power over the Normandy beaches, the Tempests of No. 150 Wing were allocated to a task of no less importance. Before the Tempest had entered service, its predecessor the Typhoon had undertaken *Noball* missions against the Pas de Calais, where many of the Fiesler Fi-103 flying bombs and their launchers were located. These initial launch complexes had been fairly large and relatively easy to destroy, so the German rocket forces had resorted to dispersing the missiles and their launchers in smaller, well camouflaged groups, thus making them harder to detect.

The 'V1' rocket itself was a small, aircraft-shaped weapon with a span of 16ft (5m) and a length of 20ft (6m). Power was courtesy of a ram jet located on pylons above the fuselage, while the warhead was located in the nose. Its speed was approximately 400mph (650km/h) in the 1,500 to 2,000ft (450 to 600m) height band, whilst its range was guided by the amount of fuel carried. Any of these missiles that had not been shot down would continue onwards with their strange puttering sound until the fuel was exhausted. At this point the rocket would begin its dive towards the

Above **Armourers bedecked with ammunition belts load the cannon magazines of this No. 501 'County of Gloucester' Sqn Tempest V that also has 45gal (205ltr) tanks under the wings. Access to the wing armament was excellent due to the large area of removable panels.** RAF Museum Collection

Below **Unusually this 'JF'-serialled Tempest of No. 3 Sqn has its D-Day invasion stripes painted round the fuselage. This photograph was taken at Newchurch; noteworthy is the cover over the canopy.** Real Wings Collection

Above **Amidst the wreckage of Volkel airfield sits a pair of No. 3 Sqn Tempests receiving much needed maintenance. The groundcrew took good care of their aircraft, as the liberal use of protective covers shows.** Real Wings Collection

ground, destroying anything close by the point of impact as the explosives detonated.

Later to become codenamed 'Divers', these missiles were first spotted during June 1944 heading towards the south of England. To combat this threat, No. 150 Wing was detached from the 2nd TAF to the ADGB, although it would remain based at Newchurch. First 'diver' patrols began on the 16 June, with a 'V1' being despatched near Maidstone, whilst another would meet the same fate in the Hythe area. By the end of that day a total of thirteen of those launched had been destroyed, and this would set the pattern for the following weeks. Throughout the daylight hours, standing patrols were flown by the Tempests of No. 150 Wing, plus Spitfires attached to the ADGB. Such were the numbers of 'V1' rockets launched against London and the south of England that claims for destruction were filed every day. To enable the Tempests to do their jobs more effectively they were fitted with Rotol propellers, in preference to the original de Havilland units that could not absorb the power output, while the maximum engine rpm was increased from 3,700rpm to 3,850rpm, and the boost from +11 to +13.

Even though British Intelligence had become aware of both the 'V1' and 'V2' after aerial reconnaissance sorties, they were unable to verify the exact details surrounding these weapons. Both missiles

and their launchers were subject to extensive bombing sorties, however only the 'V1' rocket could be intercepted, as the 'V2' travelled at high altitudes and supersonic speeds. Fortunately for the ADGB organization, the Tempest had the edge over all the other available fighters – even the Supermarine Spitfire XIVs, also assigned to this role. As well as having the extra speed, the Tempest was also a highly stable gun platform, which meant that shooting the 'V1' rockets down was far easier than the Spitfire pilots' trick of trying to destroy them by tipping the weapon under the wing-tip in the hope of destabilizing the on-board gyros.

The strike rate of the ADGB fighter force was such that by mid-August some 632 flying bombs had been shot down. However, from this point in time onwards, anti-aircraft guns with proximity-fused shells, and radar with better definition, took over the task of destroying these weapons. Radar had come of age by this time, and was able to detect these small, high speed, low level targets with some degree of success, although the systems were not refined enough to place the fighters closer than 500yd (460m) to their targets. Visual detection both in the air and from the ground was also difficult, except in the most perfect of light conditions.

While the Tempests were being successful in their newly assigned role, they were encountering problems from other, slower

fighters eager to join in the fray. To enable the Tempests to carry out their task more effectively, the area where the great majority of the flying bombs was encountered was declared a special defence zone, and all aircraft except those involved with interception duties were banned from entering it by No. 11 Group; the group's responsibility in intercepting the 'V1' also saw the Royal Observer Corps deployed around the coast within the special zone. Their task would be to fire signal flares in the direction of any flying bombs approaching Britain, thus enabling the intercepting radar-guided fighters to pick up their targets more easily. But even as the ADGB effort was stepped up, so the German rocket divisions had also increased their launch activity, to the effect that flying bombs were not only being launched during daylight hours, but night firings were becoming more common.

Although the Tempests and Griffon-powered Spitfires were more than capable of despatching the daylight intruders, their effectiveness at night was severely limited. To combat the night threat, the Mosquitoes of the night-fighter force were employed in this hazardous mission, their on-board radar being of great assistance. The night-fighter Mosquitoes initially encountered problems in intercepting the flying bombs, as judging the distance at night was difficult until they realized that approaching the missiles from the rear was far more effective.

Tempests as Night Fighters

Although the night-fighter force had achieved some success, their role would be curtailed because they were required to return to their primary duties. So that the Tempests could take over the night interception role, the lessons learned by the Mosquito crews were put into practice and modified by pilots from the Fighter Interceptor Unit. This small organization had the task of developing fighter techniques for both day- and night-fighter squadrons. The small detachment that arrived at Newchurch on 22 June 1944 was tasked with developing tactics for the Tempest. To begin with, delays caused by bad weather meant that the first shootdowns took nearly a week to achieve, though from that point on, increasing success and also an increase in pilots meant that the detachment had soon grown to a fully fledged flight.

Daytime intercepts by the Newchurch Wing would peak on 23 June, when more than two dozen flying bombs fell to the guns of the Tempests. These successes were not without casualties, as on 28 June one aircraft was shot down by British anti-aircraft fire, whilst others were damaged or destroyed by debris from exploding 'V1s'. Although every effort was made to identify the Tempests to other sections of the defence forces, the anti-aircraft guns were still claiming intercepting fighters, such as that of Flt Sgt Domanski of No. 3 Sqn, who was fatally hit by mistake while flying Tempest JN752 'JF-S' in pursuit of a 'VI'. Possibly one of the unluckiest pilots involved in chasing the 'V1' was Pilot Officer Lawless of No. 486 Sqn, who lost two Tempests in ten days: JN772 on 10 June, and JN859 on 28 June.

As June progressed, No. 56 Sqn at last managed to fully equip with Tempests, finally saying farewell to its Spitfires on 24 June. After work-up flying, and a short period spent at the Ayr APC, the squadron began operational missions on 2 July, although these operations would only continue until 28 September 1944 when the unit was despatched to Europe to join the 2nd TAF. The night-time force, the FIU detachment, was also beginning to score against the flying bomb menace,

Squadron Leader Joseph Berry DFC*

Joseph Berry was born 28 February 1920 and initially lived at Cassop cum Quarrington Teesdale before the family moved to Stampeth Nr Alnwick he attended the Duke Grammar School. Leaving school in 1936 as a 16 year old he joined the Inland Revenue, two years later he met Joyce who was working at the same branch. Joe enlisted in the RAFVR in August 1940, and in March 1942 Joe and Joyce were married.

Little is known of Joseph Berry's early service. On completion of training as a Fighter Pilot he was posted to No.256 Squadron at Squires Gate Nr Blackpool, this was a Night Fighter Squadron flying Defiants. He was commissioned in March 1942 at Squires Gate, this Squadron then transferring to Woodvale, South Port flying Beaufighters, later flying them to Setif, in the Atlas Mountains where he joined No. 153 Squadron based at Maison-Blanche Algiers.

He was awarded a DFC in March 1944 and in June was promoted Flt.Lt being posted to the FIU to fly Mosquito's. FIU formed a special flight of Tempests to intercept the V1's which had begun falling on south-east England, this flight operating mainly by night. Over the next two months Joseph was to establish himself as the top-scorer against these robots in Tempest, shooting down 52 and one shared by early August.

On 23 July he set the record for numbers destroyed, claiming seven in one night. Four nights later he pursued one at low level over West Malling airfield, closing to 100 feet in order to ensure he destroyed it before it fell on the base. His own aircraft was damaged in the resultant explosion which required a subsequent emergency landing.

On 16 August 1944 the Tempest flight moved to Manston to reform No.501 Squadron, of which Berry became commanding officer. The unit continued to hunt V1's, and he personally accounted for seven more, receiving a Bar to his DFC during September. During the night of 27/28 September, with the V1 threat mainly negated by the Allied advance in France, he led two Tempests from Bradwell Bay on 1 October on a 'Ranger' sortie over Holland, strafing trains and other ground targets of opportunity between Bad Zwischenhan in Northern Germany. While flying fast and low to their target; bursts of small arms fire struck Joseph Berry's Tempest rupturing the glycol tank. Although the Tempest was damaged Berry struggled to gain height prior to abandoning his aircraft before it crashed in flames, just over 2 miles to the East of Kibbelgaarn, the pilot failing to escape.

Joseph Berry was buried in a quiet plot in nearby Scheemda, on the simple wooden cross were written the words, 'Unknown RAF Pilot'. His overall total of V1's has been put at 60, but recorded claims appear to indicate 59½. He was awarded a second Bar to his DFC on the 20th January 1946, back dated to October 1944.

Below This unidentified Tempest V 'ZD-M' of No. 222 Sqn is the backdrop for some of the squadron's pilots somewhere on the wind- and snow-swept European mainland in the winter of 1944/45. Peter R. Arnold Collection

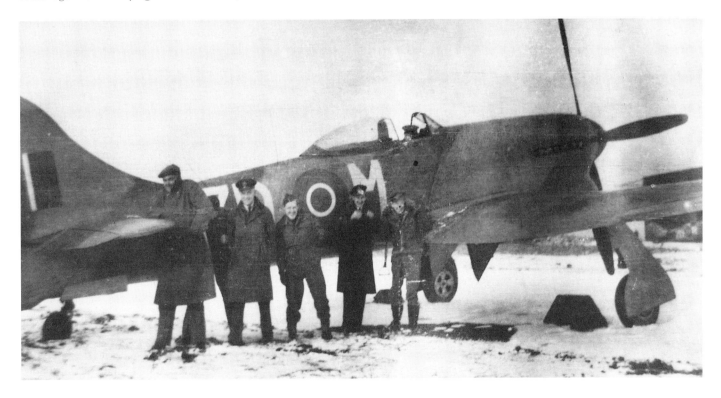

their greatest night coming in early July when one pilot managed to bring down four during one sortie. These missions were as – or more – dangerous than their daylight counterparts, at least one pilot being lost when debris from an exploding missile caused the aircraft's engine to fail, the subsequent crash killing the pilot. Others would be destroyed in foggy or inclement weather when flying close to the ground.

The Fighter Interception Unit boasted one particularly noteworthy pilot in its ranks, a certain Flt Lt Joe Berry, who successfully shot down seven 'Divers' during the night of 23/24 July, and a further four the following night. Two days later he shot down a 'V1' threatening the airbase at West Malling. Although successful, the Tempest was damaged, which required the pilot to make a force landing at the base he had just protected! At the end of July 1944, Flt Lt Berry was the top scorer in the No. 150 Wing league table, with 36.5 confirmed hits; he was closely followed by Wg Cdr Beamont with twenty-five.

Night Combat Patrols

With three squadrons fully operational with the Tempest, it was the turn of No. 501 (County of Gloucester) Sqn to re-equip with the big Hawker fighter;

sufficient numbers had by this time become available, as the pay dispute at Langley had been resolved. The date chosen for the unit to lose its battle-weary Spitfire VBs was 29 July, the location being Westhampnett. This would be a one day changeover, a most unusual occurrence, after which the squadron was stood down from active service to work up to operational status. The respite was gratefully received by the pilots, who had been in continuous action over the beach-heads since the invasion of Europe. Once the conversion and APC training had been completed, No. 501 Sqn was deployed to Manston on 2 August, with the first 'Diver' patrols being made three days later. Eight days later the aircraft of the Fighter Interception Unit amalgamated with No. 501 Sqn, this unit concentrating purely on night combat patrols.

Operations at night were flown by individual aircraft flying within a defined area, one boundary being that of the London Balloon Barrage, where anyone attempting to enter was warned off by red rockets fired by the Royal Observer Corps. The remaining boundaries were on land, and were defined by single searchlights flashing a single letter Morse code. No. 501 Sqn moved to Bradwell Bay on 22 September, this being followed by a transfer to Hunsdon on 3 March 1945, before disbandment on 20 April.

Over at Manston, a few weeks after moving from West Malling, No. 274 Sqn was also trading in its Spitfire IXs for Tempests. This was achieved on 11 August, although many of the personnel would come from No. 501 Sqn, as many of the original pilots of No. 274 Sqn were tour-expired. Both these units within No. 150 Wing made their presence felt almost immediately, racking up successes against the incoming flying bombs straightaway – although the need for Tempests to undertake these missions was slipping away.

Changes to the way the defence system had been set up were partly responsible for this. Rearrangement of the anti-aircraft belt on the coast to give a greater density of fire, improvements to the capability of the radar system, and the widespread use of proximity fuses in AAA ammunition, were all having a positive effect from the point of view of the Allies (though what the German rocket forces thought of all this is not known).

Other factors were also affecting the number of flying bombs being fired at Britain, namely the increased bombing attacks against the launch sites dotted around the Pas de Calais, the Allied armies managing to break out from Normandy, and the destruction of the German 7th Army at the Battle of Falaise. All these major events meant that by the end of August, there were few reports of incoming 'Divers', the final flying bomb being despatched by a pilot from No. 274 Sqn on 1 September 1944.

The overall score sheet was quite impressive, with 632 being officially claimed by the Newchurch Wing, although figures returned by individual units varied quite a bit from the official line: thus No. 3 Sqn would claim between 288 to 305.5 'Divers', No. 486 Sqn would declare their tally to be between 239.5 and 241, whilst No. 56 Sqn returned a total between 70.5 and 77. The smallest score, but no less meaningful, was that from the FIU, who declared their total to be 86.5 'Divers', of which all but two were destroyed during night engagements.

The Manston units also contributed over one hundred 'Divers' victories, with No. 247 Sqn destroying fifteen, and No. 501 Sqn being responsible for eighty-eight flying bombs. These victories were not without cost to the defending fighter force, as eight Tempests were lost while attacking 'V1s', either by explosion of the bomb itself, being hit by friendly AAA fire, or in

---

Squadron Leader David Fairbanks DFC**

Sqdn Ldr David C 'Foob' Fairbanks was born in the United States in 1923. After completing his schooling he ran away from home to Canada and tried to join the Royal Canadian Air Force. Initially unsuccessful he would finally succeed in February 1941 at Hamilton. After flying training he was posted to No.13 SFTS where he would stay for twelve months before pushing for, and getting, a posting to Britain. After advanced and operational training David Fairbanks was posted to No. 501 (County of Gloucester) Sqdn at Hawkinge flying Spitfire V's.

When No.501 Sqdn re-equipped with Tempest's in July 1944 Fairbanks would subsequently be posted to No.274 Sqdn which would also be equipped with Tempest's. Prior to the squadron moving to Europe David Fairbanks was engaged on combating the 'V1' menace destroying at least two. Over the following couple of months he would shoot down a further eleven and gain a half share in another.

Following on from his No.274 Sqdn posting Fairbanks would be posted to No.3 Sqdn , arriving in December 1944. His tenure with No.3 Sqdn would be short as on 9 February 1945 Fairbanks would return to No.274 Sqdn upon promotion to Squadron Leader. Within two days David Fairbanks would shoot down an aircraft initially identified as an Me 262 although this was later confirmed as an Arado Ar 234B.

On 28 February Fairbanks was airborne in command of six Tempest's indulging in a bit of ground attack and train busting after which he led his unit against a combined force of forty German fighters. During this melee David Fairbanks was shot down by a FW-190, captured and spent the rest of the war as a POW. While in captivity Fairbanks was awarded a bar to his DFC and a second one after the end of the war. Although his war was over David Fairbanks would remain as the second highest scoring Tempest pilot only being surpassed by Pierre Closterman.

After the war Fairbanks would be employed by Sperry Gyroscopes in Canada where he would fly Vampires and T-33's with the RCAF Auxiliary. A return to Britain followed where he would fly Meteors before returning to Canada to act as a test pilot for de Havilland Canada Ltd. David Fairbanks would die in 1975 of natural causes at the early age of 52.

Above **Photographed in 1943 whilst in its dispersal at Lydd, this early Typhoon IB of No. 175 Sqn undergoes ministrations from its fitters and armourers prior to a sortie over Europe.** RAF Museum

Right **Complete with yellow leading edges and black and white striping, this Typhoon 1B was on the strength of No. 257 Sqn at Tangmere when this portrait was taken.** RAF Museum

Right **Possibly one of the scruffiest Typhoons ever flown, this example has not had the rear fuselage modification, although it does sport an area of primer about the fuselage, the cannon fairings and most inconveniently the serial number.** RAF Museum

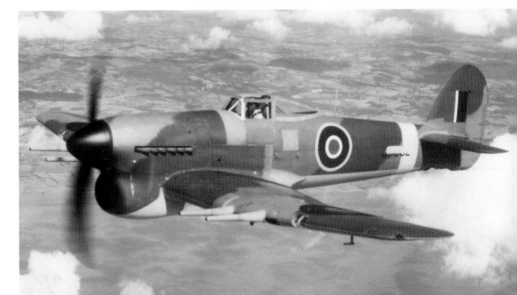

Left **Captured on film while undergoing a test flight, this Tempest V NV696 would only serve with No. 222 Sqn before being withdrawn on 10 November 1947 as 6474M. However, this view does reveal the upper surface camouflage applied to these machines.** RAF Museum

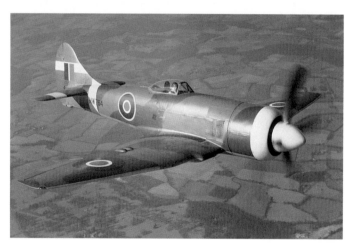

Above **Although it wears full camouflage, white identity stripes and yellow leading edges, Tempest II MW764 would never fly with the Royal Air Force, since it was sold to the Indian Air Force in May 1948.** RAF Museum

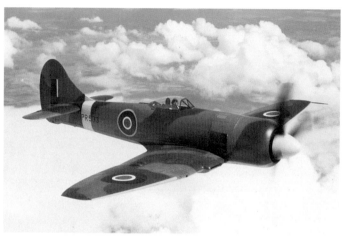

Above **In the post-war period the identification stripes were removed from many Tempest IIs. PR533 was operated by both the A&AEE and No. 33 Sqn until struck off charge in March 1951.** RAF Museum

Left **Resplendent in Korean War markings, Sea Fury FB.11 VR930 had been restored by British Aerospace at Brough before presentation to the Royal Navy Historic Flight (RNHF).** Damien Burke

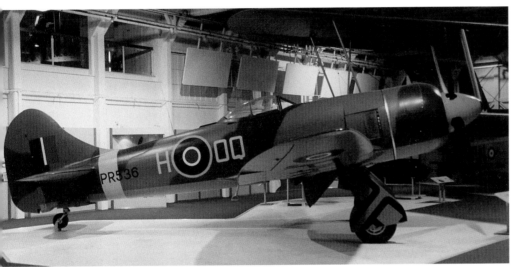

Above **Only one Tempest II, HA623, is preserved in India, in the IAF Museum at Palam AB near New Dehli; others are resident in Britain and America.** C. P. Russell Smith Collection

Left **Photographed in the RAF Museum is Tempest II PR536, which had served with Nos 20, 152 and 5 Sqns before being sold to the Indian Air Force as HA457 in September 1947. The redundant airframe was recovered from India with others in 1985. After restoration at Cardington, it was placed on display as 'OQ-H' of No. 5 Sqn.** Big Bird Aviation Collection

Left **One of the few Tempests still to retain its original markings is this MarkV EJ693. Resplendent in No. 486 Sqn marks, this particular aircraft had suffered an engine failure near airfield B.60 on 3 October 1944 while being piloted by Pilot Officer B. M. Hall. Deemed beyond economic recovery, the remains were eventually used for instructional purposes at the Delft Technical School. It was later recovered by the RAF Museum and placed in storage at Cardington, although the aircraft is now at Booker, reportedly under restoration for new owner Kermit Weeks.** Peter R. Arnold

Above **Having served with the Fleet Air Arm, this two-seater was then operated by DLB in the target-towing role before returning to Britain. This view reveals the location of the instructor's periscope and of the yellow training bands.** Nick Challoner

Right **Wearing the 109/GN coding of the Eglinton Station Flight, Sea Fury T.20 WG855 of the RNHF flies by the camera. It would remain with the flight until crashing in 1991. The remains of this aircraft were later sold to the USA, where it was last reported undergoing restoration to fly in 2000.**
Nick Challoner

Right **Sea Fury T.20 D-CATA is resplendent in its bright red overall scheme, applied by DLB to make the aircraft stand out and to deter over-enthusiastic gunners from shooting it down.** Thomas Genth

Above Target tug **D-CATA** photographed at a later date when the registration had been moved to the fin. The period fuel bowser is worthy of note for the modelling fraternity. Thomas Genth

Left Although this aircraft is an authentic Sea Fury **FB.11, VX653/G-BUCM**, it wears proper Iraqi Air Force markings more suited to the desert than temperate climes. Nick Challoner

Below Captured just after take-off, this Sea Fury, in authentic Iraqi Air Force markings, is retracting its main undercarriage units; the tailwheel will join the cycle soon after. Nick Challoner

Right **This undersurface view of the Iraqi-marked Sea Fury reveals the light blue under-surfaces and the locations of the markings. This machine is currently undergoing rebuilding at Duxford.** Nick Challoner

Right **Now reported as based in South Africa as N103FD, this ISS Fury is wearing the final colour scheme associated with the Sea Fury in Royal Netherlands Navy service. This particular machine was originally imported into Britain as G-BTTA by the Old Flying Machine Company.** Big Bird Aviation Collection

Below **This Sea Fury has worn a variety of markings in its time, but fortunately they all appear to have been authentic. In this view is WH588/G-EEMV, marked as 114-NW of No. 724 Sqn based at Nowra during 1961–62.** Big Bird Aviation Collection

Above **Although traces of its Sea Fury ancestry are still visible – it was VX368 in another life – this Sanders conversion, named 'Dreadnought', first appeared at Reno in 1983 as N20SF. It would win the Unlimited Gold race in September 1994 with Neil Anderson at the controls.** Nicholas A. Veronico

Right **Sporting Royal Canadian Navy markings, TG114 was being piloted by Dennis Sanders in 1999, during which 'Argonaut' came third in the Unlimited Silver race.** Nicholas A. Veronico

Below **One of the most radical Sea Fury conversions involved 'Critical Mass', which had started life as a T.20 WE820. Now registered as N85SF and owned by Tom Dwells, this machine took part in the Unlimited Gold race in September 1996.** Nicholas A. Veronico

Above Caught banking the angle round the pylons is Bill Rheinschild's No. 74 'Bad Attitude', which achieved fifth place in the Unlimited Silver race during September 1999. Nicholas A. Veronico

Left Once a Fury ISS of the Iraqi Air Force, this machine is now registered to Howard Pardue as N666HP; it is pictured at Reno in 1995. Nicholas A. Veronico

Below In the years prior to its importation into Britain, Sea Fury FB.11 WH857 was registered to Lloyd Hamilton as N260X. During this period it was bedecked in RAN marks, and achieved a fifth placing in the 1996 Unlimited Gold race. Nicholas A. Veronico

collisions with other attacking aircraft. As well as outright losses, the Tempest squadrons lost another twenty-three due to accidents or engine failure.

Flying Bomb Combat Intensifies

Although the launch bases on the Pas de Calais had been effectively stopped, the German forces had turned to other means by which to launch the 'flying bombs'. One of the most successful was the employment of the modified venerable Heinkel He 111H bomber, which had a pylon fitted under the starboard wing so that it could act as a launch aircraft for the 'V1'. The mission profile for these attacks would place the carrier aircraft over the North Sea where the launch would be initiated.

To counteract this threat, No. 501 Sqn remained on 'Diver' patrols, for which purpose it departed from Hunsdon to Bradwell Bay, arriving there in September 1944. Although there were a certain amount of Luftwaffe flying bomb sorties, they were not as numerous as those against the ground-based versions. To take up the slack, No. 501 Sqn took part in offensive sorties over Europe, during which they lost their commanding officer, Sqn Ldr Berry, on 1 October.

The last claims for flying bomb destruction made in 1944 were for four shot down over the night of 17/18 December. The final 'Diver' claim would be made by No. 501 Sqn on 27 March. On 1 April the war against the flying bomb menace was declared officially closed, and the squadron was redeployed to daylight attack missions. However, there was a lack of trade for this unit, and No. 501 Sqn was disbanded on 20 April 1945.

On 29 August 1944 yet another Spitfire IX unit, No. 80 Sqn, had traded in its Supermarine machines for the Hawker Tempest; this changeover was completed by 6 September, the squadron then moving to Manston to begin 'Diver' missions. As this particular phase of the war was coming to a close, the 'Diver' patrols were suspended, and the Newchurch Wing changed from ADGB-sponsored sorties of chasing flying bombs, to that of taking the war to Europe. In their first mission, No. 150 Wing went to Emden for a show of force and to tempt the Luftwaffe into the air; while in the next

Above Some of the bases occupied by the advancing Tempest squadrons were somewhat battered in nature, as is evident in this view of two No. 3 Sqn Tempests at Volkel. Of note is the heating truck pumping hot air into the radiator of the nearest aircraft. This was much needed in the winter, as the Sabre could be very temperamental in the cold. RAF Museum Collection

sortie four days later, aircraft from Newchurch strafed their counterparts on the ground at the Netherlands base at Leeuwarden, where two Messerschmitts were destroyed.

Tempest in Ground-Attack Role

With the menace of the 'V1' flying bomb no longer a threat, and the Luftwaffe virtually contained within the borders of Germany, it was time for the Tempest to practise the other part of its repertoire, that of ground attack. Its predecessor the Typhoon had carved – and would continue to carve – a niche in the combat history of the Royal Air Force, even if it did have a slightly dodgy engine and a tendency for the tail end to come adrift at inopportune moments. The Tempest had already visited Europe at the beginning . of September 1944, and they would return on the tenth of that month, this time the fighters of No. 80 Sqn accompanying a force of 9th AF Douglas B-26 Invaders to attack the airfield at Leeuwarden.

Bomber escort duties were not the only missions assigned to the Tempest

squadrons: they were also tasked to emulate the Typhoons in the ground-strafing role. The hardest mission assigned to the Manston-based Tempest units would occur on the 17 September in support of Operation *Market Garden*. Their task was the suppression of the flak defence units in the vicinity of the Arnhem, Nijmegen and Grave bridges, as well as those at Wallensee, Schowen and on the Scheldt estuary. Although the strafing attacks were successful, the attacking Tempests would return to base with three fewer aircraft than they left with.

There were various changes afoot for the Tempest squadrons: on 19/20 September, Nos 80 and 274 Sqns decamped to Coltishall, while Nos 3 and 56 Sqns would move to Matlask over the next two days. Over the following week the Tempest squadrons continued to operate in a kind of limbo, in that they were still assigned to ADGB, although their mission profiles were purely in support of the 2nd TAF operations. This position was rationalized at the end of the month when Nos 3 and 56 Sqns departed the shores of Britain for airfield B.60/Grimbergen, near Brussels; here they would come under the control of No. 122 Wing that had previously operated the North American Mustang III.

One final unit would arrive later at B.60: No. 486 Sqn with its Tempests, which brought the wing up to full strength.

On 29 September the aircraft of No. 150 Wing were airborne in support of the ground forces engaged in Operation *Market Garden*. During this engagement only one Tempest would be lost to flak, while on the profit side the fighters would shoot down four Fw 190s and damage another from a large force that had been active over the battleground. Although Operation *Market Garden* did not prove to be as successful as had been hoped, this did not stop the Allied forces pushing forwards.

As the German forces retreated, it was imperative that air support be available for the Allied armies, therefore the Tempest wings would move again to new bases. On 1 October 1944, No. 122 Wing – consisting of Nos 3, 56 and 486 Sqns – moved from Belgium to B.80/Volkel in the Netherlands. Also moving to Holland was No. 125 Wing that had acquired Nos 80 and 274 Sqns from No. 122 Wing, and would end up at Airfield B.82 at Grave. Their sojourn at Grave was to last only a week, as the two Tempest squadrons joined up with their compatriots at Volkel to bring the wing back up to its full strength of five squadrons. While they were settling into their new quarters they were visited by a flight of Messerschmitt Me 262 fighter bombers, who dropped bombs on the airfield.

Above **Swirling clouds of dust, behind them a pair of Tempests allocated to No. 274 Sqn scramble down the PSP runway at B.91 Kluis in April 1945.** RAF Museum Collection

Tempest as Bomber Escort

Bomber escort was another role given over to the Tempest squadrons, as those assigned to No. 122 Wing would find out. On 11 September 1944, three of the units from the wing – Nos 3, 56 and 486 Sqns – were assigned to escort a mixed force of Halifax and Lancaster bombers, totalling some 340 aircraft, to attack the oil storage facility at Gelsenkirchen in the Ruhr. Led by Wg Cdr R. P. Beamont, the thirty-six aircraft, complete with external drop tanks, lined up at Newchurch to depart. The Tempests would be operating at maximum range, so any entanglement with enemy fighters, or fuel tanks damaged by flak, and the fighters would be struggling to get home. Undaunted the fighters took off, and climbed up to their operating height of 18,000ft (5,500m).

Entering Germany and in sight of the Rhine, the drop tanks were jettisoned and the Tempests were cleared for any combat. Right on time, the bomber force attacked the Gelenkirchen facility, advancing through an ascending wall of flak. Although the bombers suffered losses, the Tempests departed unscathed, and landed back at base after a flight that had covered 600 miles (960km) and lasted 2hr 10min, with some of the fighters landing virtually on fumes.

Tempest in the Air Superiority Role

While the appearance of the German jet fighters might have been the precursor of things to come, their visitation was in fact a rarity, as Luftwaffe interference with air operations was kept to a minimum by superior Allied forces. This meant that the Tempests had a fairly easy life in the air superiority role, which would allow them to attack targets of opportunity – but only with their cannons, as the underwing weapons already cleared for their usage would not in fact become available to them until the closing months of the war, and meanwhile the Typhoon force was taking them all. As the Tempest was a fast and stable gun platform, it spent much of its time in combat against the German fighters; it would score numerous victories against the defending Fw 190s, although there were still losses being suffered as aircraft were brought down by flak. German jet fighters were also putting in appearances, being seen on numerous occasions during the closing months of 1944; however, as all the Allied fighter pilots would find out, catching the Me 262s was a different matter entirely. While the American fighter pilots would place their claims for aircraft shot down while taking off and landing, their Tempest counterparts decided to try it a much harder way.

Their first success was achieved on 13 October when two patrolling Tempests intercepted an Me 262 in the area of Grave. Opening fire in the chase, a lucky burst from one of the Tempests hit the jet fighter, which blew up in the most spectacular fashion. This would be the last confirmed victory for a while, although there were 'damaged' claims put in over other encounters throughout November.

Further successes were scored against the Me 262 fighters: one was claimed on 19 November whilst taking off from Rheine, and seven days later No. 3 Sqn destroyed another two on the same airfield during a ground-strafing run; furthermore the month would end on a high note when a Ju 188 and a Heinkel He 219 were shot down. But even while the Tempest squadrons were scoring successes, they were still losing aircraft to engine failures, eight going down in the last two months of 1944. Flak and Luftwaffe fighters would eventually bring the total of losses up to twenty-one aircraft and ten pilots.

Of the five units that made up No. 122 Wing, No. 56 Sqn was leading the field: not only did they manage to shoot down the more conventional fighters such as Bf 109s and Fw 190s, they were also successful against Me 262s, one being claimed on 11 December by Flt Sgt Jackson. Further combat success would come the way of all five fighter squadrons that made up No. 122 Wing, principally during the attempted German break-out from the Ardennes, later known as the 'Battle of the Bulge'. This would be the final decisive push by the German forces, both land and air forces exerting maximum pressure against the Allies. On their side was the weather, which remained inclement for much of the battle. However, it cleared on 17 December, which allowed the 2nd TAF to launch every fighter that could fly to provide much needed support for the struggling army units.

During this brief respite, the pilots of No. 274 Sqn shot down three Bf 109s, while No. 3 Sqn's pilots would claim another. The top scorers, No. 56 Sqn, were also gaining more victories, as they claimed five Messerschmitts and an He 219 'Uhu'. On a later patrol, Me 262s were encountered again, one being brought down by the commander of No. 122 Wing, Wg Cdr Wray. As always, these successes

were countered by losses, at least two aircraft being the victims of flak; however, these patrols would cease temporarily as the weather clamped down again. This allowed the German army to push forwards against the forces before them, until the Allies made a determined stand at Bastogne, where the push would finally be brought to a standstill.

The weather kept the aircraft of the 2nd TAF on the ground for the next five days, but as soon as possible the Tempests of Nos 3 and 274 Sqns were airborne again; on their first patrol they encountered a flight of Bf 109s, one of which was successfully despatched. Another two German fighters were shot down when they were spotted attacking a pair of Typhoons, both being claimed by No. 274 Sqn.

Thus both Christmas Eve and Christmas Day were ruined by the Luftwaffe, but they paid for their impudence in the loss of an Arado Ar 234 jet bomber and another Me 262. Peace reigned over Boxing Day, however hostilities resumed on 27 December; but again, the Luftwaffe paid dearly, losing fourteen fighters for the loss of one Tempest.

Above **Tempest VI NX126 was on the inventory of No. 249 Sqn based at Habbaniya when this photo was taken. The removal of many wartime restrictions meant that the squadrons could apply a bit of colour to their aircraft: thus the letters are red outlined in white, and the squadron's badge is on the fin. This aircraft would be written off in an accident in October 1949 at Deversoir.** Big Bird Aviation Collection

Below **Tempest VI NX237 was allocated to No. 8 Sqn at Khormaksar; here it is being rearmed prior to its next sortie. It would remain in service until struck off charge on 15 May 1951.** C. P. Russell Smith Collection

Tempest Combat Fortunes during 1945

January–February 1945

At the beginning of 1945 the Luftwaffe launched another attack on the Allied airfield in Europe under the codename Operation *Bodenplatte*. It began at dawn and caught everybody unprepared, although the Tempest base at Volkel seemed not to be on the roster; however, their Typhoon counterparts would bear the brunt of the offensive. To counteract this incursion the Tempests already on patrol over Hanover were hurriedly recalled, whilst others were quickly launched from Volkel. The Tempests from No. 486 Sqn would intercept the German intruders and shoot down five Fw 190s near Helmond. Further victories against the Luftwaffe would be scored by pilots from Nos 3, 56 and 80 Sqns, who would claim another five fighters.

The following few days would be quiet as the weather closed in again, which allowed both sides to replace their losses. But on 14 January the air war resumed again, with pilots from No. 122 Wing claiming another six fighters. Then nine days later the Tempests accumulated an impressive score of successes, starting early in the day with Nos 80 and 274 Sqns claiming four fighters near Gutersloh; this was followed by the pilots from No. 3 Sqn claiming four Fw 190s destroyed, and two more damaged. No 80 Sqn would feature

on the score sheet later that day, when two Messerschmitts were shot down, and another put forward as damaged. In the final engagement of that day, pilots from Nos 56 and 486 Sqns shot down six of the opposition near Rheine.

Converting to Tempest Units

As the situation over Europe changed from one of defence to attack, so the composition of the 2nd TAF itself changed, as further Tempest units formed. The first of these were two former Spitfire IX squadrons, Nos 33 and 222, who had returned to Predannack in Cornwall on 15 December 1944 where they began the Tempest conversion process. Once this was completed, both units received APC training before being sent over to Europe: they landed at airfield B.77 at Gilze-Rijen on 20 and 21 January.

Their arrival was the signal for the two remaining Spitfire IX units at the same base, Nos 349 (Belgian) and 485 (New Zealand) Sqns, to return to Britain for the same conversion process. Their base for this would also be Predannack, where they arrived on 24 February 1945. No. 349 Sqn would begin its conversion using a mix of Tempests and a few Typhoons; however, the war was progressing at such a pace that the conversion process was eventually abandoned. No. 485 Sqn was slightly luckier in that it managed to at least receive its Tempests, which it managed to hang on to for a couple of weeks, before re-equipping

with Typhoons. However, the whole conversion process was abandoned in mid-April, as the requirement for further Tempest squadrons had receded.

Operation Clarion – and Mistaken Identity

Returning to the war over Europe, No. 122 Wing had received reinforcement on 5 December 1944, when No. 41 Sqn had joined the wing with its Griffon-powered Spitfire XIVs. There was no intention that this unit would change its equipment, as its role would be that of high-level defensive cover over the following weeks, although this would be revised in September 1945 when Tempest Vs were received.

On 21 February, 2nd TAF would begin its part in Operation *Clarion*, whose premise was to totally wipe out all forms of German transportation prior to the 21st Army Group crossing the Rhine. For the Tempest units this meant strafing ground targets, and No. 274 Sqn was quickly into the fray, attacking ground targets of opportunity, plus an unlucky Ju 88.

The next day *Clarion* wound up to full speed, with No. 3 Sqn straight into the action over the Nienburg Plain. However, it was not the enemy they encountered, it was the 9th Air Force and its Mustangs, who mistook the British fighters for Fw 190s. Fortunately the Tempests outflew the Americans and continued with their mission. When the squadron had reached its target area close by Steinhuder Lake, they encountered a single B-24 Liberator, which some of the Tempests would escort over Allied lines to safety, whilst their comrades carried out their designated

Below Complete with a full load of rockets and rails, this is Tempest II, PR530, of No. 5 Sqn, at Poona in June 1946. This is one of the aircraft handed over to the Pakistani Air Force in September 1947.
RAF Museum Collection

Right **Airborne on a training sortie from Odiham is this Tempest II, MW798, of No. 54 Sqn. The aircraft's tenure with this unit was short, as the squadron re-equipped with Vampire fighters in October 1946.** RAF Museum Collection

strafing attacks. Having pulled clear of the target, the flight of Tempests encountered a pair of Messerschmitts near Rheine, one of which was shot down and another damaged. However, this attack had been seen by ten Fw 190s, who attacked the re-forming Tempests, successfully shooting one of them down. But the Luftwaffe fighters did not get away Scot free, as aircraft from No. 56 Sqn joined in the mêlée, successfully shooting one of the German fighters down, and chasing the others away.

Having cleared the Luftwaffe away, the Tempests were again bothered by P-51 Mustangs of the 9th AF: their aircraft recognition was obviously disastrously lax, as yet again the British fighters were attacked by them. Unfortunately they succeeded in shooting down the Tempest piloted by Flt Lt Green, who was nursing his flak-damaged aircraft towards base; tragically he was killed. And on yet another occasion the Americans were guilty of mistaken identity: this time the aircraft were P-47 Thunderbolts, also of the 9th AF, who attacked the Tempests of No. 486 Sqn who had been on an interception course towards a pair of marauding Fw 190s. Fortunately the P-47 pilots were bad enough marksmen, and only one Tempest was damaged. By now all the Tempest units had been warned to keep a good lookout for the Luftwaffe *and* the fighters of the USAAF. With this in mind, the Tempest squadrons continued their search for the Luftwaffe, a task in which they would score more successes.

No. 274 Sqn started this roll of success by shooting down a pair of Fw 190D-9s near Rheine; two days later a single Fw 190

was despatched, and this was quickly followed by a pair of Bf 109s by No. 486 Sqn near Bramsche. Later that day No. 274 Sqn were back in the vicinity of Rheine, where they would claim one damaged Me-262 and the despatch of a Junkers Ju 88, whilst another variant, a Ju 188, was destroyed on the ground. On the following day the Tempests were airborne again, with aircraft from Nos 33, 56 and 222 Sqns successfully shooting down four Bf 109s from a total of fifteen – although in this exchange, one Tempest was shot down and another was damaged.

Combat Fortunes in March

The following month brought a change of mission emphasis from HQ 2nd TAF, who issued orders that ground attacks were to be strongly discouraged, while flights into German airspace were to be made in strengths of sixteen aircraft or more, as the Luftwaffe was sending up intercepting fighters in greater numbers. However, pilots could never resist an easy target, so very often the ground attack rule was quietly forgotten; but inevitably this resulted in greater losses, a total of twenty-three by the end of March, many to the deadly accurate flak that the Germans were throwing up. Nevertheless, March had been a good month for the Tempest squadrons: they had brought down an Arado Ar 234B and damaged another, and shortly after had swiftly despatched four Messerschmitts that had tried to bounce the British fighters.

Below **Tempest VI NX139 undergoing low-power engine runs; it would be used by both Nos 6 and 249 Sqns before being sold to the MoS in May 1951.** C. P. Russell Smith Collection

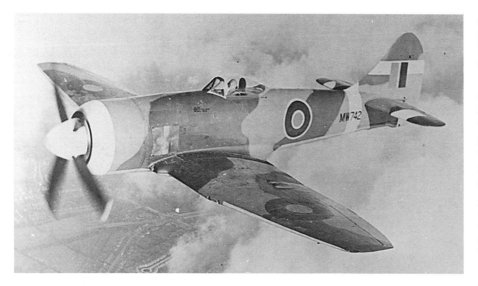

Above **Never delivered to the Royal Air Force, this Tempest II, MW742, was eventually delivered to the Indian Air Force in May 1948.** Big Bird Aviation Collection

On 4 March No. 122 Wings aircraft were on patrol in the Rheine area when they encountered a flight of four Fw 190Ds; they managed to shoot them down, though the actual combat was reported as being exceptionally difficult. Soon after, changes were made to the make-up of the Tempest wings: on 17 March No. 274 Sqn was transferred from No. 122 Wing to No. 133 Wing at B.77 Gilze-Rijen to bring them up to a fairly equalized strength.

Seven days later, the 21st Army Group began its crossing of the Rhine, with an aerial umbrella provided by the 2nd TAF. During this manoeuvre, pilots from No. 222 Sqn shot down four enemy fighters, while No. 80 Sqn despatched another one. No. 222 Sqn was on the score sheet later that day when they shot down three out of eleven Fw 190s. On the down side, the Tempests lost two aircraft to the ubiquitous flak.

Combat Fortunes in April

April 1945 was the final complete month of the war, and during this period the Tempest wings scored their greatest successes – although they would do it without the services of No. 3 Sqn, who returned to Britain to undertake an APC course at Warmwell. Within the first week of the month the Luftwaffe lost twelve aircraft, while the Tempest losses stood at four, three claimed by the Luftwaffe and one to flak.

In this month the Tempest wings moved to new airfields, following the ground forces as they advanced. No. 135 Wing, consisting of 33, 222 and 274 Sqns, decamped to airfield B.91 at Kluis near Nijmegen, arriving on 7 April. Four days later No. 122 Wing also moved forwards, only this time they landed in Germany, on the airfield complex B.112 and B.118 at Hopsten. Six days later the wing was back up to full strength again, as No. 3 Sqn had returned from its APC at Warmwell. Even though moving bases had caused some disruption, the Tempest squadrons had continued their combat patrols, and it was during one of these sorties that aircraft from No. 222 Sqn attacked the Luftwaffe airfield at Fassberg, strafing the jet fighters on the ground, plus one taking off, which crashed soon afterwards.

On 16 April pilots from No. 486 Sqn became entangled with a flight of Fw 190s, two of which were shot down, while another was claimed by a pilot from No. 80 Sqn; however, from these engagements two of the Tempests failed to return, including the leader of No. 122 Wing, Wg Cdr Brooker. Further victories were claimed by No. 80 Sqn, who brought down one Fw 190D, and marked up another as damaged; on the down side, one Tempest was lost in the exchange. No. 135 Wing would also be busy during this period, with aircraft from Nos 222 and 274 Sqns claiming a single Fw 190 and a pair of Do 217s. No. 135 Wing would move bases soon after this, when they flew to Germany to

take up residence at airfield B.109 at Quackenbruck. From here they would begin a series of offensive sweeps against the airfields in the Hamburg area.

As the amount of territory available to the German forces was constantly shrinking, the number of Luftwaffe fighters seen was increasing, both on the air and on the ground. This increase in available targets would result in the Tempest units notching up an increasing number of victories against their Luftwaffe opponents. On 20 April, two Fw 190s were shot down near Hamburg, whilst No. 486 Sqn brought down a Messerschmitt and a Focke-Wulf respectively; on the down side the 2nd TAF lost a Tempest.

Further sorties would be launched that week against the remaining German airfields, with No. 135 Wing leading the advance. To the fore were the pilots of No. 33 Sqn who, during an attack on airfields near Kiel, destroyed six German aircraft on the ground and damaged as many more. On 24 April, aircraft from all the wings' squadrons returned to the Kiel area to resume their attacks. Sweeping low across Lake Ratzenburg, the Tempests destroyed Arado Ar 196 floatplanes moored on the water. Other aircraft from the wing hit the airfield at Skydstrup in Denmark, where two enemy aircraft were destroyed and another thirteen were seriously damaged. No. 274 Sqn also joined in the fun, attacking Flensberg where four aircraft were totally destroyed and another eleven were damaged. But even though the German state was on the verge of collapse, their flak weapons were still having a devastating effect, with three Tempests shot down.

No. 122 Wing followed the rest of the Tempest force into Germany, its squadrons arriving at airfield B.52 at Fassberg on 26 April. Once the disruption of the move was over, the Tempests resumed operations, the first victory falling to the guns of No. 486 Sqn, who despatched a Junkers Ju 52. The next day, 29 April, the squadron was on patrol over Lauenburg, home of Schlachtgeschwader 151 that had recently converted from being a training establishment to being a front-line fighter unit to defend against the advancing Russians. As the Tempests approached, aircraft from the airfield rose up to meet them – which was a fatal mistake, as three Messer-schmidts and three Fw 190s were shot down in quick succession, while others were claimed as damaged. And in a further raid by the same squadron later in the day, another three Fw 190s were quickly despatched from a flight of ten. A third and final sweep that day would see the squadron's pilots claim another Fw 190. In retaliation, the German fighters claimed just one Tempest, the pilot escaping.

On 30 April the 21st Army Group crossed the River Elbe with an air umbrella provided by the aircraft of 2nd TAF. Nos 3 and 56 Sqns claimed some further enemy aircraft shot down for the month, bringing the final total for enemy aircraft destroyed to sixty-one confirmed.

Combat Fortunes in May

In the beginning of May 1945 the aircraft of No. 122 Wing patrolled over the northern coastal airfields of Germany in order to keep the fighters from interfering with the onward advance of the Allied armies, and to stop them escaping to Scandinavia. On this day, three German aircraft were shot down near Schwerin, while on 2 May another nine Luftwaffe aircraft were destroyed, seven being claimed by No. 56 Sqn. In return, the German Anti-Aircraft Force claimed at least one Tempest.

By this time aviation fuel shortages were widespread across the remaining territory held by the Germans, and in the face of this, much of the Luftwaffe was grounded; thus the opportunities for combat victories in the air were almost non-existent. However, there were still victories to be had, as a few communications aircraft were still able to fly: thus Fiesler Fi 156 Storch light aircraft would become prime targets, both in the air and on the ground. The occasional spotter plane being used in the communications role was also shot down, such as an Fw 44 Weihe destroyed by a pilot from No. 486 Sqn. Occasionally one of the few remaining fighters that was serviceable, and had fuel and ammunition, was encountered: thus on 4 May, one of the few Fw 190s still able to fly was shot down by a pilot from No. 56 Sqn.

No. 3 Sqn was also active in the air, and carried out a fighter sweep on 3 May in the area of Schleswig, where a pair of Fi 156 Storches were shot down, as was a lone Fw 44. In the course of further sorties by the same unit, in the same region, eleven more aircraft were destroyed on the ground, with fourteen claimed as damaged; the squadron itself lost one Tempest. In these last few days of the German Reich, the Tempest squadrons were claiming their final combat victories: thus No. 274 Sqn shot down a lone Do 217 bomber near Kiel, No. 56 Sqn destroyed a fleeing Fw 190, while No. 486 Sqn shot down a pair of Junkers Ju 88s flying at high speed and low level in the Tegel airfield area.

On 4 May, No. 486 Sqn claimed a Fiesler Storch on the ground, while later in the day another three were destroyed. Overall, a generous mix of aircraft was placed on the score sheet, these comprising four Dornier Do 24s, a Ju 52, a Bf 110, and a single Bv 138 flying boat.

In Conclusion

While the Tempest units were still planning and carrying out operations, negotiations were ongoing concerning the total surrender of the German forces. Even so, on this final day of hostilities, No. 3 Sqn would actually use the Tempest in the fighter-bomber role against an airfield near Kiel. Also operational in that area, No. 222 Sqn claimed four destroyed and twelve damaged aircraft. This would be the final combat sortie flown by any unit of No. 84 Group.

On 5 May, all attack sorties were cancelled, which gave the Tempest squadrons a short period of rest – although No. 3 Sqn did fly a few aircraft to provide escorts for Dakotas transporting troops and supplies to assist in the final liberation of Denmark. Two days later the war was declared officially over. Throughout this phase the Typhoons and Tempests of 2nd TAF had carried the war successfully to the Germans.

Scores Table for Tempest Pilots

The appearance of the Tempest in RAF service gave the squadrons a more manoeuvrable heavy hitting fighter that was more than capable of taking on the Luftwaffe and the 'V1' flying bomb, as the high scores table shows.

Overall the Tempests would be credited with 240 confirmed destroyed or probable aircraft victories, these being accrued between June 1944 to May 1945.

Pilot	Nationality	Unit(s)	Victories	Shared	On Ground	Probables
Sqn/Ldr D. C. Fairbanks DFC**	American	Nos 3, 274 Sqns	11 or 12	0	1	0
Sqn/Ldr W. E. Schrader DFC*	New Zealander	No.486 Sqn	9	1(0.5)	2	0
Flt Lt J. J. Payton DFC	British	No.56 Sqn	6	0	0	1
Wg/Cdr E. D. Mackie DSO DFC*	New Zealander	Nos 274, 80 Sqns No.122 Wing	5	1(0.5)	3	0
Fg/Off D. E. Ness DFC	Canada	No.56 Sqn	5	1(0.5)	0	0
Sqdn/Ldr CL Sheddan DFC	New Zealander	No.486 Sqn	4	3(0.5 ea)	0	0
Flt/Lt P. H. Closterman DFC*	French	Nos.274, 56, 3 Sqn	4	0	7	0
Fg/Off A. R. Evans DFC	New Zealander	No.486 Sqn	4	0	0	1
Fg/Off J. Garland DFC	British	No.80 Sqn	4		0	0
Fg/Off V. L. Turner DFC	Australian	No.56 Sqn	4	0	0	0
Flt/Lt A. R. Moore DFC*	British	Nos 3, 56 Sqns	3	1(0.5)	0	0.5

CHAPTER NINE

Tempest After the War

Even though hostilities ceased in Europe in May 1945, it would be a few months before any radical changes were made to the Tempest fleet; the Typhoon fleet, on the other hand, had all but disappeared by the end of the war. However, the requirement for further Tempest Vs had ceased at war's end, and this left the Royal Air Force with eight squadrons with the type, of which seven were on the strength of 2nd TAF, with the remaining unit being allocated to the ADGB. Plans to convert two further squadrons, Nos 349 and 485, at Predannack in Cornwall had eventually been cancelled after a start had been made using spare Typhoon FR.1Bs borrowed from the general support units. Both squadrons would quickly re-equip with Spitfires and rejoin the 2nd TAF to continue combat operations over Europe, although their total participation in this phase would be measured in weeks.

The Final Phase of the War

As the test flights involving the Bristol Centaurus-powered Tempest II prototype had proved successful – even though problems with the mounting of the engine to the firewall had taken some time to resolve – production contracts were soon forthcoming for Hawker's to start the construction of aircraft for RAF service. First examples of the Hawker Tempest II had begun to roll off the production lines during October 1944, although aircraft for service use did not arrive at maintenance units for pre-release preparations until March 1945, as many had been placed in store awaiting the delivery of major components, such as the power-plant.

When the Tempest IIs finally arrived at their designated maintenance units, they were immediately allocated for the emergent 'Tiger Force' that was being formed to take the war to the Japanese in the Far East. Whilst the Tempest had been chosen as the fighter component, the bomber element was initially the Avro Lancaster B.VII, although development of the enlarged Lancaster as the Lincoln B.1 was being accelerated so that it could be the primary strike weapon.

The fighter part of 'Tiger Force' began forming at Chilbolton in August 1945 under the command of none other than

Below **Hawker Tempest VI NX288 would be operated by the makers and the A&AEE, before being sold to the MoS in June 1953. Of note is the extended pitot head fitted to the port wing.** C. P. Russell Smith Collection

Wing Commander R. P. Beamont, who had recently returned to Britain after his short period of captivity. The first unit to begin equipping with the Hawker Tempest II was No. 183 Sqn; it had originally been a Typhoon unit, although it had been operating the Spitfire IX for a few months while waiting for the new version of the Tempest. On 20 August 1945, one of the last Typhoon-equipped units, No. 247 Sqn, returned home from B.158/ Lubeck in Germany to trade in its older Hawker aircraft for the newer Tempest, the first of which arrived later that month, with the whole process being completed by mid September.

But the creation of 'Tiger Force' was brought to an abrupt halt with the dropping of the atomic bombs over Hiroshima and Nagasaki, a cataclysm that brought this final phase of the war to an end. This meant that the requirement for further Tempest squadrons within Britain was shelved, although the two squadrons already equipped continued to operate the type over the following few months. But changes took place even within these units when No. 183 Sqn was renumbered as No. 54 Sqn, and re-equipped with de Havilland Vampire jet fighters, as would its companion No. 247 Sqn, both trading in their piston fighters in October and March 1946 respectively. Both units would eventually transfer from Chilbolton to Odiham, which was more suited to the operation of jet aircraft.

Just prior to its disbandment No. 54 Sqn had spent a short time converting some pilots to the Centaurus version of the Tempest prior to their deployment to the Middle East; but here, ironically, they would find themselves at the controls of the Sabre-powered version of the fighter.

This was the last time there was a permanent Tempest presence in Britain, as bases overseas would henceforth be their remit.

The Tempest in Germany

To indicate the altered status of the RAF in Germany, the 2nd TAF was renamed the 'British Air Force of Occupation'. One of the primary fighters allocated to this force was the Tempest, whose role would gradually change from keeping a watchful eye on the Germans and any possible resistance, to that of safeguarding the

Above **Normally the commanding officer's personal machine, Tempest II PR736 'EG-M' was being piloted by Flying Officer D. W. Baldock when this portrait was taken. Prominent are the Mark III rocket rails.**
Michael Baldock

West from its erstwhile allies in the east, the Russians. The Tempest wings still resident in Germany included No. 122 Wing at Fassberg and No. 135 Wing at Quackenbruck, although the squadrons themselves were undergoing some changes. No. 80 Sqn had returned to Fassberg from the Warmwell APC just in time to enjoy the benefits of VE Day in May, while No. 486 Sqn had departed to Celle on detachment before taking up a permanent posting to Kastrup in Denmark, where the other three squadrons would end up in June 1945.

The squadrons of the other wing were also undergoing changes, as exemplified by the departure of No. 222 Sqn to Molesworth on 23 October 1945 to convert to the Gloster Meteor F.3. Once converted, the squadron became part of Fighter Command, which had replaced the Air Defence of Great Britain organization. The two remaining squadrons, Nos 33 and 274 Sqns, would move to B.155/Dedelstorf on 19 August and 20 June 1945 respectively, although the tenure of No. 274 Sqn at its new base was short, as it soon departed to Warmwell for an APC refresher. As this was a period of rationalization within the Royal Air Force, many high-numbered squadrons would find their number plate changing to a lower one; this was the case that affected No. 274 Sqn, which was renumbered No. 174 Sqn on 7 September 1945 during its time at Warmwell. The previous holder of the number plate had originally been a Typhoon combat squadron.

Those units that had been resident in Denmark would eventually return to Germany to various bases, and the original mobile wing structure dispensed with, since there was now no longer any need for it. At the beginning of 1946 there was further evidence of an air force winding down from its earlier wartime strength when No. 486 Sqn finally said goodbye to Europe, parked some of its aircraft at Dunsfold in Surrey, and then departed for home, most of the squadron having gone some three months earlier.

Those aircraft that remained in Germany were passed on to No. 41 Sqn that was based at the time at Lubeck: they would lose their fairly new Spitfire XIVs for a batch of Hawker Tempests that had obviously seen better days. Also at Lubeck was No. 80 Sqn, both units constituting No. 124 Wing for the short time remaining, before it disbanded. Over at Dedelstorf, No. 135 Wing was also the short-term parent for Nos 33 and 174 Sqns, who were joined by Nos 3 and 56 Sqns, to bring the wing's strength up to four squadrons for a short period, before they transferred to Fassberg in October. No. 135 Wing would be reduced to three units when No.3 Sqn left Fassberg at the beginning of 1946 to move to Wunstorf to join No. 123 Wing, where they joined Nos 41 and 80 Sqns, once of Lubeck's No. 124 Wing. Thus Nos 123 and 135 Wings would remain as the Tempest squadron's parent organizations whilst the type remained in front-line service in Germany.

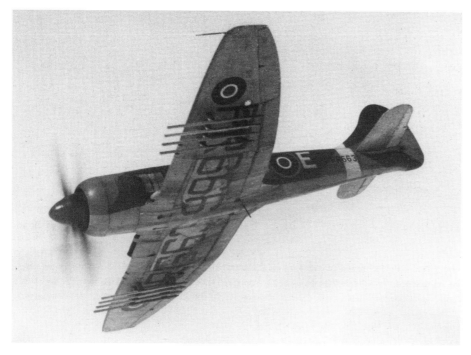

Left **Caught diving past the camera is the Tempest II PR663 – 'Echo' of No. 16 Sqn based at Fassberg in Germany. Note the incorrect underwing serial.**
Michael Baldock

The Royal Air Force, like many such large organizations, seems to thrive on the turmoil that upheaval can cause: thus, having settled on two wings with their constituent squadrons as adequate for the purposes of BAFO, the 'powers that be' obviously decided that further changes to the Tempest force in Occupied Germany was necessary. The first of these took place over the night of 30 April/1 May 1946, when all the better-known fighter-squadron number plates were returned to the custody of Fighter Command. This required that No. 41 Sqn should be renumbered No. 26 Sqn, while No 56 Sqn would become No. 16 Sqn. No. 174 Sqn was the unlucky unit in this line-up, as it was disbanded. The make-up of the two BAFO Wings was thus: No. 123 Wing at Wunstorf, with No. 3 and 80 Sqns, while at Fassberg, No. 135 Wing was parent to Nos 16, 26 and 33 Sqdns. As this was peacetime, the training regimes associated with the pilots and their qualifications to fly came to the fore. Thus Sylt and its armament practice camp became the venue for each of the Tempest squadrons in turn to let loose with cannons, rockets and bombs. The need for rocket qualification had arrived once the Typhoon had left RAF service, and there was a plentiful supply of redundant German armour lying about that needed dismantling. A rotation of detachments to Gatow near Berlin were undertaken as much as to protect British interests as to keep the Russians at bay.

Re-equipping with the Centaurus Tempests

During this period the squadrons were still equipped with Napier Sabre-powered Tempests, although this was set to change as more Bristol Centaurus-powered versions of the aircraft were beginning to roll off the Hawker production line. Thus the Tempest II began to replace the earlier version during the middle of 1946: No. 26 Sqn received its replacement fighters from 17 June at Fassberg, No. 16 Sqn received its aircraft from August onwards, while No. 33 Sqn received theirs from October. Only the Fassberg wing would re-equip with the radial-engined fighters, while over at Wunstorf No. 80 Sqn would retain their Sabre-engined Tempests until January 1948: then they moved on to the Supermarine Spitfire F.24s, with No. 3 Sqn retaining their Hawker fighters until April 1948, when the de Havilland Vampire jet fighters were received. No. 16 Sqn would manage to make the headlines on the BBC on 18 March 1947, when one crash-landed in the Russian Zone.

At this time the unit was restricted to flying within the city limits, although there were a few incursions into so-called 'friendly territory'. On one of these, Warrant Officer Angus Mackay was flying an approach into Gatow in Tempest II PR667 'EG-S' when the engine failed at 1,000ft (300m), some five miles (8km) from touchdown and over the Russian sector. Accompanying the loud bang of the engine seizing was a spray of oil that covered the windscreen panels. Although the Tempest had a reasonable glide range, the available height and distance meant that Gatow was beyond reach, so W. O. Mackay cast about for a suitable place to touch down in an area covered by pine forest. Seeing a small ploughed field, he turned the ailing Tempest towards it, and fortunately for him it had just enough forward momentum to scrape into it.

Just prior to crash-landing the pilot had called Gatow for a rescue, and was more than pleased to see a small RAF van turn up. On board was a photographer, who enjoined the pilot to stand by his battered fighter for photographs for the records. The other occupant was an armourer, who removed the still-secret gunsight, and packed it away in a special box. Both then climbed into their vehicle and departed, leaving the bewildered warrant officer behind! Fortunately for him, the squadron CO turned up and rescued him from becoming a guest of the Russians. The remains of the Tempest were returned to Gatow a few months later, where investigation of the Centaurus engine revealed that one of the sleeve valves had seized.

Having tangled with various USAAF aircraft during combat operations in the skies over Germany, it made a pleasant change for the Tempest squadrons to meet their American counterparts in happier circumstances, with neither side trying to shoot the other down. The American armed forces were also being subjected to a period of upheaval, the main beneficiary being the flying side of the US Army, which in 1947 was established as a separate service and called the United States Air Force. As this was the period before the rapid revolution in jet aircraft development, the opposition encountered by the Tempest squadrons consisted of the latest versions of the Republic P-47 Thunderbolt and the North American P-51 Mustang. The pilots of the former would especially praise the Tempest II, as it could outperform the big American fighter with ease.

The Squadrons Re-Equip

Other organized detachments would see flights of Tempests returning to Britain to take part in various exercises, including involvement in the September 1946 official RAF film covering 'Combined Operations', for which the fighters undertook rocket-firing runs over the range at Braunton Sands close to Chivenor. It was during this period that the first inklings of the Cold War – that would occupy military minds for the succeeding generations – would rear its ugly head, when in July 1947 Nos 16 and 26 Sqns were detached to the Austrian air base at Zelteg hard by the Yugoslav border to cover Russian manoeuvres. But their period of residence was short-lived, as they would return to Germany in the following month, just in time to relocate to a different base, Gutersloh. Here the squadrons would remain with their Tempest IIs until the beginning of 1949.

No. 16 Sqn was the first of the Gutersloh units to re-equip, trading in its Hawker machines for de Havilland Vampires, which were officially taken on charge in December 1948. Three months later, in April 1949, No. 26 Sqn would also become officially equipped with the de Havilland jet fighter. The final unit, No. 33 Sqn, would have to wait a little longer in its history to bid farewell to the Hawker Tempest II, as in July 1949 they would depart Germany for Renfrew near Glasgow, where the fighters would be prepared for sea passage aboard the aircraft carrier HMS *Ocean*, their destination Changi in the Far East.

Although the Tempest V had performed more than adequately during its period of combat, production of this version was terminated in preference to that of the Centaurus-powered Tempest II, soon to be the Tempest F.2, and the Tempest VI, later to be re-designated the Tempest F.6. This latter version, powered by a Napier Sabre, was modified with improved filters and system coolers for service with the squadrons in the Middle East. These units were equipped with a mixture of types such as Spitfires, P-51 Mustangs on Lend Lease terms, plus a variety of twin-engined types, including the de Havilland Mosquito: the latter was viewed with suspicion in some quarters, given its method of construction, namely formed plywood glued together. Not only did the Mosquitos need replacing, but the Spitfires were close to

Above **Although the Tempest was used more in the ground-strafing role during World War II, it was quickly cleared to use all the other weapons in the RAF inventory. This Mark VI, NX135, used by both Nos 6 and 249 Sqns in the Middle East, is being prepared for a live firing sortie. By this time the zero-length rocket rails had replaced the earlier Mark III type. This was another machine that would eventually be sold to the MoS in 1951.** C. P. Russell Smith Collection

life-expired, and the American aircraft needed to be either purchased, returned or scrapped.

Tempest VI in the Middle East

It would take until late 1946 for enough Tempest VIs to become available to replace the original mixture, but when they did, replacements arrived in droves. The new fighters were flown out to Fayid in Egypt by pilots from the Ferry Unit in groups of four, each led by a Mosquito from the same unit, that acted as a shepherd and navigation lead. The first unit to receive the Tempest VI was No. 249 Sqn based at Habbaniya in Iraq, where they arrived in December 1946. The next recipient was No. 6 Sqn based at Nicosia in Cyprus, who also re-equipped in December 1946. No. 213 Sqn, based at the same airfield, would also receive the new fighter in January 1947, while a fourth unit, No. 8 Sqn, based in Aden, would gain its new Hawker aircraft in March 1947.

Of all these units, No. 8 Sqn was the first into action, making a destructive attack against the village of Al Husein in a punitive measure to combat guerilla fighters operating in the region, who had shot and killed a local government agent. Further missions of a similar nature, seen by many as a return to the old Colonial days, would

follow. Unlike the missions of later years, these sorties were preceded by a leaflet drop possibly up to forty-eight hours earlier. The result of this was, that when the Tempests attacked, the buildings were deserted and there were no casualties.

Over on the island of Cyprus at Nicosia the two Tempest units, Nos 6 and 213 Sqns, were reformed into No. 324 Wing, which had last been active in the Mediterranean area, equipped with Spitfires. The other two squadrons, due to their detached locations, would remain as independent operational units. By the end of 1947, all four Middle East squadrons were under the command of war-time Typhoon unit commanders: thus Nos 6 and 213 Sqns came under the control of Sqn Ldrs Dennis Cowley-Milling and Colebrook, while No. 8 Sqn in Aden came under the command of Sqn Ldr Frank Jensen; the final Middle East unit, No. 249 Sqn, was placed in the hands of Sqn Ldr Peter Steib. The latter unit had spent the first year of its life as a Tempest operator, training for operational readiness and getting to grips with launching unguided rocket projectiles.

Even in late 1947 the situation in the Middle East was unstable, Israel was becoming a reality, the Arab countries were wracked by various forms of internal unrest, and the embryonic Palestine liberationists were beginning to protest violently against what they perceived to be the complicity being shown by some of

Above **Not the most dignified end to a landing, as the upside-down NX134 shows. Wearing the codes of No. 6 Sqn, the Tempest VI had swung out of control part-way through the landing and overturned at Nicosia on 11 February 1949. In the background the recovery crane can clearly be seen.** C. P. Russell Smith Collection

Left **Pictured at Khartoum is Tempest VI NX264, which had been placed in the hanger just after colliding with NX247 on take-off on 24 January 1949. After repair, the aircraft would resume its career with No. 39 Sqn, before being sold to the Ministry of Supply in April 1954.** David Howley Collection

Left **NX247 was the other machine involved in the Khartoum collision on 24 January 1949; no further service details are known about this machine, although it ended its career with No. 39 Sqn.** David Howley Collection

the Arab countries. By early 1948 No. 249 Sqn was on alert status in case of trouble in Palestine, for which purpose four of the squadron's Tempests were based at Ramat David airfield. Also on the move were the aircraft of No. 6 Sqn, who left Khartoum for Fayid in Egypt, both squadrons being charged with protecting the British forces as they withdrew from the ex-British protectorate. This would finally be accomplished during May 1948.

In order to provide further support for British forces leaving various possessions in the Middle East and Africa, No. 213 Sqn left Khartoum for Mogadishu, part of Italian Somaliland, where they arrived in August 1948 to cover the withdrawal from Ogaden. Not long after their arrival, the 90gal (410ltr) external tank became available for use by the Tempest. This modification meant that No. 213 Sqn could safely depart for Deversoir on 21 October 1948, while No.8 Sqn, still operating out of Aden, could cover the withdrawal, as the new tanks would allow patrols of some four and a half hours. As well as the Somaliland coverage during October, No. 8 Sqn was also busy on anti-guerilla sorties in the vicinity of Wadi Mirria against the Mansuri Tribe. During a three-day period a group of seven pilots flew over one hundred sorties, during which fifteen ex-Foreign Legion forts were attacked, which required the firing of four hundred and sixty rocket projectiles.

To cover the gap left by No. 213 Sqn's departure to cover the Somaliland withdrawal, the newly formed No. 39 Sqn had arrived at Khartoum on 1 April 1948. Their posting was destined to be quite busy, as the squadron was required to send a detachment of three Tempests to Asmara in Eritrea province, Ethiopia, to oversee and provide support for British troops and local militia as they hunted down gangs from the Shifta tribe that were terrorizing local village populations. But the tenure of No. 39 Sqn as a Tempest unit would be short, as it would dispense with the Hawker fighter on 1 March 1949 so that it could reform as a Mosquito NF.36 operator.

Working for the United Nations

The two units forming No. 324 Wing, Nos 6 and 213 Sqns, would eventually find themselves based at Deversior in Egypt, acting on behalf of the United Nations. This organization had negotiated hard to broker a ceasefire between the Arab nations that bounded the newly emergent state of Israel. When the squadrons had first arrived at Deversior, Spitfires of the Egyptian Air Force had, so they reported at the time, accidentally attacked RAF bases throughout the region, causing damage to aircraft on the ground, especially at Ramat David. However, their impudence would cost them dearly, with some Egyptian Spitfires being shot down in retaliation.

Over the following few months the Royal Air Force confined itself to patrols only, although the squadrons would soon find themselves embroiled in further hostilities when Israeli forces were found to be infiltrating Egypt and Jordan – the latter was regarded as a British ally, and was deemed worthy of external protection. To this end, Spitfires from No. 208 Sqn were despatched on regular reconnaissance patrols to fly along the border. During one of these patrols the participating aircraft were shot down by Spitfires from No. 101 Sqn, IAF. To protect aircraft on these patrol duties it was decided that a flight of Tempests from No. 213 Sqn would escort the next reconnaissance flight, this being a Mosquito. In support were a further four Tempests of No. 6 Sqn, in a holding pattern over the Ismalia to El Auga road. A further flight to find the missing Spitfire pilots required that the Tempests fly top cover for the No. 208 Sqn search party Spitfires. The whole force was approaching the border when further Spitfires of the Israeli Air Force jumped them, and in the ensuing dogfight a Tempest of No. 213 Sqn was shot down and a further three were damaged, one of which would later require a wing change due to main spar damage.

To compound the problem, the Tempests had departed in such haste that the cannon had not been cocked, thereby rendering them less than useless; therefore the Tempest pilots had only their speed, although this did allow them to break clear

Right **Hawker Tempest VI NX131 'A' was the personal machine of Sqn Ldr Jensen from 1947–49 when he was CO of No. 8 Sqn based at Khormaksar.**
Peter R. Arnold Collection

of the fracas. During the break-out, many of the Hawker fighters exceeded the maximum speed limit, while others were spun with fuel tanks still fitted, both being forbidden in the *Pilots' Notes*. What added to the confusion was that both sets of Spitfires were sporting red spinners, which were difficult to distinguish in the mêlée.

Greater changes were also ahead for the Tempest force in the Middle East, as in March 1949 No. 249 Sqn departed from Habbaniya to replace No. 213 Sqn at Deversior, where it would meet up with No. 6 Sqn to maintain the strength of No. 324 Wing, No. 213 Sqn having flown to Nicosia to take part in an Armament Practice Camp. By September of that year, all three units would begin re-equipping with the de Havilland Vampire, a process that would continue until March 1950, when the last Tempests departed.

Tempest IIs for India

Further from Britain the Far East would also begin to receive Hawker Tempests. Originally the Tempest II had been destined to form the fighter backbone of the 'Tiger Force', although with the latter's cancellation due to the collapse of Japanese resistance, there was less need to re-equip squadrons for this role. However,

as the fighters and fighter bombers in India needed replacing, it was decided that the Tempest II should be deployed for this. The first examples were despatched to India during 1945 for flight trials, although it wasn't until December that large numbers of Tempests were shipped to Karachi. Eventually a total of some 180 aircraft were delivered to No. 320 Maintenance Unit, based at Drigh Road, for assembly and pre-delivery flight-testing.

The first units to receive Tempests were Nos 5 (ex-Republic Thunderbolts) and 30 (also ex-Thunderbolts) Sqns based at Bhopal, which were officially equipped with the type during March 1946, while the Agra-based No. 20 Sqn (ex-Spitfire XIVs) would receive their quota during May 1946, with No. 152 Sqn (ex-Spitfire XIVs) at Risalpur doing the same in July 1946.

To help the Indian-based pilots convert to the Tempest, Hawker's had despatched a test pilot, one Frank Murphy, once a pilot assigned to No. 486 Sqn flying Typhoons, to help the Maintenance Unit pilots convert to the new type with as little trouble as possible. This did not, however, prove to be the case, as the Tempest II with its radial engine had very different handling characteristics in comparison to the Sabre-engined versions of the same aircraft. The nose profile of the Tempest II

was wider than that of the Sabre-powered aircraft, which meant that the airflow pattern over the rear fuselage followed a different flow path, making the rudder almost ineffective, even if fully deflected, with the rear fuselage in the tail-down position. Furthermore, the runways in India were often lined with monsoon drain ditches on each side, and so it was inevitable that some accidents would occur. To compound the problem there was always the possibility of a cross-wind, which in the early days would cause aircraft to run into the ditches, tearing off the undercarriage legs.

The answer was to teach the pilots to land with the tail held in the horizontal, and to keep the amount of down flap to the minimum, which would allow the rudder to remain effective until touchdown on the main wheels first. This would allow the pilot to straighten up any drift from the runway centre line before the flying speed dropped off and the tail dropped down.

Having taught the maintenance unit pilots the vagaries of flying the Tempest II, Frank Murphy would move on to the four Indian-based squadrons to give them the same lectures; but the pilots of the squadrons were far more excited about the performance of their new mounts.

APC Training

Once the squadrons had accomplished conversion flying, it was time for APC training. This entailed moving to Poona, where live-firing of all weapons was practised, and displays were laid on for the local army commanders throughout India. Once these displays of potential had been given, the Tempest squadrons were sent on armed patrols over the North-West Frontier to quell various tribal disturbances. To practise flying over the mountainous terrain the squadrons were detached to Risalpur and Peshawar; here they were also given firing practice over the ranges. Once these trials had been completed, they were sent out on general and armed patrols, complete with rockets and cannon ammunition, to intimidate the local tribesmen in an attempt to reduce their attacks against settlements in the region.

Detachments were also sent out to outlying bases, in scenes reminiscent of the 1930s when biplanes ruled the skies. In a similar manner to their antecedents, the

Below Pictured in serene flight is this Tempest VI, NX135, of No 6 Sqn, photographed in early 1949. Visible under the wing centre section is the system air cleaner unique to this version and the standard fit of zero-length rocket rails. The dark patch on the radiator inspection panel is the background to the squadron badge, while it is repeated on the fin flanked by the unit's bar insignia. C. P. Russell Smith Collection

Above **No. 33 Sqn would eventually take its Tempest Vs to the Far East. Based at Changi and other bases in the region, it would retain the Hawker fighters until June 1951. Of note are the different finishes applied to the aircraft: some retain camouflage, whilst others are unpainted.** C. P. Russell Smith Collection

Tempest squadrons would find themselves detached to such locations as Fort Miramshah, where they would occupy the accommodation built for their RAF forebears. Also from those pre-war times were the much needed 'road open patrol' days, during which the Tempests flew patrols up and down the various roads in the region in support of supply convoy trucks en route to various remote outposts. These missions were flown fully armed, with full radio communications being maintained throughout, and these were continued during daylight hours. On their return, fighters were placed in the individual hangers originally constructed in the 1930s.

The RAF Withdraws

Having satisfied the needs of the Royal Air Force in India, it was the turn of the Royal Indian Air Force to receive some of the aircraft from the Tempest production line, to replace their original equipment. This improvement to the Indian Air Force and its equipment, and the forthcoming partition of the Indian sub-continent, meant that a Royal Air Force presence was no longer required; therefore preparations were put in hand to pass over the defence of the country to the indigenous air force, and to withdraw the RAF squadrons.

The first RIAF unit to receive the

Hawker Tempest was No. 3 Sqn RIAF, their first examples arriving in September 1946, while No. 8 Sqn RIAF received its new machines during the following November. Following on from the RIAF re-equipment, the Royal Air Force began to disband its own units. The first to go was No. 30 Sqn on 1 December 1946, quickly followed by No. 152 Sqn, disbanded officially on 15 January 1947. Later that year, on 1 August 1947, No. 20 Sqn ceased to be a Tempest operator, while No. 5 Sqn followed suit the next day. Before their disbandment, the pilots of No. 5 Sqn had acted as the conversion unit for their counterparts of both the RIAF and the Pakistani Air Force.

On 15 August 1947 the official partition of India and Pakistan took place, and the era of the British Raj came to a close. However, as far as the two emergent air forces were concerned, the departure of the British did mean that they were well equipped, as most of the RAF aircraft were left behind.

A Last Fling for the Tempest

Operation *Firedog* was the last front-line fling for the Hawker Tempest, when No. 33 Sqn was transferred to Singapore instead of re-equipping with Vampires like the remainder of the BAFO squadrons. Their task would be to operate alongside

the Bristol Brigands of No. 84 Sqn in pursuit of Communist insurgents operating across Malaysia. The aircraft were transported aboard the aircraft carrier HMS *Ocean*, which was operating in the transport role at the time (it would not return to active duty until the Korean War). The carrier arrived at Seletar where the aircraft were disembarked; they were then taken to Changi, which meant that the unit was able to resume flying on 16 August 1947. The primary main base for No. 33 Sqn would remain Changi, although detachments would be maintained at Kuala Lumpur, Malaysia, up to and including the early months of 1950. From Changi the squadron moved for a brief period to Tengah, before finally departing to Butterworth in Malaya for its last period of operations, which ended in May 1951.

The sorties flown by No. 33 Sqn included strikes against the Communist insurgents, who were, however, very elusive in nature; this meant that a great many cannon shells and rocket projectiles were expended on empty jungle. Other missions were flown against fixed targets that had been identified by intelligence gathering, photo reconnaissance and other sources; thus the Tempests would attack villages and jungle encampments in an effort to flush out the insurgents and drive them into waiting ambushes. Operation *Firedog* would occupy the Royal Air Force and the other forces for at least two more years, although the Tempest itself flew its last sortie on 6 June 1951. The following day the unit began converting to the de Havilland Hornet F.3

– although there would be trouble with this aircraft because the glue in the skin suffered in the humidity of the Far East.

Target-Towing Tempests

Although the Tempest had finished its front-line career in 1951, there was still a role for it in the providing of second-line services. This would only encompass the Sabre-powered Tempest V, which would re-emerge as the capable, target-towing Tempest TT.5. Conversion work of redundant fighters for their new role began in February 1950 at Hawker's Langley works, and would continue until the final machine was rolled out in May 1952 after eighty machines had been converted. In service the converted fighters were operated by units based in Britain and Germany. Within the bounds of Britain the Tempest TT.5s were flown by the Central Gunnery School, the Armament Practice Camp at Acklington, plus Nos 226, 229 and 233 Operational Conversion Units based at Stradishall, Chivenor and Pembrey respectively.

Each of the target-tug units consisted of two target-towing flights, whose periods of flying was dependent upon the weather: this meant that in the winter, any flying was done in one shift, but in the summer the flying was done in shifts from dawn to dusk, with each pilot completing at least three sorties during a shift. This particular posting was very mundane for the pilots, as each sortie was flown to a strict pattern so there was no requirement for any violent manoeuvring except in an emergency or while undertaking post-servicing air tests. Even though the Tempest TT.5 was a purely peacetime conversion, the pilots were beset with the normal problems of oil in the cockpit which led to stained boots and coveralls, and a persistent pervasive odour.

Left **SN329 was a standard Tempest V Series 2 that was converted to be the prototype TT.5 target-tow aircraft, seen here with an air-driven winch under the wing. After extensive trials with the A&AEE from 1947 to 1949, the aircraft would lose its air-driven winch in favour of a simple release-shackle arrangement. After Boscombe Down, the Tempest was allocated to the APC at Sylt; it would be badly damaged in a forced landing on 4 June 1952.**
Big Bird Aviation Collection

Below **This side-on view of the prototype TT.5 SN329 shows the target-towing winch in greater detail. Of note are the roundels and fin stripes associated more with war than peacetime.**
C. P. Russell Smith Collection

Right **Having flown with No. 485 Sqn, Tempest V, EJ875, was returned for conversion to TT.5 standard. It would then be allocated to Sylt APC, before being sold to the MoS in 1955.** C. P. Russell Smith Collection

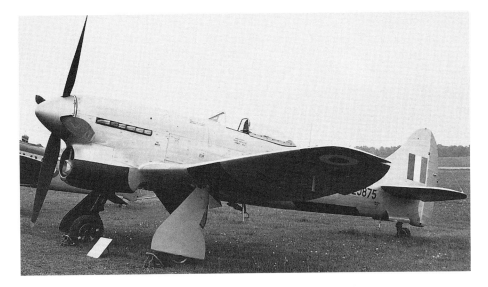

Right **Tempest TT.5 SN340 was operated by both the Acklington APC and No. 229 OCU; it was withdrawn from use in November 1954.** C. P. Russell Smith Collection

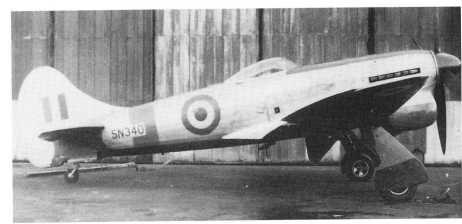

Below **At the end of their careers some aircraft ended up as training and display aids. Such a fate has befallen SN219, which had been a TT.5 with the Acklington APC and No. 233 OCU before retiring in 1955.** Big Bird Aviation Collection

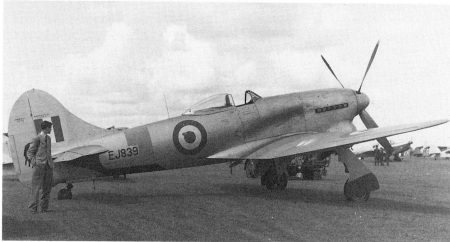

Above **As a Tempest V, NV699 served with No. 222 Sqn before being reworked as a TT.5. In this guise, periods would be spent at Andover and with Nos 228 and 229 OCUs, after which the aircraft was sold to the MoS in July 1955.** C. P. Russell Smith Collection

Left **Illustrating that target-towing could be a dangerous job is Tempest TT.5 EJ839, which served as a target tower with both the Acklington and Sylt APCs. When it was with the latter it was hit by a shell from an attacking aircraft, resulting in its being struck off charge on 6 September 1954.** C. P. Russell Smith Collection

Left **Only part of the Central Gunnery School's 'FJ-U' is visible on this Tempest TT.5 SN261, the groundcrew of which appears to be awaiting the arrival of the pilot. As with many of this version, the aircraft would eventually pass to the MoS in November 1950.** C. P. Russell Smith Collection

Over in Germany the target-towing Tempests were operated by the APC at Sylt. Both the officially converted Tempest TT.5 and the unofficial conversions of the Tempest IV were flown in large numbers in support of the target-towing role. In service the banner plus its tow cable would be laid out along the runway in the direction of take-off. Careful marshalling by ground staff would direct the pilot towards the end of the cable. Once stopped, the cable was attached to a shackle under the fuselage, after which the pilot was cleared for take-off.

Once airborne, the aircraft was directed towards the range where the pilot would pursue a preset height and course. To maximize the usage of the banner, the first leg was flown parallel to the range centreline, after which a reciprocal course was flown. This dumbell course would be followed while attack sorties were flown by squadron pilots at a rate of four per hour. Once the required attack sorties had been completed, the aircraft would be directed to a designated drop spot where the pilot would pull a release handle to drop the banner. Once recovered by the groundcrew the hits would be counted, and the result telephoned to the range officer.

Alongside the target-tug Tempest units, a handful of the type was operated by the Central Gunnery School at West Raynham, Norfolk, for the training of future squadron and flight commanders. Both Mark Vs and Mark IIs were used between 1947 and 1949, with the latter being regarded as the advanced level aircraft. Outside the Royal Air Force, the Empire Test Pilots School was also a user of the Mark II at Farnborough.

The last German-based Tempests were flown to the Maintenance Unit at Aston Down for storage and final disposal. At Chivenor, the silver Tempest TT.5s, with their black-and-yellow striped undersurfaces, would also be flown to 20 Maintenance Unit, Aston Down, during December 1954. The honour of flying the last Tempests in service fell to No. 233 OCU based at Pembrey, who would dispose of their converted Hawker fighters during July 1955, although not before many high-ranking ex-Tempest combat pilots had arrived for a last nostalgic farewell flight in the big fighter.

While the Royal Air Force was disposing of its Tempests, their counterparts in the Royal Indian Air Force were getting to grips with their new mounts. Originally many of the RIAF squadrons had been equipped with various marques of Spitfire, which were desperately in need of replacement. No. 3 Sqn was the first unit to trade in its Supermarine Spitfire VIIIs for Tempest IIs at its Kolar base during September 1946. Later that year, Nos 8 and 10 Sqns RIAF would also relinquish their earlier aircraft for the big Hawker fighter, a pattern that would be followed by No. 4 Sqn once they had returned to India after duty with the British Commonwealth Air Component as part of the Army of Occupation in Japan.

Originally equipped with the Griffon-powered Spitfire XIV, the newer Tempest's were gratefully accepted by the unit, a similar emotion being expressed by Nos. 1, 7 and 9 Sqns RIAF, who dispensed with their Spitfire VIIIs in time for the Independence Day celebration which took place on 15 August 1947. But the use of the Tempest by Nos. 1 and 9 Sqns was to be short-lived, as the partition of the Indian sub-continent into India and Pakistan meant that thirty-five Tempest IIs would be passed on to the Royal Pakistan Air Force. The remaining five Indian squadrons would form the combat backbone over the next couple of years, and would quickly find themselves in action against insurgents operating in the Kashmir state, a state of affairs that persists to this day. Many of the insurgents were Kashmiri tribesmen, and to quell their violent tendencies the Indian Army quickly deployed troops into the region, courtesy of an airlift.

Initial air support was given by a handful of Spitfires, although this was quickly changed to No. 7 Sqn and its Tempests. Their arrival, and their ability to carry both bombs and rocket projectiles, meant that they would play a decisive part in suppressing the insurgents, an offensive that would culminate in an action that became known as the Battle of Shelatung. This particular campaign would last some fifteen months before a ceasefire came into effect on 1 January 1949 bringing a fragile sense of peace to the region.

Tempests for the RIAF

Having gained the ex-RAF Tempests, the RIAF originally had a strength of 124 Tempest IIs, which would be supplemented by a further eighty-nine machines that had been purchased by Hawker Aircraft from the surplus stocks in storage at 20 MU, Aston Down. After refurbishment, the reworked fighter bombers were sold to India, with deliveries taking place during 1949. A further twenty aircraft would be purchased by the Indian government directly from redundant RAF stocks held at the maintenance units during 1951.

During 1950 India became a republic, therefore the word 'Royal' was dropped from the title of the air force, which from then on would become known as the 'Indian Air Force'. By this date the IAF had four units equipped with Tempest F.2's, these being Nos 3, 4, 8 and 10 Sqn,

Below **Once MW764 of the Royal Air Force, this Tempest II has been reworked for the Indian Air Force; thus it bears the new serial HA554 and the early version of national insignia. Photographed at Langley, the successor to the Tempest, the Sea Fury, can be seen in the background.** C. P. Russell Smith Collection

Above Tempest II HA626 pictured at Langley, awaiting delivery to the Indian Air Force; of note is the application of the now standard, three-colour roundels and fin flashes. C. P. Russell Smith Collection

known as 'Toofanis' in the service of the IAF. The Tempests did not immediately disappear from the skies of India, however, as numerous secondary roles were found to keep them usefully employed, such as pilot training and, in a similar manner to the RAF, in the target-tug role.

Tempests for the PAF

Over the border in Pakistan, the Tempest F.2s acquired from India after the division were used to equip Nos 5 and 9 Sqn of the Royal Pakistan Air Force, from its inception in 1947. In a manner similar to that of the RIAF, the Tempests of the RPAF were soon seeing action, mainly against recalcitrant tribesman on the North-West Frontier. During these policing actions, the full gamut of the Tempest's weaponry was employed: thus the tribesmen could be faced with bombs, rockets or cannon shells, or a mix of all three.

To build on the original thirty-five aircraft gained after the partition, the RPAF purchased a further twenty-four

while No. 7 Sqn had re-equipped with the de Havilland Vampire in 1949, although they were still dedicated to the fighter-bomber role. Following on from No. 3 Sqn, further Vampires were purchased to re-equip Nos. 3 and 8 Sqns for much the same duties, while in May 1953 No. 10 Sqn would trade in its Tempests for the two-seat de Havilland Vampire NF.10, for operation in the night-fighter role. The final Tempest unit, No. 4 Sqn, would retain their big Hawker fighters until these were replaced by the French-built Dassault Ouragan jet-powered fighter bomber –

RIAF Tempests

Although the war in Europe and the Far East had ended in 1945, there were still residual aircraft contracts in place; thus Hawkers would continue to roll out Tempest IIs, even though there was no real requirement for them. Many of these machines would see no service with the Royal Air Force and so went straight into storage, mainly at 5 Maintenance Unit, Kemble, and 20 Maintenance Unit at Aston Down. To soak up some of this surplus, many of these aircraft would find themselves being transferred to the emergent Royal Indian Air Force that had come into existence during 1947. The initial batch of 124 aircraft were officially handed over on 25 September 1947; all would eventually acquire RIAF serials, although no tie-ups are known.

MW405, MW406, MW407, MW410, MW411, MW412, MW413, MW414, MW419, MW420, MW421, MW435, PR527, PR529, PR536, PR539, PR540, PR541, PR543, PR544, PR545, PR546, PR548, PR551, PR552, PR553, PR556, PR557, PR558, PR559, PR562, PR564, PR567, PR584, PR585, PR590, PR591, PR592, PR593, PR594, PR595, PR597, PR598, PR600, PR601, PR602, PR603, PR605, PR606, PR607, PR609, PR610, PR612, PR614, PR617, PR618, PR619, PR620, PR621, PR647, PR651, PR652, PR653, PR655, PR658, PR660, PR664, PR666, PR668, PR671, PR675, PR677, PR678, PR681, PR684, PR688, PR713, PR714, PR717, PR719, PR721, PR722, PR725, PR727, PR728, PR729, PR730, PR731, PR732, PR734, PR735, PR739, PR740, PR741, PR747, PR748, PR750, PR751, PR752, PR773, PR775, PR780, PR783, PR787, PR789, PR791, PR794, PR795, PR801, PR804, PR808, PR813, PR814, PR815, PR830, PR835, PR836, PR837, PR840, PR842, PR843, PR849, PR863, PR868

Three of these aircraft, PR548, PR849 and PR836, were delivered for spares usage, and categorized as Cat.5 before delivery, as unfit to fly.

Six months after the first batch of aircraft was delivered to the RIAF, Hawker Aircraft would purchase, via the Ministry of Supply, a further 113 Tempest IIs that were surplus to RAF requirements, that were in storage at 20 Maintenance Unit, Aston Down. After refurbishment by Hawker's, eighty-nine were sold on to the RIAF. As before, these Tempests were drawn from aircraft in the MW and PR-serialled batches.

HA547, PR874, HA548, PR907, HA549, PR893, HA550, PR902, HA551, MW831, HA552, PR890, HA553, MW385, HA554, MW764, HA555, MW751, HA556, MW831, HA557, MW404, HA558, MW854, HA559, MW847, HA560, MW851, HA561, MW743, HA562, MW770, HA563, MW808, HA564, MW376, HA565, MW748, HA566, MW742, HA567, MW760, HA568, MW377, HA569, MW817, HA570, MW807, HA571, MW819, HA572, MW824, HA573, MW761, HA574, MW739, HA575, MW403, HA576, MW853, HA577, MW773, HA578, MW830, HA579, MW777, HA580, MW758, HA581, MW402, HA582, MW856, HA583, MW823, HA584, MW752, HA585, MW392, HA586, MW763, HA587, MW856, HA588, MW398, HA589, MW395, HA590, MW382, HA591, MW810, HA592, MW387, HA593, MW850, HA594, MW762, HA595, MW386, HA596, MW396, HA597, MW754, HA598, MW809, HA599, MW822, HA600, MW746, HA601, MW750, HA602, MW759, HA603, MW793, HA604, MW401, HA605, MW814, HA606, MW796, HA607, MW759, HA608, MW795, HA609, MW768, HA610, MW797, HA611, MW397, HA612, MW829, HA613, MW400, HA614, MW791, HA615, MW769, HA616, MW756, HA617, PR525, HA618, MW855, HA619, MW852, HA620, MW390, HA621, MW828, HA622, MW741, HA623, MW848, HA624, MW767, HA625, MW389, HA626, MW391, HA627, MW378, HA628, MW380, HA629, MW771, HA630, MW381, HA631, MW383, HA632, MW379, HA633, MW399, HA634, MW393, HA635, MW388

A further two batches of Tempest IIs would be purchased by the RIAF after service with the Royal Air Force. As before, these machines were purchased by Hawker's via the MoS from storage at No. 20 Maintenance Unit, Aston Down. Purchase dates for these two batches totalling twenty airframes were concluded on 9 July and 29 August respectively.

Batch 1: PR659, PR676, PR736, PR743, PR745, PR746, PR756, PR774, PR851, PR856, PR867, PR901, HA465 (RIAF)
Batch 2: PR555, HA407(RIAF), PR663, PR683, PR733, PR758, PR777, PR779, PR834

Eventually India would receive a total of 233 Hawker Tempest IIs.

Above **Marked as HA623, this Tempest II is the only complete restored example on display in India.**
C. P. Russell Smith Collection

Below **Hawker Tempest II PR871 spent a short period with Hawker's until being sold to the Pakistani Air Force in February 1952.** C. P. Russell Smith Collection

Hawker Aircraft refurbished machines, so the two original units achieved an establishment of sixteen aircraft each, and would allow for the formation of a further unit, numbered as No. 14 Sqn. A further twenty-one Tempest F.2s were purchased directly from redundant RAF stocks for attrition replacement purposes during 1951/52.

Although the PAF, as it had become, had built up a respectable quantity of Tempests, its days as a front-line fighter were numbered, as they would all be retired to secondary duties by 1953. The aircraft destined to replace them would be another Hawker product, the Fury FB.60. In second-line service the Tempests were used for pilot training, weapons training and finally as target tugs before finally being retired to storage. They were finally reduced to scrap during 1958.

PAF Tempests

Upon the division of the Indian sub-continent into India and Pakistan in 1947, both countries turned to Britain for equipment for their respective air forces. Those delivered to India are dealt with elsewhere, while those destined for the Pakistan Air Force would be delivered in three batches. The first group of Tempests acquired by the PAF were thirty-five ex-RAF machines handed over on 25 September 1947 just after partition. Some time after receiving their Tempests they were re-serialled into the PAF numbering sequence, which was prefixed with an A followed by three numbers.

PR530, PR535, PR549, PR560, PR563, PR565, PR566, PR581, PR587, PR588, PR589, PR608, PR611, PR623, PR648, PR649, PR656, PR661, PR662, PR670, PR686, PR715, PR718, PR723, PR724, PR737, PR754, PR755, PR772, PR796, PR799, PR800, PR810, PR831, PR832

A second batch of Tempest IIs was purchased by Hawker's from the stocks held at No. 20 Maintenance Unit, Aston Down, via the MoS in May 1948. After refurbishment these twenty-four aircraft were delivered to Pakistan.

A128, PR866, A129, PR898, A130, PR906, A131, PR892, A132, PR894, A133, PR806, A134, PR872, A135, PR865, A136, PR876, A137, PR914, A138, PR749, A139, PR809, A140, PR900, A141, PR917, A142, PR910, A143, PR615, A144, PR875, A145, PR909, A146, PR897, A147, PR891, A148, PR889, A149, PR915, A150, PR912, A151, PR899

A final batch of twentyone Tempests would be purchased by Pakistan in the period 26 November 1951 to 11 November 1952, this bringing the final total to eighty-eight aircraft. All of these aircraft were retired RAF examples purchased from stocks held at No. 20 Maintenance Unit, Aston Down, before being refurbished by Hawker's for onward delivery.

MW408, PR528, PR531, PR542, PR550, PR613, PR673, PR685, PR771, PR784, PR803, PR805, PR847, PR860, PR871, PR873, PR896, PR903, PR905, PR913, PR919

CHAPTER TEN

The Fury and Sea Fury

To most, the Hawker Sea Fury is a bit of a mystery, but it is in fact the final expression of the company's fighter design policies that stretched back to the biplane era. Prior to the Sea Fury, the Fleet Air Arm had flown a varied selection of modified land fighters for use on fleet and escort carriers, some of the better known ones being the Hawker Sea Hurricane and the Supermarine Seafire. When hostilities had ceased in 1945 the Royal Navy was faced with a choice concerning its aircraft, as a good majority of them were used on a 'Lend Lease' basis from the United States; so the choices were stark: either scrap them, buy them, or send them back. In most cases the American machines were removed from the FAA inventory very quickly. This left the Fleet Air Arm with a shortage of aircraft for its squadrons, and some of those already in service were desperately in need of replacement. Into the breach would step Hawker's, with an almost ideal replacement – which, ironically, had started life as a design for the Royal Air Force.

The Light Weight Fighter

The Sea Fury owed its development to the earlier Tempest. This fighter, although outstanding in the ground attack and heavy fighter role, was considered too big and heavy for such duties as point defence. Hawker's had already started to investigate the building of a lighter aircraft, using the Tempest as a basis. The new fighter design was intended to retain as much as possible of its predecessor and would be put forward as the 'Light Weight Fighter'. The first moves towards creating the LWF had begun in September 1942, and involved the replacement of the original wing centre section with one of shorter span, to which would be affixed modified Tempest outer wing panels. A formal presentation of the project was begun in January 1943 with the issuance of Specification F.6/42: this gave the aircraft the title 'Tempest Light Weight Fighter (Centaurus)'. A further refinement of the design by Sydney Camm and his team at Hawker Aircraft would result in Specification F.2/43 being issued by the Ministry of Supply.

Following on from the presentation of the LWF came a request from the Admiralty in April 1943 for a ship-borne fighter that would be based on the same aircraft. The specification issued by the Admiralty was N.7/43, to which Sydney Camm responded by concluding that both fighter requirements could be based on a single design, with minimum modifications being applied for each service. To cater for each service requirement, supplementary design sheets would be issued alongside the primary aircraft blueprints. It was intended from the outset that both versions of the Light Weight Fighter would be powered by the Bristol Centaurus XII piston engine, with Hawker being responsible for the design lead and the aircraft built for the Royal Air Force, while the Fleet Air Arm aircraft would be sub-contracted to Boulton Paul Aircraft based at Wolverhampton.

An Engine for the New Fighter

Although the Bristol Centaurus was the preferred engine, its popularity meant that alternatives had to be seriously considered. To cater for this, six LWF prototypes were ordered in December 1943 to Specification F.2/43. Two would have Bristol Centaurus XXIIs installed, one would have a Centaurus XII fitted, while two would have Rolls-Royce Griffon engines under the hood. The final machine was destined to spend its life as a fatigue test specimen. Catering for the naval changes would result in the issue of a supplementary specification coming from the Admiralty: N.22/43. Within the Hawker Aircraft framework the company referred to each version by its own model number; thus the P.1018 would cover the proposed Napier Sabre IV, P.1019 covered the Rolls-Royce Griffon 61, while P.1020 covered the Bristol Centaurus versions.

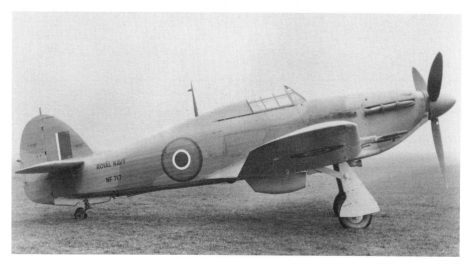

Below Prior to the appearance of the Sea Fury, the Fleet Air Arm was equipped with the Supermarine Seafire and the Sea Hurricane, as shown here. NF717 came complete with arrestor hook, wing-mounted cannon and launch spools; the only thing missing were the folding wings. Big Bird Aviation Collection

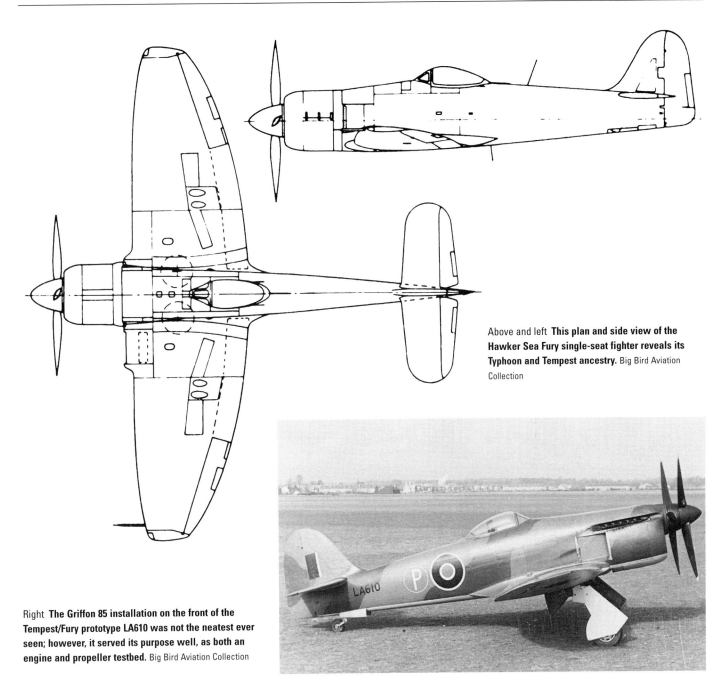

Above and left **This plan and side view of the Hawker Sea Fury single-seat fighter reveals its Typhoon and Tempest ancestry.** Big Bird Aviation Collection

Right **The Griffon 85 installation on the front of the Tempest/Fury prototype LA610 was not the neatest ever seen; however, it served its purpose well, as both an engine and propeller testbed.** Big Bird Aviation Collection

Right **When specification N.7/43 was issued, one of the aircraft produced as the Naval Fury was SR661, which was the first rolled out. This particular machine made its first flight on 21 February 1945 and was semi-navalized in that it featured an arrestor hook but lacked folding wings.** FAA Museum Collection

Above Airframe LA610 had originally been ordered as a Tempest III, although it would eventually be completed as the Sabre VII-powered Fury prototype. In this view it sports a four-bladed propeller assembly. Big Bird Aviation Collection

Left This air-to-air view of the F.2/43 Fury NX798 shows how close this aircraft was in shape to the final production Sea Fury. This particular machine had first flown on 1 September 1944, powered by a Bristol Centaurus XII engine. It would later be fitted with a Centaurus XVIII, and would end its days in Egypt after refurbishment. FAA Museum Collection

Left Although powered by the Napier Sabre VII, the F.2/43 Fury LA610 portrays many of the features that would filter through to the production Sea Fury, including the tail unit. Big Bird Aviation Collection

The maiden flight of prototype NX798 built to Specification F.2/43 was on 1 September 1944, with Hawker test pilot Philip Lucas. The powerplant installed in this machine was a Bristol Centaurus XII, although this would be replaced later in the test programme by the Centaurus XVIII. Once NX798 had successfully completed its initial flight test evaluation, it was the turn of the Griffon-powered LA610 to make its maiden flight on 7 November 1944. In contrast to the earlier machine this aircraft's engine drove a six-bladed contra-rotating Rotol propeller assembly. With both prototypes successfully airborne, the process of dispensing names began; thus the aircraft for the Royal Air Force became known as the Fury, while its Royal Navy counterpart was originally named the Naval Fury, although this was soon changed to the far more apt Sea Fury.

Post-War Development Programme

With the successful assault upon Europe well under way, it was inevitable that many aircraft contracts would be drastically cut or dispensed with altogether. One of the first contracts to go was that of the Hawker Fury, as the Royal Air Force had numerous orders outstanding for Griffon-powered Spitfires of various marques, plus great numbers of Tempests being delivered new to the maintenance units for storage. Although the RAF had decided not to pursue the Fury fighter, the Admiralty would continue pushing the development of the naval version as a much needed supplement to the Supermarine Seafires and Fairey Fireflys already available. Both types were essentially fighters, the former seen as a fleet defence fighter, while the latter was a long-range fighter, although both did have some form of ground-attack capability. The only other possible alternatives were the American aircraft already in service, although their purchase carried with it the attendant problems of spares and support costs. Given these two factors, the Fleet Air Arm would eventually say farewell to its Grumman and Chance Vought fighters once hostilities had ceased, many being disposed of by heaving them over the side of the carriers into the sea.

After the withdrawal of the RAF from the Fury programme, the two already

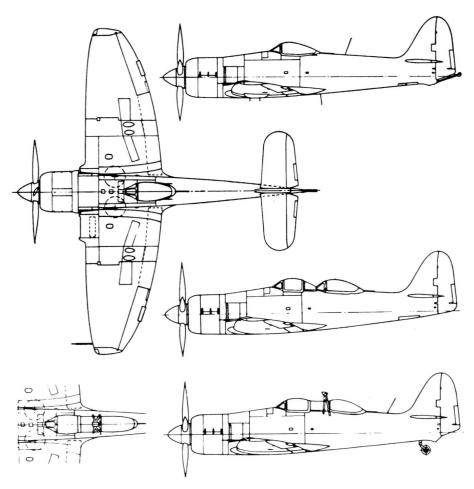

Above **The Sea Fury range of aircraft encompassed the Mark X and Mark 11 single-seaters, plus two versions of the T Mk.20 training variant, the latter three being shown in this general arrangement drawing.** Big Bird Aviation Collection

Below **Although the Sabre VII installation had smoother cowlings than the Typhoon and Tempest set-up, it still required extensive cooling, hence the enlarged intakes in the wing's leading edges.** Big Bird Aviation Collection

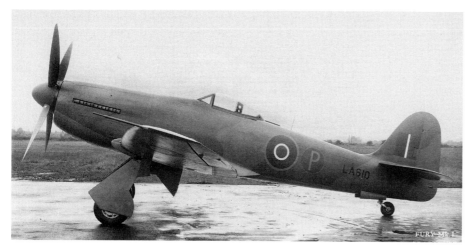

Above **This side-on view of LA610 reveals the care taken by the Hawker designers to achieve a good, clean, aerodynamic airframe.** Big Bird Aviation Collection

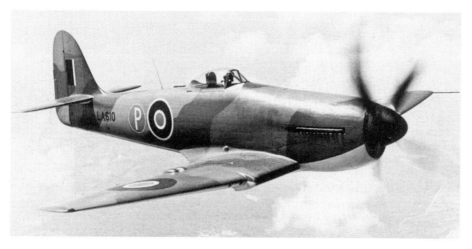

Above **During its flying history the Fury prototype LA610 was initially powered by a Rolls-Royce Griffon 85 driving a six-blade, contra-rotating propeller assembly. Once these flight trials had been completed, the Griffon was replaced by a Centaurus XV, before the Napier VII was fitted.** Big Bird Aviation Collection

the fallouts from the reductions and contract cancellations was the recall of production of the Sea Fury from Boulton Paul at Wolverhampton to the Hawker Aircraft factory at Kingston, to ensure that the primary contractor's workforce was fully occupied until the post-war manufacturing position had stabilized. Following on from the return of the contract came the partially completed prototype VB857, which was moved by truck to its new home during January 1945.

The Fury's Maiden Flight

The delay in completing the prototype VB857 at Boulton Paul meant that the first Fury prototype to make its maiden flight was SR661: it took to the air on 21 February 1945. After completion of manufacturers' flight trials, and the inevitable tweaks that this process normally engendered, airframe SR661 was transferred to RAE Farnborough for more formal evaluation during May 1945. These concentrated upon the aircraft's behaviour under simulated carrier operating conditions, and especially in the performance of the rudder throughout the entire speed range encountered during take-off and landing. The interim report from the test pilot team commented that, given the power output of the Centaurus engine, full rudder deflection to starboard was required to counteract the torque generated by the propeller under full power during the take-off run.

Problems were also encountered with the overall handling of the aircraft, as pilots complained about the lack of rudder 'feel', which was exacerbated by the behaviour of the fitted spring tab. One of the final conclusions in the report concerning rudder handling was that the 'feel' problem required urgent addressing, as it was postulated that tyro pilots could end up mishandling the aircraft if unprepared for its idiosyncrasies. This behaviour became even more pronounced when the rudder was fully deflected to the left before the take-off run began, thus as soon as air pressure was applied to the rudder surface, the rudder spring tab immediately began to compensate, which in turn caused the aircraft to swing more to the left. Should this pilot-induced swing continue, it could be reversed by the application of opposite rudder – although this would normally occur just as the Bristol Centaurus power-

completed aircraft were transferred to Navy development work. They would be joined by two further prototypes, the first of which, NX802, powered by a Bristol Centaurus XII engine, made its maiden flight on 27 July 1945. This was followed by the second airframe, VP207, which was eventually completed in 1947 and made its first flight that same year. This particular machine was one of the aircraft ordered as a back-up to the Centaurus Furies, being powered by a Napier Sabre VII. When test-flying this machine, it was found that its top speed was some 485mph (780km/h) IAS in level flight, which made it the fastest ever fighter built by Hawker Aircraft. As the Fury flight trials were

proceeding successfully, Hawker's concluded that the development programme could be safely split to follow two distinct paths: one would continue to support the Sea Fury development programme, whilst the other would concentrate upon developing the type for potential export customers.

While the Royal Air Force was reducing its commitment to buying further fighters from Hawker's, the Royal Navy, while still retaining its options for the Sea Fury, was also looking closely at its post-war aircraft requirements. After much deliberation the initial purchase of Sea Furies was reduced to a total of one hundred airframes, this later being dropped to fifty aircraft. One of

plant was achieving full power. The use of flap deflection up to thirty degrees could also cause further problems.

The engine installed in this first prototype was the Bristol Centaurus XII, which drove a four-bladed Rotol propeller assembly, and as it was purely a development machine, SR661 was built without folding wings, although it was fitted with an arrestor hook for deck-landing trials. Following on from the first flying prototype came SR666, a fully navalized aircraft featuring folding wing outer panels as well as the required arrestor-hook equipment. As this was also a development aircraft, the wing-fold mechanism was completely manual, as were the wing locking pins. This aircraft would make its first flight on 12 October 1945, being powered by a Centaurus XV instead of the proposed Centaurus XXII destined for the production aircraft, as Bristol's had encountered some manufacturing difficulties with this version. Bringing SR666 closer to the required production standard, it was fitted with a five-blade Rotol-balanced propeller assembly. What would become the third flying prototype, VB857, had been sitting in the Hawker's factory since its return from Boulton Paul. It would finally be completed in late 1945, making its maiden flight on 21 January 1946.

Engine Problems

As VB857's completion had been so delayed, it allowed Hawker's to roll it out fully navalized. With three airframes available, two fully navalized and one not, full scale development flight-testing could begin from the test airfield at Kingston to hasten the programme along. However, these good intentions would be placed under a great strain, as the Bristol Centaurus engines developed the disturbing habit of breaking crankshafts in the air. Investigation into the problem eventually traced the fault to the lubrication system that was found to be operating intermittently; this would cause the crankshaft to overheat and break under the shear load generated. Until the fault was cured by Bristol's, quite a few pilots would find themselves walking home to the test airfield at Langley after their aircraft's engine had failed. Fortunately, because the company's test pilots were so experienced, it meant there were no casualties, although there were a few bumps and bruises.

Bristol's final cure to the engine crankshaft seizure problem was the replacement of the original Centaurus with the intended production powerplant, the Centaurus XVIII. Much of the development work plus airborne trials had been carried out using the F.2/43 prototype NX802. While Bristol's and Hawker's worked hard to restore confidence in the Centaurus engine, initial land-based flight trials prior to full scale carrier trials were being carried out at A&AEE Boscombe Down during 1946, using prototype SR666. Once these trials had been successfully completed, the whole process was then moved aboard the fleet aircraft carrier, HMS *Victorious*.

Flight-Handling Trials

This series of trials would concentrate upon the behaviour of the rudder under carrier operating conditions, especially during deck landings or waved-off missed approaches. Prior to the sea-based flights with their attendant and complicated approach and landing patterns, the land-based trials had revealed that the rudder surface only remained effective

Above **Marked with Royal Navy titles and prototype markings is the second Sea Fury prototype SR666. It made its first flight on 12 October 1945, and came completely navalized as it sported both an arrestor hook and folding wings.** W. A. Harrison Collection

Below **Having completed its flight trials, SR666 then spent time at the gun butts for weapon performance and harmonization trials. For this purpose, the rear fuselage was lifted on trestles to approximate flying trim.** W. A. Harrison Collection

whilst using maximum climbing power, while the use of full power under these circumstances reduced the rudder's effectiveness.

It was also intended that these trials would investigate the reported directional instability experienced during the actual landing run after touch-down. The recommended action given to pilots was to use harsh, aggressive wheel braking to keep the aircraft moving in a straight line. To help compensate for this longitudinal drift it was recommended strongly in the trials report that a pilot-operated tailwheel lock be incorporated in the production machines after prototype flight trials. A benefit of incorporating this lock would mean that the tailwheel unit would remain fore and aft, thus allowing the tail leg unit to retract without incident. Prior to this, the castoring tailwheel had exhibited a tendency to remain off centre after take-off, which would prevent it from retracting.

One aspect of handling that had been inherited from the Tempest was similar stall characteristics, as the ailerons would lose full control authority at 98mph (158km/h) IAS in landing configuration; however, the elevators would still retain their positive handling down to 88mph (142km/h) IAS under similar circumstances.

Having cured the lubrication problems with the Centaurus engine, both Bristol and Hawker's were faced with a vibration problem in the 1,700rpm region and below, where the rigidly mounted powerplant caused serious vibrations that would continue throughout the landing approach, all the way to touch-down. Coupled to the engine behaviour was that of the propeller, which exhibited a tendency to overspeed, especially if go around or emergency power was suddenly applied.

Testing the Arrestor System

Once the flight-handling trials had been completed, it was the turn of the arrestor system to undergo extensive testing, which began during July 1945. It had already been estimated that both the pilot and aircraft would be subjected to loads of 3 gs when landing on the flight deck, as the point of hook engagement was offset from the deck centreline by some 15ft (4.5m) either way to ensure that operational Sea Furies had enough leeway to land under all seagoing conditions. During these trials there was the usual selection of missed wires, approaches and bounced wires, although the great majority of connected landings were successful. Most of the problematic landings were caused by the arrestor hook bouncing on touchdown. To improve the behaviour of the hook assembly, the aircraft was returned to Hawker's Langley factory for modifications to the hook damper, whose stiffness was increased. First evaluation flights were undertaken at RAE Farnborough, SR666 arriving on 27 July. The land and sea trials quickly proved that the modification had eradicated the fault, thus it was quickly approved for embodiment in production machines by the end of the month.

Deck-Landing Trials

Full-blown deck-landing trials began aboard the fleet aircraft carrier HMS *Ocean* on 10 August and were judged successful enough for the next stage to be started. To begin with, this next sequence was land-based, and required that SR666 be despatched to RAE Farnborough during July 1946 for deck-catapult launching trials. Initially the aircraft was launched from the establishment's land-based catapult in the tail-down hold-back position, however this arrangement generated forces of such intensity, 2.2g, that the tailwheel assembly collapsed under the load. To repair the aircraft it was necessary to return it to the manufacturers, especially as one of the runways at Langley was grass, therefore a temporary repair was instituted to allow the damaged fighter to return home and land on the less abrasive grass surface.

Investigation by Hawker's soon revealed that the collapse had been caused by the unlocked tailwheel shimmying on launch, which increased the already high load

Below Photographed overflying HMS *Formidable*, this Sea Fury X would soon join the circuit to land.
Fleet Air Arm Museum

placed upon the assembly. So that the launch trials could continue, a temporary tail leg was installed, which was locked in the down position; however, with the temporary modification in place, the maximum speed was limited to 200mph (320km/h) IAS. Although the airborne speed was limited, the trials were resumed, these being brought to a swift conclusion during the first week in October 1946. Unlike numerous other aircraft operated by the Fleet Air Arm, the Sea Fury was fitted with a centreline catapult spool, which had proved to be more efficient with the tailwheel assembly in the locked position.

Six months later the Sea Fury X, complete with folding wings, was in production for the squadrons of the Fleet Air Arm. From the early-build machines the fourth aircraft, TF989, was seconded to RAE Farnborough for catapult acceleration trials. Following on from these trials the Sea Fury was transferred to HMS *Illustrious* to evaluate the behaviour of the production machines during the critical take-off and landing phases. Successfully completed, the next sequence of trials aboard the same carrier used the sixth production machine, TF900, although these involved the full range of carrier operations. In contrast to the prototypes and the initial production Sea Furies, this aircraft had been fitted with an arrestor hook with a longer arm that was far more rigid. Fitment of this kind of hook assembly had immediate benefits, one of which was increased stability of the aircraft after connecting with the arrestor wire and during the subsequent landing run. The inspiration for this modification had been a report by the Intensive Service Trials Unit, which had strongly noted that the shorter arrestor hook had been quite flexible and had caused weather cocking on the landing run out.

Testing the Armament

Having completed the landing and take-off trials successfully, it was turn of Sea Fury X VR920 to be passed to RAE Farnborough for evaluation of the RATOG equipment; this took place during November and December 1947. While the RATOG firing and launch trials were completed with few problems, the same could not be said of the weaponry trials. The greatest culprits were the

Above **Sea Fury X TF895 was the first production machine, and is pictured here at Langley. In contrast to earlier machines, only one large intake is mounted on the wing leading edges, and the propeller assembly was still a four-bladed unit.** Big Bird Aviation Collection

underwing rocket projectiles and their zero-length launch rails. In their original manufactured condition the mounting shear pins showed a disturbing tendency to fail under the high 'g' loading generated by an off-centre line-arrested landing, which resulted in 60lb (27kg) rockets skittering across the carrier deck. Fortunately for all involved the warheads were completely inert, but even so, it would take all those involved another eleven months to correct this fault.

Maiden Flight of the First Production Machine

While the occasional glitch occurred during the Sea Fury carrier trials, nevertheless it was sufficiently advanced for production to continue. The final total of Sea Fury Xs ordered from Hawker's would reach fifty aircraft, as it was seen as an interim version and would be useful as a development and training machine. This particular variant was very similar to the prototype SR666, although its powerplant had been changed to the production Bristol Centaurus 18 engine rated at 2,480hp, which in turn drove a four-bladed propeller assembly. The first production machine, complete with a short arrestor hook, was rolled out after ground trials during September 1946, and

at the end of the month TF895 made its maiden flight from the Langley airfield, piloted by company pilot R. V. Morell.

Of the fifty aircraft manufactured, at least twenty would be diverted for test, trials and development purposes. The manufacturers retained aircraft TF895 and TF897 for general performance and handling trials, and TF900 for the specific purpose of testing the rudder spring tab to determine the best settings for its usage. The trialling of weapons was carried out using TF923, while aircraft TF898 and TF899 were used for ground- and carrier-based landing trials, and pre-service release trials were undertaken at A&AEE using Sea Furies TF902 and TF908. Further pre-release trials involving the internally mounted Hispano Mark V short-barrelled cannon armament and other external weapon loads were also undertaken at Boscombe Down, using any available aircraft. In addition, trials involving modified underwing rocket projectiles were carried out at the A&AEE, eventually sixteen being cleared for carriage on Duplex mountings.

While some of the production aircraft were involved in these trials, there was still a role for prototype SR666, which was to carry out release and carriage trials for both 500lb and 1,000lb bombs. Clearance was also obtained for other external stores already in Fleet Air Arm service, which included 1,000lb incendiary bombs, Type

2 Mark II smoke floats, plus the 45 and 90gal (205 and 410ltr) underwing fuel tanks. It fell to TF923 to act as the carrier aircraft during the trials involving the design and development of napalm tanks. Not only did this involve the behaviour of various shapes, it also included their performance when dropped from different altitudes.

Once all these numerous trials had been completed, the Controller Aircraft cleared the Hawker Sea Fury X for operational service on 31 July 1947.

Below With only its underwing serials applied, the first production Sea Fury X TF895 has emerged unpainted into the sunlight for its initial official portrait. Big Bird Aviation Collection

Above Although the Sea Fury X presents an unbalanced appearance in this head-on view, it had no effect on performance. TF895 spent most of its life undertaking trials work with Hawker's and the A&AEE. Big Bird Aviation Collection

The Sea Fury into Active Service

Having run the gamut of Hawkers, the A&AEE and the Intensive Flying Trials Unit, the Sea Fury was cleared for use by the Fleet Air Arm, whose No. 778 Sqn, based at RNAS Ford, accepted their first machine in February 1947. Observers of the FAA will instantly recognize that No. 778 Sqn was destined to act as the Sea Fury conversion and training unit. Initially it received three machines – TF905, TF906

and TF907 – although this was quickly reduced to two when TF906 was lost in a crash on 20 June, the cause being attributed to mishandling by the pilot. Following on from No. 778 Sqn, the first operational unit to receive the Sea Fury X was No. 807 Squadron based at Eglinton, whose first machines arrived during September 1947; the new fighter was replacing the earlier and slightly more docile Supermarine Seafire XVII. The contrast in aircraft behaviour was pointed up only too clearly when TF915 was lost in a crash on 21 August 1948.

As Hawker's and the Fleet Air Arm had resolved the faults of the Sea Fury X, the company felt able to offer the Admiralty the far more capable Mark 11; this featured power-folding wings as standard, amongst other innovations. One of the benefits of such a system was that it would improve the strike-down times for the deck crews trying to run a carrier flight deck under pressure. The power-folding system fitted to the Sea Fury 11 was hydraulically operated: it folded and extended the outer panels, and locking was achieved using pins driven by similar means. To enable the new version of the Sea Fury to become operational as quickly as possible, all the weapons previously trialled using the

Mark X were cleared for use with little fuss. Another change from the earlier Sea Fury version was the use of a balanced five-bladed propeller assembly driven by a Bristol Centaurus 18 engine rated at 2,480hp. These two changes would raise the basic weight of the aircraft to 9,240lb (4,190kg).

The introduction of the Sea Fury into the Fleet Air Arm brought about some changes in the make-up of the Air Wings aboard the aircraft carriers. As the Sea Fury normally flew with external tanks fitted as standard, the Admiralty decided that this aircraft would act in the fighter-bomber role, while the newly introduced Supermarine Seafire F/FR.47 would act as a short-range fleet defence fighter with a secondary reconnaissance role. Those Air Wings still operating the Fairey Firefly V would use this multi-place machine as a long-range defence fighter.

Production of the Sea Fury would be spread over a period of seven years; all in all, Hawker's rolled out 615 aircraft from its factory at Kingston. Such a production run allowed numerous Fleet Air Arm squadrons to re-equip with the heavy fighter; thus No. 802 Sqn would be the first operational unit to receive the Sea Fury 11 in April 1948, while based at Eglinton. Following on from No. 802 Sqn came Nos 801, 804, 805 and 807 Sqns, which would equip with the type in March 1951, July 1949, August 1948 and February 1948 respectively. During this period the units were based at Lee-on-Solent, Hal Far, Malta and Eglinton, although all four would embark aboard the fleet carriers HMS *Ocean*, *Theseus* and *Glory* for shake-down cruises and carrier qualifications during the period 1949 to 1950.

The Sea Fury Trainer Prototype

Since the Hawker Sea Fury was viewed as high spirited, it is surprising that a two-seat conversion trainer was not included in any of the original production contracts. The first Sea Fury trainers were actually built for the Iraqi Fury contract, and originally featured two separate canopies. The first Sea Fury trainer for the Admiralty was a diverted Iraqi machine: re-serialled VX818, this machine was reworked to the standards set in the

Admiralty Standards of Preparation manual, before making its first flight from the Hawker test airfield at Langley on 15 January 1948. After the successful completion of company test-flying, the trainer prototype was transferred to A&AEE Boscombe Down for evaluation and pre-service release.

It was during this series of flights that VX818, still with its two separate canopies, suffered a collapse of the rear bubble canopy. Investigations of this failure revealed that the rear canopy, although of similar design and construction to the front assembly, was unable to withstand the stresses and strains of manoeuvring. The answer was to construct a greenhouse affair that was basically two canopies connected by a perspex tunnel, since this assembly ensured that there would be equalized pressure between the two cockpits.

Having solved the cockpit pressure problem, attention now turned to providing a means for the instructor to monitor the student in the front seat. This was made possible by installing a periscope mounted on a framework above the tunnel.

At the completion of these trials, the trainer was cleared for production as the Sea Fury T.20. The production version of the T.20 required that some further adjustments be made to the aircraft's weights

Above Sea Fury 11 VR941 wears the early original colour scheme applied to the type in its first years, where the dark sea grey reaches most of the way down the fuselage. This particular machine was allocated to No. 703 Sqn based at Lee-on-Solent. FAA Museum Collection

Below VX818 had originally been built as one of four aircraft for the Iraqi Air Force; however, it was diverted by the MoS for use as the Fleet Air Arm prototype T Mark 20. In this view the overhead periscope has still to be installed. Fleet Air Arm Collection

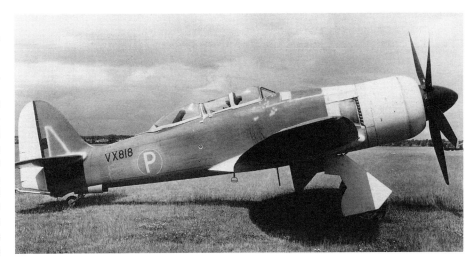

Left **Sea Fury T 20 WG655 wears the codes and tail letters of the Station Flight at Eglinton in this view taken at Yeovilton. Clearly visible under the wings are the mounting points for the zero-length rocket rail.** W. A. Harrison Collection

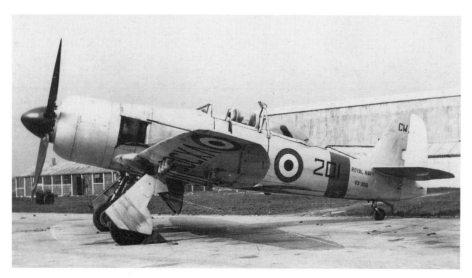

Above **Sea Fury VX652, also of No. 738 Sqn, sports a full range of practice rockets under the wings, whilst waiting for its pilot at Culdrose to begin its next mission.** W. A. Harrison Collection

Left **Also based at Culdrose was No. 738 Sqn, whose role was that of air-to-air and air-to-ground training as part of the Naval Air Fighter School. Sea Fury T 20 VX308 was employed in the conversion and training role by this unit.** W. A. Harrison Collection

and balances, hence two of the wing-mounted Hispano cannon plus ancillaries were deleted, as was the arrestor hook, since the trainer was not cleared for carrier operations. It was, however, fully capable of carrying the full range of weaponry cleared for the single-seat versions.

Overall a total of sixty Sea Fury T.20 trainers were manufactured for Fleet Air Arm usage. They would enter service during 1950, with deliveries continuing until 1952. Units operating the Sea Fury trainer included Nos 703, 736, 738, 759, 766, 771, 781, 782, 787 and 799 Sqns in the support role. The front-line units also had examples for conversion and training purposes; these included Nos 801, 802 and 809 Sqns. The Royal Navy Reserve was also equipped with the T.20, these being Nos 1830, 1831, 1832, 1833 and 1834 Sqns, plus various station flights.

Above **Sea Fury FB.50 6-16 was operated by the Royal Netherlands Navy's No. 860 Sqn, and was caught on film heading towards the aircraft carrier HrMs *Karel Doorman*.** FAA Museum Collection

Export Sales for the Sea Fury

Outside the Fleet Air Arm, Hawker's had managed to mount an intensive sales drive that would result in reasonable overseas sales. The first country to place an order for export Sea Furies was the Netherlands, who required them for the Royal Netherlands Navy. The contract, N/SF/2001, was placed on 21 October 1946, and covered the delivery of ten Sea Fury F.50 fighters that were directly equivalent to the Mark X of the FAA. Serialled 10-1 to 10-10, they were intended for service aboard the light fleet carrier HMS *Nairana*, which would eventually become the first HrMs *Karel Doorman* upon transfer to the Dutch Navy. The operating unit of the Hawker fighter would be No. 860 Sqn, which had originally been formed as a Fleet Air Arm unit before the number plate had been surrendered to the R. Neth Navy after the conclusion of hostilities in 1945. No. 860 Sqn undertook its working-up period at RNAS St Merryn before the aircraft were flown out to join their carrier. In a scenario that preceded the creation of NATO, the Sea Furies of the R. Neth Navy worked in conjunction with their counterparts of the Fleet Air Arm; thus it was quite normal practice to observe Sea Furies from both services flying from land bases and carriers belonging to both services.

During 1947, No. 860 Sqn and its Sea Furies were in action over the Dutch East Indies, where they flew in support of

Above **This excellent portrait of a Royal Netherlands Navy Sea Fury FB.50 6-34, on approach to land at Valkenburg, shows the full spread of the flaps in the fully down position, the underwing fuel tanks and the zero-length rocket rails.** W. A. Harrison Collection

ground forces trying to push out Communist insurgents. The following year this first fleet carrier was returned to the Royal Navy who, in turn, would relinquish their ownership of the vessel to its original civilian owners. The Sea Fury F.50s would remain in use by No. 860 Sqn until their retirement from the front line on 18 March 1950.

This lack of an aircraft carrier and operational aircraft was a short-lived situation, because on 15 July 1950 No. 860 Sqn RNN was reformed by the simple expedient of renaming the Gevechts-vliegopleiding – or the Fighter Pilots Combat School – which was based at Valkenburg. This unit was equipped with the Hawker Sea Fury FB.50, the equivalent

of the Fleet Air Arm's FB.11. The contract, N/SF/3001, was placed with Hawker's on 12 January 1950, and covered the delivery of twelve aircraft plus spares and support. To take the squadron to sea, the R. Neth Navy acquired the fleet carrier HMS *Venerable* and renamed it the HrMs *Karel Doorman* after transfer on 1 April 1948. Local production of the Sea Fury FB.50 was undertaken in the Netherlands by Fokker, bringing the final total of aircraft up to forty-eight. No. 860 Sqn RNN would continue to operate its Sea Fury FB.50s until disbanding on 15 June 1956, passing its machines on to the newly formed No. 3 Sqn RNN, while the replacement for the Sea Fury would be another Hawker product, the jet-powered Sea Hawk.

Above **Parked up for the night is Sea Fury FB.50 6-36, one of a batch of aircraft built in Holland by Fokker.**
C. P. Russell Smith Collection

Above **Sea Fury 10-2 was one of the first batch of ten Sea Fury FB.50 fighters sold to the Royal Netherlands Navy. It was allocated to No. 860 Sqn, and wears the earlier scheme where the dark sea grey reaches to the bottom line of the fuselage.** C. P. Russell Smith Collection

Sea Furies for Canada

Outside of a future NATO partner, Hawker's would also secure sales from countries within the Commonwealth. One of the first to benefit was the Royal Canadian Navy, which had become a separate service from the Royal Canadian Air Force in late 1945. The new service would contract for thirty-five aircraft, although no individual agreement was issued, as these machines would be diverted out of Fleet Air Arm requirements and be replaced later on. Deliveries

were made between 1948 and 1951, the aircraft used to equip No. 883 Sqn, which was part of the 18th Carrier Air Group, and No. 803 Sqn of the 19th Carrier Air Group. The first Sea Fury, basically a Mark 11, was accepted by the RCN on 23 June 1948 at the RCAF base at Rockliffe.

Having formed two carrier air groups, the Royal Canadian Navy acquired its first aircraft carrier, HMS *Warrior*, during January 1946. The previously assigned air group had originally been equipped with Supermarine Seafires and Fairey Fireflies

before the Hawker fighters arrived. A replacement for HMS *Warrior* also arrived for the RCN in the shape of HMCS *Magnificent*, a member of the Majestic class of ships, which would become affectionately known as the *Maggie* in service. The proposed air wing complement would consist of Fairey Fireflies for the anti-submarine role, with that of the Sea Furies being fleet air defence and air support for the Fireflies. Being to the same standard as their Fleet Air Arm equivalents, the RCN machines were cleared for the full range of external stores, including fuel tanks, rockets and bombs.

While the RCN flying squadrons were being given their operational work-up at RNAS Eglinton in Northern Ireland, their new floating home was carrying out a similar set of exercises in the Atlantic to prepare for the airborne complement. With both the carrier and the aircraft declared ready for service, HMCS *Magnificent* departed for Canada with the Sea Furies of both the 18th and 19th Carrier Air Groups aboard. Once in Canadian territorial waters, the aircraft assigned to the 18th CAG were transferred to the RCAF Joint Air School at Rivers, Manitoba, for further specialized training. Whilst the 19th CAG was to become the conversion and training unit for the RCN Sea Fury force, the other unit, the 18th CAG, remained aboard the carrier for operational purposes.

To reinforce the usage of the RCAF base at Manitoba, the Canadian Cabinet Defence Committee recommended in September 1948 that the facility be transferred to the RCN. This was duly done, the new base becoming known as RCNS Shearwater. During this period of changeover, the aircraft of the 19th CAG came ashore for further extensive training, while its place was taken by the 18th CAG. While the latter was acclimatizing to life aboard a bouncing airfield in the middle of the ocean, their counterparts completed their training in Canada, after which they departed to the US Navy base at Quonset Point; here they would receive training in US Navy carrier-deck landing practices. The method used by the Royal Canadian Navy involved following a maintained approach height during the landing circuit, then turning and descending at a steady rate of altitude loss, and touching down on the carrier deck under positive power. In contrast, the US Navy preferred their pilots to fly a gentle,

Above **Wearing the very first colour scheme and markings is this Sea Fury FB.11 TG120 of the Royal Canadian Navy. This particular machine, coded B-GC, was the personal machine of the Air Group Commander, 19th Carrier Air Group.** C. P. Russell Smith Collection

Right **Allocated to No. 803 Sqn RCN, this Sea Fury FB.11, VX690, coded 'BC-O', would serve on HMCS *Warrior* as part of 19th CAG, before being renumbered No. 870 Sqn on 1 May 1951.** C. P. Russell Smith Collection

Below **When No. 870 Sqn was not at sea aboard HMCS *Magnificent*, their home base was normally RCNS Dartmouth. Heading this line-up is Sea Fury FB.11 WG566/132.** C. P. Russell Smith Collection

descending curve before chopping the throttle just above the deck, and coming down under the control of the deck landing officer.

Changing from their well drilled and familiar method of deck landing caused the pilots of the RCN some serious problems. Under the original training regime, the aircraft would land in a slightly tail-down attitude; in the American fashion, the aircraft landed on the main wheels only, with the tail held higher. However, landings of this type began to cause problems for both the Sea Furies and the pilots. For the aircraft, it overstressed the airframe and caused structural damage, as the British aircraft was actually designed for a more tail-down attitude during landing; the American way saw planes bouncing as the main wheels hit the deck, this being caused by the compression returning the undercarriage leg to full extension earlier than normal. The result was that, although the Sea Fury might be lucky and engage the last deck wire, the more likely outcome was a complete failure to engage as the bounce carried the fighter over the wires.

While the aircraft of the 19th CAG were enjoying a life of bouncing over carrier wires in America, the 18th CAG was at sea practising for all eventualities – although the cruise would not be without incident, since at least one Sea Fury would be lost due to engine failure, crashing into the sea. Fortunately the pilot was rescued, damp but unharmed. This loss notwithstanding, the 18th CAG continued its work-up exercises, one of which was to practise an intercept on a target ship tran-

siting from the Canal Zone to Jamaica. The target ship was HMS *Jamaica* and would be intercepted by patrolling Sea Furies some 210 miles (340km) from the carrier. Having located the ship, the Sea Furies returned to *Magnificent* for arming with practice weapons and refuelling, before flying a further 162 miles (260km) back towards HMS *Jamaica* where a successful simulated strike was carried out.

As this was the era of records being set by military pilots around the world, it was soon the turn of the Royal Canadian Navy to make their attempt. The intended mission was to fly from Toronto, Ontario, to Halifax, Nova Scotia in the shortest possible time. The departure point was from Malton Airport and the arrival point RCNAS Dartmouth, a distance of 825 air miles (1,327km). The subsequent flight in December 1949 was attempted by two Sea Furies from No. 883 Sqn, and they took 1hr 54min at an average 435.35mph (700.48km/h) IAS.

With a routine established, the Royal Canadian Navy was subjected to interference by Canadian politicians, who decided that the aircraft and personnel of the RCN needed reorganization. The results of their deliberations were presented to the Navy in January 1951. The first changes affected the 18th CAG, whose component units would be numbered as Nos 826 and 883 Sqns, while the 19th CAG would be renamed as the Support Air Group, with Nos 803 and 825 Squadrons as the assigned units. This latter would establish itself permanently at RCNAS Shearwater as a land-based unit. Also established at this time was the new

Bombing and Gunnery Range at Chezzetcook, which would be christened by the Sea Furies of the 18th CAG before they departed to Quonset Point for a pre-cruise work-up. Once the training had been completed, the air wing then flew out to join HMCS *Magnificent*, which was cruising off Bermuda. Unfortunately this cruise was not without incident, as the group lost two Sea Furies and one pilot in accidents.

Further changes were to be inflicted upon the RCN during 1951, when the squadrons were renumbered in the Commonwealth series, which was similar in sequence to that operated by the US Navy. These alterations finally severed all links with the Fleet Air Arm. Thus Nos 803 and 825 Sqns would be renumbered to Nos 870 and 880 Squadrons, becoming in turn the air component of the 31st SAG. The 18th CAG was renumbered to become the 30th CAG, and its original units, Nos 883 and 826 Sqns, would become Nos 871 and 881 Sqns respectively. These squadrons transferred ashore to RCNAS Shearwater for intensive night-landing training, before embarking aboard the *Magnificent* for a cruise. Their place was temporarily taken by pilots and aircraft from the 31st SAG.

With its night-time training completed, the 30th CAG joined their aircraft carrier; this meant that the 31st SAG aircraft could return to Shearwater. The exercise the 'Maggie' and its aircraft were involved in was entitled Exercise *Castinets*, and required the pilots to take part in numerous night-time anti-submarine and combat air patrols, complete with the added extra hazard of a night-time landing. Exercise *Castinets* was undertaken in European waters during June 1951, and the air wing would achieve its highest total of flying hours. During the following month, the carrier and attendant ships were sailing in the Mediterranean Sea where some very unseasonal weather was experienced. The storms were severe enough to force four of the carrier's Sea Furies to divert to the Greek air base at Aroxas, as conditions surrounding the carrier made it too dangerous to attempt a landing. As the fleet progressed through the Mediterranean, the decision was made to move the Sea Furies to the Greek airbase at Ellinkon, so that another attempt could be made to rejoin the carrier. Airborne once more, the four Sea Furies made their approaches to land

---

Ex-Fleet Air Arm Sea Furies in Foreign Service

Royal Canadian Navy Sea Fury FB.11
TF985, TF993, TF994, TF995, TF997, TF998, TF999, TG113, TG114, TG115, TG116, TG117, TG118, TG119, TG120, TG121, TG122, TG123, TG124, TG125, TG126, TG127, TG128, TG129, VR918, VR919, VW230, VW231, VW563, VW571, WJ299, WJ300, WJ301, WN474, WN479

Royal Australian Navy Sea Fury FB.11
VX724, VX725, VX726, VX727, VX728, VX729, VX749, VX750, VX751, VX752, VX755, VX756, VX757, VX758, VX759, VX760, VX761, VX762, VX763, VX764, WE675, WE676, WE678, WE796

Union of Burma Air Force Sea Fury FB.11/TT.11
UB454, VR928, UB455, VR929, UB456, VW566, UB457, VW667, UB458, VW694, UB459, VW717, UB460, VX628, UB461, VX656, UB462, VX693, UB463, WE720, UB464, WF615, UB465, WH585, UB466, WH613, UB467, WH619, UB468, WJ232, UB469, WJ280, UB470, WM488, UB471, WN486

Union of Burma Air Force Sea Fury T.20
UB451, VZ368, UB452, VZ292, UB453, VZ354

---

aboard the 'Maggie'. Two made a successful touch-down, while the third reported hydraulic problems. As there was no pressing need for the aircraft to rejoin the carrier, the third machine was instructed to return to Ellinkon with the fourth acting as escort; once in sight of the Greek airfield an undercarriage emergency blowdown was used to lower the undercarriage, and the aircraft landed without further incident. HMCS *Magnificent* would later despatch a repair crew and spares in a Grumman Avenger to attend to the ailing fighter. Once the repairs had been carried out, all three aircraft were ordered to rejoin the air wing at Hal Far, Malta, which they duly did on 27 July.

Having cruised in the sun, the carrier group ended up in the North Atlantic during September 1952, to take part in Operation *Main Brace*; this was scheduled to last for thirteen days, and would act in concert with the air group from the Royal Navy Fleet carrier HMS *Theseus*. For the Sea Furies, the missions would entail combat air patrols and anti-submarine patrols, before acting as top cover escort for practice landings in northern Denmark.

Although the RCN was quite at home operating alongside its Royal Navy counterparts, the influence of Canada's larger neighbour was becoming increasingly evident. This time the squadron designations were set to change again, becoming closer in style to that of the US Navy: thus No. 880 Sqn would be re-designated VS 880, the others being similarly re-designated.

During February 1953, the aircraft of 30th CAG were ashore operating from the base at Shearwater, where they were involved in a close air support operation entitled Exercise *Assiniboine*. Having completed their part in this simulated war game, the 30th CAG was prepared for another sea-going cruise. This would be very much a flag-waving exercise, as HMS *Magnificent* and its air group were scheduled to take part in the Spithead Coronation Review flypast. Departing from Canada at the beginning of June, the carrier group arrived in time to play its part in the review on 15 June, in which eight RCN Sea Furies were involved.

Whilst the 30th CAG was at Spithead, the 31st SAG was vacating its Shearwater base for a temporary home at RCAF Scoudouc in New Brunswick, while its home base underwent major reconstruc-

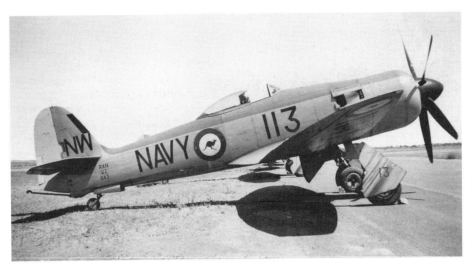

Above **Based at RNAS Nowra, Sea Fury FB.11 WZ643 wears the side code 113 applicable to No. 805 Sqn RAN.** C. P. Russell Smith Collection

tion. The sojourn of the SAG was short-lived, however, as Scoudouc was scheduled to close; therefore a further relocation to the RCAF base at Summerside on Prince Edward Island was required.

When the Korean War erupted, the Canadian forces were very keen to be a part of the action on behalf of the United Nations. However, this was not to be, as the Canadian government had stated that the role of the carrier HMCS *Magnificent* was that of anti-submarine patrols, not that of attack. Nevertheless, although denied their part in the Korean War, the carrier air group would find themselves embroiled in Exercise *Mariner*, involving some 300 vessels and over 1,000 aircraft. This exercise was one of the first put together by the nascent NATO as a show of co-operative strength. As this was a typical NATO exercise, the opposing forces were designated as blue and orange. For the Canadians this meant they would be part of the blue force, also regarded as the good guys. For the Sea Furies of VF 871, this meant flying sorties that covered long-range combat air-patrol and anti-submarine missions.

After the successful completion of *Mariner*, HMCS *Magnificent* and its air group would continue the usual round of exercises, cruises and operations until mid-1956; at this time the Sea Furies began to enter storage, prior to final disposal. Their place would be taken by the RCN's first jet aircraft, the McDonnell F2H-3 Banshee. The final official flight of a Hawker Sea Fury sporting RCN colours took place in

early 1957, when WG565 was delivered to Reserve Air Squadron VG 924 based at Calgary, Alberta.

Sea Furies for Australia

Nearly a world away, the Royal Australian Navy were also to be recipients of Sea Fury FB.11s, diverted from Fleet Air Arm contracts. The first aircraft, VW562, was accepted by the RAN in 1950, and would be followed by a further thirty-two machines. Two units were formed to operate the Hawker fighter, these being Nos 805 and 808 Sqn, both deployed aboard the fleet carrier HMAS *Sydney* and the Royal Navy carrier HMS *Vengeance* for service in the skies of Korea. No. 805 Sqn had formed at Eglinton, Northern Ireland, in late 1948 with an inventory of thirteen Sea Furies. Once the squadron had completed its working-up period, the aircraft were flown out to the carrier HMAS *Sydney*; they then sailed from the Atlantic for Australian waters. At the conclusion of the Korean War, No. 805 Sqn was deployed as the guard squadron whose role was to protect the Monte Bello Atomic Test Area. It fulfilled this task until its disbandment on 26 March, at the RAN station at Nowra.

The other Sea Fury operator, No. 808 Sqn, began its career with the Hawker fighter at St Merryn on 25 April 1950, where they too would receive thirteen aircraft. After the obligatory work-up, the squadron's aircraft flew out to join HMAS *Sydney*, where it would become part of the

Above **No. 805 Sqn had its home base at Nowra, where it wore 'NW' tailcodes while at sea aboard the carrier HMAS Sydney; the code would change to 'K' indicating that WZ649/106 had recently returned ashore to Nowra, as this portrait shows.** C. P. Russell Smith Collection

21st CAG. No. 808 Sqn split its time between the carriers *Sydney* and *Vengeance* whilst undertaking operations in the hostile skies of Korea. At the end of their active service the Sea Furies were flown to Nowra, so that the squadron could disband, on 5 October 1954. One other front-line unit flew the Sea Fury: No. 850 Sqn, which used twelve of the big Hawker fighters from January 1953 to August 1954 for a short period of service in Korean skies.

Although the Sea Fury would leave the front-line service of the RAN, it pursued a second career with No. 724 Sqn, a training support unit. At the end, the replacement for the Sea Fury FB.11 in RAN service was the de Havilland Sea Venom, although a few of the piston fighters would remain in use with No. 724 Sqn until late 1962, for target-towing duties, amongst other support roles.

Sea Furies for Burma

Outside the Commonwealth and European air forces, Hawker's managed to establish a reasonable market in the sale of refurbished machines to other air forces. One of these countries would be Burma, whose government, a more enlightened organization in those days, would order eighteen ex-Fleet Air Arm FB.11s. Contract HAL/57/B/030 was issued to cover the refurbishment of these aircraft, two of which were fitted with under-fuselage shackle points for target-towing. Although no official designation change was given for these aircraft, they were variously referred to as FB.11(TT) or TT.11s. Deliveries of these aircraft were made throughout 1958, the single-seaters being followed by three two-seat TT.20 trainers. The serials for these machines were UB454 to UB471 for the fighters, while the trainers were UB451 to UB453. Flown by the Union of Burma Air Force, the Sea Furies would remain in service until 1968, when they were replaced by Lockheed T-33s.

Below **The coding '103-K' indicates that this Sea Fury FB.11, WZ645, was allocated to No. 805 Sqn of the Royal Australian Navy during 1955–58.** C. P. Russell Smith Collection

Above **The Union of Burma Air Force purchased three T.20s from Hawker's, all being ex-Royal Navy. UB451 had originally been VZ368, and would be delivered in 1958.** C. P. Russell Smith Collection

Right **Gleaming in silver lacquer, this Union Of Burma Air Force Sea Fury FB.11, UB454, had originally been on the strength of the Fleet Air Arm before being delivered in 1958. As these were land-based aircraft, the arrestor hook was removed.** C. P. Russell Smith Collection

Sea Furies for the Middle East

The Middle East would also prove to be a fairly lucrative market for Hawker's. The first country to purchase versions of the Hawker fighter was Egypt, who took delivery of the prototype F2/43 Fury in mid-1948; it had been refurbished by Hawker's, the work including the replacement of the early type of Bristol engine by a production Centaurus XVIII. After flight-testing, the Fury was registered G-AKRY to comply with ferrying regulations. Upon arrival in Egypt the Fury was displayed to the hierarchy of the Egyptian Air Force, who were so enthused by the aircraft's performance that they immediately placed an order. But even before the ink was dry, the contract was embargoed due to the growing level of hostilities between the Arab states and the emergent state of Israel. As this arms embargo only covered exports by British firms, it is

hardly surprising that others not so affected would step into the breech. One supplier was Iraq, who supplied two Furies from their own stocks to bolster the Egyptian forces. At least one of these aircraft was lost in air-to-air combat with a Spitfire from the Israeli Air Force. Of the other two machines, the Fury prototype and the Iraqi AF machine, no further reports were forthcoming, although it is thought that they suffered the same fate.

At the cessation of hostilities the arms embargo was relaxed, which allowed the EAF finally to confirm the purchase of twelve Sea Furies to contract 17/49/USS, for delivery during 1950–51. Of this total at least one would be destroyed on the ground during the opening phase of Operation *Musketeer*, the purpose of which was to recapture the Suez Canal during the months of November/ December 1956.

Sea Furies for Iraq

In contrast to more recent times, the West enjoyed cordial relations with Iraq during the 1950s. The first order placed by Iraq was confirmed on 4 December 1946, for thirty single-seat fighters, designated as ISS or Iraqi single-seaters, and four trainers designated as IDT or Iraqi dual trainers – although this part of the order was eventually reduced to two airframes. On 21 July 1951 a further order was placed for fifteen new-build ISS fighters, followed by yet another contract on 7 March 1953 for ten refurbished FB.11s and three T.20 trainers, diverted from Fleet Air Arm resources. All these aircraft were delivered during 1952 and 1953.

The company employed to deliver the Iraqi aircraft was Airwork Ltd, who would collect each batch from the Hawker airfield at Langley and deliver them via Blackbushe, Nice, Malta, Mersah Metruh,

Above **Designated as the ISS Fury – the Iraqi single-seat Fury – this aircraft was delivered to Baghdad in 1951. These aircraft remained in service until replaced by equipment from the Soviet Union.** C. P. Russell Smith Collection

Below **Photographed at Blackbushe, this Hawker Fury would be delivered to Iraq by pilots from Airwork. Some of these aircraft would eventually go to Morocco, while others would end up in America as pylon racers at Reno.** C. P. Russell Smith Collection

Nicosia and thence to Baghdad. Immediately after touch-down, some of the waiting groundcrew would help the pilot out of the cockpit while others opened the engine cowlings to increase the rate of engine cooling. During their use by the Iraqi AF, the Furies were reportedly used in action against the Kurdish tribesman in Northern Iraq. The increasing influence of Russia in Iraqi affairs would lead to the withdrawal of the Furies, starting in 1960, after which they were placed in storage. Instead of being scrapped, however, the remaining aircraft were purchased by an American consortium during the 1970s for use in the Reno air races.

Above right The initial Sea Fury trainers built for Iraq featured a double canopy arrangement, although this tended to collapse under changing pressures. Big Bird Aviation Collection

Right Although each Baghdad Fury was fitted with external 45gal (205ltr) fuel tanks, they still required fuelling stops along the way; even so, some of the stages were a struggle against unpredicted headwinds. Big Bird Aviation Collection

Below Photographed at Nicosia, this ISS Fury on delivery to the Iraqi Air Force will stay on the ground until the early hours of the morning when it will be cooler, thus allowing the aircraft to take off fully loaded without putting a strain on the engine. C. P. Russell Smith Collection

Sea Furies for Morocco

Not all the Iraqi Furies went into storage, however: a pair was given to Morocco for the embryonic Aviation Royale Cherifienne on 4 February 1960. A further pair was presented to the same service in 1961, although the fighters saw little operational usage; they were placed in storage at Rabat, before being sold to an American dealer.

Sea Furies for Pakistan

Pakistan was one of the largest export customers for the Sea Fury after the coun- try's independence in 1947. The service doctrine adopted by the newly formed Pakistan Air Force closely followed that of the Royal Air Force, and the new fight- ers were required to replace the Tempests already in service with three squadrons. The total of Furies ordered on behalf of the PAF was ninety-three aircraft. The first was the Fury prototype F2/43, NX802, delivered in 1949 after a thor- ough refurbishment by Hawker's. Fifty production aircraft, designated as the F.60, were ordered during 1950, while a further contract for twenty-four was placed in 1951. During the period 1951–52 a final order for thirteen new- build machines was placed with Hawker's. To complete the re-equipment of the PAF, a further five fighters, all ex-FAA Sea Fury FB.11s, were ordered, these being delivered to Pakistan during 1953–54. To help with the conversion requirements of the PAF, a total of four trainers was ordered as T.61s; one came from the Iraqi contract, while the remainder were new build.

As the Furies were delivered they were used to equip Nos 5 and 9 Sqns during 1950, while in the following year No 14 Sqn would also change over to the Fury.

Left **Hawker Pakistani Sea Fury 60 L982 was one of a batch of aircraft delivered during the period 1951–52. Further machines would follow, some being ex-FAA machines refurbished by Hawker's.** Big Bird Aviation Collection

Below **Unlike in later years, the Pakistani Furies were delivered with their cannon and external fuel tanks fitted. L951 was one of the second batch of aircraft delivered during 1951.** W. A. Harrison Collection

Above **Cuban Sea Fury FB.11 541 is one of two on display in Cuba. It is seen here complete with underwing rockets, and is rumoured to have taken part in the Bay of Pigs defensive action.** FAA Museum Collection

Also equipping with the Fury was No. 2 Fighter Conversion School, based at Maripur, which received a handful of F.60 fighters and the two-seaters for conversion and training purposes. The Fury would remain in PAF front-line service until 1955, being replaced by North American F-86 Sabres; however, No. 9 Sqn would retain its piston fighters until 1960, as they were needed for patrols along the north-west frontier. They were then replaced by Lockheed F-104A Starfighters – quite a contrast! The final Furies would be retired during 1963 after employment in the target-towing role.

Sea Furies for Cuba

Only one other country would order the Sea Fury, this being Cuba, which placed a contract for fifteen FB.11s and two T.20s, all ex-FAA machines acquired by Hawker's for refurbishment from the MoS. The contract was placed in 1957, and the aircraft were delivered during 1958 by sea, when they were dismantled and crated for transit. As the Batista government was facing internal strife, the Sea Furies were the subject of exceptional security upon arrival in Havana. Once uncrated, they were assembled and test-flown, though they were unable to support the Batista

forces as they lacked armament. Whether their support would have made a difference is a moot point, as the Batista regime was overthrown by the forces of Fidel Castro on 1 January 1959.

As the Castro regime was Communist in nature, the British government immediately placed an arms embargo on Cuba. This stopped the delivery of ten further Sea Furies, cannon shells, bombs and rocket projectiles, much of which would never reach the Caribbean. In a manner similar to most violent regime changes, there was a purge throughout the armed forces, which would leave the air force with only forty-three pilots to fly all of the country's aircraft. So that some semblance of an air force could be put into the air, representatives from the Cuban government met their Hawker equivalents to open negotiations for the delivery of cannons and shells to arm the Sea Furies. By November 1959 a total of twelve fighters were declared serviceable, although this status would not last long as the aircraft batteries were stolen during an internal power struggle within the air force.

To assist the Fuerza Aerea Revolucionaria in bringing its Sea Furies up to a usable standard, Hawker's despatched a civilian maintenance team under contract

to repair the aircraft. However, some of their efforts would be in vain, as the personnel of the FAR underwent yet another purge, which would leave the air force with just six pilots, although some reinforcements would come from Chile in the short term. These events took place throughout 1960, and only the efforts of the repair team and good spares support from Langley would keep the Sea Furies flyable.

Castro's takeover of Cuba provoked a reaction from the Americans, courtesy of the CIA. Their plans would come to fruition on 15 April 1961, when a force of Douglas B-26B Invaders, painted in FAC markings and crewed by Cuban exiles, carried out an attack on the airfield at La Libertad, which would result in the destruction of one Sea Fury on the ground, and another damaged beyond repair later in the day. The few survivors would re-gather at San Antonio AB to start ground-attack sorties against ground forces at they attempted beach landings. Another Sea Fury, FAR 541, would attack the supply and support ship *Houston* with rocket projectiles, eventually sinking it. During these exchanges yet another Sea Fury was shot down, leaving only two fighters to defend the island. These two stalwarts would only fly occasionally, and were replaced in June 1961 by a large force of MiG 15s. The Bay of Pigs fiasco was the last time that any Sea Fury would see combat action.

CHAPTER ELEVEN

The Sea Fury Described

In complete contrast to its Royal Air Force predecessors, the Hawker Sea Fury had two sets of parameters to contend with: the first involved the normal stresses and strains of military flying, while the other was that of landing on a pitching and tossing carrier deck. In a similar manner to the Typhoon and the Tempest, the construction of the Sea Fury was undertaken in sections. The fuselage was manufactured in two primary sections that were bolted together at adjoining frames. Each individual section consisted of individually manufactured frames, to which were attached numerous stringers, all being covered by a stressed alloy skin riveted into position. Cut-outs for access panels, complete with reinforced landings, were placed at strategic points about the fuselage, while the panels themselves were chemically etched with reinforcing internal stringers. Attachment to the fuselage was either by fasteners, or a mounting hinge and quick-release fasteners were used.

A third major component was the tail unit assembly, which was bolted onto the aft fuselage section at the rear fuselage transport joint. This rear assembly comprised a short section of fuselage, integral with which was the fin structure. Mountings were provided for the tailplane, elevators and rudder. At the rear of this section were the reinforced mountings for the tail hook, forward of which was the bay for the retractable tailwheel unit and its covering doors. The tailwheel assembly came complete with a locking mechanism, which would keep it locked fore and aft and gave stability during the take-off run.

At the other end of the fuselage was the engine firewall, to which was mounted the Bristol Centaurus XVIII powerplant; this was encased by removable cowling panels that were located between the single cowling ring and the engine bulkhead. To maintain the shape of the cowling panels and to provide a mounting point, reinforcing straps were mounted at intermediate points around the circumference. As the exhaust system for the engine was collected into two groups, there were two cut-outs, one each side of the fuselage, to allow for their egress. To protect the area where the gases ejected, the surrounding area and immediate structure was of a monel-based alloy capable of withstanding the temperatures generated. Although the monel alloy plates were effective in controlling the heat from the exhaust system, they were subject to heat-stress cracking themselves; thus they would need to be removed for welding at intervals.

The Wings

The three-section wings for both the Mark X and the FB.11 were similar in construction, both having fore and aft spars with breaks for the wing fold. Between the spars were shaped ribs complete with lightning holes for weight reduction. Mounted on the front face of the forward spar were shaped ribs, while on the rear face of the rear spar were a series of tapered ribs with clearance cut-outs for the flaps. Mounted hard by the wing break-points on the fixed centre section were the main undercarriage units, the forward of which was attached to the front spar, while the rear mounting was attached to a false half spar. The mounting of the undercarriage units so far apart gave the Sea Fury great stability during the landing and take-off phases.

Covering each undercarriage bay were three doors. The primary fairing was attached directly to the undercarriage leg, while a smaller hinged door – the hinge at the top attached to the lower wing surface – was connected to the leg via adjustable turnbarrels, and tracked the leg into the closed position. The inboard 'D' door was activated by a series of links and bell cranks, and fitted into place after the leg was up and locked. Driving the undercarriage in both directions were hydraulically powered jacks.

As well as the undercarriage units the wing centre section also housed the four Hispano V short-barrelled 20mm cannon plus their ammunition boxes and guidance

Below Unusually clean, Sea Fury VX653 sits on the dispersal awaiting its next pilot. As many of the panels and components were painted separately from the main airframe, it is not unusual to see slight disparities in alignments, as can be observed on the engine cowling ring. Big Bird Aviation Collection

DIMENSION DATA TABLE

L x W x D

	L x W x D
SPINNER	2ft 10ins x 2ft 9ins x 2ft 9 ins
PROPELLOR	12ft dia x 1ft 6ins
POWER PLANT	7ft 10ins x 4ft 11ins x 5ft 5ins
FUSELAGE CENTRE	10ft 0ins x 3ft 11ins x 6ft 6ins
FUSELAGE REAR	9ft 4ins x 3ft 5ins x 5ft 0ins
FUSELAGE TAIL	6ft 3ins x 1ft 11ins x 8ft 6ins
TAILPLANE	14ft 2ins x 3ft 4ins x 0ft 7ins
RUDDER	2ft 11ins x 0ft 6ins x 7ft 8ins
ELEVATOR	13ft 10ins x 1ft 10ins x 0ft 9ins
WING OUTER	11ft 6ins x 8ft 4ins x 1t 4ins
WING CENTRE	18ft 0ins x 9ft 10ins x 1ft 8ins
FLAP INNER	5ft 3ins x 2ft 2ins x 0ft 6ins
FLAP CENTRE	2ft 4ins x 1ft 9ins x 0ft 2.5ins
FLAP OUTER	3ft 8ins x 1ft 9ins x 0ft 2.5ins
AILERON	8ft 2ins x 2ft 1ins x 0ft 6ins
CANOPY	4ft 11ins x 2ft 2ins x 1ft 5ins

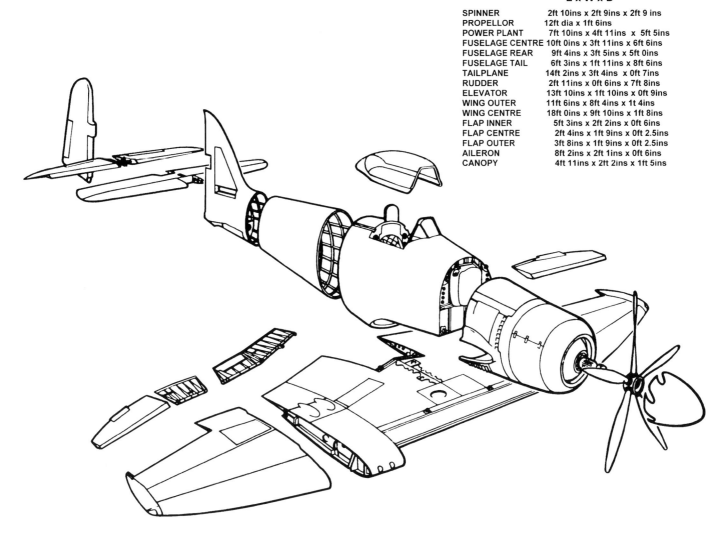

Above **This diagram shows all the major components that make up the Sea Fury, and includes all the relevant dimensions for each item.** Big Bird Aviation Collection

Right **Sea Fury X TF946 was on the strength of No. 803 Sqn of the Royal Canadian Navy during 1948 when this portrait was taken. The clarity of this view reveals the location of the fuselage footsteps, and the location of the retractable stirrup footstep.** C. P. Russell Smith Collection

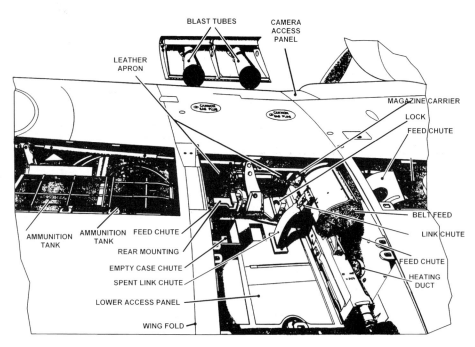

Above **The Sea Fury cannon access was borrowed from the earlier Tempest, thus armourers working on the aircraft were able to reload the cannon ammunition boxes without too much trouble.** Big Bird Aviation Collection

A) GAS DEFLECTORS
B) LOCKING NUT
C) RETAINING PIECE
D) RECOIL SPRING

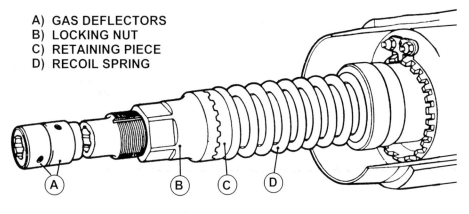

Above **Although the cannons in the Sea Fury were suppressed, they still required strong springs to absorb the recoil of firing.** Big Bird Aviation Collection

tracks; the installation was similar in both the Mark X and the FB.11. In contrast, the Sea Fury T.20 trainer had only two cannon fitted to maintain correct weight and balance. The wing structure was covered by aluminium alloy stressed skin of varying thickness riveted to the spars, stringers and ribs. In a similar manner to the fuselage, cut-outs were provided for servicing access, each having a reinforced landing. The access panels themselves were chemically manufactured and reinforced internally by stringers held in place by screw fasteners. Located on the leading edge of the centre section were intakes that provided cooling for the engine radiators and the oil coolers, the ducting for which was led along the front of the undercarriage bays to the engine compartment.

Driving the main and undercarriage units, plus the flaps, was the primary purpose of the hydraulic system. The flaps themselves were manufactured in four sections, two located under the wing centre section, with the others being fitted under the outer wing panels. On the FB.11 and the T.20 the hydraulic system also operated the wing fold mechanisms and the wing locking pins, and to extend the arrestor hook. As problems had occurred during the development of the Sea Fury, the tail hook and the undercarriage units were fitted with air/oil dampers, which were needed to control any oscillation. To provide the power to drive these systems, an engine-driven hydraulic pump was installed, which delivered a nominal working pressure of 1,800psi. Should there be a failure of the primary pump, the pilot was provided with a hand pump located to the left-hand side of his seat, which could be used to pump down the flaps, undercarriage and tail hook – although the use of muscle power would take longer. A further pump was also driven by the engine via a gearbox, this being used to supply pneumatic pressure to a dedicated accumulator at a pressure of 450 to 470psi.

The systems supplied by the pneumatic system included aircraft braking, plus the undercarriage and flap emergency blowdown systems. This particular set-up was only available for the FB.11 and the T.20, as the pneumatics fitted to the Mark X covered the braking system and the undercarriage extension assisters. Indications in all three versions were via a triple pressure gauge located in the bottom right-hand corner of the instrument panel.

The engine was also used to drive a generator that charged the Sea Fury's onboard batteries and powered the internal and external lighting units, the air-intake shutter filters plus the bomb and rocket projectile controls. Further items driven by the electrical system included the engine-cooling shutter controls, engine instrumentation, the fuel booster pump, the fuel contents gauges and the oil cooler shutters. Other equipment requiring electrical power included the gun-firing control plus the camera gun, the gyro gunsight, pressure-head heater, radio, ECM (when fitted) and the primary compass.

The Fuel System

All three versions of the Sea Fury had a fuel system that consisted of five self-sealing tanks, of which two were located in the rear fuselage, while the other three were situated in the wings. Two were interspar tanks, while the other was known as the nose tank, and was housed in the leading edge of the starboard wing. The fuselage tanks were described as being separate,

Above **Up on jacks and trestles is Sea Fury FB.11 TF963 of No. 802 Sqn, photographed at Culdrose. Given the open nature of the accommodation, the aircraft is tied down by the wing shackle points, while there is a counterweight over the tail unit, which compensates for the weight of the engine.** Big Bird Aviation Collection

Below **This excellent view of a Sea Fury T 20 reveals that there are two cannon blisters per wing, although only one cannon is fitted per wing. The size of the periscope for the instructor is clearly shown.** FAA Museum Collection

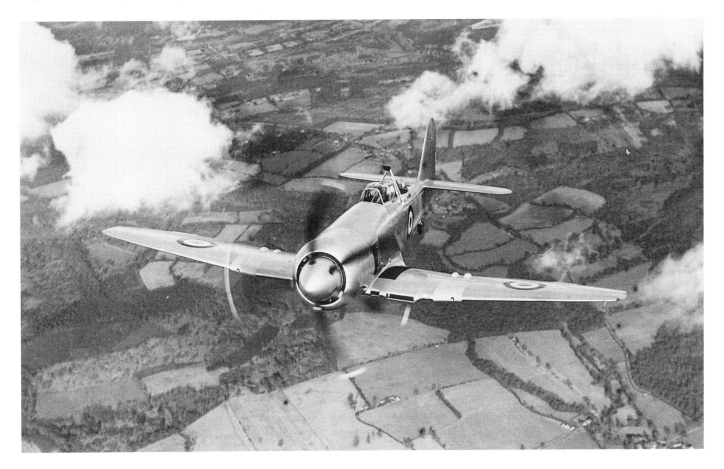

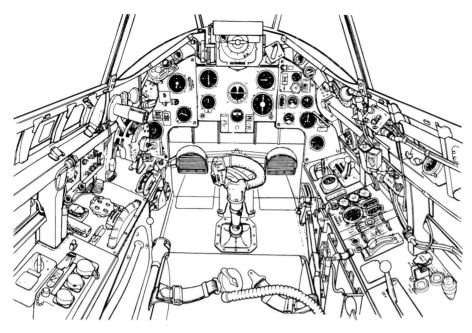

Above **Even though the Sea Fury still used a piston engine as a powerplant, it had become quite a complicated aircraft as far as the cockpit was concerned.** Big Bird Aviation Collection

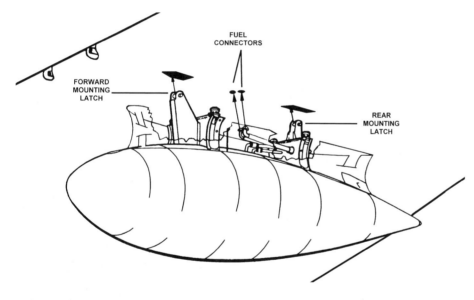

Above **In a similar manner to the Tempest, the external fuel-tank mounting for the Sea Fury consisted of a fore and aft latch, and came with fuel and air couplings.** Big Bird Aviation Collection

although their close interconnection meant that they acted as one unit.

Delivering the fuel to the engine was a Hobson/RAE injector pump, while the fuel from the other three tanks was fed to the main fuselage tank by air pressure that was supplied from the exhaust side of the vacuum pump. The main fuselage tank did not require pressurization, its fuel flow being controlled by the main fuel cock. Preventing the main tank from overfilling

was the job of a float valve that would shut off the flow at the appropriate point. Should the contents of the interconnected main fuel fall below 17gal (77ltr), the tank float valve would allow the fuel tank cock to open, so as to replenish the contents from the wing tanks.

The maximum amount held in the main fuselage tanks was 97 plus 30gal (122 plus 136ltr), while the two interspar tanks could hold a maximum of 56gal (254ltr)

each, the nose tank holding no more than 17gal. The two external fuel tanks, which helped to extend the range of the Sea Fury, came in two sizes, being rated at 45 and 90gal (205 and 409ltr) respectively. The former was the more common and was used mainly for combat purposes, whilst the latter was used mainly for transit flights.

To push the fuel from the external tanks into the main system, air pressure was provided by the vacuum pump. Should it be necessary to clear the wings for combat manoeuvring or an emergency, the underwing tanks could be jettisoned by pulling a lever in the cockpit, the action of which would close off the fuel and air supplies as the tanks pulled clear of the wings.

In contrast to the preceding Hawker fighters, the fuel system management was vastly simplified to reduce the cockpit workload; thus instead of individual tank isolation cocks, the whole system was regarded as a group feeding directly into the main fuselage tanks. This simplification meant that there would only be two fuel cocks on the pilot's panel, which were used to control the fuel flow from the external wing tanks. Selection of the external tanks using the manual levers automatically isolated the wing fuel tanks, whose pressurization was then vented overboard. Reversing the levers would then isolate the underwing tanks, which would then vent their pressure to atmosphere.

This system was not foolproof, however, as an inadvertent selection of the underwing tanks would instantly isolate the wing tanks, and if not corrected could lead to the engine shutting down when the main fuselage tanks were empty. To stop this happening, a lever lock was fitted to the tank selector cocks, which was applied when the wings were clean.

The Bristol Centaurus XVIII engine required some assistance from an electrically driven fuel-booster pump for starting purposes. This pump was located in the main fuselage fuel tank group, although it did not become effective during the automatic start sequence until the engine oil pressure had reached 30psi. Modifications to improve the capability of this system would be incorporated during the life of the Sea Fury. The first of these, modification 309, installed a manual control that required moving to the 'On' position before flight, and had to be returned to the 'Off' position as soon possible after landing

Above **This diagram not only illustrates the method of mounting the zero-length rocket launchers, it also shows how the rockets could be duplex mounted.**
Big Bird Aviation Collection

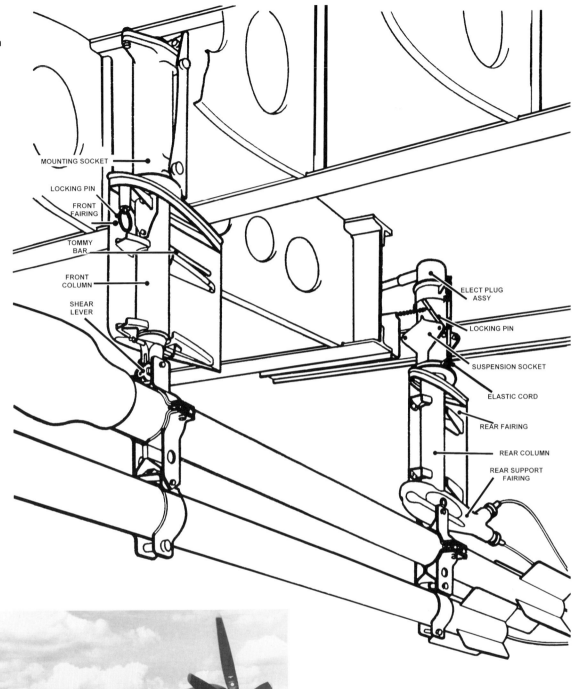

MOUNTING SOCKET

LOCKING PIN

FRONT FAIRING

TOMMY BAR

FRONT COLUMN

SHEAR LEVER

ELECT PLUG ASSY

LOCKING PIN

SUSPENSION SOCKET

ELASTIC CORD

REAR FAIRING

REAR COLUMN

REAR SUPPORT FAIRING

Left **Sea Fury FB.11 VX642 is seen here surrounded by the full range of bombs, rockets, fuel tanks and assorted paraphernalia that made the type such a flexible attack platform.**
C. P. Russell Smith Collection

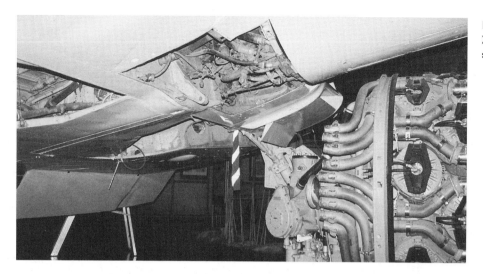

Left The heart of the Sea Fury, the Bristol Centaurus XVIII engine; to the rear can be seen the auxiliary services gearbox. Big Bird Aviation Collection

Left Just aft of the engine bulkhead is a panel that covers many of the aircraft services, such as the hydraulic and pneumatic systems. Big Bird Aviation Collection

Below This head-on view of a Sea Fury FB.11 shows how pugnacious an aircraft it is; the size of the five-blade propeller is also worthy of note. The location of the leading edge intakes on the wings is clearly shown, as is the location of the cannon ports. Big Bird Aviation Collection

and engine shut down. A further modification, N.22, added a high pressure pump to the electrical priming pump. Part of this modification also added an external connection in the port wheel bay, which allowed for external priming of the cylinders with fuel. Should the electrical pump fail for any reason, the fuel supply to the engine could be maintained by the injector pump.

Although the management of the fuel system had been simplified, the pilot was still faced by four contents gauges: these covered the main, interspar and nose tanks, and were controlled by the ground/flight selector switch, which allowed the contents to be read accurately under either condition. As it was possible for these gauges to be misread under the pressure of flying the aircraft, there was a primary Pacitor-type main gauge fitted in the main pilot's panel that gave a consolidated contents reading. However, just to make the pilot's life interesting, this gauge had the disconcerting habit of not reading correctly for at least thirty seconds while its dedicated power unit warmed up, after which it was normally reliable. In contrast, the underwing fuel tanks were not gauged, their contents being purely a matter of guesswork.

Connected to the fuel-tank gauging system was a fuel low-warning light that would come on should the total system contents drop to 107gal (486ltr), which indicated that both the wing and underwing tanks were empty. Alongside the contents indicators was a gauge that showed the system air pressure, which would read between 3.5 and 5psi when operating properly. Should the pressure drop below 3.5psi whilst flying at altitude, the pilot was recommended to reduce altitude if possible, as problems could be experienced with the wing-tank fuel feed.

Located within the forward section of the fuselage hard by the engine was the oil lubrication tank; this had a maximum fluid content of 14gal (62ltr), with a free air space of 4gal (18ltr). To ensure smooth operation of the lubrication system under all flight conditions there was a negative 'g' valve incorporated, which would maintain oil pressure even if the aircraft were fully inverted. In common with all aero engines, the Bristol Centaurus generated a lot of heat, and part of the role of the lubricating system was to help in its dispersion. To that end, Hawker's installed a ram air-cooling intake in the port wing root. To

Above With its arrestor hook deployed, Sea Fury FB.11 VR936 of No. 738 Sqn, normally based at Culdrose, undertakes a missed approach on an unknown carrier. FAA Museum Collection

reduce the workload placed upon the pilot, the operation of the complete cooling system and its thermostatically controlled electric jack was made fully automatic.

Flying Controls

Although the Sea Fury was the subject of many innovations, the flying controls were fairly conventional, being operated by rods, cables, bellcranks and pulley wheels, each run being tensioned by the use of adjustable turnbarrels. Rigging of the Sea Fury flying controls required the use of rigging pins temporarily pushed through the relevant control run neutral point, and determined locations near the control surface, after which the cables would be tensioned and checked using a tensiometer. Movement of the elevators and ailerons was courtesy of a control column topped with a spade grip, which incorporated the brake lever and gun-firing controls. The latter was also used to operate the cine camera, to release selected bombs, and fire the rocket projectiles. The operation of the rudder was via rudder pedals, whose mounting bar could be adjusted to suit the heights of various pilots, this being achieved by the use of a centrally mounted, rudder-bar adjuster

wheel. The seat could be altered vertically for the same reason.

To prevent damage to the flying controls by high winds when the Sea Fury was parked on the ground, there was a stowable control locking kit in the cockpit. To instal it, a clip was fixed to the control column, and its attached cables clipped to the seat and the rudder bar. Once all were interconnected, the pilot's seat was moved vertically to increase the tension on the locking cables. The aileron locking requirements were entirely different, as the main control surfaces were not connected to the control column. To stop these moving, specially shaped plates could be slid between the aileron and the wing trailing edge, and locked in position.

The operation of the ailerons was via the balance tabs that were attached to the column, and because they were not directly connected to the control column, it made things easier for the pilot, as well as reducing the complexity of control runs at the wing break. Trim and balance tabs were also installed on the rudder and elevators, tabs on all three axis being adjustable for better trimming in flight. Adjustment of the balance tabs was done on the ground, and they were set within prescribed limits. The trim-tab control wheels were grouped together in a control box in the cockpit, with the control wheels and indicators being the only items available to the pilot.

Operation of the Undercarriage

Even though the Sea Fury undercarriage was hydraulically driven, it was activated mechanically by a lever in the cockpit. Selection of 'up' and 'down' was through a quadrant selector in the cockpit that had a locking safety catch to stop inadvertent selection. In addition to the warning notices concerning inadvertent undercarriage selection, another was prominently displayed that warned against the retraction of the stirrup footstep under the wing root, as both the step and undercarriage were interconnected.

To indicate to the pilot the position of the undercarriage at any given time, an undercarriage position indicator, complete with lights, was located on the pilot's panel. Whilst the undercarriage was in transit, either up or down, the undercarriage lights would show red; in the fully down position the lights changed to green. When the undercarriage was up and locked, all the lights were out. Should there be a failure of the primary green light array, there was a second set that could be selected by the use of the switch on the indicator panel. During night-flying,

rotating the indicator knob in the other direction would reduce the brightness of the lights.

Backing up the indicator lights were indicator rods mounted on the top of each main leg; thus when the undercarriage legs were down and locked, not only were the green lights showing, but the indicator rods would have moved through the holes in the upper skin panel to stand proud above it. This was regarded as a useful back-up should there be a malfunction of any of the undercarriage microswitches.

Other Indicator Lights

Besides the primary indicator lights associated with the undercarriage, there were other warning lights on the panel to warn of any inconsistencies. One of these would light up should the throttle be less than one third advanced with the gear unlocked, while the other was interconnected with the port undercarriage leg and came on when both the gear and arrestor hook were fully down. To operate the arrestor hook, the pilot moved a lever in the cockpit which would lower the hook, although it could not be reset in the air. When fully deployed, a green light would come on in the cockpit.

Also requiring careful monitoring during landing and take-off were the flaps, although their position was shown using a gauge. The flap pre-selector lever in the

cockpit had four indicated positions: 'up', 'take-off', 'max lift' and 'down', although it was possible for further intermediate positions to be selected.

Pneumatic System

The electrical and hydraulic systems were not the only vital arteries aboard the Sea Fury, as it had a pneumatic system as well. This was vital for the operation of the brakes and the emergency blow-down system for the FB.11 and T.20, and the undercarriage assister circuit fitted to the Mark X. The system pressure was maintained by a pneumatic accumulator charged to between 450 and 475psi; this was reduced to 100psi at each brake unit. A ground parking facility was available via a locking lever, while differential braking for ground manoeuvring was possible using a differential braking valve inserted into the pneumatic system, which was operated by movement of the rudder bar.

Wing-Folding and Locking Systems

For those unfamiliar with the art and science of wing folding and locking, it was originally viewed as insubstantial; however, work on the technology and metallurgy needed to make the idea work correctly had been completed before the end of World War II, as a result of which Hawker's were more than confident to incorporate the technology and mechanisms into the Sea Fury. Not only were wing folding and spreading hydraulically driven, the vital spar locking pins were moved in and out hydraulically, too. Operation of the wing-folding mechanism was by a lever in the cockpit in the FB.11 and T.20 trainer, which activated the hydraulic selector valves that in turn directed fluid to the required side of the jacks. During the design of the wing-fold mechanism, care was taken to ensure that the wings could not be deployed should the flap panels be in the down position; thus a safety locking catch was built into the lever.

In the event of a hydraulic system malfunction, the pilot could use the hand pump to move the wing panels in either direction. This capability was also available for groundcrew use during main-

Below A most revealing view of a Sea Fury FB.11 shows the wing-fold mechanism in great detail, plus the location of the rocket rails. This particular machine, VX652, was on the strength of No. 738 Sqn at Culdrose when it was photographed. W. A. Harrison Collection

tenance. Visual indication of the locking pins' position was provided by a mechanical indicator rod that stood proud when the pins were withdrawn, but would lie flush when the wings were down and the pins fully home.

Engine Operation and Control

In contrast to the varied methods of operation and control employed for the airframe systems, those for the engine were purely mechanical in nature, and some of them automatic. Most of the non-automatic controls were operated by levers; thus the engine mixture control was governed by movements of the throttle lever. To get the best performance from the engine with the greatest fuel economy, pilots were recommended to maintain the power rating at 2,500rpm, with the lever in the auto position. This lever could also be moved to the alternative maximum position, which allowed the engine revs to be increased to 2,700rpm for short periods of time, although prolonged usage could cause damage to the powerplant. As the Sea Fury also had a tendency to suffer from engine vibration the throttle and rpm levers had a friction damper that could be applied to stop them moving.

Another lever that had a direct affect upon the behaviour of the powerplant was the fuel cut-off control: this had two settings, one 'normal', the other 'cut-off'. Before starting the engine this lever had to be set to the cut-off position, otherwise the push buttons for the injector and cylinder priming would not engage.

As well as the normal range of controls, the Bristol Centaurus was equipped with a supercharger that had its own range of controls: this also had two settings, (M) for low gear and (S) for high gear. To ensure that the supercharger was protected from overspeeding, there was a warning light on the pilot's panel that would come on if the supercharger were engaged in high gear below 7,000ft (2,000m).

Other ancillary controls associated with engine management included the control that operated the air intake filter: this sifted out debris that could harm the moving parts. With the air filter in operation the wing-root intakes were automatically closed off. When the wing-root intakes were open, they required a

C Flying Control Cabling
D Flexible Pylon Cabling
E Wing Fold Jack Support Structure
F Drop Tank Control Cabling
G Feed Neck Door Operating Hinge
H Wing Electrical Loom
J Feed Neck Door Operating Linkage
K Fold Jack Lower Mounting Point

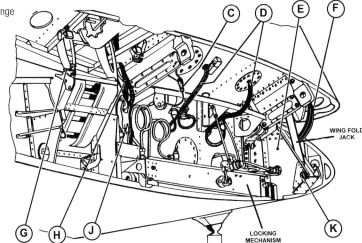

Above The wing-fold mechanism on the Sea Fury was very reliable, and due to the use of the aileron tab to control the main surface, few connections or reconnections were required. Big Bird Aviation Collection

heated air feed delivered via the warm air control valve to ensure that no freezing would take place at high altitudes or during operations in cold climates.

One further mechanical control available to the pilot was the cowling shutter control. Under normal circumstances the cowling panels were fully open during take-off; under all other circumstances in theory they were closed. There was a manual over-ride that could be operated if required, and this came in useful if the pilot wasn't sure of the cowling shutters' positioning: to check this, a quick open selection would trim the aircraft into the nose-down position.

To start the Bristol Centaurus engine was fairly simple. The ignition switches were located on the left-hand side of the pilot's panel; on the right-hand panel was a combined cartridge starter and selector, close to which were priming push-buttons.

Other Cockpit Levers

Other mechanical levers in the cockpit concerned the movement of the canopy and one of the footsteps. The main operating control for canopy movement was a crank lever to move the assembly back and forth. Attached to this mechanism was an

external open/close handle that allowed the hood to be closed from the outside, locking being achieved by a spring-loaded bolt. Also in the cockpit was a lever that moved the footstep located on the port side of the fuselage just aft of the wing. Although the footstep was controlled from the cockpit, it was required to check that it was fully closed before departure, because if the step cover were only slightly open, noxious fumes could be drawn into the cockpit. A further footstep located in the side of the fuselage would only close when the undercarriage retracted. There was one other footstep in the wing root, but this was spring-loaded to the closed position once any weight was removed.

Lighting

To provide visual identification to other aircraft, and to allow the pilot to see his instruments at night, the Sea Fury was equipped with a veritable battery of lighting. In the cockpit there were three kinds of lighting: one set of dimmable ultraviolet lights that would only illuminate the phosphorescence on the gauge indicator needles and numbers; a second set consisting of dimmable red lamps; and a single lamp that came equipped with its own independent battery.

The lights mounted around the outside of the airframe were divided into distinct groups. First there were the identification lights: red and green lights located under the starboard wing, and an amber light under the port wing. There were four navigation lamps, one at each wing-tip, and one on each side of the tail unit; these lights were also interconnected with the arrestor hook, so that when the hook was extended, the lights would come on, and so allow the carrier-deck batsman to confirm its status prior to clearing the aircraft to land.

The final lighting circuit was also aimed at helping the batsman, and consisted of attitude lights located on the port main gear leg and the port tailwheel door: these came on to confirm the undercarriage was down and locked.

Other Cockpit Controls

As well as the mechanical and electrical systems in the cockpit, the pilot was also graced with an oxygen system. The cylinders containing the gas were held in retaining cradles under the floorboards, and the system was controlled via a regulator on the right-hand side of the pilot's panel.

Controls for cockpit heating and ventilation also added to the pilot's comfort: these were operated by a handwheel that had range settings between warm and cold, although the latter selection was only available in the upper part of the cockpit. To ensure the safety of the aircraft, controls for selection of the pitot head heater and windscreen de-icing were also located in the cockpit. External windscreen de-icing was available to the pilot, and its operation would enable him to fly in the most adverse conditions. This system was fluid-based, the tank being located in the port wheel bay; a pump powered the fluid via a disperser onto the screen.

The last item in the cockpit was the pilot's seat and its combined head-rest, which could be adjusted by a lever located on the right-hand side of the seat. The other lever available for the pilot's comfort was the safety harness release lever that allowed the pilot freedom of movement without his becoming disconnected from the seat.

Above **Sea Fury FB.11 WG599 has had a bit of an accident! However, standing on its nose reveals the flap detail, the location of the rocket rails, and the bomb mountings between them. Unusually this aircraft has only one fuel tank fitted.** W. A. Harrison Collection

Weapons and Camera Control Systems

Operational weapons controls fitted to the Sea Fury were mainly under the guidance of the Mark 4B gyro gunsight; this had a reticule so that either rockets or guns could be selected, and came equipped with a camera recorder and a backlight. The Hispano cannons were electrically operated, by a switch on the control-column spade grip. This switch also controlled the release of bombs, rockets and the combat cine camera. To protect against inadvertent firing or weapons release there was a safety cut-out switch, integrated with the undercarriage weight on ground microswitches. It was possible to override these safety switches via a butt test switch located in the starboard centre wing section, which meant that an aircraft could fire the guns on the ground if required.

The cine-recording camera was situated in the port wing, and its selector control allowed the pilot to adjust it for either sunny or cloudy weather. Only one other camera was provided in the Sea Fury, for photo reconnaissance. There was also provision for the installation of both vertical and oblique cameras in the fuselage, with mountings available for a control box in the cockpit; however, no known use was made of this system.

The Sea Fury was also capable of carrying ancillary equipment such as the RATOG launch system, whose rockets were controlled by two buttons located in the cockpit: one initiated ignition, the other was used to jettison the rockets once their force was spent. As the Sea Fury was in service during the early years of the jet age, it was vulnerable to missile attack, therefore provision was made for a chaff dispenser. Operation of this system was via a controller that had a four-position speed selector. Also available to the Sea Fury was a deception flare launcher and a wing camera container.

A further indication of the Sea Fury's tangle with the jet age was its extensive avionics suite; this included a radio system based on the ARI 5491 VHF airborne relay unit, plus a standard four-channel VHF transceiver. The preferred radar unit for the Hawker fighter was the ARI 5307 ZBX system that was capable of integration with the VHF relay unit. Navigation needs were catered for by the inclusion of a radio altimeter and a G4F compass.

This, then, was the Hawker Sea Fury, an aircraft that sat comfortably between the piston-powered aircraft and those with jet engines.

Flying the Sea Fury

Given that the Sea Fury was one of the fastest piston-powered naval fighters ever built, it was inevitable that there would accidents, even though the Fleet Air Arm had purchased a batch of T.20 trainers to try to alleviate this problem. Tyro pilots facing the contents of the cockpit of the Sea Fury would almost certainly be initially overwhelmed by the plethora of switches, dials and gauges before them. Even though time had been spent in ground school, it required some practical exercise of the ingrained mnemonics and in-depth instructions before handling of the big fighter became somewhat easier.

Mastering the Fuel System

The first area on which our intrepid aviator would concentrate would be the fuel system: although simplified from its predecessors, it needed understanding, especially the management of the external fuel tanks. Most important was the position of the selector valves, which had to be in the 'off' position when the tanks were removed, otherwise the main fuel system would be isolated, and the contents gauge would read incorrectly. In contrast, the selector valves had to be in the 'on' position when the tanks were fitted. However, once fully drained, the selection had to be in the 'off' position to stop the main system feeding back.

Starting the Engine

Having mastered the fuel system, the aviator would then tackle the intricacies of engine starting and handling. As you would expect, this set of instructions began with the engine pre-start procedure. These were:

1. Ignition switches   OFF
2. Main fuel cock   ON
3. Booster pump   OFF
4. Fuel cut-off control   CUT OFF
5. Throttle   50 per cent OPEN
6. RPM control unit   MAXIMUM
7. Air-intake heat control   OFF
8. Air-intake filter control   CLEAN or FILTER
9. Engine-cooling shutters   OPEN
10. Supercharger control   M (low gear)
11. Depress the booster pump circuit if required.

When the cockpit checks had been completed, it was the turn of the ground-crew: they would turn the propeller by hand through two complete revolutions to reduce the possibility of hydraulic compression shock at the time of ignition, as this effect could cause serious damage to the engine.

With both the pilot and groundcrew ready, the fuel injector needed depressing for thirty seconds to prime the fuel system. Depending on how the aircraft were modified, the button might need to be pressed for longer: some were post Mod N.22, which was a high-pressure priming system.

With priming completed, the ignition switch was moved to the 'on' position and the starter depressed: if all was correct, the engine would start and run smoothly. Occasionally the Centaurus would misbehave and a cartridge would not exert enough force to turn the engine over; this required the pilot to select another cartridge, and depress the starter again. Should the engine fail to start after multiple attempts, the aircraft had to be turned over to the engineers. A successful start required that the powerplant be run at 1,200rpm until it was fully warmed up.

Once settled and running sweetly, further checks were required to ensure that the engine would perform throughout the flight. These mainly concerned the behaviour of the magnetos and the performance of the generator. The throttle needed to be advanced for this test, and the control column to be fully back throughout this phase to stop the Sea Fury tipping forwards onto its nose. Once the engine had been tested, the propeller had to be run through its complete range of settings; it would then be cleared for departure.

Take-Off Techniques

While designed for carrier operations, the Sea Fury was frequently flown from land bases, though special techniques then had to be followed in order for the aircraft to behave correctly. During the take-off and just after, full throttle had to be maintained to ensure that rudder control remained positive. To improve the behaviour of the rudder, the Sea Fury had to be flown off the ground with the tail in the down position; this was even more crucial should the flaps be deployed to assist take-off. Once the fighter was airborne, the wheel brakes needed to be applied gently to stop them spinning before retraction, as continued rotation could cause damage in the wheel bays. Just occasionally the Sea Fury indicator lights would show red, and the advice to correct this was to throttle back in order to slow the aircraft and allow the legs to complete their cycle.

The take-off from an aircraft carrier was completely different, as take-off flap was

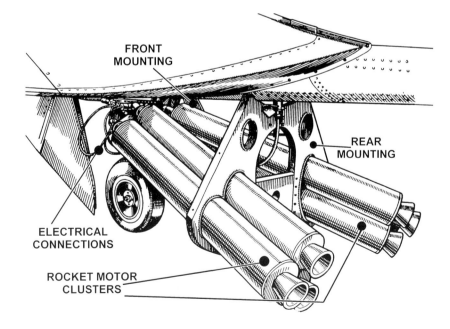

FRONT MOUNTING

REAR MOUNTING

ELECTRICAL CONNECTIONS

ROCKET MOTOR CLUSTERS

Above **The RATOG system as fitted to the Sea Fury was clustered under the centre section, whereas on other FAA aircraft they were located above the wings.** Big Bird Aviation Collection

required, with the elevators trimmed slightly nose up. So that the pilot had a margin of extra power available, the engine was run at full throttle against the brakes, while the tail was held back in the 'down' position. Just prior to the launch catapult releasing the fighter, the tailwheel had to be checked to ensure that the anti-castoring lock was engaged, while the rudder needed to be held central to stop the aircraft from crabbing during the short take-off.

Both at sea and on land the Sea Fury was capable of mounting the RATOG launch system, which gave improved take-off performance in the event of the aircraft having either a greater weapons load or a shorter take-off run. Use of this system from an airfield required that the pilot select a theoretical ignition point some way down the runway. Having identified this point, the pilot then ensured that the flaps were fully retracted, that the tailwheel was locked, and that the RATOG master switch be in the 'on' position. Once fully set, the throttle lever was advanced to full power and the brakes released. As always, the tail was held in the 'down' position with the control

column slightly offset to port. As speed advanced, the RATOG was ignited by depression of the firing button; however, should there be a misfire or ignition failure, the take-off had to be aborted. If all proceeded according to plan, the Sea Fury would become airborne, though care had to be taken if the rockets were still burning, as there was a tendency for the nose to pitch up. Once the RATOG had ceased operating, the Sea Fury would try to pitch down.

Whatever method was used to launch, all pilots were warned to be careful not to pull the aircraft off the ground, otherwise a stall would result and cause a starboard wing drop. Once airborne, the flaps needed to be raised quickly, so that a speed of 150mph (240km/h) IAS could be gained, when the pilot could dump the RATOG carriers. As the weight balance changed, there was a tendency for the nose to pitch down.

In the Air

Under normal circumstances the Sea Fury was described as nice to fly in the air at all altitudes and speeds, although there was a marked tendency for the turn to tighten at higher altitudes. Throughout the performance envelope there were few trim changes, although deploying the flaps, extending the undercarriage or opening

the cowling shutters would induce a slight nose-down attitude, while reversing the foregoing would lift the nose up.

Stalling speeds also called for careful observation, because with gear and flaps up and an AUW of 12,400lb (5,625kg), the velocity required to maintain safe flight was 105mph (170km/h) IAS; however, this limit would increase to 115mph (185km/h) IAS at an increased weight of 14,650lb (6,645kg). With the gear and flaps deployed at the lower weight, the stalling speed dropped to 90mph (145km/h) IAS, while at higher weights this increased to 100mph (160km/h) IAS. A further reduction in stalling speeds would occur during the normal power on approach as it dropped to 80mph (130km/h) IAS. Stall warning was first indicated by the tail dropping, after which the nose would drop. Correction required retarding the throttle and centralizing the controls.

Possibly one of the worst fears for all pilots is entering an unintentional spin, because not only would the occupant of the cockpit become distracted, but the airframe could be subjected to overstressing. Some aircraft are quite docile in a spin, while others have a vicious streak. For the Sea Fury, the regulations stated that intentional spinning was banned; however, should one be entered accidentally, normal recovery actions should be

Below This machine of No. 738 Sqn shows how the RATOG equipment was fitted to the Sea Fury FB.11.
C. P. Russell Smith Collection

taken, although when clearing the resulting dive, the pilot had to wait until a speed of 175mph (280km/h) IAS had been reached.

In a dive the Sea Fury made for a stable attack platform, although pilots were advised, theoretically, not to exceed the maximum limiting speed of the airframe, otherwise damage to the structure could result. During a dive the aircraft could exhibit a slight tendency to yaw, though this could be corrected by use of the trim tab.

Landing the Sea Fury

The final phase of any flight – and the one considered to be the most difficult – is a successful landing. That of the Sea Fury was no more difficult than that of any other piston-engined aircraft, as long as the agreed parameters were obeyed. Thus with everything out and down and at a weight of 12,400lb (5,625kg), an approach speed of 100mph (160km/h) IAS needed to be strictly observed; however, should the approach be flown flapless, the required speed was increased to 115mph (185km/h) IAS. The Sea Fury had a maximum landing weight of 14,000lb (6,350kg), which meant that all configurations had to be flown at least 10mph (16km/h) IAS above the approach speed. Performance when the engine was off required the pilot to adhere to a separate set of limits: therefore with gear and flaps down, careful handling was required to maintain a steady 130mph (210km/h) IAS, although this would be allowed to drop off to 115mph (185km/h) IAS just before touch-down. All pilots were warned that, if they were landing under these circumstances, descending with the flaps in the fully down position would result in a very steep glide path, followed by a heavy landing and possible damage to the airframe.

In contrast, landing on an aircraft carrier required that the pilot fly the approach and landing at a slightly higher speed, which allowed for the arrestor hook being down. As well as the hook being deployed, the tailwheel needed to be unlocked to avoid damage to the rear fuselage. Final approach speed over the carrier might be reduced to 90mph (145km/h) IAS due to the wind across the deck, although the control column needed to be held fully back if a three-point landing was to be achieved.

Above **With its RATOG units firing, this Sea Fury departs HMS Ocean. Note the flaps set to take off, and the bombs under the wings.** FAA Museum Collection

Preparing for Emergencies

Pilots trained on all aircraft types had to be prepared for all emergencies, and those flying the Sea Fury were no different. Undercarriage emergencies were one of the first areas covered in ground school, and there were numerous ways to resolve any problems. Failure of the lights to illuminate or any of the legs to lower could first be addressed by putting the undercarriage back into the 'up' position. Before any attempt was made to deploy the gear again, the flaps had to be lowered first. Should the engine-driven hydraulic pump have failed, our intrepid aviator was required to pump them down by hand, all the way to the 'max lift' setting. To achieve this state some eighty double pumps were required, and this was even more difficult if the lights were indicating that the undercarriage was unlocked.

With the flaps fully down, the Sea Fury needed to be slowed to 115mph (185km/h) IAS. Getting the undercarriage down required an even greater amount of effort, at least 120 strokes – although this instruction had the proviso, that if the gear failed to unlock within the first twelve double strokes, then another course of action would be required. This involved using the emergency lowering system, the first pull of the operating handle releasing the undercarriage uplocks and allowing the legs to drop using the draw of gravity. A second pull of the same handle would release a pneumatic charge, which would force the undercarriage into the locked position.

Should even this action fail to have an effect, the final option was to maintain a speed of 115mph (185km/h) IAS, and use the rudder to induce violent yawing; the resultant drop in the nose normally forced the undercarriage finally to engage the down locks.

Should all these efforts fail, the pilot was instructed to abandon the aircraft; though if all the lights were green and the pins were showing, a landing could be made. Fortunately for the pilot he was spared the trouble of lowering the tailwheel, as a failure of the hydraulic system would cause it to lower anyway. Changes introduced by the application of Modification N.30 meant that the emergency blow-down system became the primary means of lowering the undercarriage, although this change meant that the flaps might not fully deploy.

The lack of flaps did not cause the same sort of problems as the undercarriage did, because it was possible to land a Sea Fury on a normal-length runway as long as the wind was light. The approach had to be flown as flat as possible, and large throttle movements avoided. Given a typical service loading of 12,400lb (5,625kg), the approach speed was set at the 120mph (200km/h) IAS mark, while the landing

speed was 10mph (km/h) lower. Just over the runway threshold the throttle had to be cut, which would allow the pilot to make a three-point landing.

With only the one powerplant, the pilot of a Sea Fury would understandably become worried should it cease functioning. This might be caused by sustained negative 'g's or inverted flight, both of which could cause the fuel system to cut out. The obvious answer to this was to turn the fighter the right way up and close the fuel cut-off and throttle levers; after about ten seconds the engine injectors could be reprimed, and the Centaurus restarted. Should the cause of failure be anything but the foregoing, it was probable that either the aircraft would be lost, or the pilot would have to make a dead stick/power off landing at the nearest airfield.

Abandoning the Aircraft

If the circumstances were such that it was beyond the power of the pilot to recover the situation, the only recourse would have been to abandon the aircraft. The first step was to jettison the canopy and the fuselage cockpit side panel. The best recommended speed to clear the canopy from the aircraft was above 210mph (340km/h) IAS; however, on Sea Furies that were minus Modification 339, the pilot was recommended to open the canopy at least an inch (2.5cm) to assist the latches in disengaging (this effort was not needed on post-modification machines). Should the Sea Fury crash-land there was a jettison handle located under a perspex cover near the port wing-root fillet which, when activated, would allow rescuers to reach the pilot.

Over the sea the circumstances could be different, and training needed to be given in the art of ditching the Sea Fury. First it was necessary to clear the canopy and any external stores, so the aircraft could ditch with less difficulty. The pilot also needed to send out an emergency radio broadcast, before disconnecting the radio jack plug. Should the engine still be functioning, he would next have to lower the flaps fully, pull the control column fully back to lower the tail, and aim for the lowest possible touch-down speed. If the engine had shut down, the flap deployment was reduced to thirty degrees, as any increase would cause the sink rate to become unacceptably fast. Finally the pilot would try to land the Sea Fury along the line of the swell or into the wind, and then jump out over the port side of the aircraft.

The requirements over land were similar, although the first thing to do was to send a radio distress signal. The canopy and underwing stores then had to be cleared, before the pilot tightened his straps and lowered the flaps to the take-off setting and, maintaining a speed of 130mph (210km/h) IAS, prepared to touch down. One of the prime reasons for a wheels-up landing was a tyre burst; the Sea Fury had a strong tendency to either tip up on its nose or flip over completely, thus the wheels-up option was regarded as the lesser of the evils.

Although all of these instructions were intended to be followed under all circumstances, combat flying meant that quite frequently pilots had to write their own rules.

Specification – Sea Fury	
Type:	Mk 10, Mk 11 single-seat fighter/fighter-bomber, T.20 two-seat trainer
Powerplant:	2,480hp Centaurus 18
Weights:	Empty Mk 11 9,240lb (4,190kg), Mk 20 8,697lb (3,944kg); loaded Mk 11 12,500lb (5,700kg), Mk 20 11,930lb (5,410kg)
Dimensions:	Span 38ft 4¾in (11.7m), 16ft 1in (4.9m) folded; length Mk 10 34ft 3in (10.44m), Mk 11 34ft 8in (10.57m), T.20 34ft 7in (10.54m); height 14ft 7¾in (4.46m); wing area 280sq ft (26.01sq m)
Performance:	Max. speed Mk 11 460mph (740km/h), Mk 20 445mph (716km/h); rate of climb Mk 11 10.8min to 30,000ft (9,000m), Mk 20 10.1min to 30,000ft; range Mk 11 1,040 miles (1,670km) with 2 × 90gal (400ltr) drop tanks, Mk 20 940 miles (1,500km); service ceiling Mk 11 35,800ft (10,900m), Mk 20 35,600ft (10.850m)
Armament (fixed):	Mk 10/11 4 × Hispano 20mm cannon, Mk 20 2 × Hispano 20mm cannon
Armament (disposable)/ fuel tanks:	Mk 11/20 2 × 500lb bombs or 2 × 1,000lb bombs or 16 × rocket projectiles

Fighting in the Sea Fury

When the idea of the Sea Fury was first mooted, it was thought that its chances of engaging in any form of combat were limited, to say the least. World War II had ended with the surrender of the German and Japanese forces, and the only cloud on the horizon was that of the Soviet Union, which had revealed its intentions to carve out an empire in Europe. To counter the emerging Warsaw Pact, Britain, the United States and many of the European nations would form the North Atlantic Treaty Organization via the earlier Western Union.

The Korean War

With the Russians stopped from expanding across Europe, the Communist ethos began to look for other areas in which to express itself. The new zone that would succumb to a peculiarly oriental form of Communism was China, where General Chaing Kai Chek had lost control of the country after the 'Long March' of Mao Tse Tsung and his forces, and had retired to the Island of Taiwan. With China in the grip of its new masters, further channels were sought to spread the message. The

first outlet of any consequence would be Korea, a nation that was already divided after the expulsion of the Japanese. The south was almost defenceless, as its background was mainly rural in nature, while the north was of a militaristic tendency. As if to emphasize this difference, the forces of North Korea would launch an all-out offensive across the 38th Parallel on 25 June 1950 at 04.00hr. The Korean War had begun.

While politics were reshaping the world into two distinctive and opposing blocks, the front-line squadrons of the Fleet Air Arm were still equipping with the Sea Fury. When sufficient had entered service to allow enough units to become fully operational, separate carrier air wings were formed to equip three separate carriers. The First Carrier Group assigned to the fleet carrier HMS *Ocean* consisted of No. 802 Sqn equipped with the Hawker Sea Fury FB.11, and No. 825 Sqn flying the Fairey Firefly 5. Equipping the 17th

Carrier Group aboard the fleet carrier HMS *Theseus* were No. 807 Sqn with the Sea Fury FB.11, and No. 810 Sqn with the multi-role Firefly 5. A similar set-up was assigned to the fleet carrier HMS *Glory* whose 14th Carrier Air Group consisted of No. 804 Sqn with the Sea Fury, while No. 812 Sqn was the Fairey Firefly operator.

In response, the United Nations would assemble a multinational force that featured a large American and British contingent, whose avowed aim was to expel the forces of North Korea and their Chinese allies out of the territory of South Korea, and hold them at the 38th Parallel. The British sea-going component was drawn from the Far East Fleet that was based at Hong Kong. HMS *Triumph*, a light fleet carrier, was assigned by the Admiralty to provide the initial support to the UN forces. HMS *Triumph* would arrive in Korean waters to provide support to the UN forces, its carrier air wing consisting of No. 800 Sqn equipped with Supermarine Seafire FR.47s, and No. 827

Below **This view of HMS *Glory* photographed in calmer waters shows that much of the air wing was parked above deck. On the forward part of the carrier deck are parked the resident Sea Furies, while further aft, just behind the island, is parked the Sea Otter rescue aircraft. To the rear of the carrier deck the ships complement of Fairey Fireflies is on display.** Big Bird Aviation Collection

Sqn operating the Fairey Firefly. Complete with its support group consisting of two cruisers, two destroyers and three frigates, the *Triumph* air wing began combat operations on 3 July.

Operating alongside the Fleet Air Arm aircraft were the Vought F-4U Corsairs and Douglas Skyraiders from the USS *Valley Forge*; as both carriers were similar in design and equipment, there was a fair amount of cross-deck flying while the *Triumph* was on station for its three-month stint. During this period the carrier's air wing flew a total of 895 missions.

As combat flying was a hazardous and wearing affair to pilots, aircraft, ship and crew, it was not surprising that the HMS *Triumph* was up for replacement after three months. The carrier assigned to replace the *Triumph* was HMS *Theseus*, stationed at that time in UK waters as part of the Home Fleet. The carrier and its support fleet would depart from British waters in late August 1950, picking up its assigned 17th CAG from its home base of RNAS Lee-on-Solent on the way.

The transit journey of six weeks was put to good use, as both the carrier, its air group and the accompanying support fleet underwent a strenuous period of working up to combat readiness during the voyage to the Far East. Although each of the CAG squadrons had its fair selection of experienced senior pilots, the new boys required integration into the wing. As would be expected, the pilots of No.807 Sqn did suffer a few mishaps while making carrier landings and there were a few accidents amongst the Sea Furies – the occasional nose over onto the spinning propeller, or if the braking had been excessively heavy the aircraft would flip over completely. Once all the fuss and bother concerning the accident had been dealt with, the ship's engineering officer would decide the fate of each airframe. Those that were deemed repairable using shipboard resources were struck below for attention in the hanger, while those assessed as too badly damaged were stripped of useful parts and the shattered remains dumped over the side.

Active Service for Carrier HMS *Theseus*

HMS *Theseus* arrived in Korean waters on 9 October, passing HMS *Triumph* departing for its rest and recuperation period in the opposite direction. Once on station, the Fleet Aviation Officer, Commander E. S. Carver, was flown ashore to the Tactical Air Control Centre at Kimpo to report the carrier group's arrival. Remarkably, the centre was completely unaware of the changeover of carriers, or of the capabilities of its carrier air group, as HQ 5th Air Force had failed to inform them of the new arrivals. A very important piece of information also came back with the commander, namely the presence of a helicopter search-and-rescue flight, and the means of contacting them should the need arise. This omission was quickly rectified, and HMS *Theseus* was integrated into the offensive operations plans.

Deployed in the Yellow Sea, the aircraft of the 17th CAG began to strike at targets at Chinnampo, Pakchang, Chongju and Heiju in Hwanghai Province, these missions continuing until 22 October. Many of the strikes were aimed at Chinnampo, which had good port facilities, but was in the hands of North Koreans. However, against stiff defence the Sea Furies managed to badly damage a pair of mine-laying junks at Ho Do.

Such was the determination of the commanders in Korea to capture this port that the aircraft of the Fleet Air Arm put in a period of intensive flying: thus No. 807 Sqn Sea Furies completed 264 combat missions, while their multi-role brethren of No. 810 Sqn flying the Firefly achieved a creditable 120 sorties. However, the effort expended during this period took its toll upon the carrier and its crew, and HMS *Theseus* was withdrawn for a period of rest to the Japanese port of Iwakuni. This port was also home to the carrier's support organization, thus any defective aircraft were quickly landed, and replaced by serviceable machines ready to hand, while the engineering cadre began the task of repairing those damaged on operations.

Inspections were also carried out aboard HMS *Theseus*, where it was discovered that the running mechanism, part of the catapult launch system, was found to be worn beyond acceptable limits. As no spares were available in Japan to repair the

Below Aboard HMS *Theseus* the Sea Furies of Nos 804 and 898 Sqns prepare for training sorties prior to entering the fray in Korean waters. Note the aircraft identification striping above the wings. FAA Museum Collection

catapult, it was decided that aircraft launches should be undertaken using the RATOG system. To allow for the increased deck space needed for the take-off run, six of the Fireflies were left in Japan.

Cleared, complete with its noted limitations, for further operations, HMS *Theseus* arrived back on station on 27 October to provide support for ships engaged in minesweeping operations being undertaken in the Chinnampo estuary. These lasted until 5 November 1950, when the carrier was despatched to Hong Kong to take part in combined service exercises, although the air wing was still under strength, as its absent Fireflies were now in Korea being employed in the artillery-spotting role. The visit to Hong Kong lasted a month before HMS *Theseus* returned to the Yellow Sea on 7 December with the carrier group under the command of Vice Admiral Andrews.

For the next eight days the air wing undertook attacks against roads, bridges, airfields and railway rolling stock. Further missions were also flown against targets of opportunity, the proviso being that they must be strategic or transport in nature, as the intention behind this part of the campaign was to disrupt the supply chain in North Korea as much as possible. The carrier air wing managed to fly 332 offensive sorties without any losses – although the SAR helicopter suffered a fright when it was attacked by MiG fighters; however, a supporting patrol of Sea Furies quickly arrived and drove the enemy aircraft away, allowing the helicopter to return to the *Theseus*.

During this period of operations the aircraft of the 17th CAG encountered very little in the way of airborne resistance from the North Koreans and their Chinese allies. Their main enemy would be the intensive anti-aircraft fire thrown up by the enemy, and the possibility of technical failures with the aircraft. One who had the misfortune to experience the dubious joys of a technical malfunction was Lt D. P. W. Kelly of No. 807 Sqn, who departed from HMS *Theseus* on 24 December 1950 for a standard patrol. However, not long after launching his Bristol Centaurus began to misbehave, then failed altogether. Unfortunately for the pilot, he had failed to gain enough altitude to try a dead-stick landing back on the carrier, so he was left with two choices: to bail out, or to ditch. But as the Sea Fury had descended below

Above Illustrating well the difficulties faced by carriers in Korean waters, this photo shows the crew struggling to clear the deck for launching, while behind them sit snow-covered Sea Furies and Fireflies. FAA Museum Collection

safe parachute height, really the only option was to ditch – even though most pilots were very distrustful of this method of landing, as they were sure that the great weight of the Centaurus would pull them down into the depths of the sea.

Lt Kelly therefore followed instructions and jettisoned all the aircraft's underwing stores, before successfully ditching in the sea some four miles in front of the carrier. The US Navy destroyer USS *Sioux* was quickly on the scene and rescued the damp pilot from the sea; they returned him to HMS *Theseus*, and after a medical check-up, he resumed flying duties the next day. Although this one Sea Fury had been lost, the total of sorties flown by the air wing would reach 630 without a loss in combat. At the end of 1950 the 17th CAG was awarded the Boyd Trophy in recognition of its achievements and contributions to naval aviation during the preceding year.

Blowing up trains, bridges and ammunition dumps were not the only duties taken on by the aircraft of the 17th CAG. Both the Sea Furies and the Fireflies would find themselves engaged in combat air patrols in defence of the fleet, and on anti-submarine patrols against the submarines reported to be operated by the North Korean Navy. The primary hunter in this instance was the Firefly, although the Sea

Fury would also go on these sorties, though both needed external fuel tanks to increase their time on station. Whilst engaged on CAP duties, the Sea Furies managed over 3,900 interceptions, all of which turned out to be Allied aircraft of one sort or another. And not only did the aircraft of the 17th CAG take part in ground-attack missions, but the Sea Furies would quite often find themselves flying top cover for strike sorties flown by other air forces.

This mixture of missions continued until early 1951, when artillery spotting was added to the repertoire of the Sea Fury. These flights were concentrated around the Inchon area, where much of the naval offshore bombardment fleet was located. Shelling in this zone was intense enough to drive the enemy out, after which the fleet turned its attentions to Wonsan and Songin. Not all of the Sea Furies were engaged in the spotting role: the remainder would complete over 3,500 sorties, during which they dropped ninety-two 1,000lb bombs and 1,400 of the lighter 500lb bombs. Operating at lower levels, the Hawker fighters would let loose 7,300 rocket projectiles, and fire over half a million 20mm cannon shells. Operations off North Korea in winter were some of the hardest ever undertaken aboard an aircraft

Above **With a blizzard whipping across the deck, the groundcrew attempt to prepare a Sea Fury for a mission. Given the weather, it is highly unlikely that the sortie took place.** W. A. Harrison Collection

carrier, with blizzards frequently sweeping across the deck and hampering operations. However, dedicated work by both air- and groundcrews ensured that the sortie rate was maintained – although fourteen aircraft and pilots would be lost during this period. Some pilots would be rescued by plane-guard Sikorsky S-51 helicopters from the sea, while others were plucked from danger from behind enemy lines.

While No. 807 Sqn of the 17th CAG was flying from HMS *Theseus*, the normal operating complement of Sea Furies averaged out at twenty-three, although this would be subject to combat losses, accidents both on the carrier and into the Yellow Sea, plus the time delay experienced in receiving replacements from Britain. Those aircraft that were available would normally be airborne for an average of two and a half hours, although this required the use of external 45gal (205ltr) tanks to ensure that there were adequate fuel reserves for any mission requirements.

During combat operations from the *Theseus* the preferred launch method was the steam catapult; however, some use was made of the Sea Fury's RATOG capability, especially when it found itself employed in the bombing role. This requirement came more to the fore as the *Theseus'* tour of duty continued, as the hull was becoming encrusted with various small sea animals; these were effectively

reducing the ship's top speed, which meant that the required over-the-deck speed of twenty-eight knots was not available to launch aircraft at their heaviest weights. Unfortunately, because HMS *Theseus* had been despatched to the Far East in such haste, it had meant that a much needed period of maintenance, including a good scraping of the hull bottom, had been delayed until a later date. So, since *Theseus* was not able to steam faster than twenty-two knots, the role of the Sea Fury changed from that of fighter bomber to rocket-equipped ground attacker, as the all-up weight allowance was reduced. But even this option ran into trouble; the original intention had been to use the rockets mounted in multiples, but these had to be reduced to singletons as the generated stress of using the weapons in this form was causing cracks in the area of the wing mountings.

Although the Sea Fury was built with the capability of carrying out photo reconnaissance duties, when tried under combat conditions the results were less than satisfactory, as the lubricating oil spray thrown by the Centaurus engine was smearing and obscuring the camera port. Furthermore, it wasn't only the aircraft of the 17th CAG giving problems: the carrier itself was found to have inadequate space for the amount of ammunition being expended, although the ship's aviation fuel tanks

were of sufficient capacity. However, some careful rearrangement of life below decks soon resolved the ammunition problem.

HMS *Theseus* would resume combat operations during January 1951, however flying, even at best, would only be intermittent, as bad weather, even worse than normal for the region, hampered not only aircraft launches, but more importantly recovery. With the first twelve days of the new year lost to the inclement conditions, the carrier's problems were compounded when two days later it was discovered that the reeving of the steam catapult was worn beyond safe operating limits. What made matters worse was that this particular set-up had only managed 880 launches before failing. Undaunted, the crew of HMS *Theseus* worked round the problem; thus limitations were placed upon the launch capacity of each aircraft type, so that the Sea Furies were launched minus their external fuel tanks and weaponry, while the Fireflies used RATOG to get airborne.

These changes meant that the Hawker fighters were limited to combat air patrols, while the Fairey machines could depart with full mission loads. Given these limits, both types would give of their usual best while supporting the fighting in the Suwon–Osan–Inchon region, with minimal casualties. As the lack of a catapult was seriously hampering combat operations the carrier was despatched to the port of Sasebo for repairs. These were duly completed, and HMS *Theseus* would return to its station in the Yellow Sea on 25 January, where it relieved its temporary stand-in, USS *Bataan*. Missions began again at the end of the month, although this was not without loss; the 17th CAG lost four aircraft, and one pilot was killed during an attempted ditching. These losses notwithstanding, the air wing managed a creditable 66 sorties during the first three days of February.

Flying in support of ground forces over Korea continued, until the carrier was withdrawn for a period of much needed rest and recuperation in late March. It was during this particular tour of duty that the self-sealing tanks fitted to the Sea Fury were found to be less effective than at first supposed: one of the aircraft was hit by a half-inch armour-piercing round that caused extensive damage. Although badly damaged and leaking fuel quite heavily, the pilot managed to nurse his aircraft to Suwon, where he made a successful emergency landing.

The following month the aircraft of the 17th CAG went out on even more sorties than normal, as air and ground reconnaissance, plus intelligence gathering, had revealed that massed Communist forces were gathering on the far side of the Yula River. Missions began on 9 April and would continue over the following six days, the Sea Furies carrying out extensive strikes against road and rail bridges, vehicles and railway rolling stock, marshalling yards, supply dumps and warehouses. As well as carrying out attacks against targets themselves, the Sea Fury pilots were also employed on artillery-spotting duties for the heavy-hitting battleships and cruisers pounding targets in the Wonsan and Songjin regions. Both these sortie types were backed up by extensive armed reconnaissance missions.

Throughout this short period the 17th CAG aircraft managed 276 sorties, with no deck-landing accidents; though five Sea Furies would be lost in combat, one being shot down by US Marine Corps fighters operating out of Kimpo; another aircraft was also damaged by the same fighters during the same engagement.

Having completed its tour of duty on the eastern side of the country, the carrier was then transferred to the western side of Korea to resume combat flying. These missions would restart over the period 17–18 April, and ninety-four would be completed – although a further four aircraft would be lost during this period, thereby reducing the 17th CAG's available inventory. After this surge period, HMS *Theseus* was withdrawn from the front line for a further period of rest and recuperation at Sasebo. This was the end of HMS *Theseus'* involvement in the Korean War, and the statistics show that they achieved eighty-six flying days out of the seven months on station, while a total of 3,446 missions were flown.

On 25 April 1952 HMS *Theseus* was relieved on station by the fleet carrier HMS *Glory*.

Active Service for HMS *Glory*

The air wing aboard HMS *Glory* when it arrived in the Yellow Sea was the 14th CAG, which consisted of No. 804 Sqn with an inventory of twenty-one Sea Furies, and No. 812 Sqn flying the Fairey Firefly V. Within days of arrival, the aircraft of HMS *Glory* were engaged in the

Above **Not the best way to make yourself popular, or the normal way to arrive aboard an aircraft carrier, Sea Fury FB.11 113/T parks in a most unusual way aboard HMS *Theseus* and disrupts the resident Firefly squadron.** FAA Museum Collection

intriguingly named Operation *Strangle*, its implied intention being to finally strangle the various North Korean supply lines. This maximum air offensive began on 28 April, and initially involved fifteen aircraft from HMS *Glory* – although one Sea Fury would be lost in a crash soon after launch. The continuing rate of sorties would result in the loss of a further Sea Fury in a crash-landing on 2 May. The pilot, Lt Barlow, was successfully rescued by the carrier's plane-guard helicopter, the downed fighter later being strafed by its compatriots until it was destroyed.

A respite from combat would follow, as the carrier group was assailed by very

Below **With a brakeman in the cockpit and its wheels chocked, this Sea Fury is in the process of being struck down below the main deck of HMS *Glory* for servicing.** FAA Museum Collection

inhospitable weather, which cancelled all operations until 13 May. However, once flying was resumed, in the following three days the aircraft of the 14th CAG went out on 155 sorties, with only one loss, a Sea Fury that was brought down by anti-aircraft fire, although the pilot was rescued. After such intense exertions, HMS *Glory* departed the Yellow Sea for a period of rest and recuperation, being replaced by its American counterpart, USS *Bataan*.

The carrier returned to the combat theatre on 3 June, although on this occasion its sojourn was short, as eight days later a quick return to port was needed as water had been found in the aviation fuel tankage. It was flushed out and inspected, and repairs were carried out to the fleet carrier RFA *Wave Premier*'s forward transfer rig, which had lain unused for considerable periods of time; HMS *Glory* was then cleared to return to combat duties. This incident was duly reported in the tabloid press, although their spin on the whole story was that sabotage had been the culprit! Having sorted out the fuel problem, HMS *Glory* returned to active duty and resumed combat flying; however, at least two Sea Furies were lost on this tour.

Having completed this period of operations, the carrier returned to port in Kure for a further rest period, then returned to

active duties later in June. Just for a change, the region was blessed with good weather, which allowed the sortie rate to increase – an average of fifty sorties per day were being launched by the 14th CAG. In the last two days of this surge period the carrier's aircraft were again having to be launched using the RATOG system, as the catapult system had yet again become inoperable. Inevitably this would slow down the sortie rate slightly, though only to forty-eight per day, and the air wing still managed to drop twenty-two 1,000lb bombs and two hundred 500lb bombs, and to fire some 1,500 rocket projectiles and innumerable cannon shells. During this period virtually any moving or fixed target within the designated strike zone was considered an acceptable target, and struck accordingly.

The designation of this combined fleet was Task Force 95, with the British group being responsible for strikes against target on the western coast of Korea. The number of sorties sent out each day was intense – on one day eighty-four were logged – but amazingly only one Sea Fury was lost, and this was due to a catapult cold shot, and not enemy action. There was one close encounter, however, when a flight of Sea Furies was bounced by some USAF Lockheed P-80 jet fighters, whose pilots were not very good at aircraft recognition. Fortunately for the Fleet Air Arm

pilots, their piston-powered machines were able to out-manoeuvre the Americans, and they escaped from such unwelcome attentions without loss.

HMS *Glory* and its air wing resumed combat operations in late July 1951, and at this point in time the fighting in Korea rose to its highest level ever. Two Sea Furies were lost to intense anti-aircraft fire, and further losses occurred due to technical problems with the engines. Initially this was put down to general wear and tear, but as pilots were debriefed after missions, it transpired that the cause of failure was in fact because they were pushing their machines past their limits in order to survive in the combat arena. As a result, and to ensure that the pilots had the best chance of survival, the engineering teams put extra effort into engine maintenance, and this helped reduce the losses from technical faults.

A respite – if it could be called such – came from the fighting when typhoon 'Madge' arrived in the area in mid-August. The severity of the weather was such that any thought of flying was out of the question, at least until the storm blew itself out. By 1 September conditions had improved and flying could resume – though now the steam catapult was malfunctioning again. However, this did not stop the 14th CAG from averaging fifty sorties per day. The focus of their missions was around Han, Chinnampo and Chongchon, with all the usual target types being attacked with some degree of success.

A trip to Singapore followed during October for a much needed period of rest and recuperation, then HMS *Glory* departed to Australian waters for a work-up period in calmer, warmer climes, before her return to the Korean cauldron.

Active Service for HMS *Sydney*

While the crew of HMS *Glory* were relaxing, first in Singapore and then off Australia, the carrier was replaced on station by the Royal Australian Navy carrier HMAS *Sydney*, whose two operating units, Nos 805 and 808 Sqns, both flew the Sea Fury FB.11. Initially the Australian carrier plied its trade off the west coast of Korea, beginning on 5 October; however, its sojourn there would be short, as six days later the carrier was

Below **Complete with Korea stripes (note how they pass over the wing's leading edges) this Sea Fury, with underwing bomb load, prepares for departure from HMS *Ocean*.** FAA Museum Collection

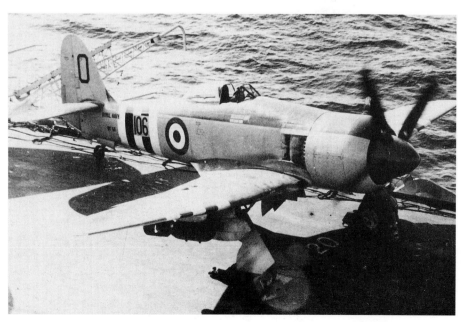

transferred to the more target-rich east coast to fly missions. On the day of its arrival, 11 October, HMAS *Sydney* launched sixteen Sea Furies to hit targets on the coast and the hills further inland. While roving over the target zone, the fighters were directed towards a force of 2,000 troops in the process of digging in. Cleared to attack, the Sea Furies began strafing the troops and the ammunition dump alongside; the latter exploded with a spectacular display of pyrotechnics, while the North Korean troops suffered serious casualties.

A short withdrawal three days later gave the carrier's crew a four-day rest period; then HMAS *Sydney* returned to the fray off the Korean coast. Shipping and troop concentrations were the primary targets of the Sea Fury squadrons, although any targets of opportunity were declared fair game. As before, the intense anti-aircraft fire damaged three fighters, all of which crash-landed upon return. Fortunately the revised fuel tank fire-protection system ensured that the pilots did not have that problem to contend with.

A Daring Rescue

It was during this period of operations that one of the most daring rescues of the Korean War took place. On 25 October, the Sea Fury piloted by Sub Lt. MacWilliams was hit by intense anti-aircraft fire. Badly damaged, the pilot made an emergency landing inland, and set off a chain of events that would be reminiscent of subsequent actions in another war in Vietnam. Recovery action by the carrier involved the use of an SAR helicopter escorted by five Sea Fury FB.11s, who in turn were given top cover against airborne intrusion by a Gloster Meteor F.8 despatched by No. 77 Sqn RAAF.

Upon arrival, the Sea Furies set about their task with enthusiasm, attacking approaching troops, and while the North Koreans were occupied dodging the cannon shells and rockets, the helicopter flew in, landed, and retrieved the pilot. Once it had flown clear, the Sea Furies and the Meteor withdrew, all making a successful landing at Kimpo airfield just as the light was fading.

After the excitement of retrieving Sub Lt MacWilliams, the combat squadrons aboard HMAS *Sydney* resumed operations. These, however, would be

Above **With its hook deployed, Sea Fury FB.11 WN474 of No. 898 Sqn, based aboard HMS *Ocean*, poses for the camera. Under the wings it carries a pair of 45gal (205ltr) fuel tanks and a pair of aerodynamic bomb carriers.** FAA Museum Collection

temporarily suspended during December 1951, as the weather was too inclement for flying. The following day the aircraft from the *Sydney* were in action again, launching a total of fifty-eight sorties involving the carrier's Sea Furies and the Fireflies. The first aircraft to depart were four Sea Furies from No. 805 Sqn, armed with cannon shells and 1,000lb bombs instead of the usual rockets. The intended target was a rail bridge north of Haeju, which was attacked as planned, although no direct hits were confirmed; then they began strafing rail vehicles, destroying at least two in the process.

While the fighters of No. 805 Sqn were hassling the Korean rail links, their counterparts in No. 808 Sqn were concentrating their efforts around the Han River area. It was during these attacks that the Sea Fury of Sub Lt Noel Knapstein was badly damaged by enemy flak. Fortunately the pilot made a successful landing on a mudflat in the estuary; he was quickly retrieved by a rescue boat from HMS *Amethyst*, and returned to his carrier.

While the Sea Furies had been troubling the Koreans, the Fireflies of No. 817 Sqn were also engaged in attacking the Korean rail links, after which they would turn their attentions to each end of the railway tunnel near Chaeryong. It was during this attack that the Firefly piloted by Sub-Lt Neil MacMillan was hit by intensive flak. Originally there appeared to be no damage to the Firefly, until fuel was seen to be streaming out of the port wing; then very quickly after the engine shut down. Left with no other option, the Firefly crew set about searching for a place to force land, eventually choosing a paddy field for

touch-down after jettisoning the canopy. As soon as possible after landing the crew abandoned their aircraft, and settled in a ditch to await either rescue or capture.

Fortunately for them, aboard HMAS *Sydney* the carrier's commander Captain Harries decided that yet again a rescue effort would be mounted, even though there weren't many hours of daylight remaining. The ship's Sikorsky rescue helicopter was quickly prepared for departure, meeting up with '99' Flight: four Sea Furies from No. 805 Sqn. Also involved in the action was a flight of Meteor F.8s, despatched, as before, from Kimpo AB by courtesy of No. 77 Sqn RAAF.

Both sets of fighters were quickly on the scene, with the Sea Furies acting in the ground-attack role to drive the enemy clear of the rescue zone, while the jet fighters flew top cover. The North Korean forces did not give up their potential prize easily, however, and at least one Sea Fury had to pull out after being damaged by ground fire; a safe landing was made at Kimpo despite the ailerons becoming increasingly unresponsive. The remaining aircraft stayed on station, although they were warned that the light was fading and that the rescue attempt was about to be called off. But the rescue flight from HMAS *Sydney* was close to arriving, so they volunteered to remain where they were, to cover the rescue. And so the Firefly crew was picked up in the dusk by the ship's helicopter. The escorting Sea Furies remained for as long as possible before having to return to the carrier, but two Meteors from Kimpo stayed with the helicopter until it landed safely in the dark at Kimpo.

Above **On patrol from HMS *Ocean*, this Sea Fury FB.11 WJ237 flies over Korea looking for targets of opportunity.** FAA Museum Collection

This was virtually the end of HMAS *Sydney*'s time in theatre, as on 7 January 1952 the carrier was relieved by the returning HMS *Glory*. *Sydney* had completed sixty-four days engaged in operations, during which some 645 sorties were made, of which 474 were offensive in nature, while the remainder were defensive. During this period two Sea Furies and a single Firefly were lost, and twenty-three aircraft were damaged by flak and small arms fire.

Reconnaissance and Bomber Duties for the Sea Fury

Once HMS *Glory* had returned to active duty, as an experiment the ship's engineers installed two F.24 cameras in a Sea Fury's underwing drop tank in an effort to give the aircraft some form of reconnaissance capability, as the one built in by Hawker's had not delivered as promised. A camera was mounted in the front and rear of the tank in an effort to give some form of panoramic coverage. After initial flight trials the reconnaissance package was cleared for use by Sea Furies from HMS *Ocean*. Although this idea was never adopted across the Fleet Air Arm, it was used successfully by the 14th CAG throughout its tour of duty for both pre- and post-strike reconnaissance.

The engineers aboard the carrier also developed bomb carriers capable of carrying 500lb bombs to replace the rocket mounts, as the 60lb rocket projectile warhead was found to be ineffective against some targets. To gain the maximum benefit from this installation, the Sea Fury pilots had to use their aircraft as dive bombers, and clear the area quickly as the fuse on each bomb was set at thirty seconds. As shown by the previous Typhoon and Tempest, the Sea Fury was found to be a very stable bombing platform.

HMS *Glory* would begin its last tour of duty on 18 April; it was replaced by HMS *Ocean* in May.

Jet Fighter Encounter

When the fleet carrier HMS *Ocean* arrived off the coast of Korea, the resident air wing was the 1st CAG, with flying units No. 802 Sqn flying Sea Furies, and No. 805 Sqn operating the Fairey Firefly. Soon after the arrival of HMS *Ocean*, the first sightings of enemy jet fighters were reported, and these quickly began to make their presence felt. The fighters were MiG 15s sporting the insignia of the North Korean Air Force, although their pilots were reported to be from Russia and China. The first encounter between the jet fighters from North Korea and the

Hawker fighters of the Fleet Air Arm took place on 9 August, when a flight of MiG 15s slipped through the defensive cordon of the United States Air Force North American F-86 Sabres. Unaware of this addition to their normal combat duties, a flight of No. 802 Sqn Sea Furies, on patrol as Wizard Flight, was bounced by the Korean jet fighters.

Alerted to the fact that they were under attack as the tracers passed their aircraft, the pilots turned their fighters towards their attackers. The leader of the Fleet Air Arm flight was Lt Peter 'Hoagy' Carmicheal, a veteran of World War II, and he and his colleagues – Sub-Lt Carl Haines, Sub-Lt Brian 'Smoo' Ellis, and Lt Peter Davies – immediately opened fire as the first aircraft passed their gunsights. Hits from the cannon of Sub-Lt Haines were seen to strike the North Korean fighter, which broke away streaming smoke and debris. In the ensuing mêlée, Lt Carmichael found another MiG filling his sights and raked it with gunfire: spewing smoke and flames, it crashed into the sea. Because the Sea Fury was very manoeuvrable the other pilots were able to take limited shots at the MiGs, although they would eventually break away; however, the Sea Furies did not escape lightly, as one of the fighters was hit by cannon fire in the wing, which ignited the fuel in the tank. To return to base, the pilot used all his skill at side slipping to put out the conflagration, enabling the wounded Sea Fury to limp back to HMS *Glory*.

There were several further encounters between the Sea Furies of the 1st CAG and North Korean jets during the following week, although of the eight MiG 15s engaged, only one would be confirmed as damaged. However, leaders such as Lt Peter Carmichael by now believed that although the MiG 15 had a 200mph (300km/h) advantage, the Sea Fury was more than a match for it, especially if flown aggressively.

After such exertions the *Glory* was pulled out of the area for a period of rest, recuperation and replenishment.

This respite only lasted a few days before the carrier returned to its duties off the Korean coast; its continued presence in the area would make it the longest-serving aircraft carrier assigned to the war effort. There was a change to the Sea Fury unit aboard HMS *Glory*, as No. 804 Sqn was withdrawn, and replaced by No. 810 Sqn, once of HMS *Theseus*; this carrier's inventory of aircraft was increased because it took over some of those left behind by its predecessors. As well as the three carrier-assigned units, the two other front-line squadrons equipped with the Sea Fury would also experience combat over Korea. However, Nos. 805 and 808 Sqns would serve aboard the Australian fleet carrier HMAS *Sydney*, where they would operate alongside their RAN counterparts.

To complete the full picture of HMS *Glory's* Korean tour, the air wing would fly nearly 30,000 sorties; however, the price for this number was the loss of twenty-two pilots killed in action. Given the defensive strength of some of these targets, it was remarkable that losses were kept so low; this was a tribute to the training and experience levels within the air wing. Besides the three carrier groups, mention must be made of the two fleet support carriers HMS *Unicorn* and *Warrior*, without whose assistance many of the air wings' exploits would not have been successful.

The Sea Fury Makes Way for the Jet Fighter

With the signing of the Korean ceasefire on 27 July 1953, and the conclusion of hostilities, the tenure of the Sea Fury as a front-line fighter would come to an end. Jet aircraft were the coming thing, and one of the first to relinquish its Hawker fighters was No. 803 Sqn, which would change over to the Supermarine Attacker F.1 during November 1951 while based at RNAS Ford. No. 806 Sqn had dispensed with its Sea Furies in September 1948, after just five months of service; they would try various early jet aircraft in turn, before settling upon the Hawker Sea Hawk.

Nos 809 and 898 Sqns traded in their Hawker fighters for the Sea Vampire and Sea Hawk respectively in January 1953. During the following year, Nos 802, 804, 807, 808, 811 and 850 Sqns would also change their Sea Furies for jet aircraft, the favourite being another Hawker product, the Sea Hawk. In the early months of 1955 the last two front-line units, Nos 801 and 810 Sqns, traded in the Sea Fury for the Sea Hawk FGA.4. Ironically the second-line support units mostly dispensed with their Sea Furies between 1948 and 1952. Of the original fourteen units to use the Hawker fighter, only six would retain the type until the middle of

Above **Opposing the United Nations forces were the North Koreans, many of whose pilots were Chinese and Russian, all of whom flew the MiG 15. This is the two-seat version, the MiG 15UTI.** Nick Challoner

the decade, these being Nos 700, 703, 738, 744, 751 and 781 Sqns.

While the combat pilots were gaining all the kudos for their exploits over Korea, there was another organization that was essential in providing training and support and defence while the events in Korea were unfolding. These were the second-line squadrons of the Royal Naval Reserve, which began to equip with the Hawker fighter during 1951, where it would replace the Supermarine Seafire F.17. The first unit to receive the Sea Fury was No.1832 Sqn based at Culham, whose new aircraft inventory began arriving in August 1951. It was quickly followed by Nos 1835 and 1836 Sqns RNR, based at Benson. All three squadrons were part of the Southern Air Division, and would move to Benson in July 1953 where the trainer aircraft plus the single-seat fighters were all operated under the common pool principle.

In Scotland, No. 1830 Sqn plus its offshoot No. 1843 Sqn would gain their share of the Sea Fury T.20 fleet in October 1952 and March 1953 respectively, to form the Scottish Air Division. Hawker aircraft had manufactured sixty Sea Fury T.20s, with deliveries beginning to the Fleet Air Arm during mid-1950, with the first examples being delivered to the Naval Air Fighting Development Unit for extensive evaluation flying. Although the Sea Fury T.20s were not fitted with an arrestor hook, which precluded their use on aircraft carriers, in most other respects they were similar in all respects to the single-seat fighters; thus they sported

powered folding wings, and could carry the same extensive range of weaponry, although the cannon installation was kept to one per side so as to maintain the aircraft's centre of gravity.

Elsewhere the Northern Air Division station at Stretton, and its reserve unit No. 1831 Sqn, gained its two-seaters in October 1950, these being joined by Sea Fury FB.11s in August 1951.

Further south at Bramcote, the Midland Air Division reserve unit No. 1833 Sqn received its Sea Fury T.20s in October 1950; these were joined by its share of single-seat fighters in February 1954. No. 1830 Sqn would dispose of its Sea Furies in October 1954, while No. 1831 Sqn relinquished both versions of Sea Fury in June 1955. Nos 1832, 1835 and 1836 Sqns disposed of their FB.11s in August 1955, while the T.20s left in June 1956.

At Bramcote, No. 1833 Sqn disposed of both versions of the Sea Fury during mid-1955, while in April 1955 No. 1834 Sqn said farewell to its Hawker fighters. No. 1843 Sqn would lose its Sea Furies in November 1955, these being replaced by Grumman Avengers. The eventual replacements for the Sea Furies included the Supermarine Attacker FB2, the Hawker Sea Hawk F.1, and the Grumman Avenger AS.6.

The United Kingdom reserve forces, including the Royal Naval Reserve squadrons, would be disbanded on 10 March 1957, some of their aircraft being dispersed amongst the few remaining Sea Fury operators, whilst the remainder were sent to the maintenance units for disposal.

CHAPTER THIRTEEN

Hawkers in Civilian Clothing

Once the Sea Fury had completed its service with the Fleet Air Arm, quite a number were purchased from the Ministry of Supply by Hawker Aircraft for possible resale to other air forces and interested parties. Military sales were achieved with Burma, the Netherlands and Egypt, among others, while a semi-military sale was made to a German organization, the Deutsche Luftfahrt Beratungsdienst. This organization had one purpose only: to provide target-tug facilities for the German armed forces.

DLB Sea Furies

The DLB order was placed with Hawker's in 1958, for the supply of ten ex-FAA Sea Fury T.20s, refurbished close to new standard. To trial the preferred towing equipment, one of the Sea Furies was fitted with a set of Swiss-manufactured towing equipment to ensure that the system worked correctly. This system utilized an air-driven winch whose generator was placed on the starboard side of the fuselage. The cables to which the banners were attached were fed out under the fuselage, there being a cable cutter incorporated to release the banner and cable in an emergency. Protecting the rear of the aircraft from cable whiplash were tailplane protection wires; these would also ensure that there were no entanglements in the vicinity of the flight control surfaces.

Not long after the first batch had finished being reworked by Hawker's, an order for a further batch of six aircraft was placed via the Ministry of Supply, this too utilizing ex-FAA Sea Furies. These sixteen aircraft, bedecked in a bright red overall colour scheme, were delivered during 1958 to 1960. Upon arrival in Germany the remaining Swiss-made target-tow equipment was installed. The main bases for the DLB Sea Furies were Lubeck, Cologne or Bonn as required by the main contractor, the emergent West German Luftwaffe, as well as providing some services for both naval and army anti-aircraft gunners. Joining the sixteen two-seat target-towing machines was an ex-Royal Netherlands Navy single-seat Sea Fury FB.11, also repainted bright overall red and fitted with target-towing equipment similar to its twin-seat siblings.

Of the total of seventeen aircraft sold to DLB, some five machines were lost in accidents; it was suspected that a percentage of these were as a result of carbon monoxide poisoning, a defect that continued to plague the type even after extensive corrective measures had been taken. The German Sea Fury fleet remained in service until they were retired during 1970. The surviving two-seat machines were sold off for further usage, while the solo single-seater was retained for display in the Luftwaffenmuseum based in Uetersen. To replace the Sea Fury, a fleet of Rockwell OV-10BZ was purchased for operation by the Luftwaffe – although these, too, have been retired, to be replaced by, yet again, a civilian-based contractor. While in use with the DLB, the two-seat Sea Furies were registered thus: D-CABY, CACA, CACE, CACI, CACO, CACU, CIBO, CAMI, CATA, COTE, CCCO, CEBO, CABU, CADA and CAFO; the single-seater was registered D-CACY.

Of the remaining T.20s, three were returned to Britain where they would again wear military markings, two under the care of the Fleet Air Arm Historic Flight, whilst the other would resume flying duties as VZ345 with the A&AEE based at Boscombe Down, although it would be badly damaged in a landing accident at its home base on 17 April 1985. The determined cause as laid out in the official accident report was excessive braking on landing, which caused the aircraft to tip onto its nose and then completely flip over. Initially categorized as 'Cat. 3 repairable', the decision was taken not to repair VZ345, as funds were not available for its rebuilding; instead it would be reduced to spares, the majority of which would be transported to the British

West German T.20s			
C/no.	FAA Serial	DLB Regn	Disposal
ES.8501	VX309	D-CIBO	FAAM
ES.8502	VX300	D-CAMI	N924G
ES.8503	VZ345	D-CATA	A&AEE
ES.8504	WE820	D-COTE	N85SF
ES.8505	VZ350	D-COCO	N20SF
ES.8506	VZ351	D-CEDO	n/k
ES.8507	VZ353	D-CABU	Cr 21.5.62
ES.8508	VX291	D-CADA	Cr 18.3.64
ES.8509	WG652	D-CAFO	N62134
ES.8510	VZ372	D-CAME	Cr 30.1.63
ES.3511	WE824	D-CABY	Cr 3.3.70
ES.3512	VZ365	D-CACA	n/k
ES.3513	VX302	D-CACE	N51SF
ES.3514	VX280	D-CACI	Cr 10.8.65
ES.3515	VX281	D-CACO	G-BCOW
ES.3516	WG655	D-CACU	FAAM
ES.3617	WG599	D-CACY	Duxford

Right **Sea Fury FB.11 D-CACY was the only single-seat aircraft procured by the DLB for target-towing duties; it was repainted bright red, and flew with 45gal (205ltr) external fuel tanks fitted as standard.** W. A. Harrison Collection

Right **The great majority of aircraft used by the DLB were two-seat T.20s. Here, D-COTE undergoes maintenance out in the sunlight. Although the cannon were removed from these aircraft, their access panels were found to be useful for entry into the wing.** Thomas Genth

Below **Target tug D-CAMI is being moved onto the flight line for the day's flying. Movement was courtesy of a tractor, while steering required an arm attached to the tailwheel. Also visible in this view is the wind-powered towing winch.** Thomas Genth

Above **Caught in the act of deploying its drogue is this Sea Fury T.20 of the DLB. Under normal circumstances the aircraft were flown by a single crewman.** Thomas Genth

Left **With all access panels open around the engine, and the propeller assembly hanging off the hand crane, the groundcrew prepare the drive shaft to accept the propeller and front plate.** Thomas Genth

Below **One of the navy systems retained by DLB was the wing-fold mechanism; this was found useful when putting the aircraft away at night, thus reducing the room requirement.** Thomas Genth

Below **This three-quarter rear view of a DLB T.20 D-CATA reveals the layout of the wires installed to protect the tailplane and fin assemblies from a flailing drogue cable. Also clearly visible in this portrait are the air-driven winch and its mountings.** Thomas Genth

Aerospace factory at Brough on Humberside, for use in the repair and rebuilding of Sea Fury FB.11, VR930, which was being restored.

Of the other redundant machines, four were purchased by a British buyer and flown to Blackbushe, where they would remain in storage before being sold on to other buyers in the United States. Two other aircraft would also end up in America via a dealer in Belgium, although their condition on delivery was described as poor. The last two aircraft were sold off by direct sales.

The Fate of the Remaining Typhoons

Although the Sea Fury had attracted the attention of many purchasers after military service, one of its predecessors, the Typhoon, was not so lucky, as very little remained in practical form of this once mighty fleet. In May 1945 the various ministries and the Royal Air Force undertook a massive census in an attempt to find out where the thousands of aircraft allegedly still available for active service actually were. The final tally of surviving Typhoons showed that 1,149 Typhoons were still on the books, with another eighty on order or undergoing delivery from the Gloster Aircraft Company. However, faster and possibly safer machines were being delivered to the fighter-bomber squadrons of the RAF, and as the squadrons re-equipped, their redundant machines were shipped to various maintenance units for disposal. Those aircraft that required major servicing or extensive repair work were immediately scrapped, while those with a possible second use were placed in storage at No. 5 MU at Kemble, and No. 20 MU at Aston Down. Such was the rapid rate of withdrawal of the Typhoon that only 748 machines survived long enough to enter storage, and of this total, only seventy-four were in flying service.

As more and more Tempests and late marque Spitfires were delivered to the Royal Air Force, the reason for retaining the Typhoon in store disappeared. Thus a mass scrapping of these airframes began, although not all would end up as saucepans, because fuselages and wing sections were shipped to the various training schools for use in instructing various ground tradesmen. The biggest user of these structural sections was the airframe repair training organizations, who would use up each component and discard it as its usefulness expired. By 1955 there was only one complete Typhoon in Britain, and this was an amalgam of parts from DN502, MN282 and MN601. Eventually even this rare machine was withdrawn and sent for processing at 60 MU at Rufforth.

Fortunately for posterity, one complete Typhoon had been spared from the mass cull of the type. This aircraft was MN235, which had been delivered to the USAAF for evaluation in March 1944. Operating out of Wright Field, Ohio, the Typhoon was tested in its fighter-bomber role and to trial its range and endurance. However, these trial flights put only nine flying hours on the airframe, better known in America as FE-401 (Foreign Experimental), before it was placed in storage. Eventually this loan specimen was ceded to the Smithsonian Institution, although there appeared to be no intention to display it in the museum. When the RAF Museum at Hendon was in the planning stage, the Smithsonian made contact and suggested that the Typhoon would be far better off in the UK – but they would like a Hawker Hurricane in exchange. The deal was finally agreed, and MN235 was returned to Britain courtesy of the Royal Air Force, who refurbished it and placed it on display within the walls of the RAF Museum.

There are other Typhoon sections still extant; for instance, the Imperial War Museum has a cockpit section on display, which is reported to have been a training aid at No.1 S of TT Halton, and there is another stored for the Jet Age Museum in Gloucestershire. There are also reported to be at least three restoration projects in private hands, at Hawkinge, Sleap Aerodrome, Shoreham Airport, Coventry Airport and Salisbury. In the main these are cockpit sections.

The Fate of the Tempest

Unlike the few Typhoon relics that are preserved, the Tempest was far more prevalent, as many examples were sold for overseas service. In Britain the cull of Tempests took place more slowly than that of the Typhoon, so greater numbers were held in storage as a potential war reserve, while others would serve with the front-line squadrons. Otherwise quite a few Mark V fighter bombers were converted for target-towing use as the TT.5. Eventually, however, the fighter-squadron Tempests were withdrawn to storage, to 5 MU at Kemble and 20 MU at Aston Down, and during November 1950 many of the stored aircraft were sold off to Hawker Aircraft for spares recovery, whilst any remaining were reduced to scrap metal.

Next it was the turn of the Tempest VI, and by 1950 the whole production run was in storage, at No. 6 MU at Brize Norton and No. 20 MU. These aircraft were disposed of in two batches, to Hawker

Below **Caught in the daylight instead of the confines of a museum, this is the sole surviving complete Typhoon IB MN235; it owes its survival to the Smithsonian Institute in America.** Big Bird Aviation Collection

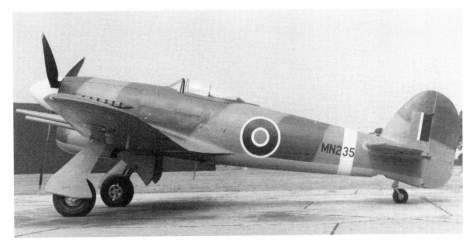

Aircraft in May 1951 for spares recovery, and to the Ministry of Supply in June 1953, for unknown purposes.

There was a more buoyant market for Tempest IIs overseas when they were withdrawn from RAF service, therefore few remained to be recovered for spares. The last Tempests to leave RAF service were the TT.5s, which were placed in storage during 1955. Yet again they were not left there long, as Hawker's and the Ministry of Supply would purchase the redundant airframes for various programmes before disposing of them to various scrapyards

around the country. This virtual clean sweep left only two examples extant within the bounds of the UK; one of these was the second prototype Mark II, LA607, which had been used as an instructional airframe at Cranfield and then sent to the Skyfame Museum at Staverton in Gloucestershire in 1966.

The other airframe was a Mark V that was given the serial SN219, although it was in fact a composite of quite a few aircraft, having been recovered in parts from the Proof and Experimental Establishment at Shoeburyness, where the

remainder had been used as targets for various weapons. The unit responsible for its recovery and restoration was No. 33 Sqn, who rebuilt it in time for it to be the centrepiece of the celebrations when the squadron received its standard in 1958. After its short moment of glory at Leeming, the Tempest was transferred to RAF Middleton St George for use as a gate guardian. Eventually common sense prevailed, and this rare specimen was removed from the ravages of the weather a few years later. Its new home was to be the RAF Museum, but before that the airframe underwent major restoration at the museum restoration facility at Cardington, where removal of the outer paint layer revealed that the fuselage bore the serial NV778. As this was far more appropriate than SN219, this is the identity displayed on the aircraft at the moment. In November 2001 Tempest V NV778 was transferred to the Cosford Aerospace Museum, where it is on display in the Michael Beetham Conservation Centre, having been in storage at Wyton.

The RAF Museum also owned the fuselage of Tempest V EJ693, which still displays its original No. 486 Sqn codes of SA-I. This particular machine had been acquired from the Technical Training School at Delft, who in turn had recovered the remains of the airframe after it had force-landed in Holland during October 1944. In storage alongside this fuselage are a set of wings from an ex-Royal Indian Air Force Tempest II, plus other spares, from which it is hoped a complete representative aircraft can be assembled. As resources were not available to complete this machine at the time, it was sold to the American aircraft collector Kermit Weeks. Now registered as N7072E it is currently stored awaiting restoration at Wycombe Air Park, Booker, in Buckinghamshire.

When the Skyfame museum closed in 1978, most of their exhibits moved to the Imperial War Museum at Duxford. One airframe, however, did not make the transition, this being the prototype Mark II, LA607, which was sold to the American collector Kermit Weeks for display in his Planes of Fame Museum at Chino. This left the RAF Museum example as the only complete surviving airframe, and the chances of this one being flown again are practically nil.

Of those Tempests that had been sold overseas, only India had extant examples,

Above After restoration by No. 33 Sqn, SN219 spent some time on display at Odiham marked as 'F', before it moved to Middleton St George for use as a gate guard. C. P. Russell Smith Collection

Below Wearing the '5R' codes of No. 33 Sqn, SN219/NV778 is seen here undergoing restoration at the RAFM workshop at Cardington, before being displayed in the museum. C. P. Russell Smith Collection

as those sold to Pakistan are reported to have been scrapped. In India there is one fairly complete example, HA623, in the Indian Air Force Museum at Palam, New Delhi. Otherwise, quite a few old airframes had been used as targets in various Indian airfields; once discovered, negotiations were put in motion to release a quantity for private sale. These efforts were ultimately successful, as eleven were put up for tender during 1977, of which six were sold to the restoration company, the Tangmere Flight; these eventually surfaced in Britain during 1985. As these Tempests had been outside

for many years without any maintenance it is hardly surprising that many components were missing, thus sourcing or remanufacture of propellers, spinners, canopies and rudders was required. Also missing were the contents of the cockpits and most of the tailplanes.

Investigations into the history of these airframes revealed that they were all a conglomeration of parts, and so the fuselage serial is accepted as the identity of each airframe. The reported serials are HA457, 557, 564, 586, 591 and HA604. The first machine to be restored was

HA591, which was then exported during 1987 to the United States for use as a static display example. Of the remainder, two machines have been selected for the initial rebuilding programme, these being HA586 and HA604, the latter being the lead machine. Tempest II HA586 eventually resumed its RAF identity of MW763 and was given the civilian registration G-TEMT. By this time both machines were at Gainsborough, and it was from here that MW763/HA586 was prepared for its test flight in mid-2002. The other aircraft is currently stored awaiting a final decision

Right **The only surviving Tempest II in Britain, at one time it was one of the prototypes LA607 pictured here at Cranfield; it would eventually move on to the Skyfame museum at Staverton, Gloucester.** C. P. Russell Smith Collection

Below **After conversion to the Tempest II, prototype LA607 was displayed at various public events. This was an early-build Series 1 airframe, so the Hispano cannon barrels protrude from the leading edge of the wing by a few inches. In Series 2 machines the barrels were fully suppressed.** Real Wings Collection

Above **Wearing the 'T/123' coding of HMS** *Theseus* **Sea Fury FB.11 TF956 is in trouble. The port leg is damaged and stuck down, so the pilot is left with no other option but to abandon the aircraft over the sea.** C. P. Russell Smith Collection

concerning its restoration. Of the remaining Indian Tempests, HA457 is currently on display in the RAF Museum at Hendon; it came via Chichester, Cardington and Duxford, during which time it was restored as PR536 of No. 5 Sqn, whose 'OQ-H' codes it displays.

Further Fortunes of the Extant Sea Furies

In contrast to the fortunes of the Typhoon and Tempest, the survival rate of the Sea Fury and its land-based counterpart the Fury was far higher, in fact sixty-five specimens were extant at one time or another, although that total has since declined due to the inevitable accidents. The airframes in the United Kingdom are mainly held by, or on behalf of, the Fleet Air Arm Museum at Yeovilton. Still extant are Sea Fury FB.11 VR930, which was restored to flying condition at British Aerospace at Brough, where it arrived during June 1994. By November 1997 the fully rebuilt aircraft had become part of the inventory of the Royal Navy Historic Flight at Yeovilton, although it is currently grounded due to problems with one of the engine sleeve valves. Prior to its new life as a display aircraft this Sea Fury had seen service with Nos 810 and 802 Sqns, amongst other units. Hopefully this aircraft will do better than its predecessor, TF956: this aircraft

had served with the Historic Flight from 1970 to 1989, before being abandoned over the sea near Prestwick in Scotland, having suffered major damage to the undercarriage after a hard landing.

A further complete example, WJ231, currently sits on display in the FAA Museum, resplendent in Korean War markings, although it does occasionally find itself being robbed for the odd spare part. Before becoming a museum exhibit, WJ231 had served with the Fleet Requirements Unit and the Yeovilton Station Flight.

One member of the Sea Fury population in private hands within Britain is FB.11 VX653/G-BUCM; it is part of the Fighter Collection fleet at Duxford, and its service record includes time with Nos 736, 738 and 811 Sqns, as well as the Fleet Requirements Unit. Also based at Duxford is Sea Fury FB.11 D-CACY, which began life as WG599 of the Fleet Air Arm. Now registered G-BWOL, this aircraft once graced the display halls at the Uetersen Museum; it arrived at Duxford during May 1995. It is reported that the Sea Fury was moved to Wycombe Air Park after purchase by the American collector Kermit Weeks.

One other Sea Fury is currently based at Colchester; it is a composite of parts from G-AGHB, G-FURY and T.20 D-CIBO. At one time there was another single-seat aircraft being flown in Britain, the all-over blue Sea Fury FB.10, which used to sport the markings of the Dutch Navy as 361. Unfortunately this aircraft suffered a bad landing and was extensively damaged; tragically the pilot was killed.

Within the bounds of Europe there is just one Sea Fury, FB.51 6-43, 6310; at one time it was at Schiphol, then it was moved to Soesterberg where it is on display in the Militaire Luchvaart Museum.

On the opposite side of the world in Australia there are six Sea Furies in preservation, all ex-Royal Australian

Below **Appearances can be deceptive, as this is in fact the F.2/43 Fury prototype NX798 on its way to Egypt; hence the civilian registration G-AKRY, applied in August 1949.** Big Bird Aviation Collection

Right **Originally Sea Fury FB.11 WJ244 with the Fleet Air Arm, this redundant aircraft became G-FURY although it would be written off on 2 August 1981. Eventually the remains ended up at Colchester with Charleston Aircraft Services, who have combined it with the ex-DLB example D-CIBO and G-AGHB; it had been deregistered in May 1974 upon sale to Canada as CF-CHB.** C. P. Russell Smith Collection

Below **This excellent view of an RNN Sea Fury FB.50 shows how well these machines were maintained by No. 860 Sqn.** W. A. Harrison Collection

Above **VH-BOU had originally been WH588 before ending up in Australia. It eventually gravitated to the UK as G-EEMV, being owned by Paul Morgan who nicknamed it 'Baby Gorilla'. On 12 May 2001 the aircraft was written off and the pilot killed.** C. P. Russell Smith Collection

Left **Out in the fresh air for a rare visit is Sea Fury FB.11 'WE726'. In reality the aircraft is WJ231.** W. A. Harrison Collection

Navy machines. Three FB.11s are in the custody of the Naval Aviation Museum at Nowra in New South Wales: VW232 is on display in the museum as 'VX730/108-K'; VW623 is marked as '102-K' and is reported as being under restoration to fly, as is the third aircraft, WG630/ 110-K. Another museum resident is FB.11 VW647; originally it was in the Camden Museum of Aviation, but was then moved to Narellan, New South Wales, where it wears the coding 127-K. This aircraft was restored and achieved its first engine ground runs in October 1976. There are also two privately registered examples: an FB.11 registered VH-HFG owned by Guido Zuccoli and based at Darwin in the Northern Territories; and an ex-Iraqi Air Force single-seat Fury FB.10, currently registered as VH-ISS to Robert H. Poynton, having been IAF 249, and based in Perth, Western Australia.

Across the Atlantic in Canada there are currently three extant Sea Furies. The FB.11 TG114 is displayed as RCN TG119/110 at the National Aviation Museum at Rockliffe, Ontario. Also a museum resident is Sea Fury FB.11 WG565, currently stored at the Calgary

Aerospace Museum. The third is N60SF, which began life as FB.11 WN480. Originally owned by Don Crowe of Delta BC, it was later sold to Crew Concepts Inc. of Boise, Idaho, in 1995. The Sea Fury would be damaged in a landing accident at Reno Nevada during the races. It was recovered, and moved by truck to Victoria in British Colombia, where it was repaired and the Centaurus engine replaced. At the time of writing this machine flies with Royal Canadian markings as 181/*Simply Magnificent*.

Down in Castro's Cuba there are reports of two Sea Furies on display, although the existence of one is in doubt. Both are single-seat FB.11s, though their correct identities are not known. One is reported to reside in the Bay of Pigs Museum at Playa Giron, and the other in the Museo del la Revolucion in Havana.

Not surprisingly, the United States of America has the largest population of Furies and Sea Furies, many of which have been used as high-speed racers at that home of air racing, Reno. Before that, many were gainfully employed in Germany as target tugs, others had been recovered from the Middle East, and yet others were retired from the Royal

Australian and Canadian Navies. Much to the chagrin of the various Hawker fighter owners, their aircraft have only won the Unlimited Class at Reno twice since 1964, and this was achieved by just one aircraft, the mighty *Dreadnought*. In 1983 the pilot was the General Dynamics chief test pilot, Neil Anderson – quite a contrast to his day-to-day occupation of flying the side-stick-controlled F-16 fighter. On this occasion the fighter achieved a top speed of 425.2mph (684.2km/h). Three years later the pilot was Rick Brickert, who brought the two-seater home at a maximum speed of 434.5mph (699.2km/h). Four years later, in 2000, there were thirteen of Sydney Camm's retired fighters on the Reno flight line.

Currently there are thirty-six Hawker fighters on the United States register, both single- and two-seaters, though not all are flyable. And although many of these machines may look fairly close to stock on the outside, there have in fact been changes to many of them, especially in the type of powerplant fitted. Usually the engine installed in the Fury and Sea Fury was the very reliable, very tolerant Bristol Centaurus, but the problem with this eighteen-cylinder, sleeve-valve powerplant was the lack of spares and manufacturers' support. In contrast, there are plentiful supplies of the Wright R-3350s, and also spares, many of which once graced the front ends of combat-proven Douglas A-1 Skyraiders.

Below Currently owned by Stolzer Aircraft in Texas, this Sea Fury contains many parts of WH589, whose registration it wears, although it is a composite of VX715 and WJ290, all being registered N4434P. C. P. Russell Smith Collection

Reno is a colourful affair, so it is hardly surprising that all the participating aircraft have unusual names. Already mentioned is *Dreadnought*, owned and operated by Brian Sanders and his company Sanders Aircraft of Eldorado Hills, California. The T.20 was recovered from Burma in 1979, and remained untouched until October 1982; conversion work then began to convert it into a racing aircraft fit to grace the pylons of Reno. Prior to its civilian career, in 1951 the Sea Fury had originally been delivered to the Fleet Air Arm as VZ368; it was later repurchased by Hawker's, refurbished, and then sold to the Union of Burma Air Force as UB451.

For its conversion, the main task was to take out the original Bristol Centaurus and replace it with a Pratt & Whitney R-4360-63A Wasp Major recovered from a Douglas C-124 Globemaster II transport. As this new engine generated even more power and therefore torque than the original, the emergent Sea Fury acquired a taller fin and rudder to counteract the powerplant's output. Registered NX20SF, *Dreadnought* was rolled out for its first flight in August 1983, beginning its racing career the following month. Since that date it has been a stalwart at the Reno races. Coincidentally this is the second Sea Fury to wear this registration: the first to wear it was an ex- German T.20, D-COCO once VZ350 of the FAA, but this aircraft had crashed on 16 December 1978, killing the pilot.

Furies fitted with the Wasp Major rejoice in the sobriquet of 'Corncob Furies'. This is an American term to describe the layout of an engine where each row of cylinders is offset from the other, in a manner similar to a corn cob. Another of this breed is known as *Furias* due to its composite nature: it includes components from the FB.11 that was once in the Technical School at Delft in the Netherlands. Also included in the make-up of N4434P are some of the parts that were once in the airframe of the ex-Royal Australian Navy FB.11 WH589. Owned originally by Ormond Haydon-Baillie, this Sea Fury had already seen service in its early days at Reno when operating from Vancouver, Canada, as CF-CHB. The Sea Fury returned to the UK in November 1973, where it became G-AGHB, complete with quasi-military camouflage scheme. But six years later, in June 1979, it was badly damaged in a crash in West Germany. It was considered a write-off,

Above **In between its time in Australia and its final destination in Britain, WH588 would spend time in America, where it would take part in the Reno races owned by Lloyd Hamilton in California.**
Nicholas A. Veronico

but the strength of the centre section and the rear fuselage was such that these were purchased for use in *Furias* by Lloyd Hamilton.

Once assembled, *Furias* was rolled out unpainted in 1983 to take part in the Reno races. Although not successful on this occasion due to an engine problem, the Fury returned to take part in later races, acquiring an enlarged fin and rudder along the way. Lloyd Hamilton continued to race the re-engined Sea Fury until his retirement in 1997. This could have been the end of this mighty machine, but Bill Rogers and Dale Stolzer of Sebastopol, California purchased *Furias*, refurbished it, and entered it in the 2000 Reno races; the pilot was Art Vance, and it clocked a respectable 397.4mph (639.5km/h).

One of the most radically rebuilt Sea Furies is *Critical Mass* owned by Tom and Peggy Dwelle. Originally a T.20, WE820, with the Fleet Air Arm, it was retired in December 1956 and was purchased from the MoS some seventeen months later. Converted as a target tug, it undertook its test flying in 'B' condition markings as G-9-49, before being delivered to DLB as D-COTE. After many years operating from Lubeck, it was sold off and arrived in America during 1980, having been purchased by Eric Lorentzen of Scottsdale, Arizona. Once in the United States, the job of creating the racer that would emerge as *Critical Mass* began. The tail feathers were completely refashioned, emerging taller and squarer in the case of the fin and rudder, while the tailplane had its span

reduced by just under 2ft (0.6m), the remaining assembly being squared off.

Further radical changes affected the pilot's position. Instead of using the original forward cockpit, this was plated over and the observer's cockpit was used instead. Covering this cockpit is the smallest canopy possible, with a fairing that blends it into the base of the fin. Further reductions affected the wings, which have been reduced from the original 38ft 5in (11.7m) to a squared-off 32ft (9.7m). The cannon bays were also put to good use, as they now house coolant radiators: these are needed for the Wright R-3350 Duplex Cyclone, which has been re-rated up to 4,000hp (2,984kw). This powerplant was originally in a Douglas B-26 Invader, and the four-bladed Aero Products H20G-162-0 propeller comes from another Douglas product, the A-1 Skyraider.

The drastic rebuild of *Critical Mass* has seen its basic weight drop from 12,500lb (5,670kg) to 11,000lb (5,000kg). Add the extra power of the engine and its performance at Reno 2000, and it is hardly surprising that the aircraft achieved 429.8mph (804km/h) during the qualifying races. Its owners are sure that under the right circumstances *Critical Mass* will eventually pass the 500mph (800km/h) mark in the near future.

In a more conventional manner Fury N666HP, carrying the name 'Fury', has visited Reno bedecked in an RAF camouflage scheme with the race number '66'. However, the aircraft is a bit of an impostor, as its full-depth rudder and lack of

Above **Originally delivered to Iraq as an ISS fighter, this aircraft was one of the cache bought by an American dealer for use in the Reno races. Currently registered as NX666HP, the racer is owned by Howard Pardue, both qualifying in 1996 and achieving a second place in the Unlimited Silver race.** Nicholas A. Veronico

Below **Once Sea Fury FB.11 WG567, this machine, now registered N878M, was once known as 'Super Chief' on the Reno racing circuit; however, since its last change of ownership it is now named 'Miss Merced'.** C. P. Russell Smith Collection

Above **The power and the glory. The only place in the world where you can see such a powerful line-up is at Reno. Here the 1999 contestants for the Unlimited Gold line up prior to take-off.**

Nicholas A. Veronico

arrestor hook mark it as a Hawker-built Baghdad or ISS Fury. Originally delivered to the Iraqi Air Force as No. 255 in December 1949, it found its way to the United States in the late 1970s where it was registered as N34SF. In 1986 this aircraft was sold to Howard Pardue, based at Breckenridge, Texas, where the original Centaurus engine was replaced with a Wright R-3350 powerplant. During Reno 2000, 'Fury' would achieve a maximum speed of 406.2mph (653.6kmh).

Another converted Hawker fighter that sports a Wright R-3350 from the front of a Skyraider was FB.11 N878M 'Miss Merced'. This Sea Fury had once been WG567 of the Royal Canadian Navy, and served with them from 1951 to 1957 before being purchased by Bob Vanderverken in 1961, who would register it as CF-VAN. Painted all red, this Sea Fury was purchased by air racer Mike Carroll in 1965. This gentleman would modify the Sea Fury by reducing the wingspan to 32ft (9.7m), this being followed by an extensive programme of filling and smoothing to reduce air flow disturbances to the minimum. The final alteration was to fit the smallest perspex canopy possible. Bedecked in a stunning flame paint finish, N878M made its Reno debut during 1967, with well known race pilot Lyle Shelton at the controls. When Mike Carroll died in an aircrash in 1968, N878M was sold to Dr Sherman Cooper of Merced, California where the Sea Fury

would get its name. Dr Cooper would fly the aircraft frequently, although in November 1971 the aircraft was badly damaged in a crash landing at Mojave after the engine seized.

The wreck was acquired by rebuilder Frank Sanders, who passed it on to Jim Mott in California, who would rebuild it close to standard. For this to happen, new outer full-span wing panels were fitted, while the reduced canopy was replaced by one of a more conventional size and shape. The original engine was removed and replaced by one from a Blackburn Beverley, which had the advantage of being more powerful than the original. Renamed 'Super Chief', the rebuilt aircraft made its first flight during 1988. Eventually the Sea Fury became available for purchase, and was bought by Steve Boulanger and Jim Michaels, whose first action was to replace the Bristol Centaurus with a Wright R-3350 power-plant. During March 2000 this aircraft was passed to Sanders Aircraft, who undertook a rebuild, re-engine and complete refit. The rebuild must have been a really good one, as 'Miss Merced' gained a bronze with a top speed of 388.4mph (625.0kmh).

The name 'Sanders' appears frequently in the field of restoring Reno racers. Based at Ione, California, this firm of expert restorers has many fine examples to its credit, including the Sea Fury TG114 which is an assemblage built around the cockpit section of the original aircraft. Currently named 'Argonaut' and registered N19SF, this is the second machine to carry this registration, the first being the ex-Fleet Air Arm FB.11 WN482, which had also seen service with the Iraqi Air Force as No.310. Bedecked in the colours of the Royal Canadian Navy colours, it would

continue flying until it crashed at Harlingen, Texas, during Airsho 81 on 9 October 1981, killing the pilot Johnny Williams. 'Argonaut' also flies in RCN colours, and achieved a maximum speed of 383.8mph (617.6kmh) during Reno 2000, piloted by Dennis Sanders.

The problem surrounding the Furies converted for the Reno racers is that some of them are a complete mish-mash of parts from two or more aircraft. One of these machines is 'September Fury', which also incorporates parts of Sea Fury TG114. This particular aircraft was delivered as an FB.11 in 1948, and served until 1956 when it and a quantity of others ended up on a farm in Ontario. There they sat until found by Canadian Brian Baird, who subsequently bought TG114. Restoration was carried out to flying condition at Uplands, Toronto, after which the registration CF-OYF was applied. Subsequently sold to J. Fornoff based in Houma, Louisiana, the Sea Fury was registered N54M, and it was wearing this number when it was damaged when landing in early 1967: after severe braking, the fighter tipped up on its nose. The original owner, Brian Baird, later recovered TG114 and began restoration using some components from Sea Fury FB.11s VR918 and VR919 at Phoenix, Arizona. However, Baird never finished his rebuild, being killed in an aircraft crash in 1969. The restoration project was purchased by Frank Sanders based at Long Beach, California.

The story of the Sea Fury and its land-based counterpart is a complicated one from the American point of view; however, these rebuilt and recycled aircraft still allow the sight and sometimes the sound of Hawker's final piston fighter to be enjoyed once more.

Tornado, Typhoon, Tempest, Fury and Sea Fury Production

Tornado

Type	Serial Numbers	Contract	Quantity	Builder	Remarks
F.18/37 Tornado	P5219, P5224	815124/38	2 Prototype	Hawker	Vulture V
Tornado I	R7936	B12148/39	1 Prototype	Hawker	Vulture V
Tornado I	R7937, R7938	B12148/39	2 Part Built	A V Roe	None fitted
Tornado I	R7939 et seq	B12148/39	197 Cancelled	A V Roe	Vulture V
Tornado	HG641	Constructed from R7937 & R7938	1 Prototype	Hawker	Centaurus CE45

Typhoon

Type	Serial Numbers	Contract	Quantity	Builder	Remarks
F.18/37 Typhoon	P5212, P5216	815124/38	2 Prototypes	Hawker	Sabre I/II
F.18/37 Typhoon	LA594	21392/41	1 Prototype	Hawker	Centaurus IV
Typhoon 1A/1B	R8198–R8200, R8220–R8231	B12148/39	15 Pilot Production Batch	Hawker	Sabre IIA
Typhoon 1A/1B 1st production batch	R7576–R7599, R7613–R7655, R7672–R7721, R7738–R7775, R7792–R7829, R7845–R7890, R7913–R7923	B12148/39	250 Production Aircraft	Gloster Aircraft Company Brockworth Factory	Sabre IIA
Typhoon 1A/1B 2nd production batch	R8630-R8663, R8680–R8722, R8737–R8781, R8799–R8845, R8861–R8900, R8923–R8947, R8966–R8981	B12148/39	250 Production Aircraft	Gloster Aircraft Company Brockworth Factory	Sabre IIA/IIB
Typhoon 1B 3rd production batch part 1	DN241–DN278, DN293–DN341, DN356–DN389, DN404–DN453, DN467–DN513, DN529–DN562, DN576–DN623	Acft/943/(C).23(a)	300 Production Aircraft	Gloster Aircraft Company Brockworth Factory	Sabre IIA/IIB
Typhoon 1B 3rd production batch part 2	EJ900–EJ934, EJ946–EJ995, EK112–EK152, EK167–EK197, EK208–EK252, EK266–EK301, EK321–EK348, EK364–EK413, EK425–EK456, EK472–EK512, EK535–EK543	Acft/943/(C).23(a)	400 Production Aircraft	Gloster Aircraft Company Brockworth Factory	Sabre IIA/IIB

continued opposite

Typhoon *continued*

Type	Serial Numbers	Contract	Quantity	Builder	Remarks
Typhoon 1B 4th production batch	JP361–JP408, JP425–JP447, JP480–JP516, JP532–JP552, JP576–JP614, JP648–JP689, JP723–JP756, JP784–JP802, JP836–JP861, JP897–JP941, JP961–JP976, JR125–JR152, JR183–JR223, JR237–JR266, JR289–JR338, JR360–JR392, JR426–JR449, JR492–JR535	Acft/943/(C).23(a	600 Production Aircraft	Gloster Aircraft Company Brockworth Factory	Sabre IIA/IIB
Typhoon 1B 5th production batch	MM951–MM995, MN113–MN156, MN169–MN213, MN229–MN269, MN282–MN325, MN339–MN381, MN396–MN436, MN449–MN496, MN513–MN556, MN569–MN608, MN623–MN667, MN680–MN720, MN735–MN779, MN791–MN823, MN851–MN896, MN920–MN956, MN968–MN999, MP113–MP158, MP175–MP203	Acft/943/(C).23(a	800 Production Aircraft	Gloster Aircraft Company Brockworth Factory	Sabre IIB
Typhoon 1B 6th production batch	PD446–PD480, PD492–PD536, PD548–PD577, PD589–PD623, RB192–RB235, RB248–RB289, RB303–RB347, RB361–RB408, RB423–RB459, RB474–RB512	Acft/943/(C).23(a	400 Production Aircraft	Gloster Aircraft Company Brockworth Factory	Sabre IIB
Typhoon 1B 7th production batch	SW386–SW428, SW443–SW478, SW493–SW537, SW551–SW596, SW620–SW668, SW682–SW716, SW728–SW772	Acft/943/(C).23(a	299 Production Aircraft	Gloster Aircraft Company Brockworth Factory	Sabre IIB

Tempest

Type	Serial Numbers	Contract	Quantity	Builder	Remarks
F.10/41 Tempest	HM595	Acft/1986/(c).23(a)	1 Prototype	Hawker Langley	Sabre II Sabre V
Tempest I Prototype	HM599	Acft/1640/(c)23(a)	1 Prototype	Langley	Sabre IV
Tempest II Prototype F.18/37	LA602, LA607	Acft/1986/(c).23(a)	LA602 LA607	Langley Langley	Centaurus IV Centaurus IV
Tempest V 1st production batch	JN729–JN773 JN792–JN882 JN854–JN877		100 Production Aircraft	Langley	Sabre II/A/B/C As available Series1/2
Tempest V 2nd production batch	EJ504, EJ518–EJ560, EJ577–EJ611, EJ616–EJ672, EJ685–EJ723, EJ739–EJ788, EJ800–EJ846, EJ859–EJ869		300 Production Aircraft	Langley	Sabre IIA/B Series 2
Tempest V 3rd production batch	NV639–NV682, NV695–NV735, NV749–NV793, NV917–NV948, NV960–NV996		199 Production Aircraft	Langley	Sabre IIB Series 2

continued overleaf

Tempest *continued*

Type	Serial Numbers	Contract	Quantity	Builder	Remarks
Tempest V 4th production batch	SN102–SN146, SN159–SN190, SN205–SN238, SN253–SN296, SN301–SN355		201 Production Aircraft	Langley	Sabre IIB Series 2
Tempest VI	NV997–NV999, NX113–NX156, NX169–NX209, NX223–NX268, NX281–NX288		142 Production Aircraft	Langley	Sabre V
Tempest II	MW374–MW423		50 Production Aircraft	Langley	Centaurus V
Tempest II 1st production batch	MW735–MW778, MW790–MW835 MW847–MW856		100 Production Aircraft	Langley	Centaurus V
Tempest II 2nd production batch	PR525–PR567, PR581–PR523, PR645–PR689, PR713–PR758, PR771–PR815, PR830–PR876, PR889–PR921		302 Production Aircraft	Langley	Centaurus V

Fury/Sea Fury

Type	Serial Numbers	Contract	Quantity	Builder	Remarks
F.2/43 Fury	NX798, NX802	Acft/264430/43	2 Prototypes	Kingston/Langley	Centaurus XII & Centaurus XVIII
F.2/43 Fury	LA610	Acft/1986/(C)23(a)	1 Prototype	Langley	Griffon 85 Centaurus XV Centaurus XVIII
F.2/43 Fury	VP207	Built from spares	1 Prototype	Langley	Sabre VII
N.7/43 Naval Fury	SR661 SR666 VP857	Acft/27022/44	1 Prototype 1 Prototype 1 Prototype	Langley Langley Boulton Paul Hawkers-Langley	Centaurus 12/18 Centaurus 15/18 Centaurus 15/18
Sea Fury F Mk.X	TF895–TF928, TF940–TF955	No.3682/44	50 Production Aircraft	Langley	Centaurus 18
Sea Fury FB.11 1st production batch	TF956–TF973, TF985–TF999, TG113–TG129	No.3682/44	50 Production Aircraft	Langley	Centaurus IX
Sea Fury FB.11 2nd production batch	VR918–VR952	No.657/46	35 Production Aircraft	Langley	Centaurus 18
Sea Fury FB.11 3rd production batch	VW224–VW243, VW541–590, VW621–VW670, VW691–VW718	No.1584/47	147 Production Aircraft	Langley & Kingston	Centaurus 18
Sea Fury FB.11 4th production batch	VX608–VX643, VX650–VX696, VX707–VX711, VX724–VX730, VX748–VX764, WF590–WF595, WF610–WF627	No.2576/48	136 Production Aircraft	Kingston & Langley	Centaurus 18
Sea Fury FB.11 5th production batch	WE673–WE694, WE708–WE736, WE785–WE806, WM472–WM482, WM487–WM495	No.3794/49	93 Production Aircraft	Langley & Kingston	Centaurus 18
Sea Fury FB.11 6th production batch	WG564–WG575, WG590–WG604, WG621–WG630	No.5042/50 (2)	37 Production Aircraft	Kingston & Langley	Centaurus 18
Sea Fury FB.11 7th production batch	WH581–WH594, WH612–WH623, WJ221–WJ248, WJ276–WJ292, WJ294–WJ297, WJ299–WJ301	No.5042/50(3)	78 Production Aircraft	Langley & Kingston	Centaurus 18
Sea Fury FB.11 8th production batch	WN474–WN479, WN484–WN487	No.6298/51	10 Production Aircraft	Kingston & Dunsfold	Centaurus 18

continued opposite

Fury/Sea Fury *continued*

Type	Serial Numbers	Contract	Quantity	Builder	Remarks
Sea Fury FB.11	WX627–WZ656	No.7408/51	30 Production Aircraft	Kingston & Dunsfold	Centaurus 18
Sea Fury Trainer	VX818	No.1998/47	1 Prototype	Kingston	Centaurus 18
Sea Fury T.20 1st production batch	VX280–VX290, VX297–VX310	No.1998/47	27 Production Aircraft	Kingston & Langley	Centaurus 18
Sea Fury T.20 2nd production batch	VZ345–VZ355, VZ363–VZ372	No.2577/48	21 Production Aircraft	Langley & Kingston	Centaurus 18
Sea Fury T.20 3rd production batch	WE820–WE826	No.3794/49	7 Production Aircraft	Langley & Kingston	Centaurus 18
Sea Fury T.20 4th production batch	WG652–WG656	No.5042/50	5 Production Aircraft	Kingston & Langley	Centaurus 18
Sea Fury F/FB.50 For Netherlands	10–1 to 10–10	N/SF/2001	10 Production Aircraft for R Neth Navy	Langley	Centaurus 18
Sea Fury ISS For Iraq	231	No.1998/47	30 Production Fighters	Langley	Centaurus 18
Sea Fury ISS/ITS For Iraq	263	No.53/1/012	25 Production Fighters, 3 Trainers All for Iraq		
Sea Fury F.60 For Pakistan	L900–L949 K857	No.2795/49 3279/PR.2259 A.1439/PR.8533 A.1782/PR.9210	50 Production Fighters 1 refurbished Fury Prototype 24 Production Fighters 13 Production Fighters	Langley Langley Langley Langley	Centaurus 18 Centaurus 18 Centaurus 18 Centaurus 18
Sea Fury Conversion For Pakistan		A.3904/PRE.1434	5 Refurbished Sea Fury	Langley	Centaurus 18
Sea Fury T.61 For Pakistan	K850–K854	No.2795/49	4 Production Trainers	Langley	Centaurus 18
Sea Fury For Egypt	703	No.17/49/U.S.S.	12 Production Fighters	Langley & Kingston	Centaurus 18
F.2/43 Fury			Refurbished for Egypt	Kingston	Centaurus 18
Sea Fury FB/TT.11 For Burma	UB454–UB471	HAL/57/B/030	18 Refurbished Fighters	Kingston & Langley	Centaurus 18
Sea Fury T.20 For Burma	UB451–UB453	HAL/57/B/030	3 Refurbished trainers	Langley & Kingston	Centaurus 18
Sea Fury FB.11/T.20	None specified	HAL/58/C/039	15 refurbished Fighters & 2 trainers	Langley & Kingston	Centaurus 18

The Survivors

Typhoon

Type	Civilian reg	Serial no.		Location	
Typhoon 1B		unknown	Cockpit section	IWM Duxford	Static
Typhoon 1B		unknown	Cockpit section	Jet Age Museum	Static
Typhoon 1B		unknown	Cockpit section	Kent BoB Museum	Static
Typhoon 1B		EJ922	Cockpit section plus rear section of Sea Fury for restoration	Kent BoB Museum	Static
Typhoon 1B		MN235	Complete example	RAF Museum Hendon	Static
Typhoon 1B		unknown	Cockpit section	Wartime Aircraft Recovery Group Aviation Museum. Sleap.	Static
Typhoon 1B		unknown	Cockpit section	Museum of D-Day Aviation, Shoreham	Static
Typhoon 1B		'JR505'	Cockpit section plus forward fuselage frame	Midland Air Museum, Coventry	Static
Typhoon 1B		unknown	Cockpit section	Air Defence Collection, Salisbury	Static
Typhoon 1B		RB396	Remains only	Museum Zuid Kamp, Netherlands	

Tempest

Type	Civilian reg	Serial no.		Location	
Tempest V	N7027E	EJ693	Remains – crashed 1.10.44	Wycombe Air Park	Static
Tempest II	N607LA	LA607	Undergoing restoration	Kermit Weeks Museum Florida	Static
Tempest II	G-PEST	HA604	Ex-IAF ex-RAF MW401	Gainsborough	Static
Tempest II		MW376		Triors, France	Static
Tempest II		MW404	Last reported at Chichester		Static
Tempest II		MW741	Ex-IAF HA?	Open storage at Poona AB India	Static
Tempest II		MW758	Last reported at Tangmere		Static
Tempest II	G-TEMT	MW763	'HF-L' ex IAF HA586	Gainsborough	Static
Tempest II		MW810	Last reported New England Air Mus	Connecticut	Static
Tempest II		MW848	IAF Museum Palam AB	New Delhi	Static
Tempest II		'PR536'	Ex-IAF HA457 'OQ-H' complete	RAF Museum Hendon	Static
Tempest V		unknown	Cockpit section	Norwich	Static
Tempest V		unknown	Cockpit section	Norwich	Static
Tempest TT.5		NV778	Complete example	Cosford Aerospace Museum	Static

continued opposite

Sea Fury

Type	Civilian reg	Serial no.		Location	
Sea Fury FB.11	N65SF	TF982	Olympic Flight Museum WA	As 737/JR	Airworthy
Sea Fury FB.11	N232J	TG114	Maruna Airplane Co. Akron.Ohio	As 'BC-L'	Airworthy
Sea Fury FB.11		TG119	National Aviation Museum Canada	As TG119/110	Static
Sea Fury FB.11		VR930	RN Historic Aircraft Flight	Yeovilton	Airworthy
Sea Fury FB.11		VW232	Naval Aviation Museum Nowra	As VX730/108K	Static
Sea Fury FB.11		VW623	Naval Aviation Museum Nowra	As VW623/102K	Static
Sea Fury FB.11		VW647	Narellan NSW	As VW647/127K	Airworthy
Sea Fury T.20	N281L	VX281	Zager Aircraft Corp CA	Ex-DLB	Airworthy
Sea Fury T.20	N924G	VX300	Sanders Aircraft Chico CA	Ex-DLB	Airworthy
Sea Fury T.20	N51SF	VX302	P I Besterveld Van Nuys CA	Ex-DLB	Airworthy
Sea Fury T.20			Yeovilton		spares
Sea Fury FB.11	G-BUCM	VX653	The Fighter Collection Duxford	Restoration to fly Iraq colours	Static
Sea Fury FB.11		VX715	L A Hamilton Santa Rosa CA	Became WH589 after rebuild	
Sea Fury T.20		VZ345	RNHAF Yeovilton ex-A&AEE	To Brough for spares	stored
Sea Fury T.20		VZ350	Sanders Aircraft CA for spares	Cr 16.12.78	stored
Sea Fury T.20		VZ351	George H. Baker FL		Airworthy
Sea Fury T.20	N71GB	VZ365	George H. Baker FL spares for	N30SF ex-IAF 325 'Skyfury'	Airworthy
Sea Fury T.20	N20SF	VZ368	Sanders Aircraft Co	'Dreadnought'	Airworthy
Sea Fury T.20	N85SF	WE820	T. A. Dwelle Inc	'Critical Mass'	Airworthy
Sea Fury FB.11		WG565	Calgary Aerospace Museum	Store as 'A-A'	Static
Sea Fury FB.11	N878M	WG567	J. A. Mott CA	'Super Chief'	Airworthy
Sea Fury FB.11	G-BWOL	WG599	Hull Aero Norwich	Ex-DLB D-CACY	under restoration
Sea Fury FB.11		WG630	NAM Nowra NAS, NSW, AU	As WG630/110K	Static
Sea Fury T.20	N62143	WG652	Aileron Inc. Damaged in fire 7.88	Rebuilt as 'Riff Raff '	Airworthy
Sea Fury T.20	N20MD	WG655	Amphip Inc. IL	Cr 1991	under rebuild
Sea Fury FB.11	N20X	WH587	Getchell Aircraft Inc CA	As RAN WH587/105	Airworthy
Sea Fury FB.11	G-EEMV	WH588	P A Morgan RAN NW/114	'Baby Gorilla' cr12.5.01	
Sea Fury FB.11	N4434P	WH589	Stolzer Aircraft TX	composite with VX715/WJ290 'Furias'	Airworthy
Sea Fury FB.11		WJ231	FAA Museum Yeovilton		Static
Sea Fury FB.11	G-FURY	WJ244	Charleston Aviation Services	Composite G-AGHB/D-CIBO	
Sea Fury FB.11	N15S	WJ288	D. W. Peeler Columbus OH		Airworthy
Sea Fury FB.11		WJ290	L. A. Hamilton CA	spares for VX715/N4434P	
Sea Fury FB.11	N39SF	WJ293	J. S. Shackleford Roanoake TX		Airworthy
Sea Fury FB.11	N26SF	WJ298	J. J. Dowd ,Syracuse NY		Airworthy
Sea Fury FB.11	N42SF	WM483	Unlimited Air Van Nuys CA	As RCN 74-B 'Bad Attitude'	Airworthy
Sea Fury FB.11	N59SF	WM484	T. Reilly FL		Airworthy
Sea Fury FB.11		WM857	unknown	As RAN '105'	Static

continued overleaf

Sea Fury *continued*

Type	Civilian reg	Serial no.		Location	
Sea Fury FB.11	N60SF	WN480	Lightfoot Aviation Inc WA	'Simply Magnificent'	Airworthy
Sea Fury FB.11	N19SF	WN482	Spares for second aircraft with this registration		Static
Sea Fury FB.11	N19SF	unknown	Sanders Aircraft CA	'Parts Fury'	Airworthy
Sea Fury FB.10	N21SF	ISS20	Sanders Aircraft AL	As DM/369	Airworthy
Sea Fury FB.11	N24SF	unknown	Status unconfirmed	'105/Spirit of Texas'	Airworthy
Sea Fury FB.11	N26S	F WJ298	J. S. Dowd NY		Airworthy
Sea Fury FB.11	N71GB	unknown	George H Baker	'Sky Fury'	Airworthy
Sea Fury FB.10	G-BTTA	ISS13	South Africa	As WV238/107Q	Airworthy
Sea Fury FB.10	N13HP	ISS25	Was N666HP Breckenbridge TX	'Fury'	Airworthy
Sea Fury FB.10	N35SF	ISS24	V. C. McAllister CO	Under restoration	Static
Sea Fury FB.10	N36SF	unknown	J Bradshaw Wroughton/Benson	RNN 361	Static
Sea Fury FB.10	N38SF	unknown	Vintage Aircraft Int NY		Static
Sea Fury FB.10	N57JB	ISS23	War Eagles Museum TX	253/K'Magnificent Obsession'	Airworthy
Sea Fury FB.11	VK-SFR		Flight watch Services Auckland NZ	Parts of WG655	Airworthy
Sea Fury FB.10	N45SF		Sonoma Valley Inc		Airworthy
Sea Fury FB.10	N46SF		Ed Jurist/Vintage Aircraft Int		Airworthy
Sea Fury FB.10	N48SF		Ed Jurist/Vintage Aircraft Int		Airworthy
Sea Fury FB.11	VH-HFG	unknown	L. D. Zuccoli Q'lands Aus	As RAN 308/K	Airworthy
Sea Fury FB.10	VH-ISS	ISS19	R. H. Poynton Perth WA	As Iraqi AF 249	Static
Sea Fury FB.10	N1324		N. J. McClain UT		Airworthy
Fury	N62SF		Ed Jurist/Vintage Aircraft Int		Static
Fury	N63SF		Ed Jurist/Vintage Aircraft Int		Static
Sea Fury FB.10	N64SF		Ed Jurist/Vintage Aircraft Int		Static
Sea Fury FB.10			Rabat Morocco		stored
Sea Fury FB.11			Bay of Pigs Museum, Cuba		Static
Sea Fury FB.11			Musea del la Revolucion, Cuba		Static
Sea Fury FB.51		6-43	Aviodome Amsterdam, Netherlands		Static
Sea Fury FB.50		06-43	Luchtmacht Museum, Netherlands		Static
Sea Fury			Valiant Air Command, FL		Static
Sea Fury			Bristol Aero Collection, Kemble	Unregistered	Airworthy
Sea Fury T.20			Kenosha, Wisconsin		Airworthy

APPENDIX III

Typhoon, Tempest and Sea Fury Units

Typhoon Squadrons

No. 1 (Fighter) Squadron Code 'JX'
8.7.42 Acklington Typhoon 1B
9.2.43 Biggin Hill
15.3.43 Lympne
15.2.44 Martlesham Heath
3.4.44 North Weald
4.44 Spitfire IXB

No. 3 Squadron Code 'QO' to 'JF' 5.6.44, to 'J5' postwar
2.43 Hunsdon Typhoon 1B
14.5.43 West Malling
28.12.43 Swanton Morley
14.2.44 Manston
2.44 Tempest V

No. 4 Squadron uncoded
10.44 B70/Duerne Typhoon FR.1B
16.10.44 B70/Deurne
23.11.44 B77/Gilze-Rijen
8.3.45 B89/Mill
17.4.45 B106/Twenthe
30.5.45 B118/Celle
31.8.45 renumbered 2 Sqn

No. 56 'Punjab' Squadron Code 'US'
9.41 Duxford Typhoon 1A
30.3.42 Snailwell
3.42 Typhoon 1B
29.5.42 Manston
1.6.42 Snailwell
24.8.42 Matlask
22.7.43 Manston
6.8.43 Martlesham Heath
15.8.43 Manston
23.8.43 Bradwell Bay
4.10.43 Martlesham Heath
15.2.44 Scorton
7.3.44 Scorton
30.3.44 Ayr
7.4.44 Scorton Spitfire IX

No. 137 Squadron Code 'SF'
1.44 Colerne Typhoon 1B
4.2.44 Lympne
1.4.44 Manston
14.8.44 B6/Coulombs
28.8.44 B30/Creton
3.9.44 B48/Amiens/Glisy
6.9.44 B58/Melsbroek
23.9.44 B78/Eindhoven
13.1.45 B86/Helmond
7.3.45 Warmwell

19.3.45 B86/Helmond
11.4.45 B106/Twente
14.4.45 B112/Hopsten
17.4.45 B120/Langenhagen
1.5.45 B156/Luneberg
7.5.45 B118/Celle
9.5.45 B160/Kastrup
21.6.45 B172/Husem
11.7.45 B158/Lubeck
20.8.45 Warmwell
26.8.45 renumbered 174 Sqn

No. 164 'Argentine–British' Squadron Code 'FJ'
1.44 Fairlop Typhoon 1B
11.2.44 Twinwood Farm
16.3.44 Thorney Island
18.6.44 Funtington
22.6.44 Hurn
17.7.44 B8/Sommervieu
20.7.44 B7/Martragny
3.9.44 B23/Morainville
6.9.44 B35/Godelmesnil
13.9.44 B53/Merville
30.10.44 B67/Ursel
26.11.44 B77/Gilze-Rijen
1.1.45 A84/Chievres
19.1.45 B77/Gilze-Rijen
21.3.45 B91/Kluis
17.4.45 B103/Ploantlunne
27.5.45 B116/Wunstorf
17.6.45 Milfield
6.45 Spitfire IX

No. 168 Squadron Code 'QC'
9.44 B66/Blankenberg Typhoon 1B
4.10.44 B78/Eindhoven
26.2.45 disbanded

No. 174 'Mauritius' Squadron Code 'XP'
No. 137 Sqn, renumbered 26.8.45
B158/Lubeck Typhoon 1B
7.9.45 disbanded

No. 175 Squadron Code 'HH'
4.43 Colerne Typhoon 1B
12.6.43 Merston
1.7.43 Lydd
10.10.43 Westhampnett
1.4.44 Holmsley South
17.6.44 B5/Camilly
19.6.44 B2/Bazenville
24.6.44 B5/Camilly
28.8.44 B24/ST Andre-de-l'Eure
2.9.44 B40/Beauvais

1.10.44 B80/Volkel
10.11.44 Warmwell
21.11.44 B80/Volkel
21.3.45 B100/Goch
10.4.45 disbanded

No. 181 Squadron Code 'EL'
9.42 Duxford Typhoon 1A
9.42 Typhoon 1B
10.12.42 Snailwell
24.3.43 Gravesend
5.4.43 Lasham
2.6.43 Appledram
3.7.43 New Romney
8.10.43 Merston
31.12.43 Odiham
13.1.44 Merston
6.2.44 Eastchurch
21.2.44 Merston
1.4.44 Hurn
20.6.44 B6/Coulombs
31.8.44 B30/Creton
3.9.44 B48/Amiens/Glisy
6.9.44 B58/Melsbroek
22.9.44 B78/Eindhoven
12.1.45 Warmwell
3.2.45 B86/Helmond
11.4.45 B106/Twente
13.4.45 B112/Hopsten
18.4.45 B120/Langenhagen
1.5.45 B156/Lueberg
7.5.45 B158/Lubeck
7.7.45 B160/Kastrup
21.7.45 Warmwell
4.8.45 B160 Kastrup
6.9.45 B166/Flensburg
9.9.45 B164/Schleswig
30.9.45 disbanded

No. 182 Squadron Code 'XM'
9.42 Martlesham Heath Typhoon 1A
9.42 Typhoon 1B
7.12.42 Sawbridgeworth
30.1.43 Martlesham Heath
1.3.43 Middle Wallop
5.4.43 Fairlop
29.4.43 Lasham
2.6.43 Appledram
2.7.43 New Romney
12.10.43 Merston
31.12.43 Odiham
5.1.44 Eastchurch
23.1.44 Merston
1.4.44 Hurn

20.6.44 B6/Coloumbs
22.6.44 Holmsley South
3.7.44 B6/Coloumbs
28.8.44 B30/Creton
3.9.44 B48/Amiens/Glisy
6.9.44 B58/Melsbroek
22.9.44 B78/Eindhoven
13.1.45 B86/Helmond
3.2.45 Warmwell
21.2.45 B86/Helmond
11.4.45 B106/Twente
13.4.45 B112/Hopsten
17.4.45 B120/Langenhagen
1.5.45 B156/Luneburg
7.5.45 B158/Lubeck
11.7.45 B160/Kastrup
5.8.45 Warmwell
19.8.45 B160/Kastrup
5.9.45 B166/Flensburg
8.9.45 B164/Schleswig
30.9.45 disbanded

No. 183 'Gold Coast' Squadron Code 'HF'

11.42 Church Fenton Typhoon 1A
11.42 Typhoon 1B
1.3.43 Cranfield
24.3.43 Colerne
8.4.43 Gatwick
3.5.43 Lasham
30.5.43 Colerne
5.6.43 Harrowbeer
4.8.43 Tangmere
18.9.43 Perranporth
14.10.43 Predannack
1.2.44 Tangmere
15.3.44 Manston
1.4.44 Thorney Island
18.6.44 Funtington
1.7.44 Hurn
14.7.44 Eastchurch
25.7.44 B7/Martrangy
3.9.44 B23/Morainville
6.9.44 B35/Godelmensil
11.9.44 B53/Merville
29.10.44 B67/Ursel
26.11.44 B77/Gilze-Rijen
1.1.45 A84 Chievres
19.1.45 B77/Gilze-Rijen
21.3.45 B91/Kluis
17.4.45 B103/Plantlunne
27.5.45 B116/Wunstorf
16.6.45 Milfield
17.6.45 Chilbolton Spitfire IX

No. 184 Squadron Code 'BR'

3.44 Odiham Typhoon 1B
11.3.44 Eastchurch
3.4.44 Odiham
23.4.44 Westhampnett
14.5.44 Holmsley South
20.5.44 Westhampnett
17.6.44 Holmsley South
27.6.44 B10/Plumetot
16.7.44 B3/Camilly
28.8.44 B.24 Andre-de-l'Eure
2.9.44 B42/Tille

4.9.44 B50/Vitry-en-Artois
17.9.44 B70/Deurne
30.9.44 B80/Volkel
4.12.44 Warmwell
18.12.44 B80/Volkel
21.3.45 B100/Goch
11.4.45 B110/Achmer
18.4.45 B150/Hustedt
7.5.45 Warmwell
28.5.45 B164/Schleswig
2.8.45 B160/Kastrup
29.8.45 disbanded

No. 193 'Fellowship of the Bellows' Squadron Code 'DP'

1.43 Harrowbeer Typhoon 1B
17.8.43 Gravesend
18.9.43 Harrowbeer
20.2.44 Fairlop
16.3.44 Thorney Island
11.4.44 Needs Oar Point
3.7.44 Hurn
11.7.44 B15/Ryes
16.7.44 B3/Ste-Croix-sur-Mer
6.9.44 B23 Morainville
8.9.44 Manston
12.9.44 B51 Lille/Vendeville
18.9.44 Fairwood Common
6.10.44 B70/Deurne
9.2.45 B89/Mill
17.4.45 B105/Drope
30.4.45 B111/Ahlhorn
8.1.45 Hildeshelm
31.8.45 disbanded

No. 195 Squadron Code 'JE'

11.42 Hutton Cranswick Typhoon 1B
12.2.43 Woodvale
13.5.43 Ludham
31.7.43 Matlask
21.8.43 Coltishall
24.9.43 Fairlop
15.2.45 disbanded

No. 197 Squadron Code 'OV'

11.42 Drem Typhoon 1A
11.42 Typhoon 1B
28.3.43 Tangmere
15.3.44 Manston
1.4.44 Tangmere
10.4.44 Needs Oar Point
3.7.44 Hurn
11.9.44 B3/Ste-Croix-sur-Mer
2.10.44 B70/Deurne
25.11.44 Fairwood Common
12.12.44 B70/Deurne
8.2.45 B89/Mill
16.4.45 B105/Drope
30.4.45 B111/Ahlhorn
9.6.45 Hildeshelm
31.8.45 disbanded

No. 198 Squadron Code 'TP'

12.42 Digby Typhoon 1A
12.42 Typhoon 1B
23.1.43 Ouston

24.3.43 Manston
15.5.43 Woodvale
5.6.43 Martlesham Heath
19.8.43 Bradwell Bay
22.8.43 Manston
16.3.44 Tangmere
6.4.44 Thorney Island
22.6.44 Hurn
1.7.44 B10/Plumetot
8.7.44 B5/Camilly
11.7.44 B10/Plumetot
19.7.44 B7/Martragny
3.9.44 B23/Morainville
6.9.44 Fairwood Common
11.9.44 B53/Merville
30.10.44 B67/Ursel
6.11.44 Fairwood Common
21.11.44 B67/Ursel
26.11.44 B77/Gilze-Rijen
31.12.44 A84/Chievres
19.1.45 B77/Gilze-Rijen
21.3.45 B91/Kluis
17.4.45 B103/Plantlunne
27.5.45 B116/Wunstorf
15.9.45 disbanded

No. 245 'Northern Rhodesia' Squadron Code 'MR'

12.42 Charmy Down Typhoon 1B
29.1.43 Peterhead
30.3.43 Gravesend
28.5.43 Fairlop
2.6.43 Selsey
1.7.43 Lydd
10.10.43 Westhampnett
1.4.44 Holmsley South
25.4.44 Eastchurch
30.4.44 Holmsley South
27.6.44 B5/Camilly
28.8.44 B/24 St-Andre-de-l'Eure
2.9.44 B42/Tille
4.9.44 B50/Vitry-en-Artois
17.9.44 B70/Duerne
30.9.44 B80/Volkel
19.12.44 Warmwell
6.1.45 B80/Volkel
20.3.45 B100/Goch
11.4.45 B110/Achmer
16.4.45 B150/Hustedt
28.5.45 B164/Schleswig
16.6.45 Warmwell
4.7.45 B164/Schleswig
10.8.45 disbanded

No. 247 'China–British' Squadron Code 'ZY'

1.43 High Ercall Typhoon 1B
28.2.43 Middle Wallop
5.4.43 Fairlop
29.5.43 Gravesend
4.6.43 Bradwell Bay
10.7.43 New Romney
11.10.43 Merston
31.10.43 Snailwell
5.11.43 Merston
31.12.43 Odiham
13.1.44 Merston
1.4.44 Eastchurch

24.4.44 Hurn
20.6.44 B6/Coulombs
28.8.44 B30/Creton
3.9.44 B48/Amiens/Glisy
6.9.44 B58/Melsbroek
22.9.44 B78/Eindhoven
13.1.45 B86/Helmond
21.2.45 Warmwell
7.3.45 B86/Helmond
12.4.45 B106/Twente
13.4.45 B112/Hopsten
17.4.45 B120/Langenhagen
1.5.45 B156/Luneburg
6.5.45 B158/Lubeck
20.8.45 Chilbolton
9.45 conv Tempest F.2

No. 257 'Burma' Squadron Code 'FM'
7.42 High Ercall Typhoon 1A
7.42 Typhoon 1B
21.9.42 Exeter
8.1.43 Warmwell
12.8.43 Gravesend
17.9.43 Warmwell
20.1.44 Beaulieu
3.2.44 Tangmere
10.4.44 Needs Oar Point
2.7.44 Hurn
8.7.44 B15/Ryes
15.7.44 B3/Ste-Croix-sur-Mer
11.8.44 Fairwood Common
30.8.44 B3/Ste-Croix-sur-Mer
4.9.44 Manston
11.9.44 B51/Lille/Vendeville
2.10.44 B70/Duerne
8.2.45 B89/Mill
5.3.45 disbanded

No. 263 'Fellowship of the Bellows' Squadron Code 'HE'
12.43 Warmwell Typhoon 1B
5.12.43 Ibsley
5.1.44 Fairwood Common
23.1.44 Beaulieu
6.3.44 Warmwell
19.3.44 Harrowbeer
19.6.44 Bolt Head
10.7.44 Hurn
23.7.44 Eastchurch
6.8.44 B3/Ste-Croix-sur-Mer
6.9.44 Manston
11.9.44 B51/Lille/Vendeville
2.10.44 B70/Deurne
13.1.45 Fairwood Common
10.2.45 B89/Mill
16.4.45 B105/Drope
30.4.45 B111/Ahlhorn
8.6.45 B6/Hildesheim
30.8.45 disbanded

No. 266 'Rhodesia' Squadron Code 'UO' to 'ZH' 4.42
1.42 Duxford Typhoon 1A
3.42 Typhoon 1B
2.8.42 Matlask
11.8.42 Duxford
21.9.42 Warmwell

8.1.43 Exeter
21.9.43 Harrowbeer
7.3.44 Bolt Head
12.3.44 Harrowbeer
15.3.44 Bolt Head
23.3.44 Tangmere
10.4.44 Needs Oar Point
27.4.44 Snaith
6.5.44 Needs Oar Point
29.6.44 Eastchurch
13.7.44 Hurn
20.7.44 B3/Ste-Croix-sur-Mer
25.7.44 B8/Sommervieu
6.9.44 B23/Morainville
8.9.44 Manston
11.9.44 B51/Lille/Vendeville
2.10.44 B70/Duerne
14.2.45 B89/Mill
16.4.45 B105/Drope
25.4.45 Fairwood Common
4.6.45 B111/Ahlhorn
8.6.45 Hildesheim
6.8.45 disbanded

No. 268 Squadron uncoded
7.44 Odiham Typhoon FR.1B
10.8.44 B10/Plumetot
13.8.44 B4/Beny-sur-Mer
1.9.44 B27/Boisny
6.9.44 B31/Fresnoy-Folny
11.9.44 B43/Fort Rouge
27.9.44 B61/St Dennis-Westrem
10.10.44 B70/Deurne
11.44 Mustang II

No. 438 'Wildcats' Squadron RCAF Code 'F3'
1.44 Ayr Typhoon 1B
18.3.44 Hurn
3.4.44 Funtington
19.4.44 Hurn
27.6.44 B9/Lantheuil
31.8.44 B24/St-Andre-de-l'Eure
3.9.44 B48/Amiens/Glisy
6.9.44 B58/Melsbroek
26.9.44 BB78/Eindhoven
19.3.45 Warmwell
3.4.45 B100/Goch
12.4.45 B110/Achmer
21.4.45 B150/Hustedt
29.5.45 B166/Flensburg
26.8.45 disbanded

No. 439 'Westmount' Squadron RCAF Code 'SV'
1.44 Ayr Typhoon 1B
18.3.44 Hurn
2.4.44 Funtington
19.4.44 Hurn
11.5.44 Hutton Cranswick
20.5.44 Hurn
27.6.44 B9/Lantheuil
31.8.44 B24/St-Andre-de-l'Eure
3.9.44 B48/Amiens/Glisy
7.9.44 B58/Melsbroek
25.9.44 B78/Eindhoven
30.3.45 B100/Goch
3.4.45 Warmwell

2.4.45 B150/Hustedt
29.5.45 B166/Flensburg
26.8.45 disbanded

No. 440 'City of Ottawa' Squadron RCAF Code 'I8'
3.44 Ayr Typhoon 1B
18.3.44 Hurn
3.4.44 Funtington
20.4.44 Hurn
28.6.44 B9/Lantheuil
31.8.44 B24/St-Andre-de-l'Eure
3.9.44 B48/Amiens/Glisy
6.9.44 B58/Melsbroek
26.9.44 B78/Eindhoven
30.3.45 B100/Goch
11.4.45 B110/Achmer
20.4.45 B150/Hustedt
23.4.45 Warmwell
8.5.45 B150/Hustedt
29.5.45 B166/Flensburg
26.8.45 disbanded

No. 486 Squadron RNZAF Code 'SA'
7.42 Wittering Typhoon 1B
27.9.42 North Weald
10.10.42 West Malling
29.10.42 Tangmere
1.44 Tempest V

No. 609 'West Riding' Squadron Code 'PR'
3.42 Duxford Typhoon 1A
3.42 Typhoon 1B
26.8.42 Bourn
30.8.42 Duxford
18.9.42 Biggin Hill
2.11.42 Manston
22.7.43 Matlask
18.8.43 Lympne
14.12.43 Manston
6.2.44 Fairwood Common
20.2.44 Manston
16.3.44 Tangmere
21.3.44 Acklington
1.7.44 B10/Plumetot
9.7.44 B5/Camilly
19.7.44 B7/Martragny
3.9.44 B23/Morainville
6.9.44 B35/Godelmensil
11.9.44 B53/Merville
30.10.44 B67/Ursel
26.11.44 B77/Gilze-Rijen
31.12.44 A84/Chievres
19.1.45 B77/Gilze-Rijen
21.3.45 B91/Kluis
17.4.45 B103/Plantlunne
27.5.45 B116/Wunstorf
2.6.45 Lasham
23.6.45 B116/Wunstorf
15.9.45 disbanded

No. 778 Squadron FAA
2.43 Arbroath Typhoon 1B

Secondary Units
No. 1 Combat Training Wing, later
No. 1 Tactical Exercise Unit

No. 3 Tactical Exercise Unit codes 'UW', 'ZX', 'EH', 'PA'
No. 4 Tactical Exercise Unit
No. 55 Operational Training Unit
No. 56 Operational Training Unit codes 'GF', 'FE',
'HQ', 'OD'
No. 59 Operational Training Unit codes 'MF', '4Q', '1I', '7L'
No. 83 Group Support Unit code '7S'
No. 84 Group Support Unit
Fighter Leaders' School codes 'HK', 'MF', 'RL'
A&AEE, RAE, AFDU, FIU

Tempest Squadrons

No. 3 Squadron Code 'QO' to 'JF' 5.6.44 to 'J5' postwar
2.44 Manston Tempest V
6.3.44 Bradwell Bay
28.4.44 Newchurch
21.9.44 Matlask
28.9.44 B60/Grimbergen
1.10.44 B80/Volkel
1.4.45 Warmwell
17.4.45 B112/Hopsten
26.4.45 B152/Fassberg
21.6.45 B160/Kastrup
18.7.45 B156/Luneburg
8.8.45 B158/Lubeck
5.9.45 B155/Dedelsdorf
14.9.45 B106/Twente
6.10.45 B170/Sylt
23.10.45 B152/Fassberg
24.1.46 Wunstorf
27.3.46 Gatow
19.9.46 Wunstorf
4.1.47 Gatow
3.2.47 Wunstorf
1.10.47 Gatow
5.1.48 Lubeck
2.48 Wunstorf Vampire F.1

No. 5 Squadron Code 'OQ'
3.46 Bhopal Tempest F.2
1.6.46 Poona
10.11.46 Poona
22.1.47 Peshwar
3.6.47 Mauripur
1.8.47 disbanded

No. 6 Squadron Code 'JV'
12.46 Nicosia Tempest F.6
5.9.47 Shallufa
26.11.47 Khartoum
5.5.48 Fayid
1.9.49 Deversior
10.49 Vampire FB.5

No. 8 Squadron Code 'RT'
3.47 Khormaksar Tempest F.6
6.49 Brigand B.1

No. 16 Squadron Code 'EG'
4.46 Fassberg Tempest F.5
1.6.46 Manston
14.7.46 Fassberg
8.46 Tempest F.2

5.9.46 Manston
16.9.46 Fassberg
4.2.47 Gatow
21.3.47 Fassberg
1.12.47 Gutersloh
12.48 Vampire FB.5

No. 20 Squadron Code 'HN'
5.46 Agra Tempest F.2
25.7.47 Mauripur
1.8.47 disbanded

No. 26 Squadron Code 'XC'
4.46 Wunstorf Tempest F.5
13.4.46 Fassberg
6.46 Tempest F.2
24.9.46 Chivenor
23.10.46 Fassberg
19.11.47 Gutersloh
4.49 Vampire FB.5

No. 30 Squadron Code 'RS'
3.46 Bhopal Tempest F.2
27.5.46 Agra
1.12.46 disbanded

No. 33 Squadron Code 'SR'
12.44 Predannack Tempest V
21.2.44 B77/Gilze-Rijen
7.4.45 B91/Kluis
29.4.45 B109/Quackensbruck
19.8.45 B155/Dedelsdorf
23.10.45 B152/Fassberg
2.1.46 Gatow
17.2.45 Fassberg
10.46 Tempest F.2
13.7.47 Zeltweg
31.11.47 Gutersloh
2.7.49 Renfrew
9.8.48 Changi
18.3.50 Tengah
30.5.50 Butterworth
5.51 Hornet F.3

No. 39 Squadron uncoded
4.48 Khartoum Tempest F.6
28.2.49 disbanded

No. 41 Squadron Code 'EB'
9.45 B158/Lubeck Tempest V
31.1.46 B116/Wunstorf
28.2.46 B170/Sylt
29.3.46 B116/Wunstorf
1.4.46 disbanded

No. 54 Squadron Code 'HF'
11.45 Chilbolton Tempest F.2
28.6.46 Odiham
5.9.46 Molesworth
1.10.46 Odiham
10.46 Vampire F.1

No. 56 'Punjab' Squadron Code 'US'
6.44 Newchurch Tempest V
23.9.44 Matlask
28.9.44 B60/Grimbergen

1.10.44 B80/Volkel
11.4.45 B112/Hopsten
26.4.45 B152/Fassberg
22.6.45 B160/Kastrup
22.8.45 B164/Schleswig
5.9.45 B155/Dedelsdorf
23.10.45 B152/Fassberg
1.4.46 disbanded

No. 80 Squadron Code 'W2'
7.44 West Malling Tempest V
29.8.44 Manston
20.9.44 Coltishall
29.9.44 B70/Duerne
1.10.44 B82/Grave
7.10.44 B80/Volkel
12.4.45 B112/Hopsten
7.5.45 B152/Fassberg
24.6.45 B160/Kastrup
6.9.45 B158/Lubeck
31.1.46 Wunstorf
17.4.46 Dedelsdorf
19.9.46 Wunstorf
1.48 Spitfire F.24

No. 152 'Hyderabad' Squadron Code 'UM'
7.46 Risalpur Tempest F.2
15.1.47 disbanded

No. 174 'Mauritius' Squadron Code 'JJ'
9.45 Warmwell Tempest V
19.9.45 B155/Dedelsdorf
19.10.45 Gatow
26.11.45 B152/Fassberg
20.4.46 disbanded

No. 183 'Gold Coast' Squadron Code 'HF'
10.45 Fairwood Common Tempest II
15.11.45 Chilbolton
15.11.45 disbanded

No. 213 'Ceylon' Squadron Code 'AK'
1.47 Nicosia Tempest F.6
3.9.47 Shallufa
22.10.47 Khartoum
17.8.48 Mogadishu
21.10.53 Deversoir
30.9.54 disbanded

No. 222 'Natal' Squadron Code 'ZD'
1.45 Predannack Tempest V
21.2.45 B77/Gilze-Rijen
7.4.45 B91/Kluis
20.4.45 B109/Quackenbruck
25.6.45 B155/Dedelsdorf
3.9.45 Manston
10.9.45 Chilbolton
23.10.45 Molesworth
10.45 Meteor F.3

No. 247 'China–British' Squadron Code 'ZY'
9.45 Chilbolton Tempest F.2
7.1.46 Fairwood Common
16.2.46 Chilbolton
3.46 Vampire F.1

No. 249 'Gold Coast' Squadron Code 'GN'
12.46 Habbiniyah Tempest F.6
13.4.48 Ramat David
17.5.48 Habbiniyah
29.3.49 Deversoir
28.6.49 Nicosia
8.8.49 Deversoir
1.50 Vampire FB.5

No. 486 Squadron RNZAF Code 'SA'
4.44 Castle Camps Tempest V
29.4.44 Newchurch
19.9.44 Matlask
28.9.44 B60/Grimbergen
1.10.44 B80/Volkel
10.4.45 B112/Hopsten
26.4.45 B150/Hustedt
6.5.45 B118/Celle
8.5.45 B106/Kastrup
6.7.45 B158/Lubeck
7.9.45 disbanded

No. 501 'County of Gloucester' Squadron Code 'SD'
7.44 Westhampnett Tempest V
2.8.44 Manston
22.9.44 Bradwell Bay
3.3.45 Hunsden
20.4.45 disbanded

Secondary Units
No. 13 Operational Training Unit codes 'FV', 'SL'
No. 83 Group Support Unit code '7S'
No. 84 Group Support Unit
No. 226 Operational Conversion Unit code 'XL'
No. 229 Operational Conversion Unit code 'RS'
233 Operational Conversion Unit
Acklington Armament Practice Camp code 'WH'
Sylt Armament Practice Camp
Central Gunnery School code 'FJU'
Central Fighter Establishment codes 'MF', 'GO', 'RE'
A&AEE, RAE, AFDU, FIU

Sea Fury Squadrons

No. 700 Squadron FAA
6.48–9.49 Yeovilton Sea Fury F.10
12.55–1.56 Ford Sea Fury FB.11

No. 703 Squadron FAA
6.48–1.52 Lee-on-Solent Sea Fury F.10
7.48–3.55 Lee-on -Solent Sea Fury FB.11
6.51–10.51 Ford Sea Fury T.20

No. 723 Squadron RAN
4.52- 10.56 Nowra Sea Fury FB.11

No. 724 Squadron RAN
5.61–10.62 Nowra Sea Fury FB.11

No. 725 Squadron RAN
1.58–5.59 Nowra Sea Fury FB.11

No. 736 Squadron FAA
8.50- 9.51 Culdrose Sea Fury F.10
5.49- 8.52 Culdrose Sea Fury FB.11
3.50- 8.52 Culdrose Sea Fury T.20

No. 738 Squadron FAA
5.50- 8.51 Culdrose Sea Fury F.10
5.50- 3.55 Culdrose Sea Fury FB.11
5.50- 3.55 Culdrose Sea Fury T.20

No. 744 Squadron FAA
5.54-10.56 Culdrose/St Mawgan Sea Fury FB.11

No. 751 Squadron FAA
8.52–3.56 Watton Sea Fury FB.11

No. 759 Squadron FAA
5.52- 6.52 Culdrose Sea Fury FB.11
2.52-1.54 Culdrose Sea Fury T.20

No. 766 Squadron FAA
9.51-7.52 Lossiemouth Sea Fury T.20

No. 767 Squadron FAA
11.49-6.52 Yeovilton Sea Fury FB.11

No. 771 Squadron FAA
7.50-12.50 Arbroath Sea Fury T.20

No. 773 Squadron FAA
1.49-3.49 Lee-on-Solent Sea Fury FB.11

No. 778 Squadron FAA
2.47- 7.47 Ford Sea Fury F.10
2.48- 7.48 Tangmere Sea Fury FB.11

No. 781 Squadron FAA
10.48-1.50 Ford Sea Fury F.10
12.53-2.55 Ford Sea Fury FB.11
5.50-9.54 Ford Sea Fury T.20

No. 782 Squadron FAA
6.48-6.50 Eglinton Sea Fury FB.11
5.51-10.51 Donibristle Sea Fury T.20

No. 787 Squadron FAA
5.47-7.48 West Raynham Sea Fury F.10
2.49-1954 West Raynham Sea Fury FB.11
1949-1949 West Raynham Sea Fury T.20

No. 799 Squadron FAA
9.48-10.49 Yeovilton Sea Fury F.10
5.49-11.51 Yeovilton Sea Fury FB.11
4.51-5.51 Yeovilton Sea Fury T.20

No. 801 Squadron FAA
3.51-1.55 Lossiemouth detachments/deployments to
Hal Far, HMS *Glory*, HMS *Ocean*, HMS *Illustrious*, Sea
Fury FB.11
12.51-1.55 Lossiemouth Sea Fury T.20

No. 802 Squadron FAA
4.48-6.48 Lee-on-Solent Sea Fury F.10
5.48-12.51 Lee-on-Solent, Eglinton Sea Fury FB.11
2.53-3.54 Arbroath detachments/deployments to Hal Far,
HMS *Theseus*, HMS *Eagle* Sea Fury FB.11
6.50-2.54 Lee-on-Solent Sea Fury T.20

No. 803 Squadron RCN
8.47- 2.50 Eglinton Sea Fury F.10
2.48- 5.51 Eglinton detachments/deployments to

Dartmouth, Rivers, Eglinton, Lee-on-Solent,
HMCS *Magnificent* Sea Fury FB.11
1.5.51 re-designated No. 870 Sqn

No. 804 Squadron FAA
7.49-1.54 Hal Far detachments/deployments to Culdrose,
Lee-on- Solent, Brawdy, Lossiemouth, HMS *Glory*,
HMS *Theseus*, HMS *Indomitable*, HMS *Illustrious*
Sea Fury FB.11

No. 805 Squadron RAN
8.48-2.49 Eglinton Sea Fury F.10
8.48-3.58 Eglinton, Nowra detachments/deployments to
HMAS *Sydney* Sea Fury FB.11

No. 806 Squadron FAA
8.48-9.48 Eglinton, HMCS *Magnificent*, Dartmouth,
Toronto Sea Fury FB.11

No. 807 Squadron FAA
9.47-12.48 Eglinton Sea Fury F.10
2.48- 5.54 Eglinton, Culdrose detachments/deployments
to HMS *Implacable*, HMS *Theseus*, HMS *Ocean*
Sea Fury FB.11

No. 808 Squadron FAA
4.50-10.54 St Merryn Nowra detachments/deployments to
HMAS *Sydney* Sea Fury FB.11

No. 809 Squadron FAA
11.51-1.52 Culdrose Sea Fury T.20

No. 810 Squadron FAA
3.54-3.55 Ford detachments/deployments to Hal Far
HMS *Centaur* Sea Fury FB.11

No. 811 Squadron FAA
8.53-12.54 Arbroath, Leuchars, Lee-on-Solent deploy-
ments/detachments Hal Far, HMS *Warrior* Sea Fury FB.11

No. 850 Squadron FAA
1.53-8.54 Nowra detachments/deployments to
HMAS *Sydney* Sea Fury FB.11

No. 860 Squadron RNN
7.50-6.56 Valkenburg detachments/deployments to
St Merryn, HMS *Illustrious*, HMS *Indomitable*
Sea Fury FB.50

No. 870 Squadron RCN
5.51-6.54 Dartmouth detachments/deployments HMCS
Magnificent, Scoudouc, Summerside, HMCS *Magnificent*,
Summerside. Sea Fury FB.11

No. 871 Squadron RCN
5.51-8.56 Dartmouth detachments/deployments to
HMCS *Magnificent*, Key West, Dartmouth. Sea Fury FB.11

No. 883 Squadron RCN
9.48-5.51 Dartmouth detachments/deployments to
HMCS *Magnificent*, Eglinton, HMCS *Magnificent*,
Dartmouth Sea Fury FB.11

No. 898 Squadron FAA
7.51-1.53 Arbroath detachments/deployments to Hal Far,
HMS *Theseus*, HMS *Ocean*, HMS *Glory* Sea Fury FB.11

No. 1830 Squadron RNR
10.52-10.54 Abbotsinch Sea Fury T.20

No. 1831 Squadron RNR
10.50-6.55 St Merryn Sea Fury T.20
8.51-6.55 St Merryn Sea Fury FB.11

No. 1832 Squadron RNR
10.50-6.56 St Merryn/Brawdy Sea Fury T.20
8.51-8.55 St Merryn/Brawdy Sea Fury FB.11

No. 1833 Squadron RNR
10.50-10.55 Bramcote Sea Fury T.20
2.54-7.55 Bramcote Sea Fury FB.11

No. 1834 Squadron RNR
10.53-4.55 Benson, Yeovilton Sea Fury FB.11
10.53-4.55 Benson, Yeovilton Sea Fury T.20

Secondary Units
11.52-9.53 Brawdy SF Sea Fury T.20
10.51-10.52 Culdrose SF Sea Fury T.20
3.52-4.52 Ford SF Sea Fury FB.11
7.50-2.55 Ford SF Sea Fury T.20
3.54-9.56 Eglinton SF Sea Fury T.20
10.52-3.53 Hal Far SF Sea Fury FB.11
5.51-4.54 Hal Far SF Sea Fury T.20
3.50-6.59 Lee-on-Solent Sea Fury FB.11
5.52-8.52 Lossiemouth Sea Fury T.20
8.51-10.51 St Merryn SF Sea Fury T.20
9.50-7.56 Yeovilton SF Sea Fury T.20
6.55-7.55 Arbroath Ferry Pool Sea Fury FB.11
4.48-2.50 Joint Warfare Establishment Sea Fury F.10
2.50-2.52 JWE Sea Fury FB.11
10.55-4.61 Airwork Fleet Requirements Unit
Sea Fury FB.11

Bibliography

Air-Britain Publications:
Royal Air Force Aircraft P1000–R9999
Royal Air Force Aircraft DA100–DZ999
Royal Air Force Aircraft EA100–EZ999
Royal Air Force Aircraft JA100–JZ999
Royal Air Force Aircraft KA100–KZ999
Royal Air Force Aircraft MA100–MZ999
Royal Air Force Aircraft NA100–NZ999
Royal Air Force Aircraft PA100–RZ999
Royal Air Force Aircraft SA100–VZ999

Aircraft Archive Vol 2 Fighters (Argus Books).

Ellis, Ken *Wrecks and Relics* 18th edition (Midland Counties).

Jackson, Robert *Hawker Tempest and Sea Fury* (Blandford Press).

Jane's Fighting Aircraft of WWII (Jane's Publishing).

Jefford, Wg Cdr C. G., MBE *RAF Squadrons* (Airlife).

Mason, Francis K., *Hawker Aircraft since 1920* (Putnam).

Mason, Francis K., *The Hawker Typhoon and Tempest* (Aston Publications).

Peel, Dave *British Civil Registers since 1919* (Airlife).

Rimell, Ken *The Typhoon at War* (Historic Military Press).

Robertson, Bruce *British Military Aircraft Serials 1878–1987* (Midland Counties).

Shores, Christopher *2nd Tactical Air Force* (Osprey).

Sturtivant, Ray *The Squadrons of the Fleet Air Arm* (Air Britain).

Magazines consulted include *Flypast, Air Pictorial, Aviation News, Air Digest*, plus snippets from numerous other publications.

Index